American Environmental Policy, 1990–2006

American and Comparative Environmental Policy
Sheldon Kamieniecki and Michael E. Kraft, series editors

American Environmental Policy, 1990–2006

Beyond Gridlock

Christopher McGrory Klyza
David J. Sousa

The MIT Press
Cambridge, Massachusetts
London, England

For information on quantity discounts, email special_sales@mitpress.mit.edu.

Set in Sabon by Publication Services, Champaign, Illinois. Printed and bound in the United States of America.

Library of Congress Cataloging-in-Publication Data

Klyza, Christopher McGrory.
American environmental policy, 1990–2006: beyond gridlock / Christopher McGrory Klyza and David J. Sousa.
p. cm.—(American and comparative environmental policy series)
Includes bibliographical references and index.
ISBN 978-0-262-11313-7 (hardcover: alk. paper)—ISBN 978-0-262-61220-3 (pbk.: alk. paper).
1. Environmental policy—United States—History—20th century. 2. Environmental policy—United States—History—21st century. 3. Environmental management—United Stated I. Sousa, David J. II. Title.
GE180.K59 2007
363.7'05610973—dc22

2007013994

10 9 8 7 6 5 4 3 2 1

to Sheila, Faye, and Isabel

to Louis Sousa (1931–2001) and Mary J. Sousa

Contents

Series Foreword

A central concern in contemporary environmental policy debates is the political difficulty of modernizing the core statutes from the 1970s, such as the Clean Air Act, the Clean Water Act, and the Endangered Species Act, to improve their coherence, effectiveness, and efficiency. Countless recommendations for sensible reforms from scholars and policymakers notwithstanding, those statutes remain largely unchanged. As a result, they cannot assist sufficiently in promoting the kind of environmental governance needed for the twenty-first century. The explanation for this failure lies largely in ideological conflicts between the two major political parties and pervasive and intensive lobbying by business interests and environmental groups. The result is that serious pursuit of a new generation of environmental policies has been all but impossible at the federal level over the past decade and more.

At the same time, one can find abundant examples of innovative action at the state and local level in areas as diverse as energy conservation, mitigation of climate change, community sustainability initiatives, and collaborative watershed management. Likewise, many leading corporations have launched impressive sustainability initiatives both to improve their bottom line and to bolster their corporate image. Even at the federal level, many important policy changes have emerged from administrative agencies, the courts, and White House decisions that have received only cursory examination by Congress. Yet the combined result still falls well short of what is needed in the years ahead.

In this book, Christopher Klyza and David Sousa offer a comprehensive and original assessment of the state of environmental policy since 1990 that captures both the prevailing national political gridlock and the many ways in which governments at all levels continue to advance the environmental agenda, often without much public visibility. Through special attention to the historical and layered construction of laws, institutions, and expectations—what they call the green state—Klyza and Sousa highlight the complexity of environmental politics and policy, the intriguing promise of new policy directions, and the uncertainties and pitfalls that many readers will recognize in their description of the contemporary political scene. They focus on the convoluted terrain of modern environmental policymaking, with its multiple and sometimes conflicting venues and pathways to policy action. They appraise this policymaking as it takes place within the White House, the budgetary process, administrative agencies and rulemaking processes, the courts, collaborative decisionmaking processes involving multiple levels of government, and state and local governments, and in conventional policymaking within Congress.

The authors argue persuasively that these multiple pathways to environmental policy advancement help to compensate for the all too obvious limitations on congressional revision of the major statutes. They see the intensified partisanship of the past decade and interest group mobilization as key drivers of policy struggles throughout the green state and across the various institutional points of access that are available to all players today. The result is a "churning process" of policy development that bears careful assessment, particularly in terms of political accountability, legitimacy, and the rule of law. We think readers will find the authors' analysis, carefully linked throughout the book to historically significant cases, both provocative and insightful. We hope it also stimulates further research on how the U.S. political system is affecting environmental policy today, and illuminates the opportunities likely to be present over the next several decades as this nation and others struggle to redefine policy suitable for addressing twenty-first century environmental challenges.

The book illustrates well our purpose in the MIT Press series in American and Comparative Environmental Policy. We encourage work that examines a broad range of environmental policy issues. We are particularly interested in books that incorporate interdisciplinary research and focus on the linkages between public policy and environmental problems and issues, both within the United States and in cross-national settings. We welcome contributions that analyze the policy dimensions of relationships between humans and the environment from either a theoretical or empirical perspective. At a time when environmental policies are increasingly seen as controversial and new approaches are being implemented widely, we especially encourage studies that assess policy successes and failures, evaluate new institutional arrangements and policy tools, and clarify new directions for environmental politics and policy. The books in this series are written for a wide audience that includes academics, policymakers, environmental scientists and professionals, business and labor leaders, environmental activists, and students concerned with environmental issues. We hope they contribute to public understanding of environmental problems, issues, and policies of concern today and also suggest promising actions for the future.

Sheldon Kamieniecki, University of California, Santa Cruz
Michael E. Kraft, University of Wisconsin, Green Bay

Preface

In early December 2006, as we were writing this preface, Senator James Inhofe (R-Oklahoma) conducted his last hearing as chair of the Senate Environment and Public Works Committee. The topic was climate change, and Inhofe, the leading climate-change skeptic in the Senate, criticized the media for "scientifically unfounded climate alarmism." The hearings illuminate the legislative gridlock on environmental policy that has been so common in the U.S. Congress since 1990. Yet two other stories having to do with climate policy unfolded within a week of Inhofe's hearing. Earlier, the Supreme Court considered a case in which twelve states sought to force the U.S. Environmental Protection Agency to regulate greenhouse gas emissions from new vehicles. At one point during the oral arguments, an exasperated Justice Antonin Scalia exclaimed: ". . . I'm not a scientist. That's why I don't want to have to deal with global warming, to tell you the truth." Yet the gridlock in Congress led to policy action on other fronts—in this case, a lawsuit. Further to the north, New York became the first state in the northeastern Regional Greenhouse Gas Initiative to unveil its draft regulations to achieve CO_2 emissions cuts through a cap-and-trade program in the region. From the Northeast to the West Coast, states have acted while Washington has not. In sum, these three events illuminate the state of environmental policy in the United States today: gridlock in Congress, but action on a variety of other pathways.

Recent writing on U.S. environmental policy frequently focuses on two themes: the gridlock on environmental policy (noted above) and the development and adoption of "next generation" environmental policy based on collaboration and pragmatism. As we read and thought about this work, we concluded that while the general themes were correct, they were also incomplete. As we thought about environmental policy more deeply, we wondered why there was legislative gridlock after 2000, with Republicans in control of the White House and Congress. Looking at policy more broadly, we saw President Clinton protecting millions of acres through the Antiquities Act, states taking the initiative on a variety of topics, and the courts issuing crucial decisions that deeply involved them in complex and chaotic disputes such as the struggles over endangered species in the Pacific Northwest. Gridlock in Congress on the environment perhaps, but certainly not policy gridlock. We also concluded that although collaborative, next generation policymaking is certainly part of the landscape, it is not the dominant policy pathway. Endangered Species Act lawsuits by the Center for Biological Diversity, for example, are just as significant in shaping policy as collaborative partnerships. In brief, environmental policymaking today is vibrant and complex, with a variety of opportunities for action. It is also full of pitfalls and ripe with uncertainty. We take you on a tour of that landscape in this book.

Acknowledgments

We thank the following individuals who read portions of the manuscript: Jeanne Nienaber Clarke, Charles Davis, Sandra Davis, Robert Duffy, Jon Isham, Bill McKibben, Martin Nie, Connie Prickett, Don Share, Jared Snyder, Bat Sparrow, and Chris Wood. We presented material in the book over the years at Colorado State University, the Middlebury College Political Science Faculty Research Group, a Southern Political Science Association meeting, and several Western Political Science Association meetings. We also thank Sheldon Kamieniecki and Michael Kraft, editors of the American and Comparative Environmental Policy series, and editor Clay Morgan and his team at The MIT Press.

Klyza offers these more personal acknowledgements: to the Trustees and administration at Middlebury College for the time—especially a well-timed leave— and resources necessary to write this book. The College continues to be a place where scholarship and teaching form integral parts of a dynamic educational community. Thanks to my colleagues in the Environmental Studies Program and Department of Political Science, especially Molly Costanza-Robinson, Diane Munroe, John Elder, Rebecca Gould, Nan Jenks-Jay, Kathy Morse, Pete Ryan, and Steve Trombulak. A special thanks to my students over the years in Conservation and Environmental Policy. You have been a testing ground for much of the material in this book, and your questions over the years have helped me to crystallize and clarify my thinking on these topics. I also thank David Brynn, Leanne Klyza Linck, Bob Linck, and Steve Mylon for numerous conversations over the years on the themes raised in the book. Most importantly, as always, I thank my wife Sheila McGrory-Klyza and daughters Faye and Isabel for their support and love.

Sousa writes: I thank my colleagues in the Department of Politics and Government at the University of Puget Sound for maintaining an exciting and collegial atmosphere in which to work. The University of Puget Sound generously supported this project with a sabbatical leave and a John Lantz Senior Fellowship that allowed me not only to work on the book but to write in wonderful places, from Monterchi near the Umbria-Tuscany border in Italy, to various places on Crete, to Bristol, Vermont. I would also like to thank Peter Wimberger of the Puget Sound Department of Biology and Karin Sable in Economics for drawing me into environmental policy studies through our work on an interdisciplinary course on the Endangered Species Act and salmon recovery on the Columbia River. Finally, and most importantly, I wish to thank my partner Jill Fuerstneau Sousa and our sons Jared and Matt for their patience and their love.

American Environmental Policy, 1990–2006

1
Environmental Policy Beyond Gridlock

Between 1964 and 1980, in the "golden era" of environmental lawmaking, the U.S. Congress enacted 22 major laws dealing with the control of pollution and the management of private lands, public lands, and wildlife. Passed with strong bipartisan support and riding a wave of legislative enthusiasm that overwhelmed most resistance, those laws triggered a profound expansion of government power in the service of emergent values and newly powerful interests. The anti-pollution laws broke new ground, giving the federal government a central role in protecting and improving air and water quality. New laws affecting the management of public lands and wildlife were layered atop existing statutes and agency practices, forcing green priorities on the Forest Service, the Army Corps of Engineers, and other agencies that had long favored extractive interests. The Endangered Species Act of 1973 typifies the politics of this moment in environmental policymaking. Growing out of concerns about the fate of the bald eagle and the bison, the Endangered Species Act was passed by a 345–4 vote in the House of Representatives and by a unanimous voice vote in the Senate. The act, which did not allow for economic considerations in decisions to place species on the endangered list, was signed into law by Republican President Richard Nixon.[1]

Soon, though, as the economic, ideological, and even cultural consequences of the "golden era" laws became clear, the new environmental laws became a focal point for political struggle. Once again the Endangered Species Act was emblematic: a 1977 controversy over whether the protection of the endangered snail darter required the Tennessee Valley Authority to abandon an expensive dam project clarified the law's disruptive force and gave a preview of later, bitter struggles. The highly visible battles over species preservation have been mirrored in other high-stakes fights over public lands and wetlands, toxic waste, water pollution, air pollution—indeed, nearly every significant environmental policy issue of the past 30 years. Scholars have noted a loose public consensus on the need for strong environmental protections, but environmental issues have divided the parties and engendered a bitter interest-group politics marked by high levels of mobilization on all sides. There is considerable political distance between the golden era, in which Congress committed itself to an ambitious, broad-based attack on environmental problems and conservatives such as Senator Jesse Helms (R-North Carolina) could support the Endangered Species Act, and the present, where reform proposals run headlong into legislative gridlock, and policy initiative and policy struggles spin off beyond Congress onto a host of other policymaking pathways.

The lawmaking revolution of the 1960s and the 1970s left many blanks to be filled in and much work for implementing agencies, the courts, and Congress in sorting out the meaning of those laws. Yet for more than 20 years fundamental environmental policy questions, major ideological disputes over the role of the state, fights about risk and lost jobs and economic inefficiencies, and now—with the emergence of concerns about global warming—looming environmental catastrophe have been channeled around Congress onto alternative pathways. This book is largely devoted to an exploration of the many paths on which environmental policy is being made, places where environmental policy-making has flourished in the context of a gridlocked Congress. These five pathways include increasing use of appropriations politics (e.g., the Salvage Rider, 1995), increasing use of executive-branch policymaking (e.g., President George W. Bush's decision to exempt electric utility plant expansions from the New Source Review program of the Clean Air Act), increasing use of the courts (e.g., to alter development through the Endangered Species Act), an increase in collaboration-based politics (e.g., the Environmental Protection Agency's Project XL), and an increase in state-focused policymaking. These different nontraditional paths indicate a vibrant environmental policy arena at the beginning of the twenty-first century, as reform impulses confront the institutional and legal legacies of more than a century of state building and the forces that in recent years have tied up Congress on environmental issues.

Choosing an Environmental Policy Future?

Legislative gridlock on the environment has generated frustrations on all sides—frustrations that were clearly evident in the 1990s. Mainstream environmental groups—sometimes called "big green"—celebrate the successes of the 1960s and the 1970s, but remain dissatisfied with a lack of progress on environmental issues, pointing to potentially catastrophic hazards like global warming, continuing risks to human health from pollutants, and rising pressures on land and water resources. They were angered by the Clinton administration's failure to press their concerns in the Democratic-controlled 103rd Congress, but that failure was predictable. President Bill Clinton had higher priorities, including economic recovery, the North American Free Trade Agreement, and health-care reform. Furthermore, legislators hostile to energy taxes and protective of the age-old regimes governing mining and grazing limited his leeway on the environment. The mainstream environmental groups seem well positioned to protect most of the gains of the past using their own substantial resources, the courts, and the considerable reservoir of general public support they enjoy. They can inflict pain to block conservative initiatives, as in 2001 when they tortured the Bush administration for its decision to review a Clinton rule (adopted in the waning days of his presidency) limiting allowable arsenic concentrations in drinking water and forced a Bush retreat. Yet their efforts to expand upon the legislative gains of the golden era in Congress have, with a few important exceptions, been fruitless: addressing global climate change; protecting the Arctic National Wildlife Refuge or other major wild landscapes; reforming existing public lands laws dealing with grazing, logging, and mining; strengthening existing pollution control laws; or establishing standards of environmental justice.

Conservatives and business interests complain about the excessive economic and social costs of environmental regulations, infringements on property rights, and the growth of government symbolized by the far-reaching authority of the U.S. Environmental Protection Agency. After the Republican victories in the 1994 congressional elections, the new Republican leadership in the House claimed a mandate to weaken environmental regulations. It pushed regulatory reforms aimed at stopping or sharply limiting enforcement of many of the nation's environmental laws. House leaders announced their intentions to rewrite the Clean Air Act, the Clean Water Act, the Superfund law, the Safe Drinking Water Act, and the Endangered Species Act, to relax restrictions on logging in national forests, and to weaken limits on pesticides in food.

This all ended in political disaster for the Republicans. The House Republican conference split on some crucial issues, with northeastern Republicans flinching at the breadth of the attack on established laws and regulations. Much of the agenda that had been passed by the House of Representatives stalled in the Republican-controlled Senate, and the assault withered as it faced presidential vetoes. Clinton successfully cast the Republicans as extremists on the environment, fueling his own political recovery and humiliating Speaker of the House Newt Gingrich (R-Georgia) and his allies.[2] The conservatives had misread their mandate and miscalculated their prospects for winning changes in the basic environmental laws. By 1996 they had moderated their goals and pulled back their efforts to undo the policy legacies of the 1960s and the 1970s. The right has continued to face difficulties moving its environmental agenda—even with Republican control of the White House and both houses of Congress. In the wake of George W. Bush's victory in the 2004 presidential election, EPA Administrator Mike Leavitt claimed a "mandate" for the administration's environmental program. Yet Bush's environmental initiatives quickly fell toward the bottom of its list of priorities, and his centerpiece "Clear Skies" proposal fell into a legislative miasma from which it is unlikely to emerge.[3] Like the greens, conservatives have pushed for significant changes to the nation's environmental policies, and, like the greens, they have been frustrated in the lawmaking process.

This legislative gridlock has been sobering to those on the environmental left and right, but it has not dampened optimism in the center that productive reform of environmental policy is possible. As battles over warming and wetlands and endangered species and arsenic in drinking water and other major issues have raged, the policy community—academics, practitioners, some stakeholders—has begun to develop a consensus on the practical problems of environmental policy and on fruitful next generation directions for reform.[4] This next generation agenda draws on green concerns about the limited success of some environmental policies in achieving environmental protection, the right's frustration with the economic and cultural costs of compliance with the golden era environmental laws, and the policy community's concerns about the inefficiencies of many current policies and excessive adversarialism in the policymaking process. Advocates of next generation reform seek more efficient, results-oriented policy and processes that will contribute to a better balancing of the many values in play in the environmental arena. These reformers think that the green wars of the 1980s and the 1990s have exhausted both sides, opening opportunities for compromise: sensible reforms of existing laws that will enhance their efficiency and improve cooperation across old boundaries.[5] Donald Kettl nicely sums up the next generation agenda: "to develop new strategies for attacking new environmental problems . . . to develop better strategies for solving old ones, and . . . to do both in ways that are more efficient, less taxing, and engender less political opposition."[6]

The next generation school's critique of the legacies of the environmental policies of the 1960s and the 1970s and its dreams of more pragmatic, incentive-based, collaborative approaches now dominate discussions of the future of environmental policy. These reformers offer a classic "both and" agenda, seeking to achieve real improvements in environmental protection while accommodating the legitimate concerns of business leaders and others about the economic and social costs of the implementation of the golden era laws. It is an attractive vision, embracing both a hard-headed pragmatism and the ideals of local collaboration and participatory regulation that have long animated democratic theorists and administrative reformers.[7] The next generation vision draws strength from three features of the political and intellectual context of environmental policymaking. First, there is a broad, if general, public consensus supporting environmental protection. Second, there is widespread agreement that the laws passed in the 1960s and the 1970s have not been entirely successful, and that the implementation of those statutes has generated excessive costs and political conflict. Third, over the years the policy community has generated innovative ideas for increasing the effectiveness and efficiency of environmental policy, both to improve its performance in achieving old objectives and to modernize policy to address emerging concerns. Yet with the great exception of the emissions trading program adopted with the Clean Air Act of 1990, next generation reformers have been as unsuccessful in Congress as environmental groups and the conservative right.[8]

Mary Graham was essentially right when she observed that

the need to resolve novel conflicts between economic and environmental interests . . . has given rise to a new pragmatism in environmental politics. In the absence of congressional action to revise basic environmental laws, workable compromises to resolve emerging problems have been jury-rigged around and within the existing labyrinth of rules. Economic incentives are employed more frequently to further federal and state objectives. In Washington, debate often remains polarized. But around the country, the nation is in the midst of a rich, experimental time in environmental policy.[9]

Yet it is important to recognize that this new pragmatism is *a* tendency, but hardly the *central* tendency in modern environmental policymaking. Debates in this area engage some of the most ideologically, culturally, and economically contentious domestic issues of our time, and neither the loose public consensus supporting environmental protection nor persuasive arguments that we can achieve higher levels of protection at lower costs can easily contain these conflicts and generate lasting momentum toward a pragmatic next generation policy.

Consider also the frustrations of some next generation policy advocates interested in increasing the efficiency of environmental policy with selected policies of George W. Bush's administration. The environmental policy analyst Jan Mazurek criticized Bush for abandoning next generation ideas, arguing that in important areas the administration ignored a broad consensus on reform, letting "progress toward a long-overdue modernization of U.S. environmental policy grind to a halt." This should not surprise anyone. The preference for more collaborative, efficient policies is an important part of modern environmental policymaking, but these approaches do not exhaust the agendas of policymakers and interest groups. All of the tactics used by the Bush administration are as much a part of modern environmental policymaking as the next generation approaches, and it is unsurprising that the administration used its authority and open policy pathways to pursue its policy agenda. Frustrated in Congress, it turned to rulemaking, litigation, appointments—to whatever tools it could find to press its goals. It is equally unsurprising that, despite the ideology of accommodation that has gripped parts of the policy community, determined environmental groups like the Center for

Biological Diversity use their resources and the leverage of the Endangered Species Act to attack development and land-management policies, typically using the courts. While the Clinton and Bush administrations were weakening enforcement of the ESA (albeit in different ways and for different reasons, with Clinton particularly citing the need for collaboration and compromise), the CBD—operating on a tiny budget—forced new species listings, new critical habitat designations, and expensive modifications to federal land management and developers' plans (see chapter 5).[10] Much like the Bush administration, the CBD has pursued an aggressive strategy rather than accepting the limitations of the consensus on pragmatism and collaboration that has such influence in the policy community. From our vantage point, President Bush's actions and those of the CBD are just as much a vibrant part of the "next generation" story of environmental policymaking as collaboration and state action.

Further, managing the conflicts that mark this field in pursuit of pragmatism and collaboration is complicated by two important institutional features of the American political system, one general and one specific to environmental policy.

First, it is true that congressional gridlock has pushed environmental policymaking onto new paths, yet not all of these paths lead to next generation reform. The American political system offers many points of access to the policymaking process, and policy initiative has moved off in many new directions, both within the legislature itself (an increasing reliance on policy riders to appropriation bills and the budget process rather than the conventional lawmaking process); to executive politics, including the use of unilateral executive authority and rulemaking; to the judicial process; as well as to state, local, and private-sector efforts at achieving efficiency, collaboration, and sustainability that have been at the center of the next generation vision. As the bitter political conflicts that mark the environmental field spread across this complex institutional terrain, following a host of policymaking pathways, specific compromises "jury-rigged within and around the existing labyrinth of rules" are vulnerable to attack and the prospects for a larger movement toward a more pragmatic, efficient, and collaborative environmental policy seem limited. Consider the fate of the Oregon Salmon Plan aimed at preserving some West Coast runs of coho salmon. Worried about the potentially devastating economic and social effects of an ESA listing, and trying to avoid the kind of train wreck caused by listings of several salmon species in the Columbia River basin, Oregon policymakers worked closely with many local groups to develop a solid recovery plan. The National Marine Fisheries Service agreed not to list the species because the local process seemed worthy and the resulting plan appeared sensible. In many ways this was a wonderful example of pragmatic collaboration in action. Yet several environmental groups and the Pacific Coast Federation of Fisherman's Association disagreed, and sued. The NMFS lacked the legal discretion to refuse to list a species and to implement a recovery process, even where it judged that locals had moved aggressively to tackle the problem. Environmentalists feared the precedent and used the courts to force the NMFS to retreat from pragmatism and cooperation to the rigidities of the law.[11] Environmentalists frustrated by the collaborative pathway found another, intersecting path that they could use to block a compromise that even some greens thought was sensible. There is no reason that the development of paths "within and around" existing rules and statutes will trump those rules or provide a stable basis for a new policy agenda centered on liberalism or conservatism or pragmatism. Without statutory changes to protect these collaborative experiments, they will often be vulnerable in a political system that offers many points of access, many points of attack.

Second, modern environmental policy choices are being made within frameworks set by the policy legacies of the 1960s and the 1970s and by even deeper legacies stretching back to choices made in the late nineteenth century and the early years of the twentieth century in what we will call "the American green state."[12] Pollution control policies, conservation policies, and natural resources policies represent basic commitments of American government rooted in statutes, the institutional structure and culture of implementing agencies, and public expectations aggressively articulated by powerful environmental groups and business corporations and various property rights interests. These laws, institutions, and expectations were built over time through policy decisions reflecting values and interests at play in particular historical periods and designed to achieve policy goals specific to those periods. The construction of these laws, institutions, and expectations—of a green state—did not proceed smoothly, or through a process of demolition of old institutions and the creation of new ones to replace them. Instead, each new movement layered new institutions and agendas atop the old and empowered new interests even while preserving many of the legal and institutional bases of the claims made by old interests.[13]

The resilience of these pre-existing policy commitments at once constrains systematic policy reform from the left, right, or the center and energizes an intense environmental politics. Conservatives' attacks on the institutions created during the golden era of environmental lawmaking merely served to highlight the strength of the policy status quo. Environmentalists have long chafed at older policy commitments privileging ranchers, miners, and loggers, among others, but they have been unable to root them out despite changes in the economy, values, and the constellation of political forces in the society. The environmental policy arena is a site for what Karen Orren and Stephen Skowronek call the crashing and grinding of "multiple orders," or "intercurrence," a politics privileging multiple and conflicting interests and values simultaneously. These values (e.g., the importance of private property and personal freedom and business prerogatives, the need for scientific management of natural resources, the value of green spaces and wild places and species protection, and rigorous protections against environmental risks) are embedded in laws and institutions that are not necessarily consistent with one another and that are not easily changed. The green state legitimizes the conflicting claims of contending interests and gives them the weight of law, at once shaping environmental politics and frustrating efforts to impose comprehensive new ordering visions.[14]

For example, the Endangered Species Act was layered atop old policy choices on water and timber and land and property rights, sometimes disturbing but not completely displacing old claims, old values, and existing laws. So when the federal government diverted water from Oregon's Klamath River Basin to help endangered fish species, farmers complained that the government had broken its commitments to them and environmentalists insisted that the ESA is the law of the land and the fish must be protected. To a large degree, both parties were correct and both had strong statutory claims. Next generation reformers rightly see the need to find some way to balance these claims, but the intensity of the conflict and the ways that competing values and interests are privileged by different laws and institutions yield a politics in which any particular policy outcome is contingent, always vulnerable to competing claims in different venues. It is hard to know what "balance" means or how to find it when policy flows from a mix of choices made in different and disconnected institutional venues at different times, and all of the choices in one way or another satisfy claims with some strong statutory, political, and cultural grounding. As Charles Wilkinson argued in *Crossing the Next Meridian*, the policies governing grazing, mining, timber, and water in the West are still dominated by the "lords of yesterday," laws and values dominant in the period of westward expansion. He is right, but it is also true—simultaneously true—that we are governed by the "lords of a little while ago," laws and institutions adopted in the 1960s and the 1970s that empower new interests and new values and new institutions to shape environmental policy.[15] This reality energizes all politics, certainly modern environmental politics, and there is no escape from the crashing and grinding of multiple orders in this field.

Norman Vig and Michael Kraft concluded their overview of contemporary environmental politics and policy with the powerful assertion that "we have no alternative but to decide what kind of future we want," and it is likely—indeed we are hopeful—that that future will draw on ideas about sustainability and the next generation vision of greater efficiency and cooperation.[16] But the possibilities of pragmatic choice, of reform driven long and hard by the next generation agenda—like the prospects for systematic reforms envisioned by conservatives or environmentalists—are sharply limited by the political realities of the present, and the ways that those intersect with the institutional legacies of the past. Environmental policy choices will be contingent, reversible, contended, reflecting both the constellation of political and ideological forces in society and the connections of those forces to different, embedded layers of the American green state.

Into the Labyrinth: Paths to the Environmental Policy Future

Far from leaving us with policy gridlock, then, the inability of Congress to respond to demands from the left, the right, or the center for changes to the laws governing pollution, conservation, and natural resources policy has ratcheted up the importance of other policymaking pathways. A sound description of modern environmental policymaking must strike out across this complex terrain, exploring all of these paths and the ways they have shaped policy. Unfortunately, most current political science research on legislative "gridlock" and its consequences has focused exclusively on lawmaking, equating this with gridlock on policy. We think that it is crucial to extend the discussion of the implications of legislative gridlock to the larger policymaking process, because, at least in the environmental field, congressional gridlock has channeled tremendous political energies down other policymaking pathways, creating considerable instability in policy as policymakers and interest groups have pursued their agendas—sometimes momentous policy shifts—in other venues.[17]

The legislative stalemate has, of course, limited the policy achievements of both greens and conservatives, and the absence of congressional sanction has decisively limited the advance of next generation reforms. Graham's "compromises . . . jury-rigged around and within the existing labyrinth of rules" are, like the Oregon Salmon Plan, typically vulnerable to challenge as they butt up against other agendas and statutory requirements. The norm is motion, continuing policy disruption, with movement from venue to venue and victory to defeat and back again for contending interests. Contrary to the expectations of those who see in modern American government the mobilization of so many contending interests that we have arrived at "demosclerosis" (hopelessly gridlocked policy), intense mobilization by interest groups has helped to move policy initiative around the stalemated Congress to multiple venues simultaneously.[18]

Similarly, the institutionalization of past environmental choices—which might at first blush be taken to yield a basic stability to policy, and some insulation of policy commitments from election results—has done neither. In part this is due to the layering of contradictory policy commitments within the American green state that will be explored in the next chapter. As Eric Schickler observed, "rather than providing stability and coherence, as the metaphor of institutions as equilibria suggests, institutions embody contradictory purposes, which provide for an ongoing, churning process of development." Orren and Skowronek find that "political reform is often incomplete, that adverse principles and methods of operation remain in place . . . the normal condition of the policy will be that of multiple, incongruous authorities operating simultaneously."[19]

And in part this policy instability results from the prominent role that presidential leadership has played on many of the pathways around legislative gridlock. Always important, the tools of presidential leadership have become even more significant in this closely fought, contentious field, despite the institutionalization of the central commitments of several generations of environmental policy. In the absence of powerful "warrants" to reconstruct environmental policy, presidents have used the many tools at their disposal in defending policy regimes with which they are associated (e.g., Clinton used executive powers to protect the Endangered Species Act and the Clean Water Act from Republican attacks; George W. Bush defended mining and grazing interests challenged by green concerns) and in trying to weaken established regimes to which they are opposed.[20] Despite the lack of significant movement in the lawmaking process in decades, and despite the institutionalization of environmental policy commitments, presidential leadership has energized movement along many of the pathways around gridlock, and has been a crucial source of policy instability.

Why does this matter? First, we think that exploring the policymaking pathways beyond legislative gridlock will provide a useful descriptive map of the current contours and patterns of environmental policymaking. Second, we think that this analysis throws up analytical challenges to students of environmental policy who see in this "rich, experimental time" in environmental policymaking harbingers of a more pragmatic and collaborative next generation policy regime. These experiments will play an important role in shaping the future of environmental policy, but we think that basic characteristics of the American policymaking system—the existence of multiple points of access and policy pathways—and the institutional legacies of the past sharply limit the reconstructive potential of the next generation reforms. There are problems with the existing environmental laws, and there is a need for reform. Yet there is no easy escape from the past, when environmental policy choices were rarely driven by pragmatic balancing, and there is no escape from politics to a world dominated by cooperation among interests still sharply divided and all empowered by various and contradictory laws and cultural premises.

Further, the movement of environmental policy initiative onto pathways around legislative gridlock raises important issues of legitimacy and accountability in environmental policymaking. In some ways this is a new problem in this field. The laws passed in the golden era, supported by both parties and powerful environmental groups, challenged business prerogatives in ways not seen since the rise of industrial unionism in the 1930s. The emergence of the modern environmental movement fed a sweeping democratization of American society and politics, altering political balances in ways that opened the system to new interests and made environmental policymaking more representative than ever before. Yet the consequences of legislative gridlock and the increasing importance of paths around the legislative process raise difficult questions about the democratic character of modern environmental policymaking.

The legitimacy issue has several dimensions. Most simply, since the environmentalists' great legislative victories in the 1960s and the 1970s there has been a decided right turn in American politics. To protect their earlier gains and to try to expand upon them, environmental groups have depended heavily on the courts and their ability to shape the rulemaking process (with the threat of legal action looming in the background). In the 1990s, at first frustrated by the low priority the Clinton administration gave environmental issues and then pushed hard by the Republican-controlled Congress after 1994, environmentalists ended up applauding Clinton for his aggressive use of executive power to protect public lands, celebrating a legacy that rested heavily on an arguably heavy-handed use of the Antiquities Act to protect large tracts of land. Under the new Bush administration, environmental interests cling tightly to the statutory language of the 1960s and the 1970s and hope that the courts, coupled with the Republicans' squeamishness about being on the wrong side of environmental issues, will rein in the backlash agenda. The environmental movement, once a powerful democratizing force, hangs on in Congress and increasingly pursues its goals outside the more democratic channels of American government.

On the other side, the populist impulse of the anti-green backlash has been channeled into some of the least visible, least well understood arenas in the policymaking process. Ronald Reagan's early appointees at the EPA and Interior pushed hard, using administrative strategies to gut environmental enforcement and to ease access to public lands for drilling, logging, and mining interests. In the 104th Congress, bold Republican "revolutionaries" came to power claiming a popular mandate to weaken environmental regulation. They suffered defeat after defeat in the legislative process and were reduced to seeking major changes to environmental policy in appropriations riders, trying to tie the rollback agenda to must-pass bills because it was obvious that they could not pass legislation to achieve these goals. Even this effort was largely unsuccessful, and the central success of the strategy—the "salvage rider" that opened vast tracts of land to logging in the Pacific Northwest—was helped along by court decisions that vastly expanded the rider's scope. (See chapter 3.) The George W. Bush administration has pursued administrative and legal strategies aimed at weakening the green state, drawing the ire of environmentalists and centrist, next generation reformers. It really is a new day for environmental policy when judicial appointments become a pressing issue, crucial both to greens and conservatives, and one must know the subtleties of lawsuits and out-of-court settlements to understand policies affecting health risks and millions of acres of public land.

Beyond this are important problems of accountability. Much of environmental policymaking has been pushed into venues—the appropriations process, executive politics, the courts—where public attention and understanding is often quite limited and where it is difficult to hold policymakers accountable. Even pathways that invite public participation, from collaborative conservation to participatory rulemaking to ballot initiatives, suffer from significant legitimacy problems. Collaboration and participatory rulemaking are attractive, but these efforts always raise serious questions about participation (who gets to participate?), accountability (how do we hold participants in these processes accountable for their choices?), and the integrity of law (should the requirements of the Endangered Species Act or the National Forest Management Act or the Clean Water Act be negotiable?). Excluded interests complain bitterly and some scholars have raised concerns that in this field we are making ad hoc "policy without law," thus handing over too much power to private interest groups.[21] Citizen initiatives have a populist flavor, but the initiative process is too often dominated by narrowly interested groups with extreme political agendas, and the use of this pathway complicates the pragmatic balancing of interests and values.[22] How will the institutionalization of the green revolution, and the inevitable reaction from the right to the environmentalists' successes, shape the future of American democracy? Advocates of localism and collaboration in rule-making and resource management have a vision of environmental democracy, but it is unclear that that vision can discipline the roiling politics of the green state and force crucial choices onto well-lit pathways.

Further, to circle back to the question of legislative gridlock, there is the difficulty of actually achieving reform—even sensible, pragmatic reform of the green state—without congressional sanction. That is, without new statutes it will be difficult to push ahead with even the tinkering and pragmatic adjustment that the next generation of environmental policy requires. This became clear in the Clinton years, when the administration's experimental efforts to bring regulated interests into the policymaking process, to create cross-media programs at the plant level and to cut pragmatic and sensible deals with polluters, often foundered on the fear that the deals would not stand up in court.[23] That is, participants needed the stamp of legitimacy on their experiments that only statutory language could provide. It will be difficult to realize changes in the basic premises of the regulatory system without changing laws, and of course changing the laws is extraordinarily problematic. The "lords of yesterday" and "the lords of a little while ago" throw up major barriers to statutory change even while their confrontations energize a vibrant, contentious, and creative politics.

The Plan of the Book

In this book we explore the pathways beyond legislative gridlock along which modern environmental policy is being made. In chapter 2 we describe the main factors leading environmental policymaking to become gridlocked in Congress. We then describe the building of the green state: the set of laws, institutions, and expectations dealing with conservation and environmental policy that have been established throughout American history. We emphasize how gridlock and the historical construction of the green state have driven environmental policymaking onto new policy pathways, and the ways that the existence of multiple points of access to the political process and the nature of the green state have contributed to considerable instability and real barriers to the development of any new order in environmental policymaking.

In chapters 3–8 we examine, in turn, several policy pathways. In chapter 3 we focus on how Congress itself has altered its environmental policymaking process as legislators have sought paths around gridlock on major environmental policy questions, relying on appropriations riders and budget politics to achieve their policy goals. We include case studies of the two most significant examples of this pathway: the Salvage Rider and efforts to allow oil drilling in the Arctic National Wildlife Refuge through the budget reconciliation process.

In chapter 4 we examine the increasing importance of executive policymaking, focusing on three cases: President Bill Clinton's use of the Antiquities Act to create or expand national monuments, Clinton's use of the rulemaking process to protect nearly 60 million acres of national forest lands from roads and logging through the "roadless rule," and President George W. Bush's use of the rulemaking process to fundamentally change the new source review program, a crucial component of the Clean Air Act. As Congress has stalemated, presidents have pressed for policy changes of great moment using their unilateral powers and broader executive authority.

In chapter 5 we turn to the role of the courts in the policymaking process. Although the courts have been major actors in environmental policymaking since the passage of the major environmental laws of the 1960s and the 1970s, with Congress gridlocked their policymaking role has become even more important. We illustrate this by examining the use of the Endangered Species Act to alter development in Arizona, industry's efforts to fundamentally re-make air quality policy through the courts in the *American Trucking Associations v. EPA* case, and the Bush administration's administrative strategies to use this pathway, through politicizing appointments and the use of the sue and settle strategy. Although there is widespread scholarly concern about the negative consequences of "adversarial legalism" for policymaking on the environment, the choices made by Congress (and courts themselves) in the 1960s and the 1970s embed adversarial legalism in the policymaking process and create enormous barriers to those trying to hack new pathways "within and around the labyrinth" of judicially-enforceable laws and rules.

In chapter 6 we examine the collaboration pathway, which is crucial to the next generation vision of environmental policymaking. This chapter highlights the strengths and weaknesses of the increasingly powerful ideology of collaboration in the environmental policy field by examining several examples of this approach in practice: habitat conservation planning through the Endangered Species Act, efforts to improve pollution control policy through the Negotiated Rulemaking Act and EPA's Common Sense Initiative and Project XL, and collaborative conservation efforts on the public lands. In many areas, we find the absence of statutory grounding for these experiments—as well as crucial questions about the quality and legitimacy of collaborative decisions—has limited their reach and potential.

In chapter 7 we explore environmental policymaking in the states. We begin with a discussion of innovative policymaking at the state level. Even at that level, innovative next-generation-style policymaking is only one part of a complex story. We examine environmental policymaking via the use of initiatives and referenda to illustrate the bitterness of struggles and the complexity of the policy labyrinth in state politics. Further, we examine conflict between the states and the federal government and the increasingly significant role of states as actors in environmental policymaking.

In chapter 8 we return to the forces leading to gridlock. We argue that these forces are unlikely to dissipate anytime soon and that, given this situation, the president and the powers at his or her disposal will be of signal importance in animating environmental policy. We next turn to a discussion of why we think the nation has moved in the direction favored by environmentalists, what we term green drift, despite this congressional gridlock and the move of the nation as a whole to the right. This green drift, we argue, is due largely to the dynamic created by the existing green state and mobilized environmental interests.

2
Creating the Current Institutional Landscape of Environmental Policymaking

Environmental policymaking now looks very different than it did in the "golden era" (that is, from the mid 1960s through 1980). In this chapter we explore the political and institutional forces underpinning legislative gridlock and the environmental politics of multiple orders described in chapter 1. The first section details political developments since the 1960s that have reshaped environmental policymaking and created legislative gridlock on the environment: increasing partisanship, hyperpluralism, a more pervasive media, the changing nature of environmental problems, and several contradictory characteristics of public opinion about the role of government and environmental policy. Legislative gridlock on the environment flows from these broad changes in the American political system as well as the ways that the golden era laws themselves reconfigured the politics of environmental issues.

After reviewing the causes of legislative gridlock, we briefly focus on the political and institutional reasons that *legislative* gridlock is not tantamount to *policy* gridlock. The logic here is simple, but it is important to note that political scientists concerned with congressional gridlock and debates over the consequences of divided government have largely ignored the impact of legislative inaction in the larger policymaking system. Understandably, students of Congress and the presidency have focused on lawmaking as an indicator of policy gridlock, yet the tremendous political energies feeding into the environmental policy arena have driven environmental policymaking onto paths around the blocked Congress. As Frank Baumgartner and Bryan Jones have observed, the many points of access available in the American political system offer interest groups and political leaders substantial opportunities to disrupt the status quo in policy. Thus a policy area featuring legislative gridlock and "stuck" statutes at its core features sharp changes in policy direction and considerable policy instability.[1]

We then turn to an examination of the construction of the American green state—the laws, institutions, and expectations concerning conservation and the environment—since the late nineteenth century. The layering of commitments, from the economic liberalism of much of the nineteenth century to the conservation era (roughly 1890–1920) to the era of environmentalism and preservation (1964–1980), has embedded conflicting impulses in public policy, and these legacies condition everything about modern environmental policymaking, from the ongoing legislative gridlock to the intense struggles that have played out on the many alternative pathways open in the American political system to debates about the limits and possibilities of reform. As Karen Orren and Stephen Skowronek wrote, "the terrain is filled from the get go, and what already exists defines the problems and substance of change."[2]

As always, achieving dramatic policy change is difficult: when under attack, entrenched institutions reveal themselves as what Skowronek called "tenacious organization(s) of power" that protect the prerogatives of old values and old interests and against new demands and emerging interests. This is the story of Charles Wilkinson's "lords of yesterday": for example, the nineteenth-century mining law persists though it does not "fit" modern circumstances or perceptions of good stewardship. Yet the process of institutional development, the layering of commitments, and the privileging of contending interests simultaneously also hinders the establishment of new policy equilibria, or any new political order. Instead, new commitments coexist with the old—the mining law grinds against the Clean Water Act—and new policy choices, like the old, become "tenacious organizations of power" that at once grind against old institutions and themselves resist reform. The layering of contradictory policy commitments yields an unstable policy terrain that has resisted the visions of new orders emerging from the greens, conservatives, and next generation reformers.[3]

Taken together, these institutional characteristics—the presence of multiple points of access to the policymaking process offering fruitful paths around legislative gridlock, and the "crashing and grinding of multiple orders" that characterizes the green state—drive environmental policy beyond gridlock. Intensified partisanship and interest-group mobilization energize this system, driving policy struggles up and down through the layers of the green state and across the many institutional points of access created by environmental laws and the larger structure of the American political system. The "churning process of development" continues on the new policymaking pathways explored in the rest of this book.[4]

The Many Paths to Legislative Gridlock on the Environment

Just as gridlock in environmental lawmaking has forced policymaking onto several new paths, many pathways have led to gridlock. All these paths follow the contours of political realities in the broader American political system, yet the characteristics of conservation and environmental policy issues create distinct routes to the legislative bottleneck. Here we focus on several main causes of legislative gridlock on the environment: partisan polarization, the weakening of liberalism in the United States, public opinion, interest-group mobilization, the increasing pervasiveness of media coverage, and the changing nature of environmental problems.

The New Partisanship in Environmental Policy

In the mid 1960s, Democrats controlling the White House and Congress laid the foundation for an increased federal role in pollution control and for an expansion of the federal government's conservation and resource-management responsibilities, but the crucial wave of environmental lawmaking occurred in the late 1960s and the 1970s, a period of divided party control. The Nixon years saw the creation of the Environmental Protection Agency and a raft of new laws as politicians from both parties responded to rising concerns about pollution, conservation, and the management of natural resources. There was remarkable bipartisanship on the environment in this period. For example, the vote on final passage of the Endangered Species Act of 1973 was unanimous in the Senate and there were only four dissenters in the House of Representatives. The Federal Water Pollution Control Act of 1972, described by *Congressional Quarterly* as then the most expansive federal environmental law in history, was passed by the Senate 74–0 and by the House 336–11. President Richard Nixon vetoed the bill on fiscal grounds, but Congress overrode that veto overwhelmingly.[5]

The record in environmental lawmaking supports David Mayhew's argument that divided government is not an insurmountable barrier to legislative innovation. Mayhew's data showed that between 1960 and 1990 more significant environmental laws, and laws of greater magnitude, were passed in periods of divided government than in periods of unified party government.[6] Why? Overwhelming public concern, intense media attention, the mobilization of environmental groups, and struggles for political advantage—Senator Edmund Muskie's (D-Maine) efforts to define himself as the national leader on the issue and Nixon's responses— overwhelmed not only the normal constitutional barriers to innovation, but those thrown up by divided government as well. Into the early 1990s many politicians on both sides of the aisle saw protecting the environment as a "motherhood issue"—that is, something that a great majority of Americans would support without question. "Moderate Republicans, upper-class voters, are with us on the environment," observed Representative Charles Schumer (D-New York). "It cuts across the old class divisions. . . . It is a great issue with new voters. . . . It is an issue with no downside."[7]

Yet even as Schumer spoke, the deepening partisan cleavages shaping legislative politics as a whole began to reach environmental issues.[8] Charles Shipan and William Lowry showed that between 1970 and 1998 the average party difference in League of Conservation Voters scores for legislators was 25 percentage points. The gap began growing in the early 1980s and now regularly and spectacularly exceeds this average.[9] (See figure.) This polarization has proceeded apace: in the second session of the 108th Congress (2003–04), Senate Democrats had an average LCV score of 85 and Senate Republicans an average score of 8. In the House of Representatives, Democrats had an average LCV score of 86 and Republicans an average score of 10.

Several developments specific to environmental policy help to explain partisan polarization on environmental issues, including the openness of the Republican Party to demands from businesses and anti-green back- lash groups for relief from the costs of regulation. The Reaganite rheto- ric of "getting government off the backs of the people" aimed squarely at the regulatory explosion of the 1960s and the 1970s, and particularly at the golden era environmental laws. This polarization also reflects other developments that have widened partisan cleavages in Congress,

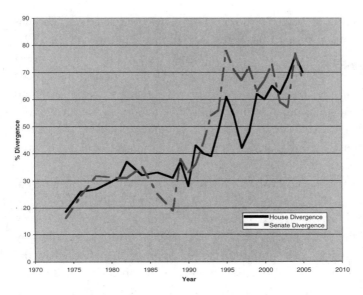

Divergence between Democrats and Republicans in congressional voting on the environment, 1974–2005. Source: League of Conservation Voters, "Past Environmental Scorecards."

particularly the Southern realignment that has reordered the party system. The Democrats have lost much of their more conservative Southern wing, and their party has become more homogeneously liberal. Democratic politicians have sought to win over economically conservative suburban swing voters by appealing to them on social and environmental issues. Simultaneously, the growing importance of the South and the Rocky Mountain West to the Republican Party has turned it to the right on environmental and natural resource issues. This process has been accelerated by the weakening of the Republican Party's moderate wing, particularly the party's loss of strength in the Northeast and on the West Coast. Southerners have, in general, exhibited a weaker commitment to environmental protection than inhabitants of other regions, and it is not surprising that a party dominated by leaders from that region would be tepid toward green concerns. Indeed, the rhetoric of a heavily Southern Republican leadership on the environment has been quite aggressive. President George W. Bush has allegedly derided environmentalists as "green, green, lima beans"; former House Majority Leader Thomas DeLay's description of the EPA as the Gestapo is well known.[10] In 1995, shortly after becoming Speaker of the House, Georgia Republican Newt Gingrich declared that the policies of the past 20 years or more had "been absurdly expensive, created far more resistance than was necessary and misallocated resources on emotional and public relations grounds without regard to either scientific, engineering, or economic rationality." Following Gingrich, House Republicans in the 104th Congress abandoned any pretense of bipartisanship on the environment.[11]

The bitter partisanship of the 1990s hindered reform of environmental policy, both in the brief period of unified Democratic control and the longer period of divided government. Clinton's efforts on energy taxation, mining and grazing reform, and global warming were largely fruitless; the Republicans' ambitious rollback program collapsed in the face of determined political opposition. George W. Bush's administration has achieved only marginal legislative gains, with intense Democratic and moderate Republican opposition holding back major legislative initiatives.

The Weakening of Liberalism as a Political Force in American National Life

Although there is now a lively debate about the future shape of the post-industrial Democratic Party, at least since 1980 the national party's liberal wing has been a frail political force.[12] Changes in demography and in the competitive strength of the parties, organized labor's decline, the increasing political activism of the business community, and a powerful intellectual assault on some of the legacies of policy liberalism have combined to create a difficult political environment for activist liberalism. The party's liberal wing has also been wracked by internal divisions. Battles between organized labor and "new politics" forces—including identity groups and environmentalists—at times divided the party and weakened the liberal impulse itself.[13]

The weakness of the Democrats' liberal wing and the growing strength of the conservative opposition have been demonstrated repeatedly at the polls. In the 1980 presidential election, the victor was Ronald Reagan, a candidate who had appeared unacceptably conservative only a few years before. And in 1984, Reagan crushed the liberal champion Walter

Mondale. In 1988, George H. W. Bush, who had made his peace with Reaganite conservatism, was easily elected over a candidate he depicted as a liberal outside the mainstream. In 1994 conservatives seized control of Congress, and Republican majorities have controlled both houses since then (except for the brief period of Democratic majority in the Senate begun by Vermont Senator James Jeffords's departure from the Republican Party in 2001). The 2000 election was controversial, but George W. Bush ran well against an experienced Democratic candidate who had every political advantage. Once elected, the younger Bush revealed himself to be deeply conservative, and behind his leadership the Republican Party gained in the 2002 midterm elections. Bush's reelection in 2004 only further underscored this trend, and Democratic victories in the 2006 congressional elections are more attributable to frustration with the Iraq War than to a resurgence of the left. Liberalism has been severely weakened as a national political force.

The exception to this trend proves the rule. Clinton, a Southern centrist elected because an economic recession had weakened his Republican predecessor, saved his presidency by renouncing "the era of big government." He benefited from both the economic recovery of the 1990s and the perception that the Republicans had taken their anti-government rhetoric too far. He signed welfare-reform legislation far to the right of anything anticipated by the Republican presidents of the 1980s and abandoned allies in the labor and environmental communities in support of the North American Free Trade Agreement. As a matter of political instinct and necessity, he steered away from the party's left wing. On the environment, Clinton found himself on the defensive, first seeking ways to "reinvent" environmental regulation and to encourage collaborative habitat conservation plans and then struggling to protect the gains of the 1970s. He was limited to the use of unilateral presidential authority to reward his allies in the environmental movement; the rest was a holding action against the rise of the right. "Great shield, no sword," said one Sierra Club official in 1996.[14] During his second term, however, stymied by Congress, Clinton made increasing use of these executive powers to conserve public land, seeking to leave something of a historical legacy. (See chapter 4.) If Nixon had to make his peace with liberal forces in Congress as a matter of political necessity, Clinton operated in a world in which the premises had changed radically, against the active use of governmental power to address pressing social and economic problems. This is a crucial point. As Shep Melnick noted, the wave of environmental laws that peaked in the 1970s followed hard upon other major statutes expanding the functions of the federal government, including Medicare and Medicaid, federal aid to education, and the Great Society.[15] Public trust in government was only beginning its steep descent, and it was easier then than now to make the case that large-scale federal intervention was necessary and likely to alleviate pressing environmental problems. The deterioration of trust has sharpened the right turn in policy debate, making major expansions of the federal government's domestic policy role—always difficult to achieve— even less likely. To the extent that reforming old environmental protection policies or tackling emerging issues like global warming or non-point sources of pollution require expansions of governmental power, the deterioration of trust and the weakness of the liberal impulse limit our ability to address those problems.

Public Opinion on the Environment and Declining Trust in Government
The electoral successes of Republicans have come despite, not because of, the party's positions on environmental issues. Public support for environmental protection remains strong. In a 2005 poll, 70 percent of Americans identified themselves as "active environmentalists" or "sympathetic to environmental concerns" and 24 percent described themselves as neutral. Only 4 percent called themselves "unsympathetic" to environmentalism. Although general support is high, most students of public opinion on environmental protection find that the issue has low salience with voters. Few citizens rank environmental issues as a top priority when evaluating government performance or candidates for office. Still, general levels of public support for environmental protection may be higher now than they were during the golden age of environmental lawmaking—certainly they are not lower. Thus, *changes* in public opinion cannot easily explain the congealing of a legislative gridlock on the environment. Instead, public opinion seems basically supportive of the policy status quo, offering no strong support for new liberal initiatives or for conservatives seeking to amend laws such as the Endangered Species Act and Superfund.[16]

Indeed, the 104th Congress's Republican leaders learned that citizens' general skepticism about government and the larger right turn in American politics did not extend to support for rolling back the federal commitment to environmental protection. Citizens perceived the Republicans to be too extreme on environmental issues; claims that the green state was inefficient and too invasive had little impact, and the party was forced to moderate its rhetoric and its agenda.[17]

Thus, the environment seems to be a settled issue in public opinion. There is strong general support for the green state, despite conservative complaints about costs and inefficiency and despite environmentalists' concerns that efforts at pollution control and conservation have been too weak. The barriers to non-incremental policy change typically give way only when there is a perceived crisis. Today—despite increasing concern on global warming—there is no widespread sense of crisis on the part of the public, no overwhelming fear about continuing environmental degradation, and no deep concern about the economic and social costs of environmental protection. Public opinion supports the status quo, reinforcing legislative gridlock.

Interest-Group Politics: Mobilization, Backlashes, and Gridlock

While public opinion on the environment has been stable over the past 30 years, the organizational politics surrounding these issues has changed dramatically. David Truman's imagery of "waves" of organization and counter-organization nicely captures developments in this sector since the late 1960s.[18] The environmental policy arena is thick with political organizations, and the intense mobilization of interests on all sides of major policy questions has limited opportunities for major legislative action.

The explosion of environmental advocacy in the early 1960s and the 1970s created a large interest-group sector.[19] Indeed, according to Baumgartner and Jones, the environmental movement was "the largest, most visible, and fastest growing part of the citizen's sector" during the period 1960–1990. The number of groups listed in the *Encyclopedia of Associations* increased from 119 to 396 between 1961 and 1990. Of even greater significance was the growth in staff and budget for these groups—resources crucial for participation in the policy process. Environmental organizations had more than nine times as many full-time staff members in 1990 as in 1961. Membership, of course, increased dramatically as well (e.g., the Sierra Club's membership increased from 16,500 in 1961 to 642,000 in 2000). In 1995, based on his study of IRS tax-exempt organizations, Robert Brulle estimated that 10,000 environmental groups existed at the national, state, and local levels. These groups had assets of $5.8 billion, annual income of $2.7 billion, and more than 40 million members. Christopher Bosso showed that 30 major national environmental organizations boasted total member-ships of 7.8 million and budgets of $2.1 billion in 2003. Bosso argued that "the breadth, density, and diversity of the environmental advocacy community give environmentalism itself greater resiliency and impact than are often recognized."[20]

Environmental groups have been minor participants in campaign finance, but their large memberships and staff resources, coupled with strong general public support for environmental protection, have made them formidable players in legislative politics. As environmental groups have proliferated, the organizational politics of environmentalism have become diverse, with groups focusing on different constituencies, issues, and strategies. This diversity has strengthened the broader movements' capacity to mobilize citizens and to operate effectively across a range of pol-icy areas. It has also, naturally, led to differences among groups over policy and strategy. The Sierra Club and the Audubon Society split on NAFTA; there is a lively debate over the extent to which the established, mainstream groups have become too institutionalized, too pragmatic and corporate. Indeed, in fall 2004 and spring 2005 the environmental movement was focused internally on a critique titled "The Death of Environmentalism."[21]

The legislative successes of environmentalists triggered two significant reactions. Business interests, knocked off balance by the environmental enthusiasm of the 1970s, quickly caught themselves and dug in against the expansion of the green state. Students of the American pressure group system noted a sharp increase in business political mobilization in the 1970s, including significant increases in lobbying, campaign spend-ing, and support for policy research and public advocacy highlighting the costs of the new social regulation. Mark Smith argued that business interests must shape public opinion in order to win on contentious policy questions, and there is ample evidence that corporate America invested heavily in such efforts as part of the larger "revolt against regulation" in the 1970s and the 1980s.[22]

One breathtaking development in this field has been the growth of corporate political spending, including both direct contributions to candidates and "soft money." In the 2003–04 election cycle, business political action committees contributed $240 million to federal candidates; environmental political action committees contributed approximately $700,000. In 2001–02, the last cycle before the ban on "soft money" contributions to parties went into effect, energy and natural resources interests gave more than $23 million, while environmental interests gave around $200,000.[23] The corporate sector's outsized fundraising capacities give it ample resources to compete with a large and powerful environmental movement.

The business mobilization has been joined by a grassroots "green backlash" movement incorporating diverse concerns, including outdoor recreationists, ranchers, farmers, property rights activists, and wise users.[24] These backlash groups have achieved few significant legislative gains, but their activism has highlighted some of the costs of new federal resource-management policies. These groups have focused attention on clashes between environmental regulations and property rights, between loggers and environmentalists, and between ranchers and advocates of grizzly and wolf reintroduction, and on other struggles. These bitter fights have crystallized national discussions about the human costs of environmental protection and environmentally sensitive resource management. The local strength of some of these interests, in particular the ties of ranching and mining interests to powerful legislators, enabled them to block changes to dated federal laws and regulations governing those industries.

In *Government's End*, Jonathan Rauch observed that entrenched interest groups have created tight gridlock in U.S. politics, blunting determined reform efforts from the left and the right.[25] Interest-group mobilization has contributed to legislative gridlock on environmental issues, frustrating environmentalists and those seeking to roll back the laws of the 1960s and the 1970s and sharply limiting the achievements of the next generation center. Green groups are powerful enough to resist changes to the basic environmental laws favored by business and anti-green backlash groups, and they can raise the political costs of attacks on

the basic environmental laws. Many greens are suspicious of next generation reforms that might weaken statutory and regulatory requirements,
and they use their power to blunt this agenda. Yet environmentalists
have been unable to overcome business resistance to green legislative
proposals. Corporate campaign contributions, lobbying, and the capacity
to summon angry grassroots support have hemmed in the environmental
movement in Congress, and fed green suspicions that next generation
reforms will be twisted to serve business interests. The level of interest-
group mobilization on the environment could not have been dreamed of
in 1970, and it has certainly contributed to legislative frustration for
allies and enemies of the green state.

A More Pervasive Media, More Responsive Politicians

Since the 1980s there have been several significant changes in how the
media cover government, changes often related to transformations in
technology. The first was the increase in the use of satellite connections
by local television stations. Many local TV stations now have reporters
in Washington who interview members of Congress on a regular basis.
This increased local coverage influences how members behave, frequently leading to an increase in symbolic stands on issues, while also
illuminating member behavior more clearly for local groups and interests. The rise of the Internet was a second important media change. This
made it easier for interest groups and individuals to track what members
of Congress were doing on particular bills, to send email action alerts to
group members, and to deluge Congress with email messages on issues
(to a lesser degree, this was done with fax messages for a time). Activists
and interested citizens seeking detailed information on what's happening
in environmental policy can easily look beyond mainstream news sources
and rely on releases from environmental organizations or economic
interests that may offer up slanted versions of the issues at stake. There
are also several environmental news services, such as the *Daily Grist,
Headwaters News,* and *Greenwire.* And third, the increase in media out-
lets due to the Internet and the growth of cable TV led to more competition to break stories and to fill pages and time. For instance, the *Drudge
Report* broke the Monica Lewinsky story, and *Talking Points Memo*
played a central role in the Trent Lott–Strom Thurmond story.[26]

These changes in the media have combined with the well-known sensitivity of politicians to constituency interests, with rising partisanship, and with increasing demands by interest groups to reduce the space available for members of Congress to engage substantive and wide-ranging legislation, especially legislation that alienates any significant population of groups. A Democrat, for example, who is thinking of supporting significant changes to the Endangered Species Act will likely be pressured by national and local environmental groups through email alerts to members in her district. Why alienate these likely supporters on a second-tier issue? Negative press and constituency pressure on environmental issues in the 104th Congress forced a Republican retreat; even now the party is seeking new, softer language in which to couch its environmental policy goals. High levels of political mobilization on all sides and strong generic public support for the status quo ratchet up the stakes for politicians considering substantive changes in environmental law.[27]

The Changing Nature of Environmental Problems

Scholars attempting to explain legislative gridlock on the environment have often cited the changing character of environmental issues. In the early 1970s, the argument goes, pollution control policy focused on curbing effluent and emissions from large, readily identifiable industrial sources. With many of these sources reasonably well controlled, and with scientific understanding of pollution problems increasing, the next generation of regulation must address new problems: highly dispersed and less visible sources of pollution. The politics of environmental policy change as the source of problems is defined as "us" (drivers of old cars, farmers, runoff from city streets, dry cleaners) instead of "them" (factory smokestacks). Developing national standards is difficult because of the complexities of the new problems; the prospects of high costs and palpable constraints on citizens' behavior change the politics of pollution issues. Legislators find it more difficult to support laws aimed at citizens and small businesses.[28]

Similarly, in resource management, new laws such as the Endangered Species Act and the Alaska Lands Act filled previously open policy spaces. Over time policymakers increasingly faced questions about the effect of federal laws and regulations on private landowners. It has at times proved difficult for national policymakers to bring federal agencies to accept the implications of the environmental law for their activities. The legislative process will be slowed by dogged defenses of private property and the legal and constitutional difficulties associated with efforts to limit property owners' discretion to use their lands as they see fit.

The emergence of new and complicated policy questions explains some part of the legislative gridlock on the environment, but it is too much to say that this is the primary cause of gridlock. Controversies and calls for legislative action have arisen in a variety of areas, from endangered species to wetlands to toxic cleanups to climate change, yet Congress has been unable to respond directly. Not only do we see the lack of an institutional "fit" between laws and agencies created in the 1970s with problems emerging in the 1990s and beyond; we see a legislature unable to address the very kind of policy questions it was tackling aggressively in the 1960s and the 1970s.

Taken together, the developments discussed above explain the difficulties that Congress has had in dealing directly with environmental issues, especially since 1990. This congressional gridlock, which has made it difficult for the political system to address new problems as well as concerns about existing laws and institutions, has been reinforced by the institutionalization of several layers of environmental policy commitments made over 100 years of political development. The "lords of yesterday" and the "lords of a little while ago" control strong points on the policy terrain and in many areas they have held the status quo against drives for policy change. Yet it is also true that the layering of the green state not only contributes to gridlock, but also energizes modern environmental politics and offers opportunities for policy to make its way up and down these layers and across the many alternative paths created by the green state and offered by the structure of the American political system. The next section examines this energized policy system in the context of legislative gridlock.

Gridlock and Policy Instability: Governing the Environment through "Institutional Disruption"

Legislative gridlock on the environment has many sources, but, as we have noted, the inability of Congress to respond to pressures for reform of environmental laws has hardly left environmental policy in stasis.

Instead, in keeping with Baumgartner and Jones's characterization of American policymaking, the existence of multiple policymaking venues offers opportunities for rapid and substantial policy change. Baumgartner and Jones argue that changing "venues," or the institutions with control over a particular policy issue, can break stable policy monopolies and reorient policy. Policy outcomes in specific areas remain stable and predictable when one set of political actors (1) successfully deploys a favorable "image" of the policy that mobilizes supporters and demobilizes opponents and (2) controls the venues in which central policy choices are made. They note that policy may remain stable for long periods, but that any policy equilibrium is vulnerable to changes in policy image and policy venue. Change occurs through "punctuated equilibrium," when contending interests successfully inject new images into debates and push choices to new venues more receptive to their concerns. These interests then establish a new policy equilibrium reflecting their agendas, which lasts until changes in policy image start the process anew. Governing in the United States occurs through "institutional disruption."[29] Thus, Baumgartner and Jones emphasize the significance of "venue shopping" by interest groups and political leaders. This has been profoundly important in environmental policymaking in the era of congressional gridlock. Congressional gridlock on land and species protection and pollution policy has shifted fundamental policy choices to non-legislative venues, from the executive branch to the courts and outward to states and local collaborative groups, and issues have moved rapidly from venue to venue in ways that have rendered every decision crucial and almost no decision final. Indeed, "institutional disruption" has become the norm in environmental policymaking. We see moments of stability (until the district court rules or is reversed or the case gets settled, until the rider is adopted or expires, until the company sues the Forest Service or the Center for Biological Diversity sues everybody, or until the administration issues the new rule, which then is challenged), but the standard is motion, movement from venue to venue and to victory and defeat and back again for contending interests. Intense mobilization on all sides of issues, coupled with policymaking processes that offer multiple points of access to competing interests, create considerable instability in the policymaking process.

There is legislative gridlock on the basic laws, but there is no stable equilibrium.

Consider the problem of determining which policy images and institutional venues now control choices about salmon runs and the hydropower system on the Columbia River. The ESA listings of several salmon species cracked open a once-stable policy subsystem centered on hydropower, irrigation, and river transport. Venue changes followed, as the listings brought new federal agencies and the courts into the flow of decisions about dam operations and the fishery. Yet 15 years after the first listings it is hard to see any new policy equilibrium, any new order on the river. Instead, we see the coexistence of powerful, competing policy images and continuing, aggressive participation by multiple interests across many venues in decisions about managing the Columbia River. Choices bounce from agency to agency and out to ad hoc groups, with the whole process occasionally punctuated by presidential elections or court decisions that send the issues back into the amazing labyrinth for another turn. The ESA listings on the Columbia were a great success for environmentalists in that they shook the old policy monopoly, but the reestablishment of anything resembling "order" has been deeply problematic. This is admittedly an extreme example of chaos in governance, but it highlights crucial characteristics of environmental policymaking beyond gridlock: multiple frames, multiple venues, significant instability. Moreover, as the next section will argue, the game is complicated by the ways that the American green state has emerged through the history of the republic.

Legislative gridlock is a feature of modern environmental policymaking. The American political system is struggling to address new or newly recognized environmental problems not engaged by existing laws, to contain bitter partisan and group conflict on environmental issues, and to address legitimate concerns about the weaknesses of statutes adopted in the 1960s and the 1970s and in earlier periods of green state building. Congress and the executive have not been able to manage these struggles in the lawmaking process, with important consequences. Legislative action could reduce uncertainty about the future of public policy; it could legitimize many of the "next generation" experiments that are now underway, creating confidence that these ad hoc arrangements can hold against judicial and administrative attack; arguably the legislative process provides greater accountability and holds greater legitimacy than policymaking on the pathways that have become so crucial in environmental policymaking. But, significantly, legislative gridlock has not created a "stuck" environmental policy. On the contrary, this is a vibrant, highly unstable area in part as a result of legislative gridlock. In the next section we explore the evolution of the American green state and the layering of often conflicting policy impulses in law and policy since the late nineteenth century.

Building the Green State

At any given moment, the different rules, arrangements, and timetables put in place by changes negotiated at various points in the past will be found to impose themselves on the actors of the present and to affect their efforts to negotiate changes of their own.
—Karen Orren and Stephen Skowronek[30]

The American green state consists of three major layers laid down over 200 years: economic liberalism, conservation, and environmentalism and preservation. (See table 2.1.) Over time, new impulses have come to dominate green state building, putting in place new laws, institutions, and political premises to guide policy. But new impulses have not completely displaced the old; instead they have layered new laws and built new institutions atop existing—and sometimes contradictory—structures. Orren and Skowronek's concept of layering is particularly useful for describing the development of the green state. "Layering, the placement of new forms of authority atop old ones left in place," they wrote, "though common, is an incomplete transfer of authority, a change likely to perpetuate controversies over exactly how much authority has shifted, over who gets to control what and how." Orren and Skowronek further noted that "the institutions of a polity are not created or recreated all at once, in accordance with a single ordering principle; they are created instead at different times, in the light of different experiences, and often for quite contrary purposes." As we discuss in greater detail below, since these past layers are not cleared away over time, there is no fresh start

Table 2.1
Building the green state.

Major Statutes	Major Institutions
First Layer, Economic Liberalism: 1800–1890	
General Survey Act (1824); regular rivers and harbors acts	Army Corps of Engineers (1802)
Mining Laws of 1866, 1870, and 1872	General Land Office (1812; became part of Bureau of Land Management, 1946)
Yellowstone National Park (1872)	Army Corps of Topographical Engineers (1838; became part of Corps of Engineers, 1863)
	U.S. Geological Survey (1879)
	Division of Forestry (1886; became Forest Service, 1905)
Second Layer, Conservation: 1890–1920	
Forest Reserve Act (1891)	Division of Biological Survey (1896; became part of Fish and Wildlife Service, 1940)
Forest Service Organic Act (1897)	Reclamation Service (1902; became Bureau of Reclamation, 1923)
Lacey Act (1900) [wildlife]	Bureau of Fisheries (1903; became part of Fish and Wildlife Service, 1940)
Newlands Act (1902) [reclamation]	Forest Service (1905)
Antiquities Act (1906)	Bureau of Mines (1910–1996)
Weeks Act (1911) [forest land purchase]	Public Health Service (1912)
Mineral Leasing Act (1920)	National Park Service (1916)
	Federal Power Commission (1920; became Federal Energy Regulatory Commission, 1977)
Conservation Interregnum: 1920–1964	
Taylor Grazing Act (1934)	Tennessee Valley Authority (1933)
Multiple Use–Sustained Yield Act (1960)	Division of Grazing (1934; became part of Bureau of Land Management, 1946)
	Soil Conservation Service (1935; became Natural Resources Conservation Service, 1994)
	Fish and Wildlife Service (1940)
	Atomic Energy Commission (1946; became Nuclear Regulatory Commission, 1975)
	Bureau of Land Management (1946)
Third Layer, Environmentalism and Preservation: 1964–1980	
Land and Water Conservation Fund (1964)	Council on Environmental Quality (1970)
Wilderness Act (1964)	Environmental Protection Agency (1970)
National Trail Systems Act (1968)	National Oceanic and Atmospheric Administration (1970)

Legislation	Agencies
Wild and Scenic Rivers Act (1968)	National Marine Fisheries Service (1971)
Clean Air Act (1970)	Nuclear Regulatory Commission (1975)
National Environmental Policy Act (1970)	Federal Energy Regulatory Commission (1977)
Coastal Zone Management Act (1972)	Office of Surface Mining (1977)
Federal Environmental Pesticide Control Act (1972)	
Federal Water Pollution Control Act (1972)	
Marine Mammals Protection Act (1972)	
Endangered Species Act (1973)	
Safe Drinking Water Act (1974)	
Federal Land Policy and Management Act (1976)	
Fisheries Conservation and Management Act (1976)	
National Forest Management Act (1976)	
Resource Conservation and Recovery Act (1976)	
Toxic Substances Control Act (1976)	
Clean Air Act Amendments (1977)	
Clean Water Act (1977)	
Surface Mining Control and Reclamation Act (1977)	
Alaska Lands Act (1980)	
Comprehensive Environmental Response, Compensation, and Liability Act (1980)	
Transition to Gridlock: 1980–1990	
Nuclear Waste Policy Act (1982)	Minerals Management Service (1982)
Resource Conservation and Recovery Act Amendments (1984)	
Safe Drinking Water Act Amendments (1986)	
Superfund Amendments (1986)	
Clean Water Act Amendments (1988)	
Ocean Dumping Act (1988)	
Clean Air Act Amendments (1990)	
Gridlock: 1990–2006	
California Desert Protection Act (1994)	
Food Quality Protection Act (1996)	

for new policies and institutions. Contradictions, conflict, and opportunity are built into the green state, with significant consequences for environmental policymaking today.[31]

The first layer of this green state, laid down from the founding through 1890, focused on developing the nation's resources, and its administrative footprint was light. The United States had a surplus of land in relation to people and capital, and many of the national policies adopted during this period focused on disposing of the nation's public lands. Indeed, the dominant idea regarding natural resources at this time was economic liberalism—society would flourish if government transferred public lands to the private sector (with some government help to release the energy within society).[32] Moving these lands into private hands would encourage settlement and economic development. Other laws, such as assorted rivers and harbors acts, sought to promote the development of water resources, again to further the growth of the nation. Until the late nineteenth century, the administrative focal point of the green state was the General Land Office, the main mission of which was to administer the disposition of federal public lands, and the U.S. Army, which managed resource development projects though the Corps of Engineers and the Corps of Topographical Engineers.[33]

This first layer of the green state is shallow and spotty, both in terms of statutes and agencies still in existence. Where the layer does exist, however, it has proved remarkably resilient. The 1872 Mining Law still governs the mining of hardrock minerals on federal public lands, with large multinationals often removing millions of dollars of minerals without paying royalties. Efforts to reform the law since the 1970s have been almost entirely unsuccessful. The Army Corps of Engineers continues to be the nation's main water development agency, hardly a rational bureaucratic choice. Other policies continue to cast a long shadow on current policy, such as R.S. 2477. This law, part of the 1866 Mining Law, granted states and localities road rights of way through public lands. Although the Federal Land Policy and Management Act (FLPMA) repealed this law in 1976, claims made before 1976 were grandfathered. Such claims are now at the center of disputes throughout the West as states and commodity interests seek to control roadways through the vast public lands, frequently clashing with wilderness advocates and those working to protect species habitat. This first layer of the green state, focused exclusively on resource development, has deep roots and when current issues encounter this first layer the discourse of development becomes central to the debate.[34]

During the decades on either side of 1900, a concentrated flurry of activity created the second layer of the green state, a layer characterized by two impulses. The first focused on conservation, namely scientific management of natural resources, with Gifford Pinchot of the Forest Service its most noteworthy proponent. The foundational idea for conservation was technocratic utilitarianism—professionals should manage natural resources for society's greatest good. Preservation of scenic and natural areas was the focus of the second impulse, with John Muir and the Sierra Club leading the way. According to the preservation idea, some places were of such moral, recreational, and scenic significance that they should be maintained in their natural state. The establishment of the second layer began a pattern for future green state building: rather than clearing away the earlier layer of the green state, reformers laid the second layer on top of the existing layer. In most cases this led to few problems, since the first layer of the green state was thin and spotty and these new laws and institutions were laid down in open political space. Furthermore, since conservation was centered on resource development, it did not conflict fundamentally with the programs of the first layer. Over time, however, this layering of the green state led to major tensions that are central to modern environmental politics. For instance, the seed of the intense political conflict over management of the national forests is found in the inherent conflict between the scientific management and preservation impulses. Those seeking sustained harvesting of these forests, a purpose for which they claim the national forests were created, run into claims of wilderness and habitat protection generally, and calls for the preservation of old-growth forests and spotted owls more specifically. Preservationists rely on new laws and institutions as well as evolving public attitudes to make their claims; both sides in these disputes root their claims in statutes and powerful—if contradictory—ideas about the role of government in resource management and environmental protection.[35]

The turn of the twentieth century saw tremendous activism on the part of the national government, particularly focused on public lands. Major conservation initiatives included the creation of the national forest system and the Forest Service and the establishment of the nation's first wildlife refuges as well as the Division of Biological Survey and Bureau of Fisheries. Water, too, was a major concern, and the federal government moved to irrigate western lands, creating the Reclamation Service to manage this work. In the preservation realm, the period saw the expansion of the national park system and the creation of the National Park Service, as well as passage of the Antiquities Act, which granted the president the power to create national monuments—a power that President Bill Clinton used vigorously. The Weeks Act, passed in 1911, allowed the Forest Service to purchase lands for national forests, establishing a precedent for the federal government to purchase lands for conservation and preservation purposes. The federal government entered the energy policy realm by passing the Mineral Leasing Act, focused primarily on coal, oil, and gas on public lands, as well as creating the Federal Power Commission to oversee hydropower projects. Lastly, although public health at this time was almost exclusively the policy responsibility of state and local governments, in recognition of an increasing federal role in this field the Public Health and Marine Hospital Service became the Public Health Service in 1912. Like its fellow state agencies, the Public Health Service was the early focal point for pollution control programs.[36]

Although the next major layer of the green state would not be laid down until the 1960s and the 1970s, state building occurred sporadically over the next 35 years, primarily following the conservation impulse. The Taylor Grazing Act established a federal grazing program and created the Grazing Service, which later merged with the General Land Office to create the Bureau of Land Management. Congress created the Soil Conservation Service to deal with soil erosion. A merger of the Bureau of Biological Survey and the Bureau of Fisheries created the Fish and Wildlife Service. And the Atomic Energy Commission was created to promote and regulate nuclear power.[37]

As this conservation layer was being laid down, Orren and Skowronek note,

the development problem . . . was not in conceiving new tasks for government, but in shifting authority to new agencies, distributing it within and among them according to new purposes and resolving conflicts over its redistribution. The entrepreneurial initiative for these shifts came from different sources, not least of which was the future managers of the new agencies themselves; but a different mix of interest behind each shift meant considerable variation from agency to agency in how much authority actually changed hands and to whose advantage. Moreover, the disruptions and displacements in the most extensive of these shifts were not clean, single-jolt affairs but repeated offensives that reverberated back and forth across agencies, building intercurrent tensions into everyday operations.[38]

As public views changed, new laws were passed, and agency missions were elaborated, these intercurrent tensions only increased, and many of these agencies came into conflict with one another. Most illustrative was the main cross-agency conflict built into the green state during the conservation era, between the Forest Service and the Interior Department. These agencies fought over the creation and placement of the National Park Service and the Division of Grazing, as well as over administration of scenic and recreation lands. The Forest Service was especially upset that many new national parks were carved out of existing national forests. Following the golden era of modern environmental policy, these internal contradictions and the nascent institutional and policy labyrinth would become far more significant.

During the period 1964–1980—the golden era of modern conservation and environmental policymaking—the third layer of the green state was created. Congress passed 22 major laws focused on pollution control, private lands, public lands, and wildlife management. Some new laws, such as the Endangered Species Act and the Wilderness Act, were layered on top of the green state from the early twentieth century, with results that, in hindsight, seem predictable. The Fish and Wildlife Service, originally focused on protecting habitat and managing species for hunting and fishing, came to administer the Endangered Species Act, a law that would see the agency clash with every other agency in the green state, especially the Forest Service, the Bureau of Land Management, and other agencies that focused on resource use. Several of these conflicts underscored contradictions built into the green state. For instance, when the government sought to reintroduce wolves to the northern Rockies, ranchers complained that the government was violating the spirit of the public lands grazing regime (part of second-layer conservation) and environmentalists complained that the Endangered Species Act is the law of the land (part of third-layer preservationism) and the wolves must return. Both the ranchers and the environmentalists were largely correct, but this did nothing to help solve the problem. Two of the conservation laws, the National Forest Management Act and the Alaska Lands Act, illustrated the growing complexities within the green state on conservation and preservation matters as environmentalists made innovative uses of laws passed decades earlier. The former law resulted from a lawsuit, *Izaak Walton League v. Butz* (1973, 1975), in which a conservation group used the Forest Service Organic Act (a second-layer law) to sue the Forest Service to prevent logging on national forests. In the process that led to passage of the Alaska Lands Act, President Jimmy Carter made unprecedented use of the Antiquities Act (another second-layer law) to protect lands in Alaska.[39]

The anti-pollution laws of the golden era were largely forays by the federal government into open policy terrain at the national level. State and local governments had been dealing with pollution issues—under the rubric of public health—for many decades, but the federal government did not enter this arena in a significant way until 1970. Hence, the air pollution, water pollution, and hazardous chemical policies crafted during the 1970s fell on largely fallow soil. The original laws and the amendments that followed were far-reaching and complex, and the pollution control portion of the green state grew quickly after its later beginnings. The EPA, pulled together by collecting preexisting programs and agencies, also found open terrain as it began its work in 1970. During this first decade of substantial national pollution control, almost all laws were based on a regulatory approach. Even though other ideas (market incentives, pollution prevention, risk management) have since flourished, it has proved nearly impossible to dislodge the regulatory programs at the heart of these pollution control statutes. Although these pollution control laws have not led to the same level of conflict within the green state, their broad economic and societal reach has made them quite controversial. The same is true for the National Environmental Policy Act, which introduced the environmental impact statement requirement for all significant federal actions. The once relatively narrow and economic-development-oriented green state had changed dramatically.[40]

With the election of Ronald Reagan and a Republican Senate from 1980 through 1986, congressional conservation and environmental policymaking slowed, but still continued. During his two terms, Reagan signed laws designating more wilderness in the lower 48 states than any other president. Furthermore, a number of significant environmental laws were enacted during this period. This is not meant to suggest that Reagan was a strong supporter of wide-ranging new conservation and environmental policies. Indeed, he pioneered a number of the new paths of environmental policymaking to achieve his goal of reducing government regulation. Nevertheless, significant environmental lawmaking did continue during his two terms in office.[41]

President George H. W. Bush sought to reinvigorate environmental policymaking. During his presidential campaign, he declared himself a conservationist and proclaimed that he would be an "environmental president." Congressional environmental policymaking under Bush culminated with the 1990 Clean Air Act amendments. Since then, Congress has passed only two significant conservation and environmental laws: the California Desert Protection Act (1994) and the Food Quality Protection Act (1996). Further building of the green state—at least at the national level—essentially stopped around 1990.[42]

This layering of multiple orders, without cleaning up past orders, has created a green state that we refer to as a labyrinth. New policies often conflict with old ones; past ideas are embedded in policy regimes, creating policy patterns especially resistant to change. This labyrinth offers opportunities as well as constraints; some of these opportunities are immediately apparent and pursued, others became visible only over time. Open paths suddenly close; new openings present themselves. In their discussion of federal public lands management, Orren and Skowronek came to a similar conclusion: "Federal land policy, once the model of flexibility and instrumental efficiency, is now the paradigmatic case of institutionally encumbered governance."[43]

As the green state has grown in the course of 100 years, it has become more and more of a labyrinth, especially because Congress has never taken the time or mustered the will to clean up and re-order the green state. Even in the few instances when it did seek to clean up the legacies of the past, such as repealing hundreds of public lands laws through FLPMA in 1976, it left openings like the previously mentioned ability to claim rights of way for existing roads across public lands. Interests seeking policy goals (in this case, resource development on the public lands) exploited this opening. The failure of Congress to sweep away past layers of the green state is deeply problematic for conservatives and business interests that would like to see the environmental laws of the 1960s and the 1970s rolled back. It also poses major challenges to next generation reformers who seek to refashion the green state to make policy more flexible and economically efficient. Reform is unlikely to restructure the green state along conservative or next generation lines. It is far more likely that when it can act, Congress will add new layers to past laws, building further complexity and contradictions into environmental policy.

What of the labyrinth and environmentalists? Although we are greatly influenced by Orren and Skowronek and are largely in accord with their analysis of American political development and public lands management, we disagree in part with their assertion that "the principle developmental effect of environmentalism to date has been to throw more authority into contention; a moving stalemate alert to momentary changes in the ideological alignment of institutions has been the rule." To be sure, the political triumphs of greens have added great instability and uncertainty to environmental policymaking, and the "momentary ideological alignment of institutions" profoundly shapes policy outcomes. But rather than a "moving stalemate," the larger pattern in environmental policymaking is of a slow, uneven movement in directions generally favored by greens. Orren and Skowronek look at the spotted owl controversy and see a "politically calculated train wreck" from which "no authority emerged secure."[44] The incomplete displacement of the old order by the new did limit green gains and did create chaos in governance. The path of policy choices since the 1990s has been tortuous and frustrating to interests on all sides. Yet from a green perspective the spotted owl train wreck appears to have been a major victory: logging levels on public lands in the Northwest dropped by nearly 90 percent, and it is unlikely they will ever recover.[45]

There are two general reasons for the broad if halting green drift in environmental policy. First, the top layer of the green state in effect covers all that developed before the 1960s and the 1970s. The pollution statutes reach across the entire economy, including once-privileged extractive industries; National Environmental Policy Act requirements touch all significant federal projects; the Endangered Species Act touches the management of huge swaths of public land, as well as private lands. The lords of yesterday are everywhere confronted by the lords of a little while ago who, in the courts at least, can ensure that the political premises of the golden era of environmental lawmaking must be accounted for in policymaking. Second, the mobilization of environmental interest groups and strong public support for the cause of environmental protection reinforce gridlock in environmental lawmaking, blocking any rollback of the commitments of the 1960s and the 1970s—commitments that, though only rarely definitive, are deeply embedded in laws, institutions, and popular expectations. (We offer a fuller discussion of these themes in chapter 8.)

This intercurrence of irrigation and endangered species, of pollution control and economic development, "produces contradictions for agents, entrepreneurs, and leaders to exploit and alternatives for them to imagine." The layering of the green state, intercurrence, and these contradictions and spaces make up a policy labyrinth. With this labyrinth in place, and with Congress currently in gridlock mode on the environment, interests seeking to reform, rollback, or extend the green state explore the labyrinth for pathways conducive to their goals. Some of these pathways—appropriations politics, executive politics, the courts— are built into the green state; others can be viewed as ways to bypass the green state—collaboration, the states—but they are all ways for pent-up policy to flow when "normal" legislative channels are gridlocked. Some interests make use of a variety of pathways; other interests find a particularly attractive pathway and make use of it for policymaking. As we will see in the chapters that follow, this labyrinth and its pathways make the green state rich in policy opportunities, but also rich in contingency, conflict, and chaos.[46]

Conclusion

Congress has largely been unable to respond to demands for significant new environmental legislation since 1990. But just as a spring freshet seeks new channels around a dammed streambed, environmental policy has sought new channels around a blocked legislative process. Advocates of new or altered environmental policy have concentrated their energies on new channels, new paths for policymaking. It is these paths—appropriations politics, executive politics, the courts, collaboration, and the states—that have become the central arenas for environmental policy in the 1990s and the early 2000s. Despite the seeming gridlock in Congress, interests have sought to use unorthodox legislative approaches, especially involving appropriations and the budget, to achieve policy goals blocked in other legislative avenues. Other interests have made use of opportunities created through the green state—executive politics and the courts. Some of these efforts have been successful, using the Endangered Species Act to alter existing policy arrangements and the Antiquities Act to create new national monuments, for instance. But many such efforts have floundered as well, running into other actors challenging rulemaking on national forests and new source review, or losing court challenges to existing statutes.

Proponents of the final two pathways, collaboration and the states, often advocate these approaches as ways to get around gridlock and the existing green state. In some cases this works, especially in areas of open policy space, but the green state is wide ranging. As we will discuss in chapter 6, many efforts at collaboration have been derailed when those opposed to the collaboration approach have managed to pull the process back into the labyrinth that the green state has become. New initiatives in the states have been especially successful in open policy space and policy arenas that the states control, such as renewable portfolio standards for electricity generation. But, the states often willingly enter the green state, for example, filing lawsuits against Clean Air Act rulemaking, or are dragged into the green state by opponents who don't like new state policies, such as automakers opposed to new state auto-emission standards.

3

Regulatory Reform, Reconciliation, and Rough Riders: Environmental Policymaking in Congress

This chapter explores avenues for environmental policymaking within Congress in the era of gridlock. There are significant pressures from many constituencies for movement on environmental policy, but legislative realities have for the most part blocked statutory changes. How have these pressures been channeled in Congress? How do legislators make, or try to make, environmental policy in the era of gridlock?

Barbara Sinclair has shown that, as a result of changes in the internal structure and political environment of Congress, the "textbook" legislative process has given way to "unorthodox lawmaking": the increasing importance of omnibus legislation, budget reconciliation bills, summits between legislative leaders and the White House, and riders on appropriation bills as policymaking tools. Sinclair raises questions about the consequences of these developments, both for the quality of congressional decisions and the legitimacy of the process yielding those decisions: "Does (unorthodox lawmaking) foster or discourage deliberation, the development and bringing to bear of expertise, the inclusion of a broad range of interests, and informed and timely decision making?"[1]

Sinclair's concerns are certainly pertinent to the quality and legitimacy of environmental policymaking in Congress, where, as the *Washington Post* editorialized in 2005, "the legislative process has ground to a halt. . . . These days only riders attached to appropriation bills can pass, or oddities such as the new budget resolution that may legalize drilling in the Arctic National Wildlife Refuge."[2] Gridlock in the lawmaking process on the environment has driven policy initiative onto "unorthodox" paths inside Congress, as lawmakers have responded to enormous political and social pressures for change in the direction of environmental policy.

This chapter focuses on environmental policymaking in the gridlocked Congress. After briefly exploring exceptions to the rule of gridlock and then the stalemate on environmental policy that marked the 103rd Congress, we investigate the record of the 104th Congress and efforts to use legislative pathways around gridlock for achieving significant policy change: the drive for general regulatory reform, budget cutting to "starve the beast," the use of the reconciliation process to break the longstanding impasse over oil drilling in the Arctic National Wildlife Refuge, and policy riders on appropriation bills. The discussion of policy riders will summarize the broad strategy of using appropriation riders in the 104th Congress, which largely failed, and then look more closely at its signature success: the "salvage rider." After investigating the record of the 104th Congress the chapter will follow these new pathways past the Clinton years to the period of Republican control of the national government initiated by George W. Bush's election in 2000.

Exceptions to Gridlock

Despite the apparent congressional stalemate on environmental issues, Congress does act on the environment—it passes bills in every session, most of them minor, and it has produced a few important bills since 1990. The most significant exceptions to the rule of gridlock were the California Desert Protection Act of 1994, the Food Quality Protection Act of 1996, and the Clean Air Act Amendments of 1990.

The explanations for the first two of these legislative breakthroughs are straightforward. The California Desert Protection Act designated 7.5 million acres of wilderness, the third greatest total of any law, following only the Alaska Lands Act in 1980 and the Wilderness Act itself in 1964, as well as creating Death Valley and Joshua Tree National Parks and the Mojave National Preserve. How did this major, controversial wilderness bill pass a divided Congress? Since 1980, the congressional norm on wilderness bills has been to designate wilderness on a state-by-state basis. When there is a consensus within a delegation—most importantly among a state's Senate delegation—that legislation moves forward. This norm helps explain why Ronald Reagan signed more wilderness legislation than any other president. Senator Alan Cranston (D-California) had first introduced the California Desert Protection bill in 1986, but opposition from his Republican counterparts in the Senate blocked action. In 1992, California elected two Democratic senators, Dianne Feinstein and Barbara Boxer, who supported the legislation. Their positions, combined with support from a majority of the California House delegation, pushed this controversial measure to enactment, though not without a struggle. Feinstein was up for reelection in 1994, and Republicans sought to block her from attaining this legislative achievement before election day. Senator J. Bennett Johnston (D-Louisiana), chair of the Senate Energy and Natural Resources Committee, remarked that the bill was "the most intensely lobbied bill" in his 22 years in the Senate. Republicans filibustered, but in the end the law passed because of the congressional norm governing wilderness designations.[3]

The Food Quality Protection Act of 1996 overhauled policy concerning pesticide residues on foods; court rulings on allowable levels of residues forced Congress to act to avoid significant economic dislocation.[4] At issue was the Delaney Clause, part of the 1958 Federal Food, Drug, and Cosmetic Act. The Delaney Clause allowed no detectable residues in processed foods of any chemical that scientists had demonstrated to cause cancer in humans or in animal tests. This zero-tolerance standard became increasingly difficult to meet with the development of instruments that could detect lower and lower levels of chemicals, from parts per million to parts per billion or even trillion. (Higher levels of pesticide residue were allowed on raw foods.) In 1988, the U.S. Environmental Protection Agency changed its interpretation of the Delaney Clause to allow some residues to remain on processed foods. In *Les v. Reilly* (1992), a federal circuit court interpreted the Delaney Clause to mean "zero risk," meaning that the EPA was required to abide by its literal meaning. Congress had to act to avoid the likely prohibition of many common pesticides.[5] Congress passed a compromise bill including a uniform standard for both raw and processed foods based on a "reasonable certainty of no harm." In practice, this meant that the EPA would set pesticide residue standards at levels that would cause cancer in no more than one in a million chances. The law included other provisions requiring the EPA to take into account the foods that children ate in large quantities, and to regulate pesticide residues accordingly; to consider whether a pesticide had estrogenic effects, and if it did, factor that into the acceptable residue levels; and to allow citizens to petition for changes to pesticide residue regulation, with the agency required to respond within a year; it also pre-empted regulation of pesticide residues by state governments.[6]

Congress overcame gridlock to pass the Food Quality Protection Act in 1996 because *Les v. Reilly* presented significant problems for agribusiness. Government registration for many common pesticides would have been revoked. This decision forced agribusiness to the bargaining table with environmentalists, who were eager to gain better protection for children, more stringent regulation of pesticides on raw foods, and stronger protections against pesticides' estrogenic effects.

The story of the passage of the Clean Air Act Amendments of 1990 was more complex because of the nature of existing air quality policy and the economic stakes. Strong political forces lined up behind the bill, with state delegations from the Northeast seeking to address acid rain problems and industries supportive of a market-based approach to air pollution regulation. Moreover, for different reasons, President George H. W. Bush and Senate Majority Leader George Mitchell (D-Maine) made passage of the bill a high priority. Both invested substantial amounts of political capital in this bill, which stands as the most significant domestic legislation enacted by Congress during the Bush administration.

Why was President George H. W. Bush committed to a bill? During his 1988 presidential campaign, Bush (then Ronald Reagan's vice president) tried to distinguish himself from Reagan in a number of areas, including the environment. Declaring that he wished to be the "environmental president," Bush focused on air pollution, including acid rain and the need for tighter controls in those parts of the country that had not met the Environmental Protection Agency's air quality standards. Once elected, Bush was committed to press for amendments to the Clean Air Act. He devoted significant time and energy to drafting a bill; even more important, he committed substantial political capital to getting the legislation through Congress.[7]

In Congress, George Mitchell's determined leadership was essential. He was personally interested in getting clean-air amendments passed, in part to deal with the acid rain problem affecting Maine, and he moved heaven and earth to do so. After the Senate failed to break a filibuster against the bill, Mitchell pushed the process into the backrooms, negotiated a unanimous consent agreement that allowed debate to go forward, and eased the way to passage. Mitchell pushed the Senate for ten weeks—"to the virtual exclusion of all other business"—on the clean-air amendments, with "most of the debate . . . conducted behind closed doors . . . in the back room of Mitchell's spacious leadership suite." As Richard Cohen remarked in his book tracing the passage of the Clean Air Act amendments, "George Mitchell's extraordinary leadership in handling the clean-air bill became a personal tour de force rarely matched in Senate history."[8]

With Bush and Mitchell pushing hard for a bill, Speaker of the House Tom Foley (D-Washington) worked for passage in the House. He pressed Representatives John Dingell (D-Michigan) and Henry Waxman (D-California), the two central House players on clean air, to work out a compromise on motor-vehicle emissions and acid rain that would hold the Democrats together, and Dingell and Waxman did so. The Rules Committee then sent the bill to the floor under a restrictive rule that blocked killer amendments. The final legislation included four main provisions: large reductions of sulfur dioxide and nitrogen oxide emissions, the main causes of acid rain, through a market-based allowance system; new rules and deadlines for parts of the country falling short of existing air quality standards; regulations leading to the phasing out of chlorofluorocarbons and other chemicals depleting stratospheric ozone; and a new program to regulate 189 hazardous air pollutants.[9]

The 1990 Clean Air Act Amendments passed in part because of the application of enormous amounts of political capital by President Bush and Senator Mitchell and in part because these leaders successfully negotiated the legislative labyrinth, using many of the tools of "unorthodox lawmaking" to defy long odds and to move the bill.

Again, Congress has managed some significant legislative achievements on the environment, but gridlock has been far more common and deeply frustrating to policymakers on the left and the right. Congress has failed to reauthorize important laws, including Superfund, the Clean Water Act, and the Endangered Species Act, and it has struggled to address emerging environmental problems. The next section briefly explores the frustrations of environmentalists in the 103rd Congress, as the Democrats were unable to translate control of Congress and the White House into significant policy achievements.

Bill Clinton and the Democratic-Controlled 103rd Congress

After 12 years of Republican control of the White House, there was a considerable backlog of policy concerns in the environmental community.[10] Environmentalists sought legislation that would reduce greenhouse emissions and encourage alternative energy; cut subsidies to the mining, grazing, and timber industries; reauthorize the Endangered Species Act, Superfund, and other laws; elevate the Environmental Protection Agency to cabinet status; and reduce pesticides in food and drinking water. President Bill Clinton was generally supportive, yet these issues were far from his highest priority and the green agenda languished in Congress. The 103rd Congress was unproductive on environmental issues—the League of Conservation Voters called it the worst in 25 years.[11] The environmentalists' ambitions ran headlong into legislative gridlock. *Congressional Quarterly* described the proposal to elevate the EPA to cabinet status as the "flagship" environmental policy initiative of Clinton's first year as president. This bill enjoyed bipartisan support and had been embraced by Clinton's Republican predecessor, Bush. Yet support collapsed at both ends of the political spectrum. Conservatives sought to attach restrictive regulatory-reform provisions to the bill. Advocates for environmental justice hoped that it would be a vehicle for environmental civil rights legislation, and their enthusiasm dampened when this proved to be politically impossible. Some environmentalists were concerned that the elevation of the EPA to cabinet status meant the end of the Council on Environmental Quality, which they valued because it brought environmental policy concerns into the White House. The bill died when the House of Representatives voted to reject a rule, proposed by the Rules Committee, that would have protected the bill from amendments carrying the conservatives' regulatory reform measures.[12] The 103rd Congress could not deliver on this largely symbolic, bipartisan bill, and its record on more difficult matters was no better.

Important parts of the Clinton agenda linked environmental concerns to one of the central economic policy issues of the early 1990s: large federal budget deficits. The administration proposed an energy tax based on the energy potential of fuels, the "BTU tax," and pitched this as a tool for deficit reduction as well as energy conservation. Again, the politics proved difficult. Environmentalists favored a tax on the carbon content of fuels, which they thought would more strongly discourage the production of greenhouse gasses, push the United States toward the use of renewable energy sources, and reduce overall demand for energy. Industries that would be negatively affected by the Clinton proposal, as well as anti-tax forces, also attacked the plan. The Clinton proposal was battered in Congress, with Democrats taking a lead role. Senator Dale Bumpers (D-Arkansas) said "It's going to be [nearly] impossible to get anything through here," and he was right. Despite Clinton's many concessions to various industries and regions that would have softened the tax's impact (and reduced its significance as an energy conservation measure), Senate opposition ultimately killed the proposal. After considerable wrangling, Congress accepted a gasoline tax of 4.3 cents per gallon as part of the reconciliation bill, a compromise that offered few environmental benefits.[13]

On public lands and resources, Clinton sought to stop wasteful subsidies, increase revenues, and address some major environmental problems simultaneously. He proposed significant changes to the management of public lands, including increased fees for ranchers whose cattle graze on public lands, the end of below-cost timber sales, and initiating royalty payments from mining companies operating on public lands. Again, these proposals promised to help address budget deficits while slowing the environmental damage that flowed from heavily subsidized grazing, mining, and logging. Secretary of the Interior Bruce Babbitt boldly declared the end of the era of "unrestrained, giveaway, environment-be-damned" use of public resources and promised the introduction of a "new American land ethic" into public policy.[14] All these proposals failed miserably. In his first economic package, Clinton proposed doubling grazing fees. He dropped this at the insistence of western senators whose votes he needed to pass the budget bill. House appropriators tried to attach the fee increase as a rider to the fiscal year 1994 Interior appropriation bill and to a Bureau of Land Management reauthorization bill, but these provisions died. Babbitt's threat to impose higher fees administratively brought intense criticism from the Senate and was withdrawn at the end of 1994. To add insult to injury, under a formula established by the Public Rangeland Improvement Act of 1978, it soon became apparent that falling beef prices would lead to a *reduction* in grazing fees, from $1.98 per animal unit month to $1.61; rates fell again for 1996, to $1.31.[15] Reform of the 1872 Mining Law suffered a similar fate. This legislation allows mining companies to extract resources from the public lands at virtually no cost. The companies may "patent" or claim title to federal lands for as little as $2.50 an acre and pay no royalties on the value of the minerals they take. By 1989, 3.2 million acres, an area roughly the size of Connecticut, had been patented by mining companies, many of which had created major environmental cleanup problems.[16] In hard budget times, events themselves seemed to make the case for reform. In May 1994, the law forced Babbitt to grant patents on federal lands in Nevada containing $8–$10 billion in gold. The mining company paid just $10,000 for the lands. At a public ceremony marking the sale Babbitt called it "the biggest gold heist since the days of Butch Cassidy."[17] Still, the entrenched power of the mining industry and its western allies in Congress, particularly in the Senate, prevented Congress from amending the law.

Across the board, the 103rd Congress failed to deliver. The journalist Jessica Matthews wrote:

. . . with respect to the environment, this Congress was pure scorched earth. Legislators could not manage to fix the lawyer-riddled, overly expensive Superfund program for cleaning up toxic waste sites, even though 80 percent of the work was done for them by a coalition of business and environmental leaders who produced a compromise plan. Administration proposals to reduce subsidies that cause environmental harm while draining the federal treasury were all defeated. . . . Reauthorization and needed improvements to the Clean Water Act, the Safe Drinking Water Act and the Endangered Species Act all failed. A harmless proposal to create a National Biological Survey to identify which species live where didn't make it out of the starting blocks. A bill to raise the Environmental Protection Agency to full Cabinet status went down. The Senate failed to ratify the Biodiversity Treaty, and the administration's proposed energy tax was slashed to insignificance.[18]

In Clinton's first two years in office, both the consensual and the controversial were caught in legislative gridlock on environmental policy.

In the 104th Congress, the balance of issues on the congressional agenda tipped decisively toward the controversial, but the results were largely the same—sound and fury and only a little legislative action.

The 104th Congress: Regulatory Reform, Reconciliation, and Riders

The stunning results of the 1994 elections opened the possibility of a break in the legislative impasse on environmental policy. The Republicans gained 52 seats in the House of Representatives and eight in the Senate, taking control of both chambers for the first time in decades. The new House majority, led by Speaker Newt Gingrich of Georgia, was the pointed spear of the conservative furies loosed in the country during the Clinton presidency. Republican Whip Tom DeLay of Texas, given some provenance over environmental issues in the 104th Congress, made his views on regulatory policy plain when he compared the Environmental Protection Agency to the Gestapo and said he could not think of a single federal regulation he would keep on the books.[19] Thomas Bliley (R-Virginia), chair of the Commerce Committee, asserted: "The American people sent us a message in November, loud and clear: Tame this regulatory beast! Our constituents want us to break the Feds' stranglehold on our economy and to get them out of decisions that are best left to the individual."[20]

Conservatives, packaging the rage of some rural Americans at laws like the Endangered Species Act and the frustrations of corporate America with the costs of compliance with environmental regulations, claimed expansive warrants for legislative change. They pushed regulatory reforms that would hinder rulemaking and enforcement of all of the nation's environmental laws.[21] They sought to rewrite the Clean Air Act, the Clean Water Act, the Superfund law, the Endangered Species Act, and the Safe Drinking Water Act; to relax restrictions on logging in national forests; and to soften limits on pesticides in food. Yet this effort failed in the face of internal party divisions in the House, Senate recalcitrance, Clinton's veto threats, and the growing realization that the conservatives were out of step with the public on these issues. At the start of the debate on Superfund revisions the leader of the reform effort, Michael Oxley (R-Ohio) boldly claimed: "If one can recognize the Superfund after we finish, then we will not have done our job."[22] The revisions languished in committee, and the project was abandoned. Clean Water Act revisions passed by the House of Representatives made no headway in the Senate. The Endangered Species Act survived intact, and there were no changes of substance to the Clean Air Act. By the end of the 104th Congress, Republicans, chastened by defeat and worried about public unease with their positions on environmental issues, sought to develop a more positive environmental policy record. They joined with Democrats in revising the Safe Drinking Water Act, did what was necessary after *Les v. Reilly* to pass the Food Quality Protection Act, and reauthorized the Fisheries Conservation and Management Act of 1976 with strengthened measures against overfishing.[23] The environmental laws of the golden era survived this assault, forcing a political retreat by conservatives and driving their initiatives onto other legislative and non-legislative pathways.

With progress on statutory changes stymied, policymaking moved onto other paths within Congress. The first was general regulatory reform, an effort—depending on one's point of view—to make regulation more efficient or to tie agencies down with new and arduous analytical requirements. The second was the attempted use of the budgetary process, including proposing massive budget cuts to weaken enforcement, the budget reconciliation to avoid possible filibusters and open the Arctic National Wildlife Refuge (ANWR) to oil drilling, and policy riders on appropriation bills.

Regulatory Reform
Beginning in the late 1970s, Marc Allen Eisner argued that a modern "efficiency regime" emerged in response to concerns about the costs of the new social regulations—including environmental regulations—adopted in the 1960s and the 1970s. Unlike earlier regulatory regimes, no single statute or set of statutes underpinned this new regime. Instead, presidents pushed its development through administrative decisions that imposed new requirements on regulatory agencies, from demands for cost-benefit analysis to centralized regulatory clearance.[24] The 104th Congress saw a serious attempt to create a statutory foundation for the efficiency regime, one powerfully influenced by the right's antipathy toward the green state. Regulatory reform legislation would have weakened the federal government's regulatory capacity, rolling back

regulations without a fight over the language of the basic environmental statutes.

As was usually the case in the 104th Congress, the House of Representatives took the point on this issue. At the end of February 1995, three reform proposals "roared through the House like an express train." HR 1022 would have imposed a complex set of risk assessment requirements on regulatory agencies, requiring them to develop detailed data analyzing health risks caused by substances or activities subject to proposed regulations. Agencies would have been required to review research on risk potentials; compare the risks at hand to other, similar risks and the risks of everyday life (e.g., being struck by lightning); and analyze the risks associated with products or activities likely to replace those being regulated. Risk assessment is difficult and all participants understood that one goal of the bill was to tie down agencies with these new requirements. Gerald Solomon (R-New York), chair of the House Rules Committee, said: "For years, business and industry have been forced through hoops to satisfy regulators. . . . Well, if this legislation becomes law, we are going to turn that around." Beyond this, HR 926 mandated that agencies produce detailed cost-benefit analyses in the rulemaking process for any rule estimated to have an economic impact of greater than $100 million. These new requirements would trump existing laws, effectively repealing parts of them. These bills, along with a property rights measure, were rolled into a single omnibus bill, HR 9, which the House passed by a 277–141 vote.[25]

Clinton's opposition and divisions in the Senate blocked regulatory reform. The administration threatened a veto, and to show its own interest in reform ratcheted up its regulatory "reinvention" project, which promised more cost-effective regulations through administrative action.[26] In the Senate, William Roth (R-Delaware) in the Government Affairs Committee and Robert Dole (R-Kansas) in the Judiciary Committee proposed competing versions of regulatory reform. Roth crafted a moderate bill that gained unanimous support from the Government Affairs Committee, but ultimately the Dole bill, which was quite a bit closer to the House version, became the focal point of the Senate fight. The Democrats filibustered, defeating three attempts at invoking cloture over an eight-day period and leading Dole—who spent the week moderating the bill to make it more palatable to Democrats—to declare the bill dead for the session. Democrats had hammered the Dole bill with proposed amendments that would have exempted high profile rulemakings on hazards like cryptosporidium in drinking water, from the new cost-benefit and risk assessment requirements. These amendments were designed to force Republicans to acknowledge that the reform would make it harder for agencies to protect citizens from certain threats. Major regulatory reform was dead for the 104th Congress and made no serious comeback for the rest of Clinton's presidency.[27]

The failure of Congress to enact regulatory reform legislation kept the initiative in the White House, where the new efficiency regime would continue to grow out of executive orders, rulemakings, and collaborative approaches to rulemaking and regulation supported by the administration. The conservative proposal pushed the Clinton administration forward, but the legislation's failure at once gave the administration a freer hand to develop its reinvention program *and* limited what could be achieved because the new Clinton initiatives program lacked statutory sanction. Former EPA Administrator William Ruckelshaus wrote: "As the legislative battles raged in 1995 and 1996, EPA launched its administrative package of regulatory reinvention initiatives. Many perceived these as largely defensive in nature, arguing that, if these were such great ideas, why did the agency wait until 1995 to do them? Congress generally has *not* seen itself as a partner in implementing EPA's reinvention package, nor has the administration sought a partnership with Congress. With one exception . . . there has been no legislation passed to support or promote the agency's reinvention efforts."[28]

Budgeting

The House leaders' strategy was to use the budget process to force the more moderate Senate and the White House to accept the conservative agenda on the environment. They hoped that Clinton, weakened by the 1994 elections, would accept large cuts in agency budgets and that major policy changes would overcome the still formidable barriers to legislative innovation using budget reconciliation and appropriation riders. The Environmental Protection Agency was a major target, but conservatives focused on many conservation programs as well, from endangered species to forest planning.

In 1995 the House of Representatives passed a bill that would have cut the EPA budget by 34 percent, by far the most significant cut for any agency. The more "moderate" Republican proposals sought cuts of around 20 percent, still a serious blow to the Environmental Protection Agency. In March 1995, shortly after passing a $17.1 billion rescissions bill aimed in part at environmental programs, Representative David McIntosh (R-Indiana) noted that this was only the beginning, with the Republican Party targeting "the most egregious areas" for cuts before revising the environmental statutes themselves based on "free market principles."[29]

Clinton, whose political standing had collapsed with the failure of his health-care proposal and with the Republican takeover of Congress, was desperate to reassert himself. Reeling, Clinton found his footing in the fight over the budget. He issued sharp veto threats and carried through with them, typically citing the effect of the Republicans' program on the environment as one reason to reject those spending bills. The budget impasse of 1995 and 1996 triggered partial government shutdowns that, when the dust cleared, damaged the congressional Republicans far more than the president. Clinton successfully framed the Republicans as out of the mainstream on crucial issues, including the environment, and beat back their budgetary initiatives, labeling them part of "an overall back-door effort by the Congressional Republicans to impose their priorities on our nation."[30] Some moderate Republicans broke with the conservatives, and by the spring of 1996 the tide had turned. The House leadership declared that it would moderate its agenda, acknowledging its defeat in this area and ending the frontal assaults on the green state.[31]

Budget data indicate that the Republican majority had some success in reining in environmental spending in its first year, but that this success did not meet their initial hopes and was short-lived.[32] Overall spending on natural resources, conservation and land management, pollution control and abatement, water resources, and recreational resources fell 9.3 percent in FY 1995, with the sharpest cuts coming in spending on water resources (down 22.8 percent) and pollution control and abatement (down 12.7 percent). However, increases in total spending in the following three fiscal years more than replaced the cuts made in 1995, and by FY 1999 total spending exceeded the levels seen at the start of the Clinton years. The Republican "revolution" may have slowed the growth of spending on environmental programs, but it hardly "starved the beast." The Republican firebrands were surprised to discover that the environmental policy regime was highly resilient and the forces creating stalemate remained in place. Still they saw opportunities, however narrow, in the budget reconciliation and appropriation processes.

Budget Reconciliation Cuts the Ice?

One "unorthodox" lawmaking pathway is the budget reconciliation process. Reconciliation is part of the congressional budget process created in 1974, and was originally conceived as a relatively minor "fallback mechanism" for reconciling tax and spending policy. It was first used in 1980, and has been used frequently since that time to drive spending cuts, to increase revenues, or to cut taxes. Reconciliation proceeds in two steps. First there is the passage of a budget resolution (not sent to the president for a signature) that instructs House and Senate committees to meet targets for spending and revenues. Second, committee recommendations are sent to the budget committees and packaged into an omnibus "reconciliation bill" to be considered on the floor. Reconciliation bills have proved to be extraordinarily powerful mechanisms for shaping budget policy and for the majority party in Congress, in part because they carry a special protection against minority obstructionism in the Senate: amendments must be germane, and these bills cannot be filibustered, so they will pass if they can gather simple majorities in both chambers.[33]

The House leadership wanted to use the budget reconciliation process to force substantial changes in policy and priorities and to drive the budget toward balance by 2002. The failure of this gambit—it "led to two historic government shutdowns, thirteen stopgap spending measures, seven presidential vetoes, and ultimately failed to produce a meaningful fiscal agreement with the White House"—is important, but not of central interest here. What matters is the attempt to use the reconciliation process to drill through one of the toughest environmental issues Congress faced: oil and gas development in the Arctic National Wildlife Refuge. As Secretary of the Interior Babbitt observed, there was ANWR drilling, "quietly stuck, like a Post-It note, on budget reconciliation measures."[34]

In 1980, the Alaska National Interest Lands Conservation Act (ANILCA) created the Arctic National Wildlife Refuge by adding millions of acres to the Arctic National Wildlife Range. Much of the area of the refuge was to be managed as wilderness, but Congress put off a decision about oil and gas development on the refuge's coastal plain. Geologists suspected that the area held significant oil and gas deposits; Congress ordered a study of ANWR's energy potential and the environmental consequences of development to be completed by 1987. There would be no drilling unless Congress acted affirmatively to open the area to development. ANILCA triggered a decades-long struggle, with ebbs and flows driven by events like the *Exxon Valdez* oil spill, which strengthened the environmentalists' position, and the 1991 Gulf War, which raised concerns about U.S. oil supplies and strengthened pro-drilling arguments.

The 1987 report recommended that the entire area of the refuge be opened to drilling, and by July the Department of the Interior had developed a plan for dividing up the area among the Alaskan native corporations that would lease the lands to oil companies.[35] Environmentalists protested that drilling would devastate wildlife and the larger coastal ecology, and Congress proved unable to move from the status quo. While greens could block drilling, they could not win permanent protection for the refuge's coastal plain. Between 1987 and 1995, there were many hearings and legislative proposals on protecting or opening the refuge, but no final legislative action. Perhaps the biggest fight came in 1991, when a major energy bill collapsed over the ANWR issue. In 1990, Bush Deputy Secretary of the Interior John Hughes observed that on ANWR environmentalists have "home-field advantage because all they have to do is block us. Blocking something is always easier than doing something affirmative, so in a 50-50 battle, that certainly could tip the scales in their favor."[36] The legacy of the 1980 ANILCA proved difficult to undo as political conditions changed.

The 104th Congress reopened the possibility of drilling in the refuge and embraced budget reconciliation as a tool for achieving this goal. Alaskans assumed powerful positions in the Senate and House, with Senator Frank Murkowski (R) taking the chair of the Senate Energy and Natural Resources Committee and Representative Don Young (R) leading the House Resources Committee. Both promised an effort to open ANWR to drilling by placing provisions in the budget reconciliation bill.[37] They introduced language that anticipated new revenues of $1.3 billion from ANWR development, and the gambit succeeded in moving the commitment to drilling through the budget process. Senator Joseph Lieberman (D-Connecticut), a leading opponent of oil drilling, said that it appeared that there were majorities in both chambers who favored opening the refuge. Murkowski and Young's tactics would prevent the minority in opposition from filibustering.[38]

The House Resources Committee adopted the language in its part of the reconciliation bill by a vote of 25–12, and the Senate Energy and Resources Committee approved its reconciliation package by a vote of 13–7. Clinton immediately threatened a veto, but this did not dissuade drilling proponents, who hoped that he would be too weak to reject the budget package. Opponents in the House failed to persuade the leadership to drop the ANWR provisions before they went to the floor, and an amendment to omit the ANWR drilling language from the Senate bill failed 51 to 48. The long battle over ANWR appeared to be over, as Congress finally passed a budget bill opening the refuge to drilling.[39]

Clinton had the final word, however, and vetoed the entire reconciliation package on December 6, 1995, citing many provisions of the budget including ANWR drilling. The budget "would open the Arctic National Wildlife Refuge to oil and gas drilling, threatening a unique, pristine ecosystem, in hopes of generating $1.3 billion in federal revenues—a revenue estimate based on wishful thinking and outdated analysis," stated the president. "I want to protect this biologically rich wilderness permanently."[40]

This veto did not resolve the issue, of course, but for most of the rest of Clinton's presidency legislative proposals to pry open ANWR were symbolic—bills without any chance of passage introduced on each side in the 105th and 106th Congresses and never coming to a vote.[41] There was more serious movement on the budgetary pathway, however. In March 2000 the Senate Budget Committee reported a budget resolution that anticipated revenues from ANWR drilling, and the Senate defeated an amendment to drop this provision from the reconciliation bill. The House of Representatives did not pass a similar provision, however, and assumptions about drilling revenues disappeared from the conference report. The reconciliation pathway appeared to be more promising than the normal legislative process. From the 101st Congress to the 106th there were three recorded votes on ANWR—all three (two in the 104th, one in the 106th) were votes to table anti-drilling amendments to budget reconciliation bills.

As will be shown below, well into George W. Bush's presidency the workings of the normal legislative process on energy and environmental legislation stymied efforts to open or permanently protect the refuge. In the 109th Congress proponents of drilling tried some new unorthodox tactics and came within a hair's breadth of success, but as of the end of 2006 the ANWR battle continued without resolution, and Democratic victories in the congressional elections all but ensure that the "home field advantage" enjoyed by drilling opponents would hold for at least two more years.

Appropriation Riders: Paths around Gridlock?

When everything else is screwed up, things do tend to reduce down to the appropriations process. —Joe White[42]

Another budget-related tool for making policy in the deadlocked Congress has been the use of "policy riders" on appropriation bills. What are riders, and why is this practice at times controversial? Congress divides the policymaking process into two parts: *authorization*, which establishes, amends, or continues policy programs, and *appropriation*, which funds those programs. In principle, substantive policymaking is left to authorizing committees, while appropriators determine funding levels. House and Senate rules prohibit legislating in appropriation bills, with the House maintaining somewhat stricter rules.[43] There is considerable flexibility, though, and this principle is violated quite regularly, with legislators attaching such directives—riders—to appropriation bills. Since appropriations must pass to fund the government, they may be good vehicles for legislation that might not be able to pass on its own. Submerged in the voluminous language and figures of a multi-billion dollar appropriation bill, riders may move through the legislative process quietly, with little or no debate. Congressional opponents may not be able to marshal their forces to fight riders when there are so many other issues at stake in a huge appropriations bill, and presidents may hesitate to veto must pass appropriation bills to kill one or a few noxious riders.

To the extent that riders become law only because they are attached to other, must-pass bills, and to the extent that they are not fully debated because they are linked to large and complex appropriation bills, they may fail Sinclair's test of good lawmaking by discouraging deliberation, the effective use of expertise, and the inclusion of a broad range of interests in decisionmaking. In environmental policymaking, riders have, with a few exceptions, not served a pragmatic, collaborative policy agenda.[44] Instead, in the 1990s and after they have most often been used to try to advance partisan objectives outside normal legislative channels, as a pathway around gridlock on the substance of environmental legislation.

Riders have been used to make environmental policy on specific issues in the past. Congress used a 1973 rider to exempt the Alaska oil pipeline from National Environmental Policy Act requirements, and in 1980 it exempted the Tellico dam project in Tennessee from the Endangered Species Act using a policy rider. They have also been used to advance environmental protection. Between 1990 and 1994, with Democrats controlling Congress, legislators used riders, with mixed success, to try to increase grazing fees, to stop the patenting of hardrock mining lands, and to block offshore oil drilling and the construction of new forest roads.[45] A prominent recent example was the congressional mandate to the Forest Service in the 1999 Interior Appropriation to implement the forest management plan hatched by the Quincy Library Group, a locally based collaborative conservation group in California.[46] Riders *can* serve the next generation approach, but the larger story shows that legislators have more frequently pursued controversial, partisan objectives using policy riders.

Lawmakers have frequently attempted to use riders to achieve environmental policy goals, especially since 1990. (See table 3.1.) Yet in the 104th Congress environmental policy riders took on new importance. Despite its sense of a mandate, the House leadership feared that it could not move legislation fast enough to achieve its goals, and anticipated difficulties in getting the Senate and Clinton to agree to their more ambitious proposals. Their experiences with traditional lawmaking showed them the difficulties of moving their agenda in authorizing legislation— regulatory reform and Clean Water Act reauthorization passed in the House but bogged down in the Senate in the shadow of veto threats. House leaders chose to use the appropriation process to evade gridlocked policymaking channels. John Aldrich and David Rohde noted that "the

Table 3.1
Major issues debated during appropriations process, 1990–2005.
Source: *CQ Almanacs*, 1990–2005.

1990	Endangered Species Act (ESA), northern spotted owl, timber harvesting
	Mining patent moratorium
	National forest logging roads
	Offshore oil and gas leasing moratorium
	Public lands grazing fee increase
1991	ESA, northern spotted owl, timber harvesting
	Public lands grazing fee increase
	Wolf reintroduction blocked
1992	ESA, northern spotted owl, timber harvesting
	Forest Service logging appeals
	Mining claim fee
	Mining patent moratorium
	National forest logging roads
	Public lands grazing fee increase
	Reducing below-cost timber sales
1993	Mining patent moratorium
	National Biological Survey
	Offshore oil and gas leasing moratorium
	Public lands grazing fee increase
1994	EPA ethanol rule
	ESA implementation
	Mining patent moratorium
	National Biological Survey
	Offshore oil and gas leasing moratorium
	Tongass National Forest management
1995	Abolish Bureau of Mines
	Abolish National Biological Survey
	Block EPA enforcement of provisions of the Clean Air Act, Clean Water Act, Delaney Clause, Resource Conservation and Recovery Act, Safe Drinking Water Act, Toxic Release Inventory, wetlands development
	Block public lands roads rulemaking (R.S. 2477)
	California Desert Protection Act implementation
	ESA listing moratorium
	National forest salvage logging
	Offshore oil and gas leasing moratorium
	Prevent EPA from issuing rule on radon in drinking water
	Public lands grazing rules
	Tongass National Forest management

Table 3.1
(*continued*)

1996	Block EPA enforcement of wetlands development
	ESA and marbled murrelet
	ESA and Mount Graham squirrel
	ESA listing moratorium
	California Desert Protection Act implementation
	Mining patent moratorium
	National forest logging roads
	National forest salvage logging
	Public lands grazing fee increase
	Royalties from oil on public lands
	Tongass National Forest management
1997	ESA and grizzly bear reintroduction
	Exporting timber from national forests
	National forest logging roads
	Public lands mining rules
	Road building in wilderness areas
	Royalties from oil on public lands
	United Nations Biosphere Program
	Waive ESA provisions for flood-control projects
1998	Chugach National Forest road
	Columbia Basin Ecosystem Management Plan
	EPA education, outreach, policy development on global climate change
	EPA rules: mercury emissions, regional haze, water dredging
	Glacier Bay National Park and commercial fishing
	Helicopters in Alaska wilderness
	Increasing national forest logging
	National forest logging roads
	Public lands grazing leases
	Public lands mining rules
	Road construction through Izembek National Wildlife Refuge wilderness
	Road construction through Petroglyph National Monument
	Royalties from oil on public lands
	Tongass National Forest logging
1999	Block BLM and Forest Service from conducting wildlife surveys for management plans
	Clean Water Act and coal mining
	ESA and grizzly bear reintroduction
	Glacier Bay National Park and commercial fishing
	Limit global climate change policy activities
	Mark Twain National Forest lead mining
	National forest logging roads
	National forest planning process

Table 3.1
(*continued*)

	Public lands grazing leases
	Public lands mining rules
	Reducing national forest logging
	Royalties from oil on public lands
	Washington state gold mine
	Wetlands management
2000	Below-cost national forest logging
	Block EPA ozone rule
	Columbia Basin Ecosystem Management Plan
	Creation of national monuments
	EPA rules: arsenic in drinking water, ozone, water dredging
	ESA and pollock/cod fishery
	Limit global climate change policy activities
	Management of national monuments
	Missouri River management plan
	National forest roadless areas
	Pesticide use in national parks
	Public lands grazing leases
	Public lands mining rules
	Snake River dam removal
	Yellowstone National Park snowmobiles
2001	Arctic National Wildlife Monument oil exploration
	EPA rule on arsenic in drinking water
	ESA citizen petitions
	Glacier Bay National Park and cruise ships
	Great Lakes oil and gas exploration
	Limit global climate change policy activities
	Missouri River management plan
	Public lands mining rules
	Offshore oil and gas leases
	Oil exploration in national monuments
2002	Black Hills National Forest logging
	Healthy forests initiative
2003	Block California rule to reduce lawn mower emissions
	Competitive outsourcing reviews for Forest Service and Interior Department
	ESA, silvery minnow, New Mexico water
	Flathead and Kootenai National Forests logging
	Limit Tongass National Forest logging lawsuits
	National forest fire management
	National forest planning process
	National forest roadless areas

Table 3.1
(*continued*)

	National Marine Fisheries Service fish habitat protection program
	New source review
	Prohibit federal funds to kill bison
	Public lands roads (R.S. 2477)
	Remove National Park Service authority to block bridges over wild and scenic rivers
	Yellowstone National Park snowmobiles
2004	Cumberland Island National Seashore wilderness roads
	ESA and HCPs
	ESA and pesticides
	Exempting factory farms from environmental reporting rules
	Missouri River management plan
	Moratorium on killing bison
	Public lands grazing leases
	Reclassification of nuclear sludge
	Siskiyou National Forest logging
	Tongass National Forest logging road ban
	Yellowstone National Park snowmobiles
2005	Arctic National Wildlife Monument oil exploration
	Delay EPA rule on small engine emissions
	EPA studies of pesticide exposure using human subjects
	Offshore oil and gas leasing moratorium
	Sale of wild horses from public lands
	Tongass National Forest logging road ban

decision was made not only to use [the Appropriations Committee] to slash spending on programs the [Republican] majority did not support, but also to enact substantive legislative changes that could, under regular procedures, only be considered by standing committees."[47] *Congressional Quarterly* reported: "[Republican] conservatives bent on reshaping government have found that spending bills are the handiest way to restrict, cut, remake, and in some cases simply eliminate federal programs and agencies that have irritated them for years."[48] The "revolution" would come in part in the form of riders on must-pass appropriation bills.

Riders Rebuffed: The Failure of the Frontal Assault

In 1995, conservative legislators made a frontal assault on the green state using riders, with their major proposals in two bills, one for the Veterans

Administration (VA), Housing and Urban Development (HUD), and Independent Agencies (including the Environmental Protection Agency), and the other the Interior appropriation. Seventeen major riders on the VA-HUD bill would have prohibited the EPA from spending FY 1996 funds for programs and activities listed by Congress.⁴⁹ Riders aimed at water regulations would have blocked the EPA from issuing standards for drinking water contaminants (including arsenic and radon) and for wetlands protection and enforcement, stopped enforcement of stormwater permits, barred implementation of the Great Lakes Initiative (a complex program involving water quality standards for 29 pollutants aimed at protecting humans and wildlife in the Great Lakes region), weakened industrial effluent guidelines, and relaxed pressures on cities affected by EPA orders on stormwater overflows.

Several riders were aimed at air quality regulations: eliminating the Environmental Protection Agency's capacity to enforce its trip reduction and vehicle inspection programs, blocking the imposition of "maximum available control technology" rules to reduce toxic emissions from oil refineries, and preventing the EPA from extending risk-management-plan requirements imposed on industry by the Clean Air Act Amendments of 1990. Other riders would have blocked the EPA from spending on some right-to-know and toxic release data gathering, delayed standard setting for pesticides on foods, and prevented the EPA from obtaining voluntary audit reports undertaken by industries. Most of these riders anticipated that eventually there would be permanent legislation changing policy in these areas. But, as the Congressional Research Service reported, it was unlikely that Congress would deliver such legislation soon. These riders, and others attached to additional appropriation bills, would be the leading edge of the conservative agenda.

The VA-HUD bill generated immediate controversy. Even while he worried about the difficulties of passing appropriation bills laden with riders, Appropriations Committee Chair Robert Livingston (R-Louisiana) saw the riders as satisfying "hungry Republicans" anxious for action after years in the minority. Jerry Lewis (R-California), chair of the subcommittee handling the VA-HUD bill, acknowledged that he was uncomfortable with so much legislation in an appropriation bill, but said it was necessary because authorization was so slow and because the EPA had "run roughshod over the American public." David Obey (D-Wisconsin) argued that the Republicans were "trying to bury all these policy issues so their (authorizing) chairmen don't have to take these issues on frontally." John Dingell (D-Michigan) called the VA-HUD appropriation bill "a calculated attempt to eviscerate the environmental statutes."[50]

It was apparent that the riders would have hard going in the Senate. Clinton threatened to veto this "stealth attack on our environment in the form of a budget bill." Clinton's Chief of Staff, Leon Panetta, went farther, warning that Congress and the White House were on a collision course and that Clinton would risk a government shutdown to stop these unacceptable provisions.[51] Senate Appropriations Chairman Mark Hatfield (R-Oregon) warned that his committee would need to "clean up" the House bill. Environmentalists mobilized against these "riders from hell," and there was considerable commentary in newspapers across the country.

Moderate House Republicans read these signs and balked at the riders, hesitating on the substance and fearing that being on the wrong side of environmental issues would hurt the party in the 1996 elections. The leader of this revolt in the House of Representatives, Sherwood Boehlert (R-New York), noted that the environment "was the one area where Republicans are getting clobbered across the country."[52] In late July, by a vote of 212–206, the House (with the votes of 51 Republicans) voted to strip the 17 riders out of the FY 1996 appropriation bill. The coalition of Democrats and moderate Republicans thought it had turned the anti-green tide. Two days later, however, determined House leaders pushed the issue to a second vote and—without changing a single vote, but depending on changes in attendance—restored the riders with a 210–210 tie.[53]

The House leadership essentially invited a humiliating defeat. In September the Senate voted to strike all but one of the 17 riders from the bill, retaining only the prohibition against using FY 1996 funds to implement a "trip reduction program" aimed at increasing carpooling. In early November, the House adopted a nonbinding motion instructing its budget conferees to drop the riders on a 227–194 vote, 58 Republicans having voted with the majority. Boehlert, the leader of the Republican defectors, said "Republicans can read the polls." Speaker Gingrich conceded that the Republicans had "mishandled the environment all spring and summer" and promised renewed thinking and renewed effort for 1996.[54]

Like the VA-HUD appropriation, the Interior bill's environmental provisions became a matter for public debate. In October 1995, Secretary Babbitt went public with his opposition to the riders. In a *Washington Post* column titled "Springtime for Polluters," he wrote:

These issues were never discussed in the last election, and for good reason: There aren't any voters out there saying we have too many parks, or our water is too clean. Yet without public debate, Republicans have engaged a quiet agenda to dismantle environmental and public resource protection. Their program is being rushed through Congress at dizzying speed, which is troubling, for in the frenzied blur, few people outside the committee chambers know how, much less why, it is being carried out at all. If the Republican leadership has decided that it is in the national interest to roll back three decades of conservation legislation, irrespective of public opinion, it is their prerogative. . . . But the least they could do is work in the open, using the constitutional process that we all learned about in high school civics. . . . Instead, their leadership is moving surreptitiously, circumventing the process by inserting legislation into the appropriation process and the related "reconciliation bill," both of which move on an expedited, debate-restricted, all-or-nothing track.[55]

The Interior bill carrying the riders passed on December 14, 1995. Clinton vetoed it, citing concerns about its impact on environmental protection, energy efficiency programs, and other programs. The veto meant that funding for most operations at Interior, for the Forest Service, for Department of Energy research programs, and for other programs ran out, and these agencies and programs closed down as part of the larger government shutdowns that took place from mid-December to early January 1996. When Republican firebrands continued to push for changes in wetlands policy, logging in the Tongass National Forest, and changes in management of the Mojave National Preserve after the new year, Vice President Gore played what *Congressional Quarterly* called the "environmental trump card," demanding that they drop these riders or face another government shutdown. They did so. The FY 1996 Interior Appropriation became "a study in policy controversies avoided," and the larger forces blocking significant legislative policy change on the environment held fast.[56]

Salvaging Success

The highest-profile success of the riders strategy was the Emergency Salvage Timber Program, also known as the "salvage rider," attached to the

1995 Rescissions Act. The central purpose of the Rescissions Act was to repeal spending that had already been approved for 1995 as the new Republican majority's first move toward a balanced budget. It was the largest rescissions bill ever passed, cutting $16.3 billion from the 1995 budget. It also provided $7.2 billion in new spending for earthquake relief in California, recovery from the Oklahoma City bombing, and other humanitarian efforts, making it difficult to oppose the bill. The act cut spending for several environmental agencies and programs, including Superfund cleanup, Fish and Wildlife Service endangered species projects, the National Park Service, the Bureau of Land Management, and the National Biological Survey.[57] It also contained a rider affecting management of the Tongass National Forest. But as an environmental law, the Rescissions Act is most remembered for the "salvage rider."

The "policy window" for the rider was opened by wildfires that spread across the West in the early 1990s, devastating forests and threatening property.[58] The fires seemingly gave credence to arguments that poor management and delays in harvesting dead and dying timber had undermined forest health and heightened wildfire dangers. Senator Larry Craig (R-Idaho) argued: "The forests of the inland West are sick. They are the product of eight years of drought and decades of mismanagement that have resulted in one of the largest fuel buildups, acre by acre, ever in the history of the U.S. Forest Service."[59] While proponents emphasized the salvage issue, the rider was not focused only on salvage timber. It also took on two central issues in the ongoing struggle over logging and endangered species in the Northwest, and reflected conservatives' larger concern with the ways that environmentalists had used administrative appeals and litigation to block access to timber in that region. Much more than "salvage timber" would flow out this policy window.

The first issue was the partial failure of an earlier policy rider that had aimed to maintain a steady flow of timber to loggers in the face of judicial injunctions that had halted harvest to protect the spotted owl. Congress responded to these injunctions with the "Northwest Timber Compromise," Section 318 of the 1990 Interior Appropriation. Section 318 opened access to old-growth timber in thirteen national forests in Oregon and Washington and on Bureau of Land Management lands in Oregon, all known to be owl habitat. It did so by asserting that the forest management plans at issue in the courts gave "adequate consideration for the purpose of meeting the statutory requirements that are the basis" for the judicial injunctions, effectively overturning the injunctions. Further, the rider suspended the application of the National Environmental Policy Act, the Federal Land Policy and Management Act, the National Forest Management Act, and the Migratory Bird Treaty Act to the timber sales and replaced them with less restrictive safeguards; prohibited injunctions against the logging; and asserted that actions taken under the Forest Service and Bureau of Land Management plans "shall not be subject to judicial review by any court of the United States." [60] Judge William Dwyer nicely summarized the rider's purpose: Congress could create "geographical" and "temporal" exceptions to environmental laws, and the rider "would provide a short-term supply of national forest timber to mills in Washington and Oregon without having the usual type of agency action subject to judicial review." [61]

The rider was not wholly successful in removing judicial barriers to logging, however. Section 318 was challenged on constitutional grounds and some sales were stopped until the Supreme Court issued the definitive decision. Some sales were blocked by challenges to their adherence to the specific terms of Section 318 (which, for example, required the agencies to avoid fragmenting the remaining owl habitat in allocating timber sales). The Endangered Species Act still applied to timber sales, and others were stopped by concerns about their impact on the spotted owl and the marbled murrelet.[62] So, despite Section 318, a considerable number of timber sales were stalled due to litigation or other problems. The 1995 salvage rider tried to shake those sales loose.

Second, the salvage rider grew out of some legislators' frustrations with implementation of the Clinton administration's Northwest Forest Plan. During his 1992 campaign, Clinton had promised action to resolve the region's timber wars. In April 1993 he convened a "Forest Summit" in Oregon to seek ways to break the stalemate on timber policy. The conference involved stakeholders, environmentalists, and scientists as well as officials from the White House and relevant management agencies, and informed Clinton's effort to balance economic and environmental interests. The administration unveiled the Forest Plan in summer 1993, governing management of 24.5 million acres in Washington, Oregon, and

California. This plan was not submitted to Congress—it was a "paradigmatic example of changing course without statutory change"—but instead evolved as an agreement between the Forest Service and the Bureau of Land Management to amend forest management plans on the 19 national forests and 7 Bureau of Land Management districts in the region.[63] As the agencies' Record of Decision indicated, this was the first time that they had "developed and adopted a common management approach to the lands they administered throughout an entire ecological region," and while satisfying no one completely the deal represented an important achievement for the Clinton administration.[64]

The Forest Plan attempted to balance demands for timber harvest and species habitat. It set a target for harvest of 1.1 billion board feet per year, far below the levels seen in the go-go 1980s, but a marked improvement for loggers over the no-go injunctions that had come with the owl listing. The Forest Plan barely withstood judicial challenge, with Judge Dwyer stating that any logging above the levels projected in the plan would likely be illegal, and asserting that it would have to be reconsidered if the government failed to meet its commitments for planning and monitoring species health.[65] Environmentalists challenged the plan's implementation, and for this and other reasons the Forest Service failed to deliver the targeted harvest levels. This angered logging interests and legislators representing timber communities. Senator Slade Gorton (R-Washington), a sponsor of the salvage rider, complained:

But do our people have 1.1 billion board feet of harvest? No . . . they do not. . . . They are nowhere close to that because the Forest Service in its personnel cuts has cut mostly the people who work in the woods preparing these sales and because the Clinton administration knows that almost no single action taken pursuant to this option will escape an appeal within the Forest Service and a lawsuit being stretched out forever and ever.[66]

The salvage rider aimed to speed Forest Plan timber sales by limiting administrative and judicial appeals of agency decisions. Gorton observed that the rider would "help the administration carry out its own promises" to deliver timber sales to logging interests in the Northwest.[67]

No legislation, even a rider, dealing with logging in the Pacific Northwest in the 1990s could have passed through Congress quietly. When the salvage rider emerged in the House Appropriations Committee, there was open debate on the merits of the proposal. Representative Charles Taylor (R-North Carolina) bluntly stated:

This means, for example, that the [Secretary of the Interior] cannot be sued for violation of the Clean Water Act, the provisions of the NFMA concerning species' viability, unsuitability, or consistency with resource management plans, or the jeopardy or take provisions of the Endangered Species Act. Furthermore . . . a sale can be offered that does not comport with a resource management plan, or interim guidelines, or management directives. . . . Finally a sale can be offered even if it would be barred under any decision, injunction, or order of any federal court.[68]

Opponents objected strongly. David Skaggs (D-Colorado) observed that under the rider "all environmental review, all judicial review, for all practical purposes, is gone." Sidney Yates (D-Illinois) saw the rider as "license for unregulated timber harvest," declaring that behind the "emergency" provisions for salvage there was a broader agenda:

. . . this amendment literally suspends every law governing management of the public forests, including those that protect fish, wildlife, water quality, and recreation and jobs that depend on such critically important forest resources. But this amendment does not stop there. It turns off judicial due process in standing court cases by overturning every past court decision in the country that protects timber sales. It bars public comment on these timber sales and eliminates administrative appeals.[69]

A similar fight occurred in the Senate, where Senators Gorton and Hatfield pushed hard for the rider, and Senator Patty Murray (D-Washington) vainly attempted to weaken the proposal by protecting some roadless areas from harvest and maintaining judicial and administrative reviews of timber sales. Murray acknowledged that there was a legitimate salvage timber issue in the forests, but argued that the approach to the issue taken in the timber rider was unnecessarily extreme, noting: "There is a history of waiving environmental laws to solve timber problems; that strategy has not worked."[70]

Senators Gorton and Craig defended the use of riders in a *Washington Post* editorial, focusing particularly on forest issues. The use of the riders, they claimed, "underscored the need for reform of the authorizing statutes that govern the U.S. Forest Service" and the difficulties of achieving those changes. They proposed that Clinton "join us in seeking legislation that will modernize the now-antiquated laws that govern federal forest management," but saw policy riders as a useful tool for circumventing gridlock in the absence of statutory changes. Obviously environmentalists would not support opening up the language of the environmental laws in a Republican Congress, and Clinton undoubtedly thought that he had already established a model for a more balanced policy with the Northwest Forest Plan.[71] The salvage rider moved ahead in Congress and around the legislative gridlock on forest policy.

Newspapers editorialized and environmentalists mobilized—Clinton received 50,000 letters on the issue. Still, while it was openly debated the salvage rider was just a small part of a multifaceted bill that included Oklahoma City relief money, other disaster relief spending, and billions in budget cuts. In 1995, Republicans were determined to put the federal budget on a fast track toward balance, and many Democrats, shocked by the results of the 1994 elections, were willing to cooperate. Still, Clinton threatened to veto the rescissions bill before it passed, mentioning that the salvage rider "would basically direct us to make timber sales to large companies, subsidized by taxpayers . . . that will essentially throw out all of our environmental laws and the protections we have that surround such timber sales."[72] This did not dissuade the Republican leadership, however, and the bill carrying the rider was passed by the House of Representatives (235–189) and by the Senate (61–38) on May 25, 1995. Clinton delivered the promised veto on June 7, citing many concerns about the policy priorities reflected in the bill. Again, he explicitly mentioned the salvage rider as one reason for the veto: "I continue to object to language that would override existing environmental laws in an effort to increase timber salvage. . . . It is not appropriate to use this legislation to overturn environmental laws."[73]

Republican leaders lacked the votes to override the veto, so they entered into negotiations with the White House, using "summitry" to try to produce an acceptable package. They made some concessions to Clinton on spending, but the salvage rider remained in the bill with what Senator Gorton called "only slightly more than superficial" changes.[74] The revised Rescissions Act carrying the salvage rider was passed by the Senate (90–7) and by the House (276–151) and was signed into law on July 27, 1995.[75] Environmentalists were stunned, complaining that they had been "stabbed in the back." Clinton's failure to kill the salvage rider—particularly the language that extended the rider's reach beyond salvage timber sales—reflected his political weakness and his need to back spending cuts. Further, administration officials claimed that they did not fully understand the implications of the salvage rider. Obviously the salvage rider could not have become law without being carried by some other, inexorable legislative vehicle. Senators Patrick Leahy (D-Vermont) and Joseph Lieberman, who opposed the salvage provision, voted for the bill, noting that they had to set aside those concerns because of the importance of deficit reduction.[76] Sierra Club Executive Director Carl Pope observed of Clinton's decision to sign the bill: ". . . political expediency is the only explanation for Clinton's flip-flop. The President evidently calculated that the risks of failing to pass the Republicans' spending bill were greater than those of failing the forests."[77]

Indeed, the rider worked better than its supporters could have imagined. Almost immediately upon its passage its expansive reach became clear. Environmentalists complained that the law—which had been debated in Congress, mentioned in a presidential veto message, and subject to negotiations in a budget summit involving White House and congressional officials—was a "Trojan horse" and its passage a "clear-cut case of slipping a fast one through Congress."[78] The editorial page of the *Seattle Times*, which had supported the rider, accused Gorton of engaging in a "bait and switch" on timber salvage, citing a press release he had sent to the paper that repeatedly mentioned "salvage logging" but did not mention logging old-growth timber. "We're not talking about clear-cuts in the Olympics," Gorton had written. "These operations will pull dead, dying, burnt, diseased blown-down, and bug-infested timber out of the forest, and reforest the salvaged areas. It's an important part of restoring these forests to health." At the moment that the *Times* published this piece, loggers were aiming to clear cut in areas on Washington's Olympic peninsula, where fire was not a particular danger.[79]

What were the major provisions of the salvage rider?[80] Proponents emphasized the need to remove fuel for wildfires by increasing loggers' access to "salvage timber," dead or dying trees affected by fire or insects. Congress ordered the Secretaries of Agriculture and the Interior to increase salvage timber harvests to the "maximum extent feasible" over and above programmed levels. Most commentators claim that the rider's definition of "salvage timber" was unusually broad—so much so that Senator Bill Bradley (D-New Jersey) joked that it covered "any tree made of wood."[81] Loggers would be allowed to take healthy trees as well, as long as salvage harvest was an "important reason" for the timber sale and these trees were either in imminent danger of fire or insect attack or lacked "the characteristics of a healthy and viable ecosystem for the purpose of ecosystem improvement or rehabilitation."[82] Despite the rider's appearance in a rescissions bill, the harvest of salvage timber was not to be limited by budgetary concerns: sales would proceed even if the costs to the treasury would exceed revenues.

The rider also contained provisions that had nothing to do with timber salvage, pushing the Department of the Interior to proceed with delayed or cancelled sales under the Northwest Forest Plan and the Northwest Timber Compromise. The rider set aside the environmental laws that were delaying Section 318 sales and ordered the agencies to move forward with those sales quickly. This was the central issue. Advocates of the rider wanted all of the sales—salvage sales, Forest Plan sales, and Timber Compromise sales—to proceed quickly. The sales would require only streamlined environmental reviews, one document combining the environmental impact statement required by the National Environmental Policy Act and the biological assessment required by the Endangered Species Act.[83] Judicial review would be constrained, with strict timelines and a ban on injunctions and restraining orders. The rider suspended the application of the Endangered Species Act, the National Forest Management Act, the National Environmental Policy Act, the Federal Land Policy and Management Act, the Forest and Rangeland Renewable Resources Planning Act, and the Multiple Use Sustained Yield Act, and ordered federal courts to intercede against timber sales only if agency actions were "arbitrary and capricious." This language largely insulated the Forest Service and the Bureau of Land Management from citizen suits and gave them enormous discretion: as the Congressional Research Service delicately put it, "[The salvage rider] does not direct the agencies to comply with current laws, and substantially insulates agency decisions from review under the laws that govern forest and species management."[84] Furthermore, the rider freed the agencies from regulations providing for administrative appeals of timber sales, blocking another pathway environmentalists used to impede timber cuts.

Greens complained that the salvage rider led to "logging without laws," suspending the application of the major environmental laws in the affected areas of the Northwest for the period the rider was in effect.[85] Freed from legal constraints, in some cases the Forest Service showed itself to be a creature of its history: a Fish and Wildlife Service field office described the Forest Service's attitude as "these sales are exempt from the ESA, etc, and from public/legal appeal, so let's rock and roll."[86]

Section 2001(k) promised to be a fulcrum that would leverage the power of the salvage rider beyond that anticipated even by some of its congressional supporters. That section read:

> Notwithstanding any other provision of law . . . the Secretary shall act to award, release, and permit to be complete in fiscal years 1995 and 1996, with no change in originally advertised terms . . . *all* timber sale contracts offered or awarded before that date *in any unit of the National Forest System or district of the BLM subject to section 318.* (emphasis added)

On the day the rider was adopted, several Republican legislators sent a letter to Secretary of the Interior Babbitt and Secretary of Agriculture Dan Glickman emphasizing just this point. These lawmakers insisted that the rider applied not only to timber sales developed under the requirements of Section 318 during the fiscal years 1989 and 1990 in which the 318 rider was in effect, but to all sales offered but not finalized on all Forest Service lands in Oregon and Washington and all sales on Bureau of Land Management lands in western Oregon between 1989 and the date of the salvage rider's passage.[87]

The Clinton administration's interpretation was narrower. It believed that this provision applied only to timber sales awarded or offered under the Northwest Timber Compromise rider during 1989 and 1990, and that the salvage rider required only the release of sales that met environmental and procedural standards set in the Northwest Compromise rider. Under the Clinton administration's interpretation, the salvage rider would require the release of about 410 million board feet of timber in green tree sales, some of which would come in old-growth forests. Under the legislators' interpretation—also the industry position—the rider would force the sale of about 660 million board feet of timber, a difference of 250 million board feet.[88]

This issue was litigated almost immediately by the Northwest Forest Resources Council, an industry group, which demanded the release of

660 million board feet of timber in delayed or blocked sales. A district court's decision supporting the industry was upheld in the appeals court, forcing the Forest Service and the Bureau of Land Management to move on the blocked sales. The courts ordered the "resurrection" of sales that had been cancelled due to litigation and required the agencies to seek other qualified bidders where the original high bidder had proved unwilling or unable to proceed. Jason Patlis observed: "Courts ruled that the language in the rider was explicit in waiving existing environmental laws and, being left with no law to apply, they had to rely on the plain terms of the rider itself, which essentially mandated the sales."[89] The result—"logging without laws"—was surprising to many who had followed the debate and even to at least one legislator who had worked to pass the rider in the House of Representatives. Congressman Norm Dicks (D-Washington) renounced the rider and observed that its reach was "broader than any of us thought possible."[90]

The salvage logging permitted by the rider was controversial, but the 318 sales were another issue entirely. The *Seattle Times* reported that the provision led to the region's first old-growth clear-cuts since the spotted owl listings, and noted the reversion to discredited logging practices given the relaxation of environmental standards:

Today, few clear-cuts are done on federal land, and large strips of trees must now be left around streams to protect fish. But Congress said this logging could proceed as it would have when first offered for sale in 1989. In many cases, that means clear-cuts, streams stripped of tree cover, and few amenities such as snags or ground cover left for wildlife. . . . On federal land, [one logger observed] "We simply don't do logging like this anymore."[91]

The Clinton administration, stung by criticism and arguing that it had been duped (or at least dense) about the reach of the salvage rider, tried to limit the damage. Clinton and Gore admitted that signing the rescissions bill carrying the rider was a mistake, Gore calling it the biggest mistake of Clinton's first term.[92] Clinton called for legislation to repeal the rider and an effort led by Senator Murray to "fix a mistake made a year ago" failed on a 54–42 vote. The salvage rider would then be handled on non-legislative paths, moving to administrative politics, the courts, and dealmaking between the Clinton administration and timber companies.

The salvage rider did increase timber harvests—a considerable part of this harvest included green, healthy trees—between July 1995 and the end of December 1996. The total harvest was 4.6 billion board feet, 1.2 billion more than had been planned by the Forest Service. Challenges to these salvage sales generally failed, with courts declaring in an Arizona case involving the impact of a sale on the Mexican spotted owl that Congress had "created a blanket exemption to environmental laws that otherwise would apply," and in a Montana case involving cuts in grizzly country that the Forest Service had "discretion to disregard entirely the effect on the grizzly bear habitat."[93]

A July 1996 order from Secretary of Agriculture Glickman, reflecting the administration's growing concerns about the reach of the salvage program, limited the harvest considerably. Glickman demanded that salvage sales for which bids had not yet been opened meet the same environmental standards that they would have absent the salvage rider language, and that Forest Service officials determine that salvage sales they offered would survive normal appeals and reviews. This order, anticipating the expiration of the salvage rider, delayed 224 timber sales of more than 700 million board feet of timber. About 309 million board feet in these delayed sales would have come from roadless areas, 51 million contained too much green timber, 206 million were not imminently in danger of fire or insect infestation, and more than 100 million were green tree sales not originally advertised as salvage cuts but "repackaged" as salvage harvests.[94] The effects of the rider on 318 sales were substantial, but eventually blunted by the federal courts. In June 1996 an appeals court decided *Northwest Forest Council v. Pilchuck Audubon Society* involving access to old-growth timber in forests thought to be habitat for the threatened marbled murrelet. The salvage rider allowed 318 sales to go forward "notwithstanding any other provision of law," but it left one important environmental constraint: sales could not go forward "if any threatened or endangered bird species is known to be nesting within the acreage that is the subject of the sale unit." Marbled murrelet nesting sites are difficult to find, and government biologists had long used indirect methods (the accepted practice) to surmise the presence of such sites. Timber companies argued that when Congress said that the tracts could be spared only if they were "known" nesting sites, it meant to hold the agencies to a higher standard, requiring them to produce "physical evidence such as eggshell fragments, fecal rings, or dead chicks present on or below a tree." Since little such evidence was ever available, the timber industry's interpretation would have pried open 176 million board feet of cuts blocked by the Endangered Species Act. The appeals court upheld the agency's methodology, preserving substantial tracts of coastal, old-growth timber.[95] Bonnie Phillips of the Audubon Society said: "Thank God for the courts. They stood up for science and common sense. Now if only Congress could do the same." Timber representatives were as frustrated as Phillips was pleased, claiming that the decision was a "huge blow" and that the courts' decision subverted congressional intent.[96]

The Clinton administration moved to soften this blow and meet timber production goals through dealmaking. In September 1996 it announced an agreement with 15 timber companies to exchange 44 tracts of the old-growth marbled murrelet habitat for access to timber in other, less sensitive locations, cuts that would be subject to environmental laws.[97] These exchanges would themselves become controversial, since matching the timber volumes lost in the coastal murrelet habitat would require major cuts elsewhere. But this deal, along with the *Pilchuck* decision protecting marbled murrelet habitat and Glickman's memorandum on salvage sales seemed to signal a new, if temporary, truce in the timber wars.

What is most striking about the reconciliation and riders tactics adopted by the Republicans in the 104th Congress is that they failed to achieve their central policy goals. ANWR drilling could not survive a presidential veto, and the symbolic and substantive importance of the issue to environmentalists and Democrats virtually guaranteed that Clinton would reject the gambit. The salvage rider did succeed, essentially suspending "intercurrence" in the Northwest forests for a brief period by negating the golden era laws governing resource management on public lands. A few other minor riders survived over the years, but the bold effort to use the 1996 appropriation process to dramatically curb environmental enforcement (anticipating future legislation making these changes permanent) was thrown back by the basic political and institutional forces that have long stalemated environmental policymaking.

Yet the struggles of the 104th Congress did not end these battles. As will be shown below, drilling advocates nearly succeeded in using budget reconciliation to win legislative language that would pry open the ANWR, winning a temporary victory in spring 2005 before finally failing in December 2005. And, as table 3.1 shows, the use of policy riders to try to shape environmental policy continued after 1995, with only limited success. Indeed, in a series of articles in the *National Journal*, Margaret Kriz wrote that after the failed frontal assaults on the green state in the 104th Congress, "governmental officials are finding backdoor ways to change federal policy." The budget and appropriation arena, she continued, were "the most active venue for sneak attacks." Senator Craig, in response to this change in approach, commented, "To be able to move a major bill dealing with environmental law, or any adjustment to the law, is very difficult. Congress doesn't want to focus on it, doesn't want to put up with the heat." Most of these riders continued to generate controversy, and most failed. By the late 1990s and even into the Bush administration it appeared that the Interior appropriation in particular had become an arena for symbolic politics, with legislators proposing riders that were designed more to please attentive constituencies than to actually reshape environmental policy.[98]

The Republicans in Power, 2001–2005

The legislative gridlock of the Clinton years left a full plate of environmental issues for the incoming Bush administration, and the ferment of the 104th Congress left a ready-made agenda for significant policy change. For Bush, however, environmental policy was at best a second-tier concern, well behind tax cuts and, after the terrorist attacks of September 11, 2001, domestic security and war. The new president did not take a seat at the table set by the "revolutionaries" of 1995 and 1996. Serious overhauls of the Clean Air Act, the Clean Water Act, the Endangered Species Act, Superfund, and laws governing forest management remained high on the agenda of some congressional conservatives, but the Bush administration pursued a more modest course. Total budgets for natural resources and pollution control actually increased in its first years, though by 2005 spending in most environmental policy areas had been reduced to or below 2002 levels.[99] The Republican-controlled Congress made only a little legislative headway on major issues. For example, in 2005 the House of Representatives passed a major revision of the Endangered Species Act, but this bill went nowhere in the Republican-controlled Senate. Bush and the Republican Congress did enact three noteworthy laws, but gridlock on major issues continued into the Republican era. Highly controversial issues—the most visible and apparently successful being drilling in ANWR—moved to budget reconciliation and the appropriation process, though the use of policy riders diminished considerably from the peak in the mid 1990s.

Legislating on the Environment in a Republican Era

The highest environmental policy priorities of the Bush administration were amendments to the Clean Air Act and energy legislation. Bush's Clean Air amendments, called the "Clear Skies" initiative, aimed to introduce cap-and-trade provisions for nitrogen oxide, sulfur dioxide, and mercury emissions from power plants.[100] This proposal made little progress in Bush's first term, but Republican gains in the 2004 elections brightened its prospects and the administration made it a priority early in 2005. The legislation immediately stalled in the Senate Committee on Public Works and the Environment, where the central issue was whether the bill should address carbon dioxide emissions as well as the pollutants addressed in Bush's proposal. Bush had committed himself to regulating carbon dioxide emissions in the 2000 campaign as part of a multi-pollutant power plant plan and then backed away from this promise, infuriating environmentalists worried about global warming and contributing to Senator Jim Jeffords's departure from the Republican Party. The Senate Committee was badly divided. Senator George Voinovich (R-Ohio) noted: "Chafee (R-Rhode Island) thinks (global warming) is the biggest problem in the world and the chairman has a sign in his office saying (warming) is a hoax." Chairman James Inhofe (R-Oklahoma) complained that the bill was killed by "environmental extremists." Jeffords (I-Vermont) retorted: "This legislation denies plain scientific evidence of human health damage from toxic air pollution and of global warming from greenhouse gas emissions."[101] This priority bill stalled despite solid Republican majorities in Congress and widespread support for the cap-and-trade concept. Frustrated in Congress, the administration moved to achieve some of Clear Skies through rulemaking; its contro-versial mercury rule was quickly challenged in the federal courts.[102]

Energy legislation stalled until 2005. In 2001, the Republican House passed an industry and administration-supported bill that emphasized increasing domestic production of oil and gas, including more than $33 billion in tax incentives for production and other incentives for off-shore drilling. The bill also pushed an old hot button by calling for open-ing ANWR to oil and gas exploration. The Senate bill focused more on conservation, rejected ANWR drilling, and included (among other issues not addressed in the House bill) provisions mandating the use of ethanol. The House-Senate conference to resolve these differences made no progress, and supporters abandoned the energy bill in October 2001.[103]

Congress took up the energy bill again in early 2003. The House of Representatives passed a bill focused on increasing production and calling for ANWR drilling. The bill also provided some incentives for alternative fuels, seed money for the hydrogen-vehicle program sup-ported by President Bush, and new provisions for energy deregulation. The Senate, now controlled by the Republicans, still proved to be diffi-cult terrain for energy legislation. The Senate rejected an attempt to achieve drilling in ANWR through budget reconciliation, and deep divisions opened on several other issues, including ethanol, the possibility of banning the use of MTBE (a cancer-causing gasoline additive that was found to be leaching into groundwater across the country) and liability waivers for producers of that chemical, and fuel economy standards for light trucks. To get the bill past the Senate gridlock to conference, Senate Minority Leader Tom Daschle (D-South Dakota) proposed that senators pass the energy bill that they had adopted in 2002, in the second session of the 107th Congress. It was clear that Republicans would completely rewrite the bill in conference, but the compromise was not enough to get the bill to the House-Senate negotiations. Senator Charles Schumer (D-New York) led a successful filibuster, and the energy bill once again failed. Schumer's filibuster was opposed by several Democrats (including Daschle, seeking to expand the use of ethanol for his South Dakota farm constituents), but was supported by six Republicans, five of them from the Northeast. The major issue for these northeastern Republicans was the bill's inclusion of a liability waiver for the manufacturers of MTBE.

Cost estimates for cleaning up water supplies and homes contaminated with the chemical had risen to $29 billion, and these legislators could not stomach a broad waiver of liability for its producers.[104]

In 2005, Congress finally adopted a broad energy bill that earned bipartisan support. *CQ Weekly* noted that the bill was "notable for its omissions" on the most contentious environmental issues. It included no provisions on ANWR drilling and dropped most protections for MTBE producers; it did nothing to force reductions in greenhouse gases, to require power companies to use more renewable sources of energy, or to increase mileage standards for vehicles. Critics argued that the bill did little at all to protect the environment, and derided the legislation as a giveaway to energy producers.[105] While this is a bit too strong—the bill encouraged energy conservation and the development of cleaner technologies—passage was greased by billions in subsidies to the energy industry. Indeed, these subsidies were the heart of the bill. It contained provisions to encourage extraction of oil, gas, and coal, and significant supports for electricity producers, ethanol interests, and the nuclear industry. All told, the bill contained $15 billion in tax cuts over a decade; one group estimated that the total cost of the bill could exceed $80 billion.[106] Representative John Dingell (D-Michigan), an ally of the auto industry, acknowledged, "This is not a perfect bill," but claimed it was a "solid beginning of an energy strategy for the 21st century." Environmentalists and their congressional allies were much less sanguine. Edward Markey (D-Massachusetts) called the law a "moral and political failure because it's what's not in this bill that was important." Sierra Club Executive Director Carl Pope complained: "Instead of cutting America's oil dependence, boosting production of renewable energy and lowering energy prices, this bill funnels billions of taxpayer dollars to polluting energy industries, and opens up our coastlines and wild lands to destructive oil and gas activities."[107] Congress proved that it could offer significant subsidies to energy producers with some sweeteners on the side for cleaner energy production; it did not prove that it could address the most pressing environmental issues of the day.

Congress handed Bush two other notable legislative successes.[108] The first was passage of a "brownfields" bill. State and local governments, environmentalists, environmental-justice advocates, and others had long sought federal help in cleaning "brownfields"—areas where property development was "complicated by the presence or potential presence of a hazardous substance, pollutant, or contaminant."[109] Brownfields legislation had long stalled in Congress because of controversy over the larger Superfund cleanup program, but a compromise bill won unanimous support in both houses of Congress and was signed into law. The legislation pleased business interests by offering some exemptions from liability for cleanups, and by restricting the Environmental Protection Agency's authority to either reevaluate a site after it had been declared clean or to tag a Superfund site where there were ongoing cleanup efforts. The modest price tag—$1.25 billion over five years—was acceptable to budget hawks, state and local officials welcomed the influx of federal dollars for economic development, and Democrats won Davis-Bacon prevailing-wage protection for workers at cleanup sites.[110] The second notable success in the legislative process was passage of a forest management bill, labeled the "Healthy Forests Initiative" by the Bush administration. The proposal gained legislative momentum from wildfires that raged in 2000, when 8.4 million acres burned in more than 100,000 fires, and in 2002, when fires covered 7.1 million acres. More than 2,000 homes burned, and 21 people died, in 2002. President Bush and his allies argued that excessive environmental reviews, constant administrative appeals, and litigation had hindered the Forest Service's efforts to remove the fuel that sparked hazardous wildfires; the Forest Service itself complained of a "process predicament" that undermined its efforts to maintain forest health.[111] The basic approach of the salvage rider—suspending or weakening procedural requirements that slowed timber cuts—returned with the healthy forests proposal.

The Bush administration proposed its Healthy Forests Initiative in August 2002, stressing the need to reduce administrative burdens created by the environmental laws bearing on forest management. Part of the initiative was administrative, instructing the Department of Agriculture, the Department of the Interior, and the Council on Environmental Quality to streamline regulations and environmental reviews, essentially exempting fire management projects from the National Environmental Policy Act (NEPA). The Healthy Forests Initiative also called upon Congress for legislation. Bush's proposal exempted fire management projects on

nearly 10 million acres of public land deemed to be at high fire risk from
NEPA requirements as well as administrative appeals; it repealed the
Administrative Appeals Act of 1993, a policy rider that had established
a process for handling appeals of forest management decisions; it
speeded interagency assessments of the impact of projects on ESA-listed
species; it limited judicial review, forbade temporary restraining orders
and preliminary injunctions against thinning projects, and required
courts to defer to agency findings that the benefits of thinning projects
exceeded their costs; and it authorized the Bureau of Land Management
and the Forest Service to develop long-term "stewardship contracts"
with loggers, nonprofit groups, and communities. "Stewards" would
thin forests of small trees and deadwood, and would have the rights to
sell or use the wood they took. [112] The first effort to win forest legislation
came in the appropriations process, with a Senate rider to the Interior
Appropriation bill debated in September 2002. Senators Pete Domenici
(R-New Mexico) and Larry Craig (R-Idaho) proposed the rider, which
would have waived NEPA requirements for thinning on up to 10 million
acres of public land and limited judicial review of those projects. An
amendment proposed by the Democrats would have allowed cuts on
approximately half as many acres, focused thinning efforts on areas near
buildings, and waived NEPA requirements only for thinning in these
"wildland-urban interfaces." A compromise effort failed, and Democrats
filibustered the Interior Appropriation bill. Several votes to end debate
failed, and the dispute over the rider led to Congress's failure to pass an
Interior appropriation that year. While it failed as a rider, though, the
Healthy Forests Initiative moved forward on a more conventional, if
complicated, legislative track. [113]

Legislation resembling the Bush proposal was passed by the House of
Representatives easily in May 2003, but the bill ran into trouble in the
Senate. Democrats and some Republicans opposed waiving NEPA requirements for thinning projects conducted far from communities and
questioned the extent to which the House bill relaxed environmental
restrictions on logging. [114] A compromise emerged in the Senate after
six weeks of negotiation and provided the basis for the final bill. It authorized $760 million for forest thinning ("hazardous fuel reduction projects"),
with at least 50 percent of the funds to be spent in areas within 1.5 miles

of at-risk communities. The bill also allowed thinning near municipal reservoirs, on listed species habitat, and in areas subject to insect infestation. In those areas, it limited the number of environmental reviews normally required for logging projects. The law also restricted administrative appeals and imposed limitations on judicial review of these thinning projects. Preliminary judicial injunctions would be permitted, but they would have to be reviewed every 45 days; courts were instructed to defer to agencies' assessments of the benefits of the threat reduction projects, and to consider the potential environmental consequences of inaction in the face of fire risk. The bill nearly failed in conference, but was saved by leadership negotiations outside the formal conference structure. The compromise drew criticism from conservatives who thought that it gave away too much of the Bush proposal, but it was the best deal the conservatives could get. Interestingly, one controversial part of the bill, the "stewardship contracting" provision, passed into law not as part of the Healthy Forests Restoration Act, but as a rider to the FY 2003 omnibus appropriation bill.

Reconciliation in a Republican Era

Soon after the Republican victories in the 2004 elections, supporters of drilling in ANWR renewed their efforts to open the refuge.[115] Achieving energy legislation allowing drilling was impossible; budget reconciliation offered a way to break the decades-long impasse in the Arctic.

The Republicans gained four Senate seats in 2004, leaving them with too few votes to break a filibuster but enough votes to push ANWR drilling through the budget reconciliation. Environmentalists again decried this back-door approach to opening the refuge, and the *Washington Post* editorialized: "Whatever you think of drilling in the reserve, and we are skeptical, this kind of important vote on a matter of national policy shouldn't be crammed into the budget bill and deprived of the usual procedural protections."[116] Senator Ted Stevens of Alaska defended the approach. "It's the only way around a filibuster. It's become a way of life with the Democrats. They refuse to accept a majority vote."[117]

The provision moved quickly in the Senate, with the decisive vote on an amendment offered by Senator Maria Cantwell (D-Washington) to strip the provision from the budget, which would have stopped the move toward drilling. Cantwell objected to drilling on environmental grounds, but also complained about the use of reconciliation by the Republican majority, worrying about the precedent being set for environmental policymaking:

Why not expedite timber sales by simply recognizing revenues in the budget? Why not open drilling in coastal regions of the country by simply recognizing revenues in the budget? Why not open drilling in Yellowstone National Park by recognizing revenues in the budget? Do we . . . simply subvert the normal process that would allow us to debate and consider whether we should have these oil sources recognized?

Senator Judd Gregg (R-New Hampshire) defended the use of Senate rules and the larger majority rule principle: "We are using the rules of the Senate. . . . All this rule of the Senate does is allow a majority . . . to take a position and pass a piece of legislation. . . . Is there something wrong with majority rules?"[118]

Pro-drilling forces narrowly defeated the Cantwell amendment, and at the end of April Congress adopted a budget including the provision calling for revenues from ANWR drilling. Representative Richard Pombo (R-California) said "I think it's going to happen, after 25 years of fighting over it."[119] The issue was not closed, however. In November 2005, a group of more than 20 moderate House Republicans demanded that ANWR drilling be removed from the House reconciliation bill. The Republican leadership needed their votes since the Democrats were unified in opposition to the overall reconciliation bill due to tens of billions of dollars in cuts to domestic programs, so they dropped the drilling provision. With ANWR drilling pulled from the bill, it was passed by the House by a 217–215 vote. Despite efforts by the White House and pro-drilling Republicans, ANWR drilling was not included in the conference version of the reconciliation bill since House leaders still needed the moderate Republican votes. In a last effort for the year to open ANWR, drilling advocates added language to open the refuge to the defense appropriations bill. It was passed by the House overwhelmingly, but it was blocked by a filibuster in the Senate. The provision was removed from the defense bill, much to the consternation of Senator Stevens, who had once noted that he had been "on this track like a white rat for 24 years."[120]

Congress's ANWR wheels kept spinning in 2006, but the status quo held firm, and drilling was dropped from the energy legislation that was passed in 2005.[121] Although ANWR is certain to be the subject of further legislative action in coming years, for the time being what is notable is that the Republican majority, seeing normal processes for handling legislative questions frozen, used the reconciliation process in an effort to circumvent gridlock and resolve—if any environmental policy question is ever resolved—one of the most contentious environmental policy disputes since 1980. Although they came extremely close to victory, they discovered that gridlock is a factor even in the budget reconciliation pathway.

Appropriation Riders in a Republican Era

The Republicans' use of policy riders to achieve environmental policy goals diminished after the Republicans took control of the White House. The Bush administration could use its authority to rein in the Environmental Protection Agency and to break through the complex administrative requirements that came with the golden era environmental laws affecting resource management, and Republican legislators saw less need to use riders to rein in rogue environmental bureaucrats. Further, in confidence that the Bush administration would pursue policies they could live with, Republican legislators could avoid the political heat that came with controversial environmental policy riders. "The era of riders is in abeyance for the time being," said R. Scott Lilly, top aide for House Appropriations Democrats in mid 2003. "They kind of decided that is not good politics for them."[122]

Two cases involving riders that did *not* appear in the 2001 VA-HUD appropriation illustrate the changing politics of policy riders in the Republican era. First, previous VA-HUD bills had contained language forbidding the Clinton administration from using funds to implement the Kyoto Protocol. Congressional Republicans knew that the Bush administration would not go down this path, so the 2001 VA-HUD appropriation bill included no such language. Second, responding to the public outcry that occurred after the Bush administration announced that it would delay implementation of Clinton-era standards reducing allowable levels of arsenic in drinking water, both houses of Congress passed riders that would have pushed the Bush EPA to implement the Clinton standards. Democrats saw an opportunity to achieve a policy goal while embarrassing the Bush administration on a controversial issue; a small number of Republicans joined them, seeking to avoid the political problems they had suffered on environmental issues in the 1990s. When the Bush administration announced that it would not delay implementation of the Clinton standards, the need for these riders disappeared. Congress did, however, order the Environmental Protection Agency to be flexible with deadlines set for small communities faced with high costs for controlling arsenic levels in their drinking water.[123]

Despite an overall decline in the significance of riders, legislators continued to raise important policy issues in the appropriation process in the Republican Congress. In 2004, for example, Congress, with strong bipartisan support, adopted a rider allowing the reclassification of high-level nuclear waste stored in Idaho and South Carolina as less hazardous. For the most part, though, the riders represented efforts to achieve partisan agendas. Several important Republican-sponsored riders failed, including efforts to push through the "Healthy Forests" program, to block a California rule limiting air pollution from lawnmowers and similar small gas-powered motors, to make ESA listings more difficult, and to exempt Alaska from the Clinton "roadless rule" that stopped the building of roads in previously roadless forests (though a court challenge succeeded in exempting Alaska from the rule; see chapter 4). Republican-supported riders carrying the "stewardship contracting" provision mentioned above and blocking legal and administration appeals of the 1997 management plan from the Tongass National Forest in Alaska—allowing logging on 676,000 acres there—passed. In 2005 debate over riders focused on several issues, including ending the moratorium on offshore drilling on the Outer Continental Shelf and efforts to block road building in the Tongass National Forest. Only two were finally adopted, one ratifying a compromise on an EPA rule on small engine emissions, and the other governing EPA studies of pesticide effects using human subjects.

Democratic-sponsored riders typically aimed at blocking Bush initiatives. In 2001 Democrats proposed riders to stop the expansion of oil and gas drilling in national monuments, a policy being considered by the Bush administration; to stop offshore drilling leases; to block a Bush administration proposal to make it more difficult for citizens to gain ESA species listings; and to relax regulations of hardrock mining.[124] These issues promised to provoke tough fights in Congress, but the September 11 terrorist attacks muted partisanship for a time, leading legislators to postpone most of these battles. Still, Congress did adopt riders that prevented the administration from increasing the acreage available for oil and gas drilling in national monuments and stopped an initiative that would have made it more difficult to list species under the Endangered Species Act.[125]

What does all of this mean? Perhaps reinforced by the political embarrassments of 1995 and 1996, the Republicans' increasingly firm grip on the national government as a whole seems to have diminished their interest in pursuing environmental policy goals through riders. Under a Republican administration, the agencies take fewer actions the congressional majority opposes, and they can count on the White House to press for policies in the administrative process—for example, the effort to extend drilling into new national monuments—that might otherwise be sought through riders. Still, as evidenced by the failed healthy forests rider and the successful stewardship contracting rider, Republican legislators have continued to see riders as useful tools for evading gridlock. Democratic legislators have sought to use riders to block administration proposals and, perhaps, to highlight proposed agency actions that would be controversial if there was any public awareness of those actions. The issue of expanding oil and gas drilling in national monuments again illustrates the point. Republican legislators did not need to offer a rider to achieve this, since the Bush administration would move this way. Democrats used a rider to block this gambit, and to try to make a public issue out of a proposal that might, otherwise, have gone largely unnoticed outside the policy community. We are unlikely to see a repetition of the aggressive Republican strategy of the 104th Congress, but riders remain an important avenue around real and perceived legislative gridlock.

Conclusion

This analysis of congressional politics on the environment since 1990 yields three main conclusions.

First, in the aftermath of the golden era of environmental lawmaking, the normal legislative process has proved to be a difficult pathway for most reforms of the basic environmental laws, and for the passage of new laws addressing new environmental problems. Yet there has been considerable action on environmental issues within Congress. A few laws have passed, but persistent gridlock on the substance of major environmental legislation has pushed policy initiative onto alternative legislative paths. It is unlikely that the Republicans' bold effort in the 104th Congress to crack open the green state with riders will be repeated anytime soon, and it remains to be seen whether budget reconciliation can pry open ANWR. Yet, in view of the pressures for change in policy direction, the intensity of partisanship on these issues, the constraints that hinder changes in the language of the basic statutes, and the availability of viable and successful pathways around the normal legislative process, we should expect a vibrant legislative politics on environmental issues despite continuing gridlock, as legislators use the rules and unorthodox processes to push their agendas.

Second, the record of environmental policymaking in Congress since 1990 should give pause to those who see in the legislative gridlock on these issues basis for a new, more pragmatic approach to environmental policymaking. Congress has been unable to reauthorize statutes, to adopt new laws to address emerging environmental problems or—since the 1990 Clean Air Act Amendments—to give sound statutory grounding to pragmatic experiments. Indeed, environmental policymaking on these alternative legislative pathways has rarely reflected pragmatic impulses—there are few indications that the use of riders and reconciliation have served "next generation" policy goals, and the budget cuts and regulatory reform proposals of the mid 1990s were hardly measured efforts to rebalance economic and environmental values. [126] Worse, in important cases—witness the impact of the salvage rider on the Northwest Forest Plan and the possibilities for compromise in the region—congressional action has undermined rather than strengthened or supported pragmatic reform. Struggles over salvage, ANWR, arsenic in drinking water, roadless areas in national forests, recreational vehicles in national parks, air quality regulations, wetlands, and other issues have been conducted in new legislative venues, but on the same contentious ideological terrain that they have occupied for years. [127] The significance of this point is magnified by one of the most important consequences of congressional gridlock: policy initiative has been driven onto other, nonlegislative pathways, ratcheting up the significance of executive politics, the courts, various forms of collaboration, and states in environmental policymaking. As we noted in chapter 1, congressional stalemate hardly produces policy gridlock. From a next generation perspective, this development is at once promising—as Edward Weber has shown, for some actors the legislative stalemate of the 1990s increased the perceived benefits of cooperation over the costs of bitter conflict—and troubling. The failure of Congress to mark out clear statutory pathways leaves in place institutional and legal legacies rooted in more than a century of policy development, and a politics of multiple orders drawing legitimacy from different laws and different strains in the political culture. What remains in place is as likely to pulverize next generation innovations as it is to translate them into new directions in public policy. The reality is that, given the depth, expanse, and internal contradictions that mark the green state, Congress itself would find it extremely difficult to impose a new ordering vision if it set out to do so. In the absence of such congressional action, environmentalists, conservatives and business interests, and next generation reformers struggle for the future in an institutional system marked by considerable stability in the basic legal structure and instability and contingency in policy outcomes. To use Karen Orren and Stephen Skowronek's language, the "intercurrence" that characterizes the green state encompasses a host of institutions and values and interests, but—aside perhaps from a long-term drift toward greater environmental awareness and protection—lacks a central, rationalizing tendency.[128]

Even in areas in which Congress manages to act on alternative pathways, those actions enter into an institutional labyrinth that renders major decisions contingent at best. The recent use of budget reconciliation to try to open the way for drilling in ANWR is an example. If pro-drilling forces ever do get final legislative victory, there is no doubt that there will be continuing challenges in Congress, the courts, and the administrative process that will complicate the sinking of wells. This goes deeper than the challenges of hyperpluralism, where public authority cannot be exercised without challenge from some aggrieved interest; it goes to the evolution of an institutional system and even a culture that legitimizes contradictory environmental policy claims simultaneously, *an intercurrent state*.[129] The Northwest Timber Compromise (Section 318) and the salvage rider are other significant examples. Congress, having failed to address the critical situation that had evolved around the unsustainable timber cuts allowed in the 1980s, dissatisfaction with the Endangered Species Act, the listing of the spotted owl, and the desperate political conflict that gripped the Pacific Northwest, cut into the conflict with temporary riders returning throwback logging to the region. This lasted only until the courts hemmed in the riders' effects and the Clinton administration found ways to slow implementation to play out the clock. Congress *can* set broad new directions for policy—the Clean Air Act Amendments of 1990 are a case in point. Yet 15 years after that bold stroke those anticipating significant changes in the character of the American green state are still waiting for innovations that would establish such broad new directions for environmental policy in the United States. In the meantime, interests of all kinds will work in the green state labyrinth, seeking opportunities to advance their goals along any available pathway. Policy outcomes will continue to be less stable and less predictable, dependent on court decisions and administrative rulemakings that frequently change across circuits and across administrations.

Third, gridlock in the "textbook" legislative process on the environment has changed the game in Congress and the broader American political system. In the 1960s and the 1970s, Congress enacted a host of major environmental laws, at times—as in the case of the Wild and Scenic Rivers Act and the Wilderness Act—overcoming considerable opposition to mark out significant new policy directions. These laws marked significant changes in societal values and the balance of power in American politics, with the organizational and legislative success of the environmental movement striking a hard blow against arguments about the endemic biases of American pluralism. That is, the golden era environmental laws grew out of the democratization of the political system, a process that enhanced the legitimacy of political outcomes by enhancing political representation and forces that at least for a time seemed to balance the political influence of the business community. There were many compromises in the legislative processes that produced the golden era laws, and they were hardly perfect from the perspective of environmentalists. But the Congress of the 1960s and the 1970s responded to popular demands and, in environmental policymaking, ratified the broad democratization of the political order that took place after mid-century.

And now? Since 1980, congressional policymaking on the environment has shifted decisively onto less visible, less legitimate tracks, with legislators seeking to attain their objectives by stretching and bending settled rules and procedures and artful packaging of controversial proposals ("regulatory reform" to curb big government, "Healthy Forests," "Clear Skies") the order of the day. For example, in the 104th Congress, House conservatives sought to tie major rollbacks of the green state that could never have survived the legislative process on their own to "must pass" appropriation bills; the salvage rider carried in the slipstream of legislation to relieve victims of the horrific Oklahoma City bombing. To describe this development is to raise questions about its legitimacy. Recognizing that the prohibition against legislating on appropriation bills has long been a weak constraint on determined members of Congress and acknowledging that the normal legislative process is typically not a model of democracy in action, it still appears to be the case that gridlock pushed important choices onto some somewhat less democratic pathways. This point holds even though some riders—the salvage rider in particular— were openly debated and widely publicized. The use of budget reconciliation to open the coastal plain of ANWR to oil drilling raises another kind of legitimacy issue. The House embraced drilling in an up or down vote (although in the end it was the House that stripped it from the reconciliation bill), and the Senate would have if the issue could have come to the floor. But the Republican leadership in the Senate understood that Democrats would rely on the Senate's norm of unlimited debate and the filibuster rule to block this controversial move, and used the budget procedure in a controversial way to win the day. From an institutional perspective these gambits—sometimes successful, sometimes not—hardly set the stage for compromise and "next generation" thinking about environmental policy problems over the long haul. More significant is the transformation of environmental policymaking in Congress from a major outgrowth of the democratization of the American political system in the 1960s and the 1970s to something else, a game played on unconventional legislative pathways and, arguably, at the boundaries of political legitimacy in service of decidedly partisan and ideological objectives.

The chapters that follow track the movement of policy initiative on the environment beyond the gridlocked Congress to other institutions and into the labyrinth of the American green state.

4

National Monuments, Roadless Forests, and Aging Electric Utilities: Executive Policymaking through Statutory Discretion and Rulemaking

Since the beginning of significant national-level conservation policymaking in the late 1800s and the early 1900s, presidents have made use of a variety of approaches to shape policy. President Theodore Roosevelt made the greatest use of these tools. Under the administrative discretion granted the president by Congress in the 1891 General Revision Act, Roosevelt created more than 100 new forest reserves, consisting of approximately 150 million acres. (Congress passed a law rescinding this power in six western states in 1907.) Roosevelt also made substantial use of his discretion under the Antiquities Act of 1906. He stretched the limits of the new law in designating 18 national monuments, including the Grand Canyon and Mount Olympus, each hundreds of thousands of acres in size. A final example was his establishment of Pelican Island as the first national wildlife refuge in 1903. Roosevelt went on to create 50 other bird reserves and four wildlife reserves, establishing the National Wildlife Refuge system without any congressional authority, reasoning that since he was not specifically prevented by law from creating such refuges that he could do so. The use of such executive pathways to make conservation and environmental policy has waxed and waned since Roosevelt's presidency, but in the context of a gridlocked Congress it has taken on increasing importance as a policymaking path for Presidents Bill Clinton and George W. Bush.[1]

Although Roosevelt's successors have enjoyed considerable discretion in environmental policymaking and modern presidents have substantial resources for managing the policies of the government they head, these modern presidents also face a large and complex green state and intense political mobilization around environmental issues, and their freedom of action to shape environmental policy is more limited. To use Stephen Skowronek's imagery, the green state has "thickened," and despite a long-term increase in the resources available to presidents for shaping policy, they must struggle to impose new environmental priorities. They can use unilateral authority in some cases, but driving environmental policy also requires taking control of the administrative apparatus of the green state and turning that apparatus to the president's purposes. Thus from the perspective of presidents, environmental policymaking has been bound up with the elaboration of the administrative presidency, including the increasing politicization of appointments to important positions in the Environmental Protection Agency and the Department of the Interior and attempts to use the Office of Management and Budget to coordinate and control the far-flung regulatory system. Terry Moe argued persuasively that all modern presidents are driven to politicize administrative arrangements because they find that too many crucial decisions are "lost to the permanent government" and they want to gain control of those choices. This has clearly been the case in environmental policymaking, where presidents have aggressively used the tools of the administrative presidency to shape policy. Changes in party control of the White House have meant dramatic shifts in the backgrounds and ideologies of people appointed to central political positions in the environmental policy bureaucracy. Indeed, all presidents since Gerald Ford have tried to use the OMB to reorient environmental regulation.[2]

The importance of executive politics—the use of unilateral executive authority and an emphasis on shaping rulemaking and policy implementation—is increased by legislative gridlock on environmental issues. As we showed in chapters 2 and 3, except in rare cases presidents have been frustrated in the use of their formal and informal legislative powers to advance their policy agendas, and, despite two shocks to agency budgets since Ronald Reagan's election, the green state itself has not been seriously weakened by these budgetary attacks. The current structure of laws is essentially given, and the institutional field is thick with agencies and organizations with stakes in pieces of the status quo. Presidents seeking to shape environmental policy must find ways around this reality, exercising unilateral powers and focusing on implementation and the articulation of those laws in rulemaking.[3]

Modern presidents do not operate on the open fields that were available to Theodore Roosevelt, but, despite legislative gridlock and the density of the institutional and legal structures governing the environment, they were able to drive environmental policymaking in new directions, even after the end of the golden era of lawmaking. Their formal and informal legislative powers may not give them much leverage over the direction of policy in the era of gridlock, but they still control a host of other powers that have allowed them to move policy despite gridlock in Congress. Indeed, despite the thickened institutional environment presidents now face there is considerable volatility in policy, much of it driven by the increasing importance of executive powers in this field. After an overview of the various powers that presidents can bring to bear in the search for pathways around gridlock, we will present three case studies of the uses of executive politics to attempt to achieve significant conservation and environmental policy goals: Bill Clinton's use of the Antiquities Act and the roadless rule designed to block road building in roadless national forest areas, and George W. Bush's rulemaking to alter the New Source Review provisions of the Clean Air Act.

Presidents have several major powers outside of the legislative process.

First, using constitutional or statutory authority, presidents can issue executive orders, commands to agency and department heads typically aimed at carrying forward the president's statutory obligations or enhancing operational management of the executive branch. These orders have the force of law 30 days after they are published in the *Federal Register*. Presidents have sometimes used orders to make crucial policy decisions; in the environmental arena, for instance, the U.S. Environmental Protection Agency was created by executive order in 1970. Typically, though, executive orders have not been used to mark out specific new directions for environmental policy. As Jonathan West and Glen Sussman wrote, "executive orders are most often used to establish agencies in the executive branch, to alter administrative rules or actions, to modify the decision-making process, or to flesh out and enforce laws." West and Sussman's analysis of executive orders from Franklin Roosevelt through the first two years of the Clinton administration showed that the percentage of orders dealing with the environment ranged from a high of 38 percent during Roosevelt's second term to 7 percent during both of Ronald Reagan's terms. They further reported that of these environmental executive orders, 71 percent were used to implement congressional statutes, 24 percent to reform or reorganize the bureaucracy, and only 5 percent to adopt new initiatives.[4] Our analysis of the executive orders issued in Clinton's two terms and in George W. Bush's first term revealed similar results. Among Clinton's executive orders, 13 percent during his first term and 12 percent during his second term dealt with the environment. Most of these 45 executive orders concerned implementation and the creation of advisory councils and other matters of bureaucratic structure. Clinton's most significant conservation and environmental policy orders required the use of federal purchasing power to further energy conservation, recycling, and water conservation; committed the Environmental Protection Agency and the federal government generally to work on behalf of environmental justice; encouraged the EPA and other agencies to use negotiated rulemaking; established the American Heritage Rivers Program; protected coral reefs; established the Marine Protected Areas Program; and created the 84-million-acre Northwest Hawaiian Islands Coral Reef Ecosystem Reserve. Bush issued only 16 executive orders dealing with the environment in his first term (9 percent). All focused on bureaucracy and implementation, with the most significant ones seeking to expedite permitting and regulatory review of energy projects.[5] The executive orders issued since 1980 that have had the most far-reaching effect on conservation and environmental policy, however, have dealt with OMB oversight of regulation more generally: Reagan's E.O. 12,291, requiring a regulatory impact analysis for proposed regulations, and E.O. 12,498, requiring agencies to submit regulatory calendars to the OMB, and Clinton's E.O. 12,866, which replaced the Reagan regulatory executive orders with a new process that reduced the significance of strict cost-benefit analysis in regulatory evaluation. Under the Clinton and George W. Bush administrations, presidents have moved beyond efforts to better manage the overall rulemaking process through the OMB to using rulemaking to make significant policy changes, policy initiatives often stuck in the congressional morass.[6]

A second tool available to presidents for making conservation and environmental policy is discretionary authority granted to the president by various statutes. Although Congress has guarded its powers much more vigilantly in the post-Watergate era, several earlier statutes remain that grant the president wide-ranging power. In the conservation arena, far and away the most significant such statute is the Antiquities Act. As will be discussed in a case study below, Clinton and his Secretary of the Interior, Bruce Babbitt, made aggressive use of the this law, designating 19 new national monuments and expanding several existing ones. All told, Clinton protected nearly 6 million acres through the Antiquities Act. These national monuments could well be the chief conservation accomplishment of Clinton's presidency, and one of his chief policy legacies overall. Babbitt also made significant use of his discretionary authority as Secretary of the Interior in reorienting implementation of the Endangered Species Act through the use of habitat conservation plans (see chapter 6), as well as spurring reforms in river management throughout the nation.[7]

Third, administrations can use the open language of statutes and the implementation process to drive policy in new directions. For example, one of the most significant resources policy initiatives of Clinton's first term, the Northwest Forest Plan, was developed in negotiations among management agencies and other stakeholders, with the agencies responding to Clinton's political direction and operating under the freedom of action allowed by the panoply of forest management laws. The 1994 Record of Decision sealing the deal between the Forest Service and the Bureau of Land Management embraced an "ecosystem management" approach, and found authority to do this in the "broad discretion to . . . rely upon our expertise to manage the lands under our administrative authority" afforded by the Endangered Species Act, the Federal Land Policy and Management Act, the Forest and Rangeland Renewable Resources Planning Act, Forest Service Organic Act, the Multiple Use Sustained Yield Act, and the National Forest Management Act.[8] These statutes did not mandate the management approach adopted in the Forest Plan. Instead the plan reflected the Clinton administration's efforts to balance the demands of environmentalists and the timber industry in the Northwest, and its use of flexibility in the statutes to try to achieve this objective. Importantly there was no effort to involve Congress in this attempt to end the timber wars; the Clinton White House sought this important goal through the implementation process.

Shaping the enforcement of environmental laws, within constraints set by political necessity, statutory language, and the courts, is a fourth tool for presidential administrations. David Ullrich, a former EPA regional manager, observed:

The people who work on enforcement are very sensitive to signals about what they are doing. Because enforcement has always been and will always be controversial and contentious, it is very critical that the people working on it have entirely clear signals that enforcement is important, that compliance with environmental laws is important, and that the people who do the work will be supported. Those signals have to come from the top. They have to come from the Administrator and the Assistant Administrator [both political appointees].[9]

Comparative assessments of enforcement in different administrations show considerable variation in enforcement activity. One study of the Environmental Protection Agency showed a 58 percent drop in violation notices to polluters—the EPA's most important enforcement tool—between the Clinton and George W. Bush administrations. The same study also found a significant drop in fines. The Bush EPA did issue more administrative orders to stop polluting to violators, a tool historically used to address simple, routine problems. This reflected the Bush administration's emphasis on voluntary business efforts to control effluents and emissions.[10] In another study of the Clinton and Bush years, Joel Mintz found a much greater emphasis on enforcement in the Clinton administration. The most compelling case involved the Clinton EPA's enforcement of New Source Review requirements for modifications at coal-fired power plants, and the Bush administration's more industry-friendly approach (see the case study below). Presidents have not had much luck in changing the basic environmental statutes, or at achieving new legislation. But they can shape policy, sometimes at the margins and sometimes more fundamentally, by affecting the nature and aggressiveness of enforcement.[11]

Fifth, in recent years there has been increased attention to the strategic positioning of presidential administrations in litigation around environmental issues. Critics of the George W. Bush administration have cited its failure to contest a challenge to the roadless rule in federal court, its failure to appeal a ruling adverse to the federal government in a case involving mountaintop removal mining in West Virginia, and what they viewed as industry-friendly settlements of lawsuits involving logging restrictions under the Northwest Forest Plan, snowmobile access to

Yellowstone National Park, and the opening of BLM lands being managed as wilderness in Utah.[12] Senator Charles Schumer noted the policy implications of some of these actions, arguing that the failure to appeal several cases left "far-reaching decisions on the books that re-interpret core legal principles, including constitutional standards (such as whether the 11th Amendment bars citizen suits when a federal regulatory program is delegated to a state), statutory interpretations (including the application of federal reserved water rights) and regulatory procedure (including how many studies must be done prior to a regulation going into effect)."[13] If Bush's critics—and those who argue that the Clinton administration pursued the same course in the courts, only usually on behalf of environmentalists—are correct, strategic positioning in the judicial process is an important tool available to presidents for shaping policy in the era of gridlock.[14]

Finally, and most significantly, since 1995 rulemaking has emerged as the primary way presidents have wielded their power to make conservation and environmental policy. According to the Administrative Procedures Act of 1946, a rule is "the whole or part of an agency statement of general or particular applicability and future effect designed to implement, interpret, or prescribe law or policy." Some statutes, such as the Clean Air Act, require agencies to engage in substantial, time bound rulemaking. In these instances, presidents and agencies do not have the discretion to make or not make a rule, though they do have some discretion in terms of the content of the rule. (See the case study on ozone and particulate standards in chapter 5.) In other situations, however, presidents can make significant discretionary use of rulemaking; in such instances, they can use rulemaking to achieve policy goals. The Administrative Procedures Act requires certain procedures and public participation in the rulemaking process, and the rules are subject to judicial review. (Courts can reject rules if they are "arbitrary, capricious, an abuse of discretion, or otherwise not in accordance with law.") But in cases where the law is vague or unclear, agencies have potentially wide leeway in making rules—and policy. With deadlock in Congress, this makes rulemaking a popular pathway for presidents.[15]

With little in the way of new conservation and environmental laws to mark his eight years as president, Clinton oversaw a host of policy initiatives made through rulemaking. Although some of these new rules were required by statute, such as issuing maximum achievable control technology standards for dozens of air toxics and issuing emission standards for heavy duty trucks and gasoline emission standards, both required by the 1990 Clean Air Act Amendments, or by court cases, such as writing total maximum daily load standards under the Clean Water Act, the majority of Clinton's most important rulemaking initiatives were discretionary. In the conservation arena, Clinton's most significant policy via rulemaking was the effort to protect nearly 60 million acres of roadless national forest lands from future development. Although this rule is still in legal limbo, if implemented it would be one of the largest conservation initiatives in the nation's history. Rebuffed in Congress in other efforts to reform additional aspects of public lands management, the Clinton administration used rulemaking to issue new grazing standards and guidelines as well as environmental regulations for hardrock mining. Indeed, in a section of his overview of the Babbitt legacy subtitled "Who Needs Congress? Activism without Legislation," John Leshy, Solicitor for the Department of the Interior during the Clinton administration, wrote: "While Babbitt had some successes dealing with Congress, he was perhaps at his best in filling the vacuum left when Congress was gridlocked and could not act." Clinton also made use of rulemaking to tighten wetlands regulation and to alter implementation of the Endangered Species Act by adopting rules aimed at reducing private landowner opposition to the law. Regarding pollution, the Clinton administration increased the scope of the Toxic Release Inventory program and adopted strict new ambient air quality standards for ozone and particulates. Although the Clean Air Act required the Environmental Protection Agency to revisit its ambient air quality standards every five years, it did not determine how the administration should judge ambiguous evidence. Indeed, an early analysis of the Clinton administration's environmental legacy noted that these stricter standards "could turn out to be one of the Clinton Administration's most enduring environmental legacies."[16]

When George W. Bush entered the White House, his first rulemaking action was to put a 60-day hold on all Clinton rules, such as the roadless rule, that had not yet gone into effect. As time passed, the Bush administration used the rulemaking process to reverse or try to reverse a number of policies established by the Clinton administration via rule-making: protecting roadless lands in national forests, public lands grazing (proposed) and hardrock mining regulations, snowmobiling in Yellow-stone National Park (in legal limbo), reducing allowable arsenic levels in drinking water, and lowering the standards for air conditioner efficiency (blocked by a lawsuit). These actions demonstrated just how tenuous it could be to make policy through rulemaking; a change in party control of the White House could unravel much of the policy work done through rulemaking, an unraveling that would be less likely if Congress had enacted the policies through the legislative process. The persistence of legislative gridlock—the inability of Congress to move off the status quo—increases the importance of other policy pathways, where insta-bility may be common. Beyond these actions, however, it seemed unlikely that Bush would need to make much use of rulemaking to make conser-vation and environmental policy, since Republicans enjoyed a majority in both the House and the Senate. Rather, he could work with sympa-thetic majorities in Congress on these issues. But the Bush administration soon discovered that making policy in the environmental realm was not so easy. Many moderate Republicans had views on environmental policy that differed from those of the administration. Most significant among this group was Senator James Jeffords (R-Vermont), chair of the Com-mittee on Environment and Public Works. With Jeffords opposing Bush's Clear Skies legislative initiative (and then dropping his affiliation with the Republican Party), and with only two Republican co-sponsors of the bill in the Senate, the Bush administration moved farther down the rule-making policy pathway.[17]

The administration has been boldest in the air quality arena, where Bush has sought to use the rulemaking process to bypass Congress. In perhaps its most important rulemaking effort, the administration pro-posed exempting most older utilities and factories from the Clean Air Act's New Source Review (NSR) standards, which will be examined in more detail in a case study below. Rules are also pending to control mercury pollution from utilities, rules that downgrade mercury from a hazardous pollutant and make use of emissions trading, as well as rules controlling nitrogen oxide and sulfur dioxide through a cap-and-trade program via the Clean Air Interstate Rule. Among regulations required by the Clean

Air Act Amendments, the administration has issued a strong rule to control pollution from non-road heavy-duty diesel engines, but issued several weak air toxics rules. In the realm of water quality, the Bush administration issued a rule that legalized the blending and release of treated and untreated sewage from waste treatment plants, and one that environmental groups claim exempted factory farms from the Clean Water Act. In the natural resources arena, rules have been promulgated allowing the dumping of mountaintop coal mining debris into streambeds and making claims for rights of way on public lands easier. The administration has expanded the categories of logging activities in national forests that do not need to meet certain environmental standards as well as issuing new rules for managing the national forests. A new rule removes the requirement that the Environmental Protection Agency consult with the Fish and Wildlife Service regarding potential harms to endangered species from new pesticides. In response to opposition from hunting and fishing groups, the Bush administration shelved draft wetlands rules that would have significantly reduced federal wetlands jurisdiction. And just before the 2004 election, the administration proposed a rule allowing only dam owners the right to appeal Department of the Interior rulings on how hydroelectric dams are re-licensed and operated, shutting environmental groups, Indian tribes, and states out of the process.[18]

According to many environmental leaders, the Bush administration has had something of a free ride in making unpopular conservation and environmental policy through rulemaking. "The effect of the administration's concentration on war and terror has been to prevent the public from focusing on these issues," claimed Carl Pope, executive director of the Sierra Club. Other analysts point more directly to gridlock in Congress to explain the widespread use of rulemaking to make policy on the environment and numerous other issues. In a major study of Bush's regulatory politics, the *New York Times* journalist Joel Brinkley wrote: "The administration has often been stymied in its efforts to pass major domestic initiatives in Congress.. . . . So officials have turned to regulatory change. . . . Bush administration officials and their allies say they use regulations because new laws are not needed for many of the changes they have made and going to Congress every time would be needlessly complicated."[19]

Although presidents have used the executive politics pathway to make conservation and environmental policy since the early twentieth century, the circumstances of using the pathway have changed dramatically since the late nineteenth century. Theodore Roosevelt was acting in a wide-open policy terrain, one in which the green state was just being created. Indeed, his actions enlarging the national forest system and creating national monuments and wildlife refuges were central components of the second layer of the green state and laid the foundation for the next century of public lands conservation policy. Bill Clinton and George W. Bush, in stark contrast, faced a policy terrain that was anything but open. The green state was by then vast and labyrinthine, created through a series of laws, regulations, and court rulings designed to further commodity development and conservation, to stimulate economic development and protect public health, to protect private property and public goods. This green state is populated by a host of federal and state agencies, surrounded by thousands of corporations and nongovernmental organizations interested in advancing their goals, and embedded in a world of public expectations that the laws and policies of the years since 1900 have shaped. Furthermore, since 1990 Congress has become increasingly unable to make policy in this arena. This congressional gridlock has made executive politics even more attractive to frustrated presidents and societal interests. After 100 years of institutional thickening, Roosevelt's use of the Antiquities Act should be viewed quite differently than Clinton's.

Monuments to Executive Power: Clinton Climbs out of the Labyrinth

In a 1995 ceremony at Yellowstone National Park, President Bill Clinton announced that he had used his executive authority to block a gold mine at the boundaries of the gem of the national park system. Immediately after the formal ceremony Clinton reportedly turned to an aide and said, "It's fun to be president; let's do some more of this."[20] As chapter 3 showed, Clinton's early environmental agenda was stymied in Congress, and since the Republican victories in 1994 he had been on the defensive, reduced to blocking conservative initiatives and, as in the case of the salvage rider, accommodating the new congressional majority. He was desperate for policy openings to mollify his environmentalist constituents and to prove, given the politics of that Republican moment, that he deserved reelection. Secretary of the Interior Babbitt had ideas about how Clinton might follow up on the Yellowstone decision by doing "more of this"—using unilateral executive authority to achieve key political and environmental policy goals. He turned Clinton's attention to the potential of the Antiquities Act of 1906 as a tool for land protection and environmental policy leadership.

Clinton took Babbitt's suggestion, and his environmental policy legacy hinges in part on the use of his powers to create national monuments under the Antiquities Act. He largely ignored the increasing preference for collaboration with locals in environmental policymaking and used his legal prerogatives to force land protections on recalcitrant legislators and locals. His actions required no public notice or comment, no environmental impact analysis, and no agreement from Congress. Operating outside the strictures of legislative gridlock and beyond the premises of next generation environmental policymaking, Clinton protected vast tracts of land, nearly 6 million acres in all. This is vital testimony to the importance of the executive politics pathway, which seems as much a part of the current policymaking landscape as regulatory "reinvention," the use of economic incentives to achieve greater efficiency, or collaboration to achieve greater consensus.

Clinton was not the first president to use the Antiquities Act aggressively, and he was not the first to encounter resistance from Congress. Yet his actions do mark a new direction in the use of the act. First, they highlight the new partisanship on land-protection issues. Since 1969, Democratic presidents Jimmy Carter and Clinton used the Antiquities Act to undertake dramatic actions involving huge swaths of public land. Among the five Republican presidents since 1969, only George W. Bush used the act, both times in 2006. Second, no president has pinned more on the use of unilateral powers under the Antiquities Act than Clinton. Carter's intervention in the struggle over Alaska lands was critical (see below), but the weight of his action cracked just one hard congressional nut and led to new legislation. Clinton's spate of monument designations circumvented a much broader and tighter gridlock, cracking a whole bag of nuts and establishing him as a major figure in the history of American conservation. Unlike in Carter's case, no law followed Clinton's actions.

Given his administration's general commitment to next generation approaches, it is significant that Clinton's legacy rests heavily on the exercise of unilateral powers under a 100-year-old law. Third, the Clinton administration envisioned "national landscape monuments" protecting "complete landscapes and whole ecosystems that are 'distinct and significant.'"[21] Protecting ecosystems with the Antiquities Act marked a "paradigm change" stretching the law beyond even the wide boundaries established by previous administrations.[22]

The Antiquities Act was the product of lobbying by early-twentieth-century archeologists concerned about the loss of Native American archeological sites in the Southwest. They pushed for legislation to empower presidents to protect "aboriginal antiquities located on federal lands."[23] The law's language, however, opened the possibility of broader use:

The President of the United States is authorized, *in his discretion*, to declare by public proclamation historic landmarks, historic and prehistoric structures, *and other objects of historic or scientific interest* that are situated upon the lands owned or controlled by the Government of the United States to be national monuments, and may reserve as a part thereof parcels of land, the limits of which in all cases shall be *confined to the smallest area compatible with the proper care and management of the objects to be protected.*[24] (emphasis added)

The law placed no limit on the size of monuments; the italicized passages emphasize the president's discretion and expand the reach of his powers beyond archeological sites to "objects of historic or scientific interest." Aggressive monument designations by Theodore Roosevelt, culminating in the creation of the 818,560-acre Grand Canyon National Monument in 1908, showed the potential of the law. Judicial decisions upholding the Grand Canyon monument and Franklin Roosevelt's creation of the Jackson Hole National Monument firmly established expansive presidential authority for land protection under the Antiquities Act.

Theodore Roosevelt's immediate successors used the law quite actively, but after the Jackson Hole controversy monument designations tailed off. Presidents from Taft through Franklin Roosevelt created 65 new monuments. Most were small, but there were important exceptions: Woodrow Wilson and Calvin Coolidge created monuments in Alaska that exceeded 1 million acres each (Katmai and Glacier Bay), and Herbert Hoover and Franklin Roosevelt designated monuments exceeding 800,000 acres in

California (Death Valley and Joshua Tree). After FDR, though, the Antiquities Act was lightly used until Jimmy Carter picked it up in late 1978. Presidents Truman through Ford created just six monuments, the largest of which was 26,000 acres.[25]

Why did the Antiquities Act recede in importance in this period? First, the areas most obviously in need of protection under the act had already been designated monuments, so there were few easy, uncontroversial areas left to protect. Second, Congress had grown somewhat obstreperous, fighting FDR at Jackson Hole, Eisenhower over the C & O Canal between Washington, DC and Maryland, and Lyndon Johnson's Marble Canyon monument in Arizona. Third, Congress grew more active in land protection in this period, expanding the national park system and, after 1964, using the Wilderness Act to protect public lands. The purposes of the Wilderness Act and the Antiquities Act overlapped to some degree, and presidents interested in protecting large tracts of land could hope that the legislative process would deliver that protection.[26]

If the law had been slumbering, it woke with a start on December 1, 1978. Carter roused the Antiquities Act as part of a successful effort to break a legislative logjam on the Alaska lands bill. In 1971 Congress had enacted the Alaska Native Claims Settlement Act (ANCSA), which gave the Secretary of the Interior nine months to identify up to 80 million acres of Alaska lands for possible designation as national parks, wildlife refuges, wild and scenic rivers, and national forests. In December 1973 Nixon Secretary of the Interior Rogers Morton proposed protecting 83.5 million acres. Under ANCSA these lands would be protected from development for five years while Congress considered the proposal. In mid 1978 the House of Representatives passed a strong lands bill, but supporters could not overcome opposition from the Alaska delegation in the Senate. Carter had described the Alaska legislation as his highest environmental policy priority, and with the five year deadline fast approaching the White House threatened administrative action to protect the lands. Still the Senate could not be moved.[27]

Carter took strong action to force the Senate's hand. In November 1978, Secretary of the Interior Cecil Andrus used his powers under the Federal Land Policy and Management Act to protect 105 million acres for three years, aiming to block mining claims and other actions that might further complicate the issue in Congress. He called his withdrawal an "insurance policy" against the "deliberate obstructionism" that had thus far blocked action in the Senate, and vowed that the administration would protect the land from "the all-out-for-development-at-any-cost groups: oil and gas representatives, some mining and real estate interests . . . the rape, ruin, and run boys, as I call them."[28] On December 1, Carter further demonstrated the administration's resolve by using his powers under the Antiquities Act. He created or expanded 17 national monuments in Alaska covering almost 56 million acres of land; unlike Andrus's actions, which carried a time limit, the monument designations could be permanent.

The Andrus withdrawal and the monument designations were strategic moves on Carter's part. He stressed that he had been forced to act by the impending ANSCA deadline, and that he had done so in the expectation that Congress would soon pass an Alaska lands bill.[29] In 1980, Alaska Governor Jay Hammond (R) acknowledged that the administration had purposely moved slowly developing regulations for the monuments; it had "lain back, waiting for a final bill" from Congress. Hammond understood that if there were no bill in 1980, the administration would move aggressively to protect the monument lands.[30]

Reactions in Alaska were negative, but Carter's actions moved Congress, persuading the Alaska delegation that it had to come to the table to have any leverage over the disposition of millions of acres of land in the state.[31] Congress adopted the 1980 Alaska National Interest Lands Conservation Act (ANILCA), a sweeping law designating 25 wild and scenic rivers and drawing vast tracts of land into protected categories: 56 million acres of wilderness overlaid on 44 million acres in national parks and preserves and 54 million acres of wildlife refuges. Congress did grant the Alaskan state legislature a veto over future withdrawals of public lands in the state greater than 5,000 acres, and the law did revoke the monument designations. Still, it essentially ratified Carter's actions by giving legislative protection to almost all the lands he had designated as monuments.[32] Carter's moves survived two legal challenges, and the revival of the Antiquities Act proved to be decisive in driving what Representative Morris Udall (D-Arizona) called "one of the most important pieces of legislation in the conservation annals of our country" through the legislative process.[33]

Clinton's Monuments: Grand Staircase and Beyond

Like Carter, Clinton used the Antiquities Act to break through legislative gridlock, but most often Clinton had no realistic expectation that Congress would respond by passing protective lands legislation. The administration did occasionally (and at times successfully) threaten to create monuments to move Congress, but deepened legislative gridlock forced Clinton to rely heavily on raw executive power. Secretary of the Interior Babbitt bluntly told a House committee in October 1999, "I am not prepared to sit back and let this Congress do what it has done for the last seven years on these areas, which is virtually nothing."[34] Clinton backed Babbitt's threat with decisive actions, lending credence to Interior Solicitor Leshy's 2000 remark that the Antiquities Act was "one of the most successful environmental laws in history."[35]

Clinton's first use of the Antiquities Act came on September 18, 1996, when he cut through a deadlocked debate over wilderness designations in the Red Rock region of southern Utah (see chapter 5) and created the 1.7-million-acre Grand Staircase-Escalante National Monument. The 22-million-acre Red Rock area turns the eye of conservationists because of its great natural beauty, and is courted by economic interests for the kind of magnificence that lies under the surface—vast mineral resources. The Kaiparowits Plateau, at the heart of the disputed area, held an estimated 62 billion tons of coal, and a Dutch concern was working toward the permits necessary to dig into this rich reserve. Conservationists sought to protect the area from development and sought designation of nearly 6 million acres of wilderness; Utah political leaders were determined to open these lands to development, and proposed about 2 million acres of wilderness.[36]

After the Republicans captured control of Congress in 1994, Utah legislators saw the possibility that they could resolve the issue on their terms. In 1995 they introduced bills in the House and the Senate that would have protected 1.8 million acres in 49 patches in the Red Rock area, excluding the Kaiparowits and falling far short of the conservationists' goals. Senator Orrin Hatch (R-Utah) said: "We have really selected the crown jewels . . . [and] we have not included any BLM lands that have high resource development potential." Congressional delegations traditionally have considerable leverage over wilderness designations in their states, but local and national environmental organizations were heavily invested in protecting these lands. The *Washington Post* reported: "Perhaps not since the fight in the late 1970s over Alaska wilderness has there been a debate with higher stakes for both sides than the upcoming legislative battle over southern Utah, which has more acreage with wilderness potential than almost any other area in the lower 48."[37]

The Utah delegation's bill met staunch opposition not only because conservationists viewed the area to be set aside as too small. It also contained provisions that would weaken protections for the newly designated wilderness areas by mandating that roads remain open to use by motorized vehicles, and by allowing the construction and maintenance of pipelines, power lines, and other facilities within the wilderness areas. Environmentalists feared the precedent of these provisions for Wilderness Act protected lands nationally. Further, the proposal mandated federal-state land swaps that gave Utah acreage valued at 5–10 times that of the lands to be received by the federal government. Most controversial were the "hard release" provisions of the bill, which, after the wilderness designation, forbade the Bureau of Land Management from managing any of its additional lands in Utah as wilderness—it was required to allow "nonwilderness multiple uses" on all of its lands. Historically the Bureau of Land Management had the authority to manage for multiple uses including wilderness, with an eye toward maintaining the suitability of wild lands for wilderness designations in the future. The Utah bill would have been the first wilderness legislation forcing the Bureau of Land Management to manage its lands for anything legal *but* wilderness.[38]

The Clinton administration joined with the Southern Utah Wilderness Alliance and other organizations to fight the bill, which was passed in the House but which failed in the Senate in May 1996 despite Hatch's effort to link it to popular parks legislation.[39] In testimony to the House in favor of the bill, Utah Governor Mike Leavitt (R) had warned that if it were not passed "the same old debate will continue—5.7 million acres or zero acres."[40] The bill's failure did leave the legislative debate there, hopelessly gridlocked, despite Republican control of both House and Senate and a bill strongly favored by Utah politicians.

But there was movement on other policy paths. On one, the bulldozers were rolling: Andalex, a Dutch mining company, was moving forward on its mining in the Kaiparowits Plateau, awaiting the imminent completion of the environmental impact statement (EIS). On another path, the Clinton administration was working on a plan to circumvent Congress entirely.

For at least a year the administration had been working on the possibility of a national monument designation at Grand Staircase. It did not consult with any Utah officials, and the state delegation was surprised on September 7 when the *Washington Post* reported that the administration was considering using the Antiquities Act in the Red Rock region.[41] Utah legislators had met with administration officials on wilderness issues the week before the story broke, and at that time they had heard nothing about a monument. On September 10, just eight days before Clinton's announcement of the monument, a story in the *Salt Lake City Deseret News* reported that administration officials had acknowledged that a "serious review" was taking place, but that they had given assurances that "nothing was imminent," that the process would take several years, and that "no decision as big as this would be made without consulting people in the state." The story concluded that a monument was "likely years away—if it happens at all—but it is a serious proposal," and that "Utah's members of Congress [had] wondered aloud whether a press leak about it was a groundless election year ploy to win votes from environmentalists."[42] Democratic Representative Bill Orton (UT) was told at a meeting on September 13 that no monument designation was imminent, and there are reports that Governor Leavitt heard the same thing from the administration that week.[43]

On September 18, Clinton announced the Grand Staircase-Escalante National Monument, which effectively blocked mining claims on the Kaiparowits Plateau and offered immediate protection to lands that had been at the heart of the bitter Utah lands fight. The president did not visit Utah to make this major announcement. Instead, he held the ceremony at the Grand Canyon in Arizona, effectively lobbing a political bomb across the state border. Few Utah officials attended the ceremony. Among them were three men wearing black lapel ribbons, representatives from Utah's Kanab County, which would be directly affected by the monument. County residents held a "Loss of Rights" rally, flying the flag at half-mast and launching 50 black balloons as a symbolic warning to other states about abuses of the Antiquities Act.[44]

Republican officials from Utah and across the West decried the designation in the strongest terms. Senator Hatch called it "the mother of all land grabs," and Senator Robert Bennett (R-Utah) called it an "outrageous, arrogant approach to public policy." Senator Frank Murkowski (R-Alaska), chair of the Senate Energy and Natural Resources Committee, called the designation "the most arrogant, hypocritical, and blatantly political exercise of federal power affecting public lands ever," and, straining further, said that the monument designation "had the feel of Pearl Harbor." Craig Peterson, majority leader of the Utah state senate, likened the experience to "what a woman must feel like when she has been raped" and said "I feel violated." Representative Helen Chenoweth (R-Idaho) called the monument the "biggest land grab since the invasion of Poland."[45] The House Resources Committee staff launched a nine month investigation of the White House decision culminating in two reports: "Behind Closed Doors: The Abuse of Trust and Discretion in the Establishment of the Grand Staircase-Escalante National Monument" and "Monumental Abuse: The Clinton Administration's Campaign of Misinformation in the Establishment of the Grand Staircase-Escalante National Monument." The reports argued that the Grand Staircase designation was entirely political, and criticized the administration for keeping legislators in the dark and actively misleading the Utah delegation until the eleventh hour.[46]

Administration officials and defenders of the monument rejected the argument that there had been no consultation with Utah's political leadership on this issue. They cited the longstanding debate over the Utah wilderness bill, and argued that when the legislative process failed to resolve the issue—and when the Utah delegation failed in its own brute-force solution to the wilderness debate—Clinton acted to block mining operations on land he thought should be protected.[47] "The creation of the monument," Bill Hedden of the Grand Canyon Trust argued, "was a reaction to the fact that we are so polarized in this state that we can't communicate at all with each other. We have failed to come up with a solution on our own, so basically we took ourselves out of the debate."[48] Yet it is easy to see why—even setting aside the substance—opponents of the Grand Staircase decision would have been frustrated. The move was at odds with legislative expectations about consultation, the norm that NEPA-style public input will precede major federal actions affecting the environment, and the next generation *gestalt* on the importance of collaborative decisionmaking.

Carter's Alaska designations led to legislative attacks on the Antiquities Act, all of which failed, but they also led to lands legislation Carter could accept. In the case of Grand Staircase-Escalante, there was no serious discussion of a new lands bill after the monument was created. The political furor led in only one direction—to legislative proposals to curb presidential power under the act and attempts to deny funding for the Utah monument. All of these efforts failed, in part because the designation was quite popular among most citizens and legislators not fighting the federal government in the "war on the West."[49] Clinton's orders bypassed the congressional gridlock on land-protection issues, and hostile legislators could not block this pathway.

Not only did legislative attacks on the Antiquities Act fail to make headway; the lawsuit attacking Grand Staircase was resolved in favor of presidential authority. The district court wrote: "The record is undisputed that (Clinton) used his authority under the Antiquities Act to designate the Grand Staircase Monument. The record is also undisputed that in doing so the President complied with the Antiquities Act's two requirements, (1) designating, in his discretion, objects of scientific or historic value, and (2) setting aside, in his discretion, the smallest area necessary to protect the objects. With little additional discussion, these facts compel a finding in favor of the President's actions in creating the monument. That is essentially the end of the legal analysis."[50]

Clinton did not designate any more monuments until 2000, but there was significant action in the interim period. Secretary Babbitt pursued a "no surprises" policy with respect to monument designations. He promised to visit areas under consideration, to meet with local officials and interested citizens, and to give Congress a chance to adopt legislation protecting lands under consideration for monument status.[51] Legislators perceived a threat, and Babbitt did not shrink from making the threat explicit. In response to questions from a House subcommittee about the future of Arizona's Shivwits Plateau, he stated: "If Congress does not act and produce an acceptable bill on protecting these lands, I will consider asking the president to use his power."[52] Surveying the Clinton years, a history of the Department of the Interior celebrated the results of this kind of pressure: "Assuming that protection would be given to these areas through presidential action if Congress did not act to do so, Congress created three new national conservation areas, one national monument, and one cooperative protection area in 2000."[53] Senator Ben Nighthorse Campbell (R-Colorado), who sponsored the creation of the Colorado Canyon Conservation Area under the shadow of the Antiquities Act, grumbled that Babbitt's new participatory process gave him the opportunity to introduce legislation to protect lands that Clinton would have protected anyway.[54]

The rush of new monument designations began in mid 2000 and ended just as Clinton left office in 2001. He announced 18 new monuments, 15 of which protected significant tracts of land in the West. "Chasing Teddy Roosevelt's ghost," Clinton designated 19 of the 123 monuments announced since 1906, and expanded three existing national monuments; his total Antiquities Act "haul" was nearly 6 million acres.[55] (See table 4.1.) Secretary of the Interior Babbitt had pressed Clinton on the land-protection issue, holding him to a kind of scorecard and encouraging him to use his powers to build a legacy as a conservationist. The early ambivalence of environmentalists toward Clinton gave way to high praise: Sierra Club head Carl Pope said that Clinton would be remembered as "one of the great defenders of the environment."[56]

Many of these monument designations were controversial. For example, the Upper Missouri River Breaks National Monument was strongly opposed by many locals and much of Montana's political leadership, though some polls showed that at least half of the state's citizenry supported the designation. Babbitt said that he hoped that the Montana congressional delegation would agree to legislation protecting the Breaks. At a public meeting in the state, he said: "I would prefer all of us to walk out of here tonight and say 'We agree the Montana congressional delegation should introduce legislation, and that'll keep Bruce Babbitt and his monument crowd out of here.'" But Congress did not act. Clinton used his Antiquities Act powers, though Babbitt agreed to adhere to "Montana Principles" suggested by Senator Max Baucus (D-Montana), including preserving access to the monument lands for grazing and hunting.[57] Time and again Clinton swept aside local opposition and announced new monuments.

Table 4.1
National monument designations and expansions in the Clinton years. Adapted from Ranchod, "The Clinton National Monuments: Protecting Ecosystems with the Antiquities Act," *Harvard Environmental Law Review* 25, 2001: 535–589.

Monument	State	Acres	
Grand Staircase-Escalante	UT	1,700,000	September 1996
Agua Fria	AZ	71,700	January 2000
California Coastal	CA	Unknown	January 2000
Grand Canyon-Parashant	AZ	1,014,000	January 2000
Pinnacles (expansion)	CA	7,900	January 2000
Giant Sequoia	CA	327,769	April 2000
Canyons of the Ancients	CO	164,000	June 2000
Cascade-Siskiyou	OR	52,000	June 2000
Hanford Reach	WA	195,000	June 2000
Ironwood Forest	AZ	128,917	June 2000
President Lincoln and Soldiers' Home	DC	2.3	July 2000
Craters of the Moon (expansion)	ID	661,000	November 2000
Vermilion Cliffs	AZ	293,000	November 2000
Buck Island Reef (expansion)	U.S. VI	18,135	January 2001
Carrizo Plain	CA	204,107	January 2001
Kasha-Katuwe Tent Rocks	NM	4,147	January 2001
Pompeys Pillar	MT	51	January 2001
Upper Missouri River Breaks	MT	377,346	January 2001
Minidoka Internment	ID	73	January 2001
Virgin Islands Coral Reef	USVI	12,708	January 2001
Governors Island	NY	20	January 2001
Sonoran Desert	AZ	486,149	January 2001

The judiciary proved to be no barrier to the monument designations. A coalition of groups with interests in using areas of the Sequoia National Forest in California challenged Clinton's designation of the 327,769-acre Giant Sequoia National Monument, arguing that Clinton had abused his authority under the Antiquities Act in many ways. In *Tulare County v. Bush* (2001) a district court dismissed the case, noting the president's discretion under the law and the history of monument designations. An appeals court upheld the district court decision, and the Supreme Court denied a petition for a writ of certiorari in 2003.[58]

Once again there was consternation in Congress, but no legislation to overturn the monuments. Opponents of the Clinton designations hoped that the incoming Bush administration would aggressively roll back the monuments. This would of course be quite difficult politically. Clinton's press secretary, Joe Lockhart, said: "To get something enacted, to get something changed, is very difficult because the forces of the status quo are enormous, but to undo something is just as difficult or more difficult. And for a new president, Republican or Democrat, to stand up and say, 'I believe that we should let these big companies go in and take this land back from the American public,' is almost impossible politically. It's never been done."[59]

At her confirmation hearing, Gale Norton, Bush's nominee for Secretary of the Interior, expressed skepticism about the process that led to the Clinton monuments. Yet early in her tenure at Interior she signaled that, while the Bush administration might push for changes to boundaries and management, it would not try to reverse the monument designations.[60] Proposals to open some of the new monuments to oil and gas exploration failed in the 107th Congress (see chapter 3), and while they may someday yield changes on the ground, it is important to note that Norton was working from a new status quo created by the aggressive exercise of unfettered presidential power.

It is hardly news that legislative gridlock on public lands issues has led presidents to seek other paths toward their political and policy objectives. On public lands, Democrats Carter and Clinton were drawn to the Antiquities Act, which gave them a way around formidable barriers to policy change. What is notable, however, is that this reaction to gridlock and intense partisanship in Congress is hardly in the next generation policy mold. The law's open language gives presidents considerable discretion. The deference of the courts, divisions in Congress, the absence of requirements for public participation in the decisionmaking process, and general public support for land protection reinforced their autonomy. Both Carter and Clinton used that autonomy aggressively to advance their policy and political agendas. Yet it is also crucial to note the differences between Carter's and Clinton's actions. Carter, working at the end of the golden era of environmental legislation, used the Antiquities Act as a tool in the legislative process. Congress ultimately acted to protect enormous tracts of land in Alaska despite the frustrations of the Alaska delegation to Congress. Clinton had no illusions that the legislative process would yield the land protections that he sought, so he used the Antiquities Act primarily as a tool for circumventing rather than driving the legislative process.

This does not look like the "morning after Earth Day" in Mary Graham's sense, where there is a consensus and policymakers are seeking pragmatic ways to achieve goals more efficiently and effectively, or leaders are trying to adjust the green state to new kinds of problems.[61] There was no collaboration with local officials on Grand Staircase-Escalante. The process that Babbitt put in place after 1996 for seeking local input on proposed monuments was hardly deliberative—locals knew that if they failed to protect lands of interest to the administration Clinton would take action. In addition, the dispute over wilderness in Utah was not a new kind of environmental issue, straining old processes and old institutions created to address different kinds of concerns. In the 1990s Congress could not process familiar problems involving wilderness designations and conflicts over the appropriate uses of public lands because of the intensity of political mobilization on the issue. Facing this, with the stroke of a pen Clinton created a new reality on the ground, serving the interests of land protection but also serving his own political needs. It is remarkable that a crucial part of the Clinton conservation legacy rests on the exercise of unilateral executive authority—he used the Antiquities Act to climb out of and above the policymaking labyrinth, to overcome a Republican Congress even as he was being impeached. And it is difficult to argue that executive actions that protected nearly 6 million acres of public land in the 1990s are not a crucial part of the story of American politics on the morning after Earth Day.

The Roadless Rule and the National Forests: Making Conservation Policy through Rulemaking

Policy focused on national forest lands without roads dates back to the 1920s, when the Forest Service administratively designated the first wilderness area in New Mexico and created a set of national wilderness standards. Wilderness policy evolved over the next several decades, culminating in passage of the Wilderness Act in 1964. This law established a procedure whereby Congress could designate wilderness areas on public lands managed by the Fish and Wildlife Service, the Forest Service, and the National Park Service. These areas would, by definition, be roadless and no timber harvesting would be allowed there. Despite numerous compromises made to gain passage of the law, these areas received significant protection from commodity exploitation. Over the next several decades, Congress designated more than 100 million acres of wilderness.[62]

Despite the tremendous preservationist success through the Wilderness Act, protection of roadless lands—especially those managed by the Bureau of Land Management and the Forest Service—has remained a center of political controversy. Wilderness advocates have sought to prevent roads from being built on existing roadless lands to protect their wild character, and, perhaps, to have them protected as wilderness in the future. Commodity interests have sought, in general, to have such roadless lands treated as multiple use lands open for various types of development rather than as another system of protected lands or wilderness in waiting. The last major round of congressional wilderness designation came in the mid 1980s, when Congress passed a series of wilderness laws flowing out of the Forest Service's second Roadless Area Review and Evaluation (RARE II). Wilderness advocates have been stymied, especially since 1994 when the Republicans took control of both chambers of Congress, in their efforts to gain wilderness protection for the more than 50 million acres of roadless national forest land. Although wilderness supporters continued to press their goals in Congress, they also sought other pathways to achieve these goals. In the Clinton administration's second term, they found willing partners in the Forest Service and the White House. Making use of the rulemaking process, the Forest Service published a final rule in January 2001 protecting more than 58 million acres of national forest from road building and, in almost all instances, timber harvesting—one of the grandest conservation policies in the nation's history. The roadless rule, however, was finalized just as the Clinton administration was leaving office and, in a clear demonstration of the challenges of making major policy via rulemaking, the rule quickly fell into an administrative and legal morass.[63]

The impetus for the roadless rule was twofold. First, as noted above, preservationists were pressing to protect the remaining national forest roadless areas. By the second half of the 1990s, this goal found support at the top levels of the Forest Service. Second, these same Forest Service leaders had a pragmatic rationale for elevating roads and roadless policy to the top of the agency's agenda. By the 1990s, the Forest Service administered a network of 380,000 miles of roads, a road system requiring an estimated $8.4 billion of maintenance and reconstruction. From the late 1980s through the late 1990s, the percentage of adequately maintained national forest roads declined from 47 percent of the system to 38 percent. Furthermore, wilderness advocates, blocked in their efforts to have new wilderness designated by Congress, turned to an alternative pathway—the congressional appropriations process. Forging a coalition of environmentalists and conservative budget cutters, the wilderness advocates sought to drastically reduce the agency's road budget as a way to prevent it from building new roads into roadless areas. This culminated in 1997 when the House nearly voted to cut the Forest Service's road budget by 80 percent. The following year the purchaser road credit program—the main source of funds for building new roads—was terminated. For the leading architects of the roadless rule, Chief of the Forest Service Mike Dombeck and his senior staff, this vote served as the catalyst for action within the agency. In the fall of 1997, Dombeck sought to move the Forest Service in a new direction, focusing on a Natural Resource Agenda centered on watershed health and restoration, ecologically sustainable forest and grassland management, recreation, and roads.[64]

Forest Service officials and their supporters cited many reasons for protecting roadless areas. Their rationale included protecting "high quality or undisturbed soil, water, and air," "sources of public drinking water," "diversity of plant and animal communities," "habitat for threatened, endangered, proposed, candidate, and sensitive species and for those species dependent on large, undisturbed areas of land," "primitive, semi-primitive . . . dispersed recreation," "reference landscapes," "natural appearing landscapes with high scenic quality," "traditional cultural properties and sacred sites," and ecosystem health more generally. Conversely, national forest roads, especially when not properly maintained, led to erosion and landslides that damaged watersheds valuable for critical habitat and drinking water. The agency also argued that development in roadless areas made little economic sense due to the backlog on existing road maintenance as well as due to the costs associated with planning, litigation, harvesting, and road building in these typically remote and less productive areas. The Forest Service also noted that proposed development in such roadless areas almost always generated controversy, and that only a limited amount of timber came from these roadless areas (less than 1 percent of national production).[65]

Of course the forest products industry and its supporters viewed the roadless issue differently. Industry opposed the rule, as it opposed the Wilderness Act and most wilderness designation, because it would reduce lands available for timber harvesting. Leading industry groups such as the American Forest and Paper Association emphasized the need for roads to protect forest health (that is, to protect forests from fire and to allow access to diseased and insect-infested forests) and community stability (the need to supply local mills), in addition to general statements about the importance of multiple use, sound science, and local management of national forests.[66]

The policy process began in earnest in January 1998 when Chief Dombeck proposed a temporary suspension of new road construction into roadless areas. Dombeck argued that the Forest Service needed time to develop a new, comprehensive road and roadless policy and the suspension would give the agency time to do so. This proposal drew immediate scorn from western commodity interests and their allies in Congress. "You don't start a good-faith dialogue by first rolling a hand grenade under the door," said Senator Larry Craig (R-Idaho), chair of the Senate Forests and Public Lands Management Subcommittee. In February 1999, the Forest Service finalized the proposed policy, prohibiting new road construction into inventoried roadless areas for 18 months, with the exception of national forests that had recently revised their forest plans under the National Forest Management Act. The response was predictable. Wilderness advocates were supportive, arguing that the moratorium should be made permanent. Commodity interests and their allies in Congress, especially western Republicans, opposed the moratorium and threatened to reduce the agency's budget if it continued. John Porter (R-Illinois) and other representatives who were interested in cutting the agency's road budget were more receptive. The Forest Service's road budget began to increase after years of decline. For Dombeck and his senior policy advisor Chris Wood, "the moratorium separated the issues of roadless area protection from the need to reform management of the 386,000-mile road system," helping to achieve one of their pragmatic policy goals.[67]

What next? Dombeck and staff had meetings with the White House staff on this question. The answer became public on October 13, 1999, when President Clinton delivered a speech in a Virginia national forest. "I direct the Forest Service," Clinton said, "to develop, and propose for public comment, regulations to provide appropriate long-term protection for most or all of these currently inventoried 'roadless' areas." The rule-making process within the Forest Service began immediately, with an EIS notice of intent published less than a week later. Dombeck and Wood later wrote: "With the White House investing significant political capital in its success, not completing the Roadless Rule was never an option for the Forest Service." In addition to the rule focusing specifically on road-less areas, the Forest Service also developed a related comprehensive road rule and new forest planning regulations dealing with roadless areas.[68]

The main actors in the policy process openly acknowledged the venue shopping at work in the roadless issue. "They are doing through a regu-latory process what they can't do legislatively," said Michael Klein of the American Forest and Paper Association. "They don't have the votes, so they are doing an end-run around Congress to jam this elitist policy down the throats of the American people." Environmentalists knew they had friends in the White House and elsewhere in the administration, as well as a second term president in search of policy legacies as he faced a Republican Congress and impeachment. "If this is done right," said Ken Rait of the Heritage Forest Campaign, "it will be the boldest conserva-tion move of the century, sheerly because of the magnitude."[69]

The Forest Service assembled a special team and moved quickly on the roadless rule. The agency issued a draft environmental impact statement and a proposed rule in May 2000. Of the 54.3 million acres of invento-ried roadless lands, the rule called for no road building on 43 million acres. The 2.8 million acres of inventoried roadless lands with existing roads would be exempted from the rule and a decision on whether or not to include the 8.5 million acres of inventoried roadless lands in Alaska's Tongass National Forest, the largest national forest in the country, would be deferred until April 2004, when its current management plan was due for review. In addition, the rule was silent on timber harvesting. In other words, if it did not require new roads, timber harvesting could occur on the roadless lands. The proposed rule generated more than a million comments, most of them preprinted postcards from the members of environmental groups, and more than 90 percent favored increased protection for roadless areas. These groups wanted two changes to the rule: they wanted the Tongass National Forest included and they wanted timber harvesting explicitly banned from the roadless areas. The Forest Service had decided to exclude the Tongass (as it had been excluded from the temporary road construction moratorium) because the Tongass had recently completed a new forest plan. Most of the opposition to the rule came from the timber industry, which argued that roads were needed to protect forest health (and to allow them access to timber), and from users of off-road vehicles, who were worried about the loss of potential access to these roadless areas. The response of state and local governments varied; some strongly opposed, some strongly supportive of the rule. The roadless rule, in any form, was widely opposed in the rural West. "The scum in Washington, DC, are taking our freedom away from us once again," said Gaylen Hamilton, a logger, at one of the 30 public meetings held in Idaho. There, Boise Cascade and other timber companies bused workers to hearings, and Governor Dirk Kempthorne (R) and Senator Larry Craig led efforts to block the rule from going into effect. While Kempthorne had some success through the courts (see below), Craig was unsuccessful in Congress. As the administrative process continued, Vice President Al Gore was running for president and promising that if elected he would make sure the roadless rule applied to the Tongass and banned timber harvesting.[70]

During the summer and fall of 2000, the Forest Service analyzed public input and examined the alternatives, focusing especially on the Tongass and timber harvesting issues. The agency's top leadership moved in the direction advocated by the environmental groups. "The Forest Service could not reasonably call for protection of fragmented roadless areas in the lower 48 while leaving unprotected the one national forest where they existed in abundance," wrote Dombeck and Woods. "Not only that but the Tongass road system was in notoriously poor condition." The timber harvesting issue was more difficult for the agency to resolve. "The Forest Service's senior leadership believed that banning all timber harvest would eliminate management tools that could be used to restore forest ecosystem health and lessen the risk of unnaturally intense fires," they wrote. The agency did not ban all timber harvesting; the final rule allowed forest thinning projects without roads, but "the rule made it clear that cutting, selling, or removing small-diameter trees would be rare and consistent with preserving the ecological values of roadless areas."[71]

When the final environmental impact statement was completed and a final rule was recommended to President Clinton just after the election in November 2000, it offered more protections for roadless areas than the proposed rule of May 2000. The rule would apply to all Tongass National Forest roadless areas as of 2004, timber harvesting was prohibited with only limited exceptions, and the rule was expanded to cover 58.5 million acres—the 2.8 million acres of inventoried roadless lands with roads, an additional 4.2 million acres of roadless lands that were not inventoried, and the Tongass lands. The rule also included a proposed six-year, $72 million economic assistance program for affected communities. Overall, the environmental groups and Gore succeeded in making the final roadless rule even stronger than the draft rule; indeed even stronger than the rule proposed with the final EIS since the final rule applied immediately to the Tongass. The final roadless rule was announced on January 5, 2001, published in the *Federal Register* on January 12, 2001, and scheduled to go into effect on March 13, 2001. Environmentalists were ecstatic: "This is a great moment in history, and it is something for which our children will express gratitude," said Ken Rait. This jubilation would prove to be short-lived.[72]

The final roadless rule ran into trouble almost immediately. When President George W. Bush took office on January 20, 2001, Chief of Staff Andrew Card, directed that all pending regulations be postponed 60 days for presidential review. This postponed the effective date of the rule until May 12, 2001. Although it was unlikely that the Bush administration would have developed such a rule, administrative law limited its options. Since the final rule had gone through the proper procedures and been published in the *Federal Register*, the Bush administration could not simply ignore it. Rather, to repeal or significantly alter the rule the administration would have to go through the proper administrative process. Instead of using its political capital on this issue, the administration announced in May that it would implement the roadless rule, but seek to amend it to address some of the concerns raised by critics of the rule.[73]

On another front, almost as soon as Chief Dombeck announced the final roadless rule, opponents began to file lawsuits against it. During the 60-day Bush postponement, the first of the legal challenges bore fruit. In *Kootenai Tribe of Idaho v. Veneman* and *Idaho ex rel. Kempthorne v. U.S. Forest Service*, Idaho District Court Judge Edward Lodge issued a preliminary injunction blocking the roadless rule from going into effect. Lodge argued that the plaintiffs in both cases were likely to be successful on the merits because the Forest Service had violated numerous provisions of the National Environmental Policy Act during the rulemaking process: failure "to analyze a reasonable range of alternatives," "the comment period was grossly inadequate," and a "failure to adequately analyze the cumulative impacts of its proposal." This injunction began on May 10, 2001, just days before the rule was scheduled to go into effect.[74]

With the roadless rule in legal limbo, the Bush administration began a rulemaking process to amend the rule in July 2001. The Forest Service received more than 700,000 responses, the overwhelming number favoring the final roadless rule. New Chief of the Forest Service Dale Bosworth also issued a series of interim directives on roadless areas and roads to guide the agency until the administrative and legal status of the roadless rule was clarified. The main theme of these directives was that only the chief had the authority to approve or disapprove timber harvests and road construction in inventoried roadless areas until a new national forest plan or revision was adopted.[75]

Meanwhile, the Bush administration declined to appeal the district court's ruling and injunction. The timber industry acknowledged that it sought to convince the administration not to appeal the case; it was an easy way for the administration to undo a policy it disliked with virtually no effort. The interveners, a number of environmental groups, did appeal, however, with successful results. The Ninth Circuit Court of Appeals overturned the Idaho district court injunction in December 2002. The appeals court ruled, first, that the interveners could indeed appeal this case even though the government declined to do so, and second, that Judge Lodge had abused his discretion in granting the injunction, concluding that the plaintiffs had not demonstrated a strong likelihood that the Forest Service had violated the National Environmental Policy Act. The court reversed the injunction and remanded the case back to the Idaho district court. The injunction was lifted in April 2003.[76]

Two months later, the Bush administration announced it would retain the roadless rule. The administration also announced, however, that it had settled a lawsuit against the rule brought by the State of Alaska. The settlement, finalized in December 2003, meant that the roadless rule would not apply to the Tongass National Forest until the Forest Service had adopted a final special rule for Alaska. Administration officials also proposed amending the rule to allow governors to seek exemptions to certain activities in roadless areas within their states, though nothing came of this proposal until the following summer.[77]

The courts, however, soon returned to center stage. In July 2003, nearly seven months after the Ninth Circuit dissolved the roadless rule injunction, a district court in Wyoming—in the Tenth Circuit—issued a new injunction enjoining implementation of the rule across the country. Agreeing with much of the reasoning of Judge Lodge in Idaho, and dismissing much of the reasoning of the Ninth Circuit's decision, Judge Clarence Brimmer noted numerous serious violations of the National Environmental Policy Act and of the Wilderness Act, leading to a likelihood of success for the plaintiffs. He issued not just a temporary, but rather a permanent injunction against the rule. The Bush administration not only declined to appeal this case to the Tenth Circuit Court of Appeals, but also actively argued that environmental group interveners should not be allowed to appeal the decision, as they had in the Ninth Circuit. In May 2004, the Tenth Circuit agreed to hear the appeal, and while the court deliberated on the case, Brimmer's injunction was the law of the land and the roadless rule was blocked. The court's decision came in July 2005. Since the Bush administration had adopted a new roadless rule that superseded the Clinton rule, the court concluded "the new rule has mooted the issues in this case and [we] therefore dismiss the appeal." The Clinton roadless rule appeared to be dead.[78]

The next twist on the roadless rule came in July 2004. At an event in Boise, Secretary of Agriculture Ann Veneman announced that the Bush administration was proposing a new rule to deal with roadless areas. While pledging to conserve these areas, she announced that the new rule would invite governors to petition the Forest Service to keep specific roadless areas free of roads. After considering these petitions, the agency would make decisions on a state-by-state basis. Hence, the entire process offered no guarantee that a single acre of roadless national forest land would not be developed. Veneman said: "The prospect of endless lawsuits represents neither progress, nor certainty for communities." The new rule will allow the administration to work "closely with the nation's governors." The proposed rule reversed the proposal from the previous summer, which would have allowed governors to seek exemptions from the roadless rule. Governor Kempthorne and Senator Craig, two leading opponents of the Clinton roadless rule, joined Veneman at the Boise event. "We now have a roadless process that can be accomplished by respecting state sovereignty," Kempthorne commented. The proposal also garnered support from western Republicans in Congress. "It injects common sense and local control into Clinton's eleventh-hour mindless edict," commented Richard Pombo (R-California), chair of the House Resources Committee.[79]

Environmental groups and Democratic politicians were outraged. "This is the biggest single giveaway to the timber industry in the history of the national forests," said Phil Clapp of the National Environmental Trust. "It would be unprecedented," said Tiernan Sittenfeld of the U.S. Public Interest Research Group, "to give governors power over federal public lands that belong to all Americans." New Mexico Governor Bill Richardson, a Democrat, pledged to seek protection for all roadless acres in his state. Even former President Clinton got into the act, writing an op-ed piece in the *Los Angeles Times* supporting his roadless rule and opposing the Bush administration's proposal. The rulemaking process stretched on through the fall election, with the new rule finalized in May 2005.[80]

After more than five years, hundreds of public meetings, millions of comments, and numerous lawsuits, how did things stand on roadless national forest lands? For supporters of the Bush administration approach, the new proposed rule put the roadless issue on the proper track, one likely to lead to less conflict. "This new roadless initiative begins with a much stronger chance to succeed," according to Senator Mike Crapo (R-Idaho), "because it offers local input and suggestions from stakeholders, land use managers, local elected officials and state leaders. Collaborative efforts closest to the ground are they key to wise public lands management and eliminating gridlock. . . . The Bush administration is wiping the slate clean and erasing Clinton's legacy of locking up our land," he added. "The Clinton roadless rule further polarized the public land debate, with the only benefactors being the fundraisers of environmental groups." Despite Crapo's comments, the new Bush roadless initiative did anything but lessen the conflict over roadless areas.[81]

Just three months after the new Bush rule was finalized, California, New Mexico, and Oregon filed suit against the Bush roadless rule, arguing that it would harm water quality and endangered species in the states. Similarly, in October 2005, twenty environmental groups filed another lawsuit seeking the restoration of the Clinton roadless rule. The groups claimed the Bush rule violated the National Environmental Policy Act and the Endangered Species Act. In her September 2006 ruling on these cases, U.S. District Court Judge Elizabeth Laporte overturned the Bush roadless rule and reinstated the Clinton rule, agreeing with the states and environmental groups that Bush's rule did violate the National Environmental Policy Act and the Endangered Species Act. In a familiar refrain, environmentalists rejoiced, the timber industry filed a new lawsuit, and the Bush administration struggled to respond.[82]

Through the end of 2006, no roads have been built in areas covered by the roadless rule since it was finalized, despite the legal and administrative changes. And given the inability of Congress to act in a decisive way on this or any other environmental issue, the administrative and legal guerilla warfare that has constituted the roadless rule policy process will likely continue on this issue and others. As Dombeck and Wood watched their work unravel from outside the Forest Service, they wrote: "That a federal rule entailing such minor economic costs could generate such a huge public response demonstrates that, like so many other conservation issues, the roadless debate has more to do with values than with environmental protection or economic prosperity." "Regardless of the legal and political wrangling," they concluded, "the era of road building in the Forest Service has come to an end." The catalysts to the original roadless rule—environmental group opposition to any development of roadless areas and budget shortfalls for Forest Service roads—remain very much in place.[83]

The case study of the roadless rule illustrates several advantages and disadvantages of using the executive politics pathway to make policy.

The great advantage is that once the Forest Service and President Clinton decided to act, they could do so with relatively little standing in their way. They had to follow the relevant legal and administrative procedures, but they did not have to negotiate with Republican governors or members of Congress. With their environmental group allies, they dominated the public participation process, giving the roadless rule a sheath of democratic legitimacy. Through the rulemaking process, the Clinton administration came close to preserving the greatest amount of land through one act in the nation's history.

But of course, with the change of parties in the White House in January 2001, opponents of the rule could also use executive politics. Although the Bush administration was hesitant to expend the political capital necessary to reverse the rule, it offered at first a limited and then no defense of the rule in the courts. The administration settled a case in Alaska to exempt the Tongass National Forest from the rule, and eventually proposed a new roadless rule that would gut the Clinton rule. Thus policy governing tens of millions of acres of forests was highly unstable despite congressional gridlock. Policies made using executive power, especially rulemaking, are vulnerable to revision by new administrations.

Opponents of both roadless rules were also quick to turn to alternative pathways and were extremely successful in their use of the courts. District courts in both Idaho and Wyoming issued injunctions blocking the Clinton roadless rule from going into effect; a district court in California blocked the Bush roadless rule and reinstated the Clinton rule. With increasingly partisan judges (see chapter 5) and the complex plethora of laws and regulations that constitute the green state, policy advocates can often convince a judge somewhere that new rules violate either a law or a procedural process. In the roadless rule cases, Clinton opponents have thus far been most successful in arguing that the rulemaking process violated the National Environmental Policy Act, a law designed to make sure the environment was considered in the federal policy process. The National Environmental Policy Act has long been employed by environmental groups to block or slow policies they opposed; the roadless rule cases demonstrate that development interests have discovered that they can also use the law to block or slow policies they oppose. Even if Al Gore had become president in January 2001, the court cases discussed above would have created substantial hurdles to the implementation of the roadless rule. But, as Robert Keiter noted, "the courts have generally sustained the Clinton administration's ecologically oriented reform initiatives," such as the Antiquities Act and the roadless rule in the Ninth Circuit and the California district court, so the courts remain a wild card for the executive politics policymaking pathway.[84]

And what of Congress? Where was it when "the boldest conservation move of the century" was being adopted? Largely on the sidelines. Legislators using the appropriations politics pathway helped to get the issue on the agenda. But despite Republican control of both chambers and the outraged cries of western Republicans, Congress did little but hold committee hearings (a total of seven) before the roadless rule was finalized in January 2001. Since then, in response to Bush administration actions and legal decisions, members of Congress have unsuccessfully sought to bypass the problem by enacting the roadless rule into law and to block the administration's Alaska court settlement and other administrative changes. But just as opponents of the roadless rule could not gain enough support to block the Clinton rule, supporters cannot gain enough support to protect it. Recently, however, roadless advocates and their congressional allies have returned to a pathway where they found success in the late 1990s. In June 2004 and May 2006, the House of Representatives passed an amendment to the Interior Appropriations bill that barred the use of federal money to build new roads in the Tongass National Forest. Although the Senate did not pass a similar provision either year, the House action indicates that the roadless issue is far from settled. [85]

So, despite Senator Crapo's views, the Bush administration has hardly wiped the slate clean and eliminated gridlock. Rather, until Congress acts with some degree of authority and clarity on the roadless issue, supporters and opponents of roadless national forest land protection will continue to probe the green state for successful pathways to further their policy goals. And until that congressional action, the outcomes of these policy forays will, in all likelihood, be as complicated and unstable as in the roadless rule case.

New Source Review: Reaching the Limits of Making Policy by Rulemaking

Due to the 1970 Clean Air Act and major amendments to the law in 1977 and 1990, emissions of most major air pollutants in the United States have declined in the last 35 years. Some air quality problems, however, have been slower to respond to the provisions of these laws, including acid rain, regional haze, and mercury pollution. Electric utilities, especially coal-fired plants, are the primary stationary source of these pollutants nationally, emitting 67 percent of sulfur dioxide (SO_2), approximately one-third of mercury, and 25 percent of nitrogen oxides (NO_x).These plants also account for approximately 40 percent of all CO_2 emissions, implicating them in the increasingly contentions debate over climate change. Not surprisingly, these coal-burning electric plants—most of them built between 1950 and 1980—have become a focal point for debates over air pollution policy.[86]

Although members of Congress have introduced several bills focused on controlling emissions of pollutants from power plants, including President George W. Bush's Clear Skies proposal, these bills have gone nowhere in the gridlocked body. Instead, air pollution policy for these coal-burning utilities has focused on New Source Review, a seemingly obscure provision of the 1977 Clean Air Act Amendments. The Bush administration proposed a dramatic overhaul of NSR rules in 2003, but several northeastern states challenged these rules and the Court of Appeals for the District of Columbia blocked certain aspects of the rules from going into effect. In his efforts to follow a new pathway for air pollution policy, Bush appears to have run into the limits of the rulemaking pathway, limits established by the courts and state governments—and by clear statutes enacted by Congress during the golden era of modern environmental policy.

The 1970 Clean Air Act featured four main components designed to improve the nation's air quality. First, for major, widespread air pollutants, the Environmental Protection Agency would establish National Ambient Air Quality Standards (NAAQS) to protect public health and other values. There are now standards for carbon monoxide, ground-level ozone, lead, nitrogen dioxide, particulate matter, and sulfur dioxide. (For more on NAAQS, see chapter 5.) The additional three components of the act addressed how the nation would meet these standards. National technology-based standards were established for mobile sources. As new cars were produced and sold, they needed to emit substantially less pollution. Similarly, national, technology-based New Source Performance Standards (NSPS) were established for new stationary sources; that is, new factories and power plants. And finally, acknowledging that different states have different economies, geographies, and pollution sources, each state was to devise a State Implementation Plan (SIP) explaining what methods it would use—beyond the national mobile and new stationary source performance standards—to achieve the national ambient air standards. Congress explicitly chose not to require existing stationary sources to control air pollution (until passage of the 1977 Clean Air Act Amendments, as discussed below). Requiring existing plants to adopt new pollution control equipment did not make economic sense when these plants would be phased out in 10–15 years. As older factories retired and industry built new factories, the NSPS would be imposed. Thus, within a generation, older, dirty sources that had been "grandfathered" out of national Clean Air Act standards would be closed and no longer relevant to air quality policy.[87]

The 1977 Clean Air Act Amendments added another major component to air quality policy. In response to a series of judicial decisions, Congress codified the Prevention of Significant Deterioration (PSD) program. This program sought to protect those parts of the country that have air quality better than the national ambient air quality standards. Environmental groups—subsequently supported by the courts and Congress—feared that industry would shift operations to parts of the country with cleaner air, spreading pollution around the country. The PSD program made clear the national goal to improve air quality where it was poor without reducing air quality where it was good. In order to implement this program, new sources in areas meeting national air quality standards (attainment areas) were required to go through New Source Review and obtain a permit in order to protect air quality under the PSD program.[88]

Also added to the Clean Air Act in 1977 was the non-attainment New Source Review program. NSR was deemed necessary for two reasons. Since large parts of the nation were not meeting the national ambient air quality standards, Congress decided that before any new stationary source of air pollution could be added in areas not meeting standards (non-attainment areas), it must undergo New Source Review to receive a permit. This permit would require the new source to employ technologies leading to the lowest achievable emission rate and to offset any increased emissions with reductions from some other source in the area. So, after 1977 there were two New Source Review programs, one for non-attainment and one for PSD.[89]

The most controversial and perhaps most crucial part of the New Source Review program is determining when it applies to existing stationary sources of pollution undergoing some modification. The Clean Air Act defines modification as "any physical change in, or change in the method of operation of, a stationary source which increases the amount of any air pollutant emitted by such source or which results in the emission of any air pollutant not previously emitted." Any modification that leads to increased emissions—defined as 40 tons per year for both SO_2 and NO_x— triggers the New Source Review permitting process, and is almost certain to lead to an order for additional pollution control equipment at the affected plant. The Environmental Protection Agency decided, from the outset, that activities classified as "routine maintenance, repair, and replacement" (RMRR) would be exempt from NSR provisions. But this simply changed the question from what was a modification to what counted as routine maintenance? The U.S. Court of Appeals for the District of Columbia, in *Alabama Power Co. v. Costle* (1979), upheld the agency's ability to exempt certain activities from New Source Review, but these activities were limited to minor exceptions (those increasing emissions by fewer than 100 to 250 tons per year). After this decision, the EPA issued a new NSR rule in 1980, but rather than include a clear definition of what counted as routine maintenance and what counted as a modification requiring New Source Review, the agency called for a common sense analysis, which over time became a test examining the nature, extent, purpose, frequency, and cost of the activities in question. This 1980 New Source Review rule continues to be the main rule governing the program, despite numerous court challenges and proposed revisions.[90]

By the mid 1990s, northeastern states were increasingly frustrated on the issue of ground-level ozone, which created significant problems for them in the summer. These states were working aggressively to reduce ozone emissions within their own borders, but NO_x emissions from Midwestern power plants were aggravating their problems. Unless these plants reduced their emissions, the Northeast could not meet national standards for ground-level ozone in a timely manner. These states continued to be concerned about acid rain and, increasingly, about mercury emissions. They launched a two-pronged strategy to force changes on these upwind utilities.

The first approach included pushing the Environmental Protection Agency to require Midwestern states to revise their state implementation plans to require greater reductions in NO_x emissions. Furthermore, several northeastern states petitioned the EPA for action on emissions at specific facilities in the Midwest and the Southeast. Lawsuits from both the states and the electric utilities led to a settlement in March 1998, in which the EPA agreed to move ahead with this SIP revision process. Since then, the SIP revisions have moved forward sporadically, often stalled by litigation and changes in EPA direction.[91]

Second, these states focused on New Source Review. All of these air quality issues were complicated by the economics of the electric utility industry. Economic and technological considerations increasingly made it cost-effective to extend the life of old power plants rather than replace them, undermining the assumption of the Clean Air Act that many of these old, dirty plants would soon be out of service. The utilities launched what they termed "life extension" programs designed to keep older plants operating. These life extension programs would require significant modifications at the old power plants, leading to a major test of the EPA's distinction between routine maintenance at power plants, which would not require new permits, and "new source" activities, which would require new permits and, almost certainly, major investments in pollution control technology.

This led to a legal battle over these life extension projects, *Wisconsin Electric Power Company v. Reilly* (1990). The utility sought assurance from the Environmental Protection Agency that it did not need a PSD New Source Review permit for replacement of significant equipment at its plant, arguing that the replacement amounted to routine maintenance. The EPA disagreed, countering that the work sought to extend the life of the plant, thus it was beyond RMRR and the utility required a New

Source Review permit. Wisconsin Electric filed a lawsuit challenging the EPA's decision. The Court of Appeals ruled in favor of the EPA; the equipment replacement was not routine maintenance and required a permit.[92]

The agency did, however, change one central aspect of New Source Review in light of the case in a 1992 rule. Previously, in determining whether to require new source permits, it had used the modified plant's "potential emissions" as the standard for evaluating changes in emissions levels. Now, instead, it would use the modified plant's "projected actual emissions" as its standard. The utilities successfully argued that this was a more accurate gauge of emissions since plants rarely run at full capacity and the "actual-to-potential trigger" did not accurately portray a plant's emissions profile. The Environmental Protection Agency floated a new definition of RMRR in 1994, as well as proposing a comprehensive overhaul of the New Source Review program in 1996, but neither the definition nor rule was finalized under the Clinton administration as discussions among the agency and interested parties dragged on. Other changes occurred in the NSR context in the 1990s as well. With the passage of the 1990 Clean Air Act Amendments, the EPA had a new program designed to deal specifically with the acid rain precursors SO_2 and NO_X. But with the adoption of stricter NAAQS for ozone and particulate matter finalized in 1997, the agency looked for further reductions in emissions from coal-fired plants. The electric utility industry, meanwhile, engaged in an ongoing dance of language and engineering. It dropped the use of life extension to describe projects at plants during the time of *Wisconsin Electric Power Company v. Reilly*, preferring to describe projects in ways meant to suggest routine maintenance—and exemption from New Source Review.[93]

In late 1996, the Environmental Protection Agency began an examination of coal-fired utilities, which led the agency to begin New Source Review enforcement actions against seven utilities for violations at 36 power plants in the Midwest and Southeast. The EPA filed suits in November 1999, arguing that these facilities underwent major modifications without proper permitting. The agency worked with sympathetic states as well, suggesting that the states should evaluate New Source Review compliance by the utilities. Later in the month, Connecticut and New York filed NSR lawsuits of their own (under the Clean Air Act's citizen suit provision) against American Electric Power Company for violations at ten of its power plants (a suit joined by six other states). In the next several months, the EPA notified numerous other utilities of pending NSR enforcement actions, as well as issuing an administrative order against the Tennessee Valley Authority. Several utilities, including Tampa Electric and Virginia Power, settled with the EPA. These settlements typically included billion dollar investments in pollution control technology at the relevant plants.[94]

There was disagreement over how much reduction of emissions, if any, these NSR enforcement cases would deliver, as well as whether the Environmental Protection Agency had changed its interpretation of RMRR. Environmental groups, northeastern states, and the EPA argued that the reductions would be significant. EPA Administrator Carol Browner claimed that "Controlling the sulfur dioxide and nitrogen oxides from these plants could lead to an 85 to 95 percent reduction respectively in these pollutants." Industry disagreed, claiming that New Source Review discouraged utilities from reducing emissions by investing in equipment that would make plants more efficient. Industry further argued that the Environmental Protection Agency had changed its interpretation of RMRR. "For years we'd asked the EPA for guidance about how we should meet NSR requirements," claimed Dan Riedinger of the Edison Electric Institute. "That guidance never came. Instead the agency just began suing power plants." The agency denied the charge, and environmentalists countered that the industry had enjoyed a free ride for many years because of lax EPA enforcement. They claimed that there had been no change in interpretation, but that industry had been violating NSR without penalty for years. Sylvia Lawrence, the EPA's head of enforcement and compliance, called this "the single most significant noncompliance pattern EPA had ever found."[95]

Although environmentalists and many northeastern states were thrilled with the Environmental Protection Agency's more aggressive NSR enforcement, the utility industry was not. Its legal challenges went nowhere, however, and the industry then unsuccessfully sought relief through an appropriation rider in the Republican-controlled Congress. Representative C. W. "Bill" Young (R-Florida), chair of the Appropriations Committee, rejected the rider, however, arguing that it was not relevant to an appropriations bill. But with Bush's victory in 2000, the utilities saw an opportunity to alter NSR policy. The utility voice was loud and clear, and it was heard. The Bush administration pursued three options. First, the Justice Department was ordered to evaluate whether or not the existing NSR enforcement actions were consistent with the Clean Air Act. This review, directed by a Bush political appointee, concluded in January 2002 that the existing NSR enforcement actions were indeed consistent with the CAA. Second, President Bush sent his Clear Skies legislation to Congress. This proposal addressed SO_2, NO_x, and mercury emissions from power plants, and would have eliminated the NSR program as redundant. As noted in chapter 3, this bill languished in Congress, earning only two co-sponsors in the Senate in his first term and not making it out of committee in his second term. Finally, the President's National Energy Policy Development Group, headed by Vice President Dick Cheney, recommended that the Environmental Protection Agency, in consultation with the Department of Energy, "review New Source Review regulations, including administrative interpretation and implementation, and report . . . on the impact of the regulations on investment in new utility and refinery generation capacity, energy efficiency, and environmental protection."[96]

With complete control over this third option, the Bush administration decided to remake the NSR program through rulemaking. The Environmental Protection Agency issued two reports in response to the issues raised by Cheney's National Energy Policy Development Group. The first, the "NSR 90-Day Review Background Paper" released in June 2001, provided an overview of the NSR program and supplied preliminary data on the program, costs, and the utility industry. At a public hearing that was part of the process, utility executive Paul King of Cinergy Corporation expressed the industry view: "The way the EPA is interpreting these rules is creating havoc with electrical generation around the country." A year later, in June 2002, the EPA released the more comprehensive "New Source Review: Report to the President." The report concluded:

As applied to existing power plants and refineries . . . the NSR program has impeded or resulted in the cancellation of projects which would maintain and improve reliability, efficiency and safety of existing energy capacity. Such discouragement results in lost capacity, as well as lost opportunities to improve energy efficiency and reduce air pollution.

The EPA did, however, state that "with regard to environmental protection . . . preventing emissions of pollutants covered by NSR does result in significant environmental and public health benefits." Furthermore, the EPA noted that it had been developing a revised NSR rule since the mid 1990s, and that it would continue to work to improve the program.[97]

Jeffrey Holstead, Assistant Administrator for Air and Radiation at the Environmental Protection Agency and a former lobbyist for the utility industry, guided the rulemaking process at the agency, a process that included substantial input from the Department of Energy. Indeed, a significant battle took place within the administration and the Republican Party over reforming NSR. Pushing for industry-friendly reforms were such Republican powerhouses as Haley Barbour and Marc Racicot— both lobbyists for a group of coal-fired electric utilities organized as the Electric Reliability Coordinating Council during the debate. Notably, Barbour was a past chair of the Republican National Committee, and Racicot would hold that post in the future. Cheney and Energy Secretary Spencer Abraham strongly supported the industry position in the administration. EPA Administrator Christine Todd Whitman, although open to revising the rules, fought to maintain the integrity of the Clean Air Act. Whitman was to lose this battle, as well as a number of others, and soon resigned her post at the EPA.[98]

On the last day of 2002, the Environmental Protection Agency published a final rule and a proposed rule that would significantly change the NSR program and air quality policy. The final rule, a culmination of the process begun in the mid 1990s, revised how baseline emissions and emissions changes are calculated, established an alternative method of compliance known as plantwide applicability limits, and included exemptions from NSR for clean units, pollution prevention, and control projects. The rule was quickly challenged in court by more than a dozen states and a number of environmental and public health groups. The American Lung Association and a coalition of environmental groups called the rule changes "the most harmful and unlawful air pollution initiative ever undertaken by the federal government." Since the emissions calculations proposed had already been adopted for electric utilities in

1992, however, this rule was not as important to the industry as it was to other industrial sectors. The proposed rule, though, was extremely important. It would redefine what counted as routine maintenance, dropping the existing case-by-case approach for a new method that would establish an annual allowance for the cost of all maintenance, repairs, and replacement at each source. Any RMRR activities that cost less than the allowance would be exempt from NSR. The EPA also sought comments on another approach: replacing existing equipment with equipment of the same design that served the same purpose would be exempt from NSR—defined as RMRR—if it did not exceed a certain yet-to-be-determined percentage cost of the relevant unit.[99]

The final RMRR rule, released in August 2003 and published in the *Federal Register* in October, was substantially different from the rule proposed eight months earlier. Relying heavily on industry comments, the Environmental Protection Agency dropped the annual maintenance provision of the rule and instead relied on exempting from NSR replacement of equipment, repairs, and maintenance that cost less than 20 percent of a generating unit's replacement cost per year. That is, any individual project is exempt from NSR as long as it cost less than 20 percent of the plant's replacement value (for example, a plant could have three projects that cost 15 percent of replacement value in any given year and they would all be exempt from NSR since none exceeds the 20 percent threshold). Environmentalists and their supporters were outraged, arguing that the new rule gutted the NSR program and greatly favored coal-fired electric utilities that caused significant pollution problems. They argued that the new rule keeps the NSR program in place, but sets the threshold for New Source Review so high that in reality NSR will never be applied to any existing sources, allowing them to be forever exempt from the requirement to install pollution controls. Former EPA officials were shocked at the 20 percent threshold. "What I don't understand is why they were so greedy," commented previous head of the EPA's Office of Regulatory Enforcement Eric Schaeffer. "Five percent would have been too high, but 20? I don't think the industry expected that in its wildest dreams." Senator James Jeffords (I-Vermont), a leading foe of Bush's air quality proposals, claimed the new rule was "just one more flagrant violation of the Clean Air Act and every court's opinion on this matter."

New York Attorney General Eliot Spitzer (D), whose office has led the legal challenges of both NSR rule changes, said that the "20 percent threshold eviscerates the statute."[100]

The Bush administration and its supporters defended the proposed rule. In a September speech to utility workers and executives in Michigan, the president said: "We simplified the rules. We made them easy to understand. We trust the people in this plant to make the right decisions." Supporters further argued that the rule reduced uncertainty for operators of existing sources and that increasing the NSR threshold would lead operators to pursue improvements under RMRR that could lead to increased reliability, efficiency, and safety. "Today's regulations will lift a major cloud of uncertainty, boosting our efforts to provide affordable reliable electric service and cleaner air," maintained Thomas Kuhn, president of the Edison Electric Institute, the electric utilities' main trade association.[101]

Fourteen states and several cities and towns challenged the new rule in court. In announcing the lawsuit, Spitzer said: "It was a sad day in America when a coalition of states must go to federal court to defend the Clean Air Act against the misguided actions of the federal agency created to protect the environment." The fundamental legal question was whether or not the EPA had the authority to exempt certain activities as "routine maintenance, repair, and replacement" beyond those approved by the courts in the *Alabama Power* decision.[102]

The EPA contended that it had used its discretionary authority to issue the RMRR rule. Under current administrative law, such authority is based on the *Chevron* theory, which flows from the 1984 Supreme Court case *Chevron v. Natural Resources Defense Council*. Briefly, *Chevron* established a two-step test to determine whether courts will defer to agency discretion in interpreting and implementing statutes. First, the court must find the statute to be vague or ambiguous on the issue in question. If the statute is clear, the agency's claim to discretionary authority fails. If the statute is found to be vague or ambiguous on the issue in question, the court moves to the second step of the test, whether the agency's interpretation of the statute is reasonable. The court will defer to an agency if it determines that the agency reasonably interpreted the statute. So in this case, the EPA claimed that the Clean Air Act was vague enough on New Source Review issues to give it discretion, and that the new rule reflected a reasonable application of the law.[103]

It is here where the Bush administration overreached in its efforts to make policy via rulemaking. It could not convince the court that the relevant language of the Clean Air Act was ambiguous enough for the Environmental Protection Agency to succeed in *Chevron* step one. The State of New York *et al.* convinced the Court of Appeals for the District of Columbia Circuit that their challenge to the EPA's claim to broad discretion was strong enough to warrant a stay of the rule, which the court granted on December 24, 2003, two days before it was to take effect. "The Rule," the petitioners argued, "is a radical departure from twenty-five years of judicial and agency precedent regarding the applicability of the NSR requirements to plant modifications." They continued: "Twenty-five years after Congress enacted the NSR provisions, EPA has reversed course and contends that the statutory definition of modification can be read to exclude extensive multimillion dollar equipment replacement projects that increase emissions significantly. Because this interpretation conflicts with the plain language of the statute and clear Congressional intent, it is invalid." Spitzer called the decision by the D.C. Circuit Court "one of the most important environmental victories in many years."[104]

The president's efforts, both in Congress and via rulemaking, also had a chilling effect on lawsuits and settlement negotiations among utilities sued over previous NSR violations; the utilities were less willing to settle when the NSR program might disappear or be radically changed. This didn't necessarily help the utilities in court, however. Ohio Edison challenged the Environmental Protection Agency in court, but a district court judge found in favor of the EPA's former interpretation of NSR, ruling that none of the activities at issue were exempt as routine maintenance. Faced with the ruling, the utility negotiated a $1.1 billion settlement with the agency in March 2005. Of the NSR cases launched by the Clinton administration, nine utilities have settled with the EPA, agreeing to reduce emissions by nearly a million tons. The EPA lost one case; three additional cases are still in preliminary stages. Once the new NSR rule was promulgated in 2003, however, the EPA announced it would initiate no new NSR lawsuits. Rather, the utilities' actions would be judged against the standards of the more lenient new rule. The Bush administration had hardly been aggressive on NSR before the rule change, filing only one new NSR case since it took office. In light of the EPA announcement and the Bush record, several northeastern states, led by New York, took up the legal challenges. In June 2005, the Fourth Circuit Court of Appeals upheld a lower court's ruling that struck down a Clinton era NSR enforcement case against Duke Energy, leading to judicial confusion on other NSR enforcement cases. In October 2005, after that decision, the Environmental Protection Agency proposed another new rule dealing with NSR. The rule would adopt the industry position, upheld in the *Duke Energy* case, that NSR should only be triggered by an increase in a plant's hourly emissions, not its annual emissions. Environmental groups and several states contended that the new rule would mean that NSR would never be triggered, and they vowed to file suit to block the rule if it were to be finalized. This issue grew more complicated when the Seventh Circuit Court of Appeals issued a contradictory ruling in an NSR case in August 2006. This confusion may be cleared up somewhat when the Supreme Court issues its ruling in the Duke Energy case in 2007.[105]

The District of Columbia Court of Appeals issued its final verdict on the NSR rule in March 2006. In its 3–0 decision, the court vacated the rule "because it is contrary to the plain language of . . . the Act." In other words, the Environmental Protection Agency's proposed rule did not pass the first part of the *Chevron* test. Since the rule had been stayed for more than two years, the ruling was not particularly surprising. The Bush administration's request for a rehearing of the case by the entire Court of Appeals panel was denied in July 2006, and in November the administration and industry groups appealed the decision to the Supreme Court.[106]

In a *New York Times Magazine* cover story on changing the NSR rules, Bruce Barcott wrote:

Of the many environmental changes brought about by the Bush White House, none illustrate the administration's modus operandi better than the overhaul of new-source review. . . . While its legislative initiatives have languished on Capitol Hill, the administration has managed to effect a radical transformation of the nation's environmental laws, quietly and subtly, by means of regulatory changes and bureaucratic directives. Overturning new-source review . . . represents the most sweeping change, and among the least noticed.

Even after November 2004, when Bush was reelected and Republicans increased their majorities in the House and the Senate, the president's Clear Skies proposal did not emerge from a Congress that remains gridlocked on environmental matters. (See chapter 3.) Hence, rulemaking continues to be the administration's main pathway for changing air pollution policy. Although the RMRR New Source Review rule was blocked in the courts, and other NSR rules are in litigation, the administration unveiled two sweeping new rules using cap-and-trade systems to reduce emissions from power plants in March 2005. The first rule, focused on SO_2 and NO_x in the eastern United States (the Clean Air Interstate Rule, CAIR), aims to reduce these pollutants by more than 70 percent and 60 percent, respectively, by 2015. The mercury rule seeks a 70 percent reduction in emissions by 2018. The first rule has been grudgingly supported by environmental groups and northeastern states, which favor the reductions but argue that CAIR does not go far enough quickly enough, and by utilities, which support the emissions trading provisions. The mercury rule, however, was strongly criticized by environmentalists and several states quickly challenged it in court. Critics argued that the cap-and-trade approach is unsuitable for toxic mercury, because it will lead to dangerous hot spots. They contend that mercury should have been regulated as a hazardous pollutant with strong controls at each utility, leading to deeper, quicker, and more uniform reductions. Of course it is too soon to know how the legal challenges to all of the NSR and other air quality rules will turn out, but it is clear that there are limits to making policy via rulemaking. Bush's policymaking efforts ran into the past—a clear statute from the golden age of environmental policy—as well as other policy pathways. Fourteen states were quick to make use of the courts in an effort, successful so far, to block these changes. This is a story on the limits of using rulemaking to make policy, and for advocates of next generation reform it demonstrates that states are as likely to go to court as to craft new pragmatic approaches to further their interests.[107]

Conclusion

As we noted at the beginning of this chapter, presidents have made use of the executive pathway to make policy for more than 100 years. But

when Theodore Roosevelt made the greatest use of this executive authority, he did so in a relatively open political landscape with, at first, the
blessing of Congress. Congress explicitly granted presidents the power to
create national forests and national monuments, and when Congress
thought Roosevelt was going too far, it rescinded his power to create
national forests beginning in 1907. This issue of balance between congressional and presidential power to protect public lands arose again in
particular cases of the Antiquities Act and during the eight year debate
over passage of the Wilderness Act. But this focus on executive conservation and environmental policymaking did not reach the level it had at
the beginning of the twentieth century until the late 1970s, when Carter
made bold use of the Antiquities Act to prod Congress into protecting
tens of millions of acres of Alaska public lands. Reagan made tremendous use of the executive politics approach as well, but with different
goals than Carter. Rather than fighting a quixotic battle to change the
basic statutes passed during the golden era, he instead relied on using
appointments, budget cuts, and OMB control over agency rulemaking to
gain some control over this governmental Leviathan. Moving into the
presidencies of Bill Clinton and George W. Bush, however, we see presidents making increased use of executive politics to affect specific policies.

This more fundamental move onto the executive politics pathway is
largely a response to the gridlock in Congress. With Congress unable to
move on land protection or revisions to the Clean Air Act—and on a
host of other issues—presidents took action themselves. Indeed, increasingly it is presidential leadership that energizes this and other environmental policy pathways. Although this legislative gridlock blocked certain
actions, it also presented new opportunities. By entering the green state,
presidents could pursue significant policy changes without Congress, at
the same time knowing that the gridlocked body would be unlikely to
respond legislatively to such actions. In the three cases examined here,
many members of Congress were outraged by presidential actions. Yet
Congress never passed legislation to overturn these initiatives.

This, of course, does not mean that Clinton and Bush were able to act
without constraint. Indeed, their rulemaking policy initiatives have
proved to be entirely contingent: Clinton's roadless rule was first blocked
by the courts and then replaced by a Bush roadless rule and then

reinstated, and the NSR rule was blocked by the courts as well. Although Congress may not be able to respond, other actors in the environmental policy realm have made use of other pathways—namely the courts—to challenge these departures from the status quo.

The case of the Antiquities Act is especially illuminating for a variety of reasons. First, it vividly demonstrates the layering of the green state over time. The law was passed in 1906, a time when Congress was far more willing to grant discretionary power to protect lands to the president. It was also passed at a time when land preservation was not as central—or divisive—an issue on the conservation agenda. Indeed, it is hard to imagine such a law passing today, or even during the golden era. (Congress would have likely reserved the right to designate national monuments for itself, as it did in the Wilderness Act.) Nonetheless, the law remains in place, substantially unchanged. Despite congressional opposition in response to specific national monument designations over time, Congress has never mustered the will to clear away this part of the green state. Second, despite the outrage over Clinton's wide-ranging use of the Antiquities Act, the courts have repeatedly upheld these actions as valid. This stands in stark contrast to the experiences of the roadless and NSR rules, where the courts have prevented the rules from going into effect. The Clinton experience with the Antiquities Act underscores the point that policy made through Congress has greater legitimacy and stability within the American political system.

Of course, designating national monuments through the Antiquities Act can be criticized on a number of grounds. To many citizens and politicians in Utah, for example, Clinton's actions under the law lacked legitimacy. There were no public hearings or public comment period; there was simply presidential proclamation. We can also question the rationality of a policy process that gives one figure the power to make policy, without the usual open process that can examine trade-offs and develop compromises. Yet there is no denying that these actions conform to a clear and long-standing statute.

The rulemaking cases—roadless and NSR—demonstrate more clearly the limits of the executive politics pathway. As both Clinton and Bush discovered in their venue shopping, although this path takes you around a gridlocked Congress, it also takes you deep into the green state labyrinth. Although this green state provided the opportunities to create new policy, it also provided opponents of these polices numerous opportunities to block them. In the case of the roadless rule, opponents of Clinton's rule turned to another pathway—the courts—and argued that the roadless rule violated the Administrative Procedures Act, the National Environmental Policy Act, and the Wilderness Act. Foes of the Bush roadless rule followed the same path in challenging that rule. Opponents of the NSR rules have argued that they violated clearly worded sections of the Clean Air Act. Both presidents have run into the past.

Critics of making policy via rulemaking are quick to question the legitimacy of such policy, arguing that it is often made in the offices of Washington agencies (and lobbyists), outside of the public realm. The two cases offer different takes on this critique. Given the hundreds of hearings and millions of public comments received, it is hard to argue that the roadless rule was made without adequate public discussion and input. A fairer criticism of the roadless rule is that the policy process failed to deliver a rational, stable policy. The process instead created a contingent and open-ended policy. More than five years after the final rule was published in the *Federal Register*, national forest roadless policy is still in flux. Court injunctions twice blocked the Clinton rule from being implemented. The Bush administration then developed its own roadless rule, which was in turn blocked by a judge who then reinstated the Clinton rule. And, after seemingly succeeding in decoupling the forest road budget from the roadless issue, it appears that environmentalists are returning to this appropriations pathway to achieve policy goals they thought they had achieved via the roadless rule. In sum, the ten-year odyssey of the roadless rule underscores the difficulties of making policy through rulemaking. But it also underscores that pressure on issues does not easily dissipate. Congress's inability to deal with wilderness and national forest management issues did not mean no action on these issues; rather it pushed action onto other pathways, ones that have proved less stable and legitimate than congressional action.

The NSR rule was largely crafted outside of the public eye, elevating concerns about legitimacy. From its genesis in the secretive National Energy Policy Development Group through its release in August 2003 with a 20 percent threshold that the public had never had a chance to comment on—these concerns were real. Just as problematic as in the roadless rule case is the rationality of the NSR policy process. Although the Bush administration did not have to fear that a new administration would unravel its rule when it took office, as was the case with Clinton and the roadless rule, opponents were quick to make use of the courts. These opponents included a significant number of states, especially from the Northeast, that disagreed with the Bush vision on air quality policy. Although rulemaking and a gridlocked Congress may have allowed Bush to get around northeastern opposition to Clear Skies in Congress, the many paths of the green state allowed these opponents to attack and block his initiatives in court. Just as with the roadless case, the failure of recent congressional action on air quality has led to a rulemaking process with a contingent and open-ended result. Six years after taking office, and more than three years after finalizing the RMRR rule, the administration's efforts to substantially alter air quality policy appear to be played out.

For those interested in moving conservation and environmental policy away from the status quo—whether mainstream environmental groups, conservatives and business interests, or advocates of next generation reform—these stories underscore the importance of understanding the green state. Reform projects are only likely to move forward when they can follow a path that is part of the green state, but the paths of the green state constitute a labyrinth, with some paths leading to other laws and institutions that may block reform efforts. In general, though, environmentalists are most likely to be successful when they have a strong, clear, existing law embedded in the green state, laws such as the Antiquities Act, the Clean Air Act, and the Endangered Species Act. These laws allow environmentalists and their allies to block rollbacks or advance protections. Without such legal support, however, new initiatives via the executive pathway, such as the roadless rule, are likely to run into the same type of gridlock reflected in Congress, making their ultimate success unlikely. For conservatives and business interests, the green state offers a host of opportunities to block new initiatives on the executive pathway, but very little to anchor new reforms that they favor. Finally, this pathway runs counter to the future that advocates of next generation reform envision. But they must realize that environmentalists, industry, and presidents will seek their goals however they can. Even states—celebrated actors in the move to the next generation—will not hesitate to protect their interests via any open pathway. So, as we enter the next generation of environmental policymaking, we are likely to see as many roadless rules and NSR revisions as we are collaborations and negotiated rulemakings. Indeed, they are all parts of the next generation of environmental policymaking.

5

From "Who Has Standing?" to "Who Is Left Standing?": The Courts and Environmental Policymaking in the Era of Gridlock

In the 1978 Endangered Species Act case *Tennessee Valley Authority (TVA) v. Hill*, the Supreme Court halted the construction of the nearly completed Tellico Dam on the Little Tennessee River to protect the habitat of the endangered snail darter. Dam advocates balked at the costs of protecting the tiny fish, but the Court reasoned as follows: "It is clear from the Act's legislative history that Congress intended to halt and reverse the trend toward species extinction—whatever the cost. [The ESA's language] reveals a conscious congressional design to give endangered species priority over the 'primary missions' of federal agencies."[1] Important in its own right, the *TVA* decision illustrated the crucial role played by courts in environmental policymaking in the wake of the golden era in lawmaking. Relaxed standing rules and provisions for citizen suits included in the major environmental laws opened the courthouses to environmentalists' claims. Judges have played a major role, case by case, in defining the practical meaning of the green state, both through interpreting statutes and in countless administrative law cases when they rule on agency procedures and the validity of new rules.[2]

In this chapter, we argue that while the courts have long been crucial actors in this arena, continuing legislative gridlock has increased the significance, complexity, and contentiousness of the judicial pathway. *TVA v. Hill* forced the federal government to face up to the implications of the Endangered Species Act, but there is considerable distance between that stunning decision and the story of the law and its implementation since the early 1970s. Despite widespread criticism and occasionally explosive political conflicts over endangered species, Congress has been unable to reform the law significantly, failing to pass a reauthorization pending since 1991. The implementing agencies lack the budgets and political support necessary for aggressive action, and find themselves reacting to a flood of legal challenges. Most species listings have come as a result of legal pressures on the implementing agencies, and from 2000 to 2003 *every* species listing resulted from a lawsuit. Kieran Suckling, the leader of the organization whose lawsuits are responsible for 95 percent of the species listings since 2000, observed that "the only place the ESA exists today is in the federal courts."[3] This is a major development in environmental policymaking, and hardly unique to the Endangered Species Act. The intersection of policy designs aimed at involving the courts in the new administrative law and deadlocked politics has heightened the role of the judges and intensified the politics of the judicial process in environmental policymaking. The legislative gridlock on this issue has led interests on all sides to see the courts as more important venues in which to achieve central policy goals. And as legislative deadlock has ratcheted up the policymaking role of the courts, Congress has found it ever more difficult to react to court decisions, either by reversing or endorsing them.[4]

This represents a considerable change in the significance of the courts for making environmental policy. In the 1970s and the early 1980s, when the courts issued far-reaching decisions on interpretation and administrative law, Congress, not yet gridlocked, debated and often responded to these decisions with new legislation. In response to *TVA v. Hill*, for instance, in 1978 Congress amended the Endangered Species Act to create the "God Squad" to provide an opportunity to exempt projects from the law. Another noteworthy example of judicial decision and congressional response was the development of the Prevention of Significant Deterioration (PSD) program under the Clean Air Act through *Sierra Club v. Ruckelshaus* (1972) and *Natural Resources Defense Council v. Environmental Protection Agency* (1974). According to Shep Melnick, "the statutory basis for both sets of judicial decisions was slim at best," but when the Clean Air Act was substantially amended in 1977, Congress thoroughly debated the PSD program and "the 1977 amendments ratified the core of the judicially developed policy. . . . PSD did not merely survive congressional review, it flourished." So, despite Melnick's concerns regarding the effects of an activist court on air quality policy in the 1970s, Congress actually took up the courts' decisions and ratified them in amendments to the Clean Air Act. By the early 1990s, the gridlocked Congress faced more difficulties in responding to judicial policymaking, as evidenced by the failure of Congress to respond directly to the bitter controversy over the spotted owl or salmon recovery in the Pacific Northwest. Judicial decisions are more likely to stand as policy since Congress is gridlocked, making these judicial decisions even more important than they were in the past.[5]

After exploring the movement of the courts into environmental policymaking, we present three case studies illustrating the new politics of the judicial process in the environmental arena. The first case focuses on the role of the courts in the struggle to gain effective ESA protections for the pygmy owl in the Tucson metropolitan area, highlighting the use of the law as an instrument of what Frank Baumgartner and Bryan Jones call "institutional disruption."[6] The case highlights the role of courts in both driving policy change and mediating bitter policy disputes in a highly contentious political environment marked by intense political and legal mobilization. The second case investigates gridlock over Clean Air Act rulemaking in the 1990s, and how, in *American Trucking Associations (ATA) v. EPA* (1999), a political stalemate on air pollution issues opened the way for a legal assault on the entire complex of air pollution regulation that came surprisingly close to success. Far from seeking accommodations and greater efficiencies in regulation, ATA aimed at the heart of the regulatory apparatus to gain relief. The third case highlights the increasing importance of administrative strategies in the judicial process, focusing on the new environmental politics of judicial appointments and the positioning of the federal government in controversial litigation, including the "sue and settle" strategies that have drawn fire in recent years. Far from the evolution of a more pragmatic approach to policymaking and incremental movement toward "what works," developments in the judicial process— like those in the executive arena—reflect the deep contentiousness and basic instability of environmental policymaking at the turn of the century.

Standing and Fighting on the Judicial Pathway

A kind of double movement made the courts important actors in environmental policy in the 1960s and the 1970s.

First, judges eased standing requirements for individuals and groups seeking to protect the environment. In *Scenic Hudson Preservation Conference v. Federal Power Commission* (1965) a federal appeals court granted conservationists standing to sue to block a hydroelectric facility slated to be built at Storm King Mountain on the Hudson River. Oliver Houck noted that the power company dismissed conservationists' claims that they would suffer aesthetic and cultural injury from the facility as the "self-centered complaints" of a "few local dreamers."[7] Yet the environmentalists' success in blocking the project showed the power of such dreamers in a world in which the courts are open to their claims. The ability of environmental groups to make their "self-centered" complaints effective in the courts was firmly established in *Sierra Club v. Morton* (1972) and expanded in a broader line of cases.[8] In *Morton* the Sierra Club sought to challenge the construction of a ski resort in California's Mineral King Valley. The group claimed standing based on its "special interest in the conservation and the sound maintenance of the national parks, game refuges, and forests of the country." The Supreme Court rejected this broad claim, insisting that the group would need to establish that some member or members would suffer "individualized injury" as a result of the project. The Court did, however, acknowledge that the resort's potential impact on citizens' and future generations' enjoyment of the area might constitute an "injury in fact" sufficient to prove standing. This opened the door to widespread litigation by environmental groups, which now would only have to show that some member or members would suffer injury to press their legal claims.

Second, because legislators feared that federal bureaucracies would not forcefully implement the new environmental laws, virtually all of the major bills passed in the 1960s and the 1970s included provisions for citizen suits against private parties and federal agencies. That is, Congress expected that citizen lawsuits would help to hold agencies accountable for their performance in protecting the environment. "The regulatory statutes of the 1960s and 1970s," Melnick wrote, "offered the courts an invitation to engage in searching oversight of newly created programs and agencies," and the courts took up this invitation with considerable verve.[9] For example, the courts transformed the National Environmental Policy Act from a vague directive to a powerful legal force when it rejected the Atomic Energy Commission's limited interpretation of NEPA requirements in the *Calvert Cliffs* case (1971).[10] Circuit court judge Skelly Wright wrote:

Several recently enacted statutes [such as NEPA] attest to the commitment of the Government to control, at long last, the destructive engine of material "progress." . . . [There is no] escape hatch for foot dragging agencies. . . . Congress did not intend the Act to be such a paper tiger. . . . Considerations of administrative difficulty, delay, or economic cost will not suffice to strip the section of its fundamental importance. We believe that the Commission's crabbed interpretation of NEPA makes a mockery of the Act. . . . NEPA was meant to do more than regulate the flow of papers in the federal bureaucracy. . . . [The Commission's] responsibility is not simply to sit back, like an umpire, and resolve adversary contentions at the hearing stage. . . . It remains to be seen whether the promise of this legislation will become a reality. Therein lies the judicial role. . . . *Our duty, in short, is to see that important legislative purposes, heralded in the halls of Congress, are not lost or misdirected in the vast hallways of the federal bureaucracy.*[11] (emphasis added)

These openings created powerful incentives for environmental groups to use the courts. The Environmental Defense Fund (EDF) was formed in the late 1960s to, in the words of its founder, "Sue the bastards." The Natural Resources Defense Council (NRDC) was established in 1970 as an environmental law practice modeled on the ACLU and the NAACP Legal Defense Fund. In 1971 the Sierra Club formed its Legal Defense Fund (now Earthjustice) that involved the Sierra Club deeply in both litigation *and* the administrative process, where the Sierra Club used its legal expertise to shape agency rulemaking. All of these groups have participated extensively in litigation, and new organizations have entered the field. The Center for Biological Diversity (CBD) has been especially aggressive in using litigation to achieve its goals, and some of its results have been stunning. As we noted above, in the first two years of George W. Bush's administration CBD lawsuits were responsible for *every* new species listing under the Endangered Species Act.[12] "Since the 1960s," the *High Country News* noted, "the courts have been the backstops for environmentalists. When corporations or agencies have flouted federal laws protecting wilderness or rivers or forests or endangered species, environmentalists have gone to the courts, asking judges to be the law's enforcers."[13] The relaxed standing provisions and the receptivity of courts to environmentalists' demands yielded a profound change in the balance of power in the American political system.

Environmentalists' successes in the courts led to a counter mobilization by business and conservative interests. For example, property rights groups have been particularly active in litigating against the expansion of government's regulatory powers, focusing on the problem of regulatory takings. In a 1998 law review article, Douglas Kendall and Charles Lord sketched the outlines of a conservative "takings project" that emerged in the 1980s. The project was given its intellectual rationale by law professor Richard Epstein's work on property rights and its impetus by the expansion of environmental regulation. Financed by the National Association of Home Builders and other development interests, and working through such organizations as the Pacific Legal Foundation, the Mountain States Legal Foundation, and the Defenders of Property Rights, these advocates won several major judicial victories and worked to turn the regulatory debate by focusing on property rights. Dubbing property the "civil rights issue of the 1990s," the groups adopted an "ACLU-type constitutional litigation strategy" and marshaled considerable resources for future litigation—by 1998 the dozen most prominent nonprofit organizations working this legal field boasted budgets exceeding $15 million and were involved in a host of new takings cases around the country.[14]

The result of the dramatic expansion of the federal government's regulatory powers with laws providing clear direction to implementing agencies, statutory and judicial invitations to litigation holding agencies accountable, and the intense mobilization of interests around policy questions has been the deep penetration of what Robert Kagan calls "adversarial legalism" into environmental policymaking.[15] The judicial arena has become a site for bitter and fundamental policy conflicts whose outcomes have veered sharply between poles rather than converging on the pragmatic center. This instability is as much of a reality of modern environmental policymaking as the efforts to develop more pragmatic, efficient mechanisms for addressing policy problems. Indeed, the courts provide an important vantage point from which disaffected groups can attack "next generation" solutions to environmental policy problems, and it appears that the openness of the judicial pathway poses a real challenge to the jury-rigging of new governance structures. In recent years the Supreme Court has inched toward limiting standing for citizen groups to challenge agency actions under major environmental laws (see below). If the Court moves more forcefully in this direction it would, perhaps, tame the adversarial legalism that has shaped policy for decades. Yet this move, by dramatically shifting the balance of power in this arena against environmental groups, might not serve the "next generation" governance agenda particularly well.

The Endangered Species Act, the Courts, and Policy Change: The Center for Biological Diversity, the Pygmy Owl, and Creating Chaos through Law

The Endangered Species Act has proved to be an especially attractive tool for environmental groups to access the courts in an effort to achieve policy change—change the groups often could not achieve through the legislative process or any of the other policy pathways. The Endangered Species Act is a strikingly clear law; it includes a number of steps that invite litigation—namely listing and the designation of critical habitat—and it requires that no federal action jeopardize an endangered or threatened species. As the Supreme Court made clear in *TVA v. Hill*, the clarity of the ESA's language limited the discretion of the judges. The Court's opinion stated: "Our individual appraisal of the wisdom or unwisdom of a particular course consciously selected by Congress is to be put aside in the process of interpreting a statute." Environmental groups did not miss the implications of this language. The Endangered Species Act came to be viewed by many groups, often small groups with limited funds, as their most attractive tool for policy change. In the language of Baumgartner and Jones, these groups found a venue for policy change to their liking and went to work. Their greatest success at achieving policy change was the case of the northern spotted owl.

Environmental groups successfully used the courts to force the U.S. Fish and Wildlife Service (FWS) to reconsider its decision not to list the spotted owl and, relying on the Endangered Species Act, the National Environmental Policy Act, and the National Forest Management Act, forced the Forest Service and the Bureau of Land Management to drastically alter their timber harvesting throughout the Pacific Northwest. The change to forest policy leveraged by the Endangered Species Act and the courts was sweeping. Timber harvests on the national forests in the region declined from a 1987 peak of 5.6 billion board feet to 570 million board feet in 1997—a decline of nearly 90 percent in a decade. Although this case has been described as a legal train wreck—and for many in the region it was—it was far from that for environmental groups. It was a phenomenally successful policy victory. Let us now turn to a case study of a group that has specialized in using the Endangered Species Act and the courts to achieve policy change.[16]

Tremendous population growth in the fragile and diverse ecosystems of the southwestern United States generated problems for many native plant and animal species. The Center for Biological Diversity has used the Endangered Species Act to disrupt settled patterns of resource exploitation and to change policy in the region. A profile of the CBD published in the *New Yorker* concluded:

The Southwest, and the agencies that control so much of it, have moved in the center's direction. People who want to use the land to make money have less influence; people who want to preserve it as an aesthetic treasure have more influence. Precisely by being so self-righteous and impossible, the center has been an important part of the change. This isn't quite the same thing as ushering in an era of biodiversity, though. Another metaphor, more appropriate to the history of the region, captures better what Kieran Suckling and his mates have done. They're outlaws. Outlaws cause trouble, alter the established order, and make authority figures angry. And, in the end, they get dealt with.[17]

The imagery is provocative, but it is important to recognize that CBD leader Suckling and his colleagues are not outlaws; they are using a powerful law that—so far at least—is almost impervious to change and the access to institutional venues it affords to push development interests toward the outlaw category. The case presented here focuses on the CBD's efforts to use the Endangered Species Act to protect the cactus ferruginous pygmy owl and to fundamentally alter development in southern Arizona.

The CBD is a regional group based in Tucson focused on protecting endangered species—and altering conservation and natural resources policy in the Southwest. The group was born in the late 1980s though the efforts of three individuals: Peter Galvin, Kieran Suckling, and Robin Silver. Galvin and Suckling were working on contract with the U.S. Forest Service, surveying national forests in Arizona and New Mexico for Mexican spotted owls. Both became disillusioned with the agency because they thought it was ignoring the Endangered Species Act and the agency's own regulations. In 1989, with Silver, they founded the Greater

Gila Biodiversity Project in Reserve, NM. The group first focused on the Mexican spotted owl, helping to get the species listed as threatened. Six years later, looking for more money, more staff, and a more receptive community, the group moved to Tucson and became the Southwest Center for Biological Diversity.[18]

The SCBD was a lean operation using science and litigation to achieve its goals. Its strategy was to gather the necessary scientific evidence, and then to petition the FWS to list a species as endangered or threatened. If successful, the SCBD often followed up with further lawsuits—to force the FWS to designate critical habitat for a species or to force the Army Corps of Engineers, the Bureau of Land Management, or the Forest Service to analyze its actions for the effect they might have on endangered species. This approach has been startlingly effective. As of August 2001, the group had won 59 Endangered Species Act cases and lost one, with 15 still pending. Executive director Suckling clearly sees the ESA as a way to achieve change, especially on the public lands: "These [public lands] agencies are not going to fundamentally change their approach to managing public lands unless they, themselves, recognize they have to change. That's what the legal train wreck is." A train wreck indeed for public lands managers, but it is an extremely effective venue for policy change for the CBD.[19]

This success was achieved at a pittance of the budgets of national environmental groups or the resources of the ranching, timber, mining, or development industries. In 1997 the SCBD had 13 full-time employees and 4,000 members, half from Tucson. A little less than half of its budget of $384,000 was supplied by members and individual donors; foundations and contract work supplied the rest. With its successes in the Southwest, the SCBD changed its name to the Center for Biological Diversity in 1999 and expanded its operations, primarily to California. Its 2005 budget had increased nearly tenfold to $3.0 million, with its membership rising to 25,000. Foundation funding came from the Patagonia Foundation, the Pew Charitable Trusts, the Rockefeller Family Fund, and the Turner Foundation. Besides its main office in Tucson, the CBD had offices in California, New Mexico, Oregon, and Washington, DC, and the staff remained a lean 40.[20]

To achieve its biodiversity goals, the CBD generally focused on changing logging, grazing, and development policy. Efforts by the SCBD, and other groups, to protect the Mexican spotted owl led a federal judge to block all timber cutting on all national forests in Arizona and New Mexico from August 1995 to December 1996. Although this did not capture national attention the way the spotted owl in the Pacific Northwest did, and it didn't have nearly the effect on the volume of timber cut, it was a far more sweeping ruling and has had a greater effect on the forest products industry in the Southwest. Eleven sawmills in Arizona and New Mexico closed in 1992, including all but one of the biggest, due to decreased timber cutting on national forests because of appeals of timber sales and forest management plans. In 1990, the national forests in the two states sold 320 million board feet of timber. By 1996 it was 33 million board feet. Although harvesting rose to 73 million board feet in 2002, some suggested the work of the CBD could be a mortal blow to commercial logging in the Southwest.[21]

Grazing policy has been an even more important target for the CBD. Group leaders were clear: grazing on public lands in the Southwest needed to stop. Period. The focus was on the effects of grazing on the scarce and ecologically vital riparian habitats throughout the region. The CBD challenged virtually all Bureau of Land Management and Forest Service grazing allotments in the Southwest, claiming that they negatively affect critical habitat for a host of endangered species. They have succeeded in winning substantial reductions in cattle on these allotments, and in fencing cattle out of riparian zones. But it is not just grazing in riparian areas that the CBD seeks to end. Cattle grazing "is the single most devastating impact on the ecosystems of the Southwest. It just doesn't belong here," Suckling argued. The CBD has the attention of the already economically marginal livestock industry, and there is no confusion between the CBD and livestock interests as to what the CBD wants to do. C. B. "Doc" Lane of the Arizona Cattlemen's Association said: "They want to get rid of grazing. Period. That's it. End of discussion. They have no interest in meeting with us at all." Caren Cowan, executive secretary of the New Mexico Cattlegrowers' Association, commented: "They've put extreme pressure on the ranching industry. Your economy's gonna go. Your families are leaving. They're doing economic genocide to rural counties. And ethnic cleansing of rural residents."[22]

More recently, the CBD began to challenge development, a conflict we examine more thoroughly through the pygmy owl case. The cactus ferruginous pygmy owl (*Glaucidium brasilianum cactorum*) is a small bird, averaging less than three ounces in weight and fewer than seven inches in length. It nests in the cavities of trees or large columnar cactus. One of four subspecies of the pygmy owl, it is the only subspecies located in the United States, with distinct populations in lowland central Arizona and southeastern Texas. In Arizona, the pygmy owl's primary habitats are riparian cottonwood forests and mesquite thickets or bosques; secondary habitat is in Sonoran desert scrub. Scientists estimate that 90 percent of the riparian habitat in Arizona has been destroyed, primarily due to grazing, farming, and development, and remaining riparian habitat— home to a disproportionate share of the animals and plants on this northern edge of the Sonoran desert—is under especially intense pressure for development in the Phoenix and Tucson metropolitan regions.[23]

The story of the pygmy owl and the Endangered Species Act begins in the late 1980s. In January 1989, the Fish and Wildlife Service listed the pygmy owl as a Category 2 candidate species throughout the range of the bird. Category 2 candidate species were those that the FWS had enough information about to indicate the species might be worthy of protection under the ESA, but for which the agency lacked sufficient information to make such a determination. After further study and examination of existing evidence, the FWS moved the pygmy owl to a Category 1 candidate species in November 1991. A Category 1 species was one that the FWS had enough valid evidence to list as threatened or endangered, but the species was not listed because the agency was focusing its limited resources on other listing activities.[24]

The Category 1 program served as an invitation to interest groups that sought to have a species listed. The FWS as much as admitted that plants and animals designated Category 1 deserved to be listed; they simply were not high enough among the agency's priorities. Given the petition option for listing, such an invitation virtually guaranteed a shift in FWS priorities and a successful listing. The pygmy owl did not linger as a Category 1 species. In May 1992, several conservation groups led by the SCBD petitioned the FWS, asking the agency to list the pygmy owl as endangered and to designate critical habitat for the owl as well. Once such a petition is received, the Endangered Species Act requires the FWS to determine within 90 days whether or not there is substantial information indicating the species "may be warranted" for listing. It took the FWS until March 1993 (nine months) to find that there was such substantial evidence and to begin a status review. Once such a finding is made, the FWS has one year to make a decision on listing, but the agency continued to miss the deadlines stated in the law. The proposal to declare the pygmy owl as endangered was published in the *Federal Register* in December 1994, nine months late.[25]

The rule proposed listing the pygmy owl as endangered in Arizona and threatened in Texas, and proposed designating critical habitat in Arizona. Following publication of this proposed rule, the FWS held two public hearings and received comments on the proposal for several months. Perhaps the most relevant comment, as interpreted by the FWS, was that "Without an immediate halt to the urbanization of the Phoenix and Tucson metropolitan areas, the potential impacts from such limiting factors will only increase in intensity and quite possibly negate any positive advance made rehabilitating this habitat." The agency's response in the final rule did not embrace this claim, but did acknowledge its magnitude: "While the urbanization of the Phoenix and Tucson metropolitan areas have resulted in a decline in riparian areas where the pygmy owl was historically found . . . it is not the intention of the Act to halt urbanization."[26]

The Endangered Species Act requires that a final rule be published within a year of the proposed rule. With the FWS five months late and no sign of a final rule, the SCBD notified the agency that it would sue over its failure to list the pygmy owl. The SCBD followed through and filed suit in August 1996. The final rule was eventually published in March 1997, 15 months late. The final rule differed from the proposed rule in two main ways. First, evidence gathered in Texas since the proposed listing of the pygmy owl as threatened suggested that the population there exceeded 1,300 and was viable. Furthermore, habitat in the coastal plain was stable or increasing. Hence, the FWS decided that a threatened listing of the pygmy owl in Texas was no longer warranted. Second, the FWS dropped the proposed designation of critical habitat for the pygmy owl in Arizona. The agency's rationale was twofold: (1) identifying critical habitat would bring increased threats to pygmy owls from birders and (2) identifying critical habitat would make pygmy owls and their nests more vulnerable to vandalism.[27]

When state biologists located nearly 20 pygmy owls northwest of Tucson in 1996, area developers saw the significance of the listing and the possibility of critical habitat designation. The main areas of conflict included Honey Bee Canyon, site of 500 potential houses, and the 9,000-house Red Hawk project in the foothills of the Tortolita Mountains. FWS officials thought that it was unlikely that listing the pygmy owl would stop development in the region; rather developments would be altered, moved, or reduced.[28]

The FWS's reversal on critical habitat did not last long. The SCBD filed a lawsuit in October 1997 over the failure of the FWS to designate critical habitat for the pygmy owl and the Huachuca water umbel (a plant). A year later, in October 1998, federal judge Alfredo Marquez ruled that the FWS should designate critical habitat "without further delay." When the SCBD requested clarification of the judge's ruling, he ordered the FWS to propose critical habitat for both species within 30 days and to issue final rules within six months. In late December 1998, the FWS published a proposed rule designating 730,565 acres of critical habitat for the pygmy owl in Conchise, Maricopa, Pima, and Pinal counties. Once habitat is officially designated as critical, no activity funded, authorized, or undertaken by a federal agency can destroy or significantly modify that habitat.[29]

The proposed FWS critical habitat "attempted to form an interconnected system of suitable and potential habitat areas extending from southern Arizona to the northernmost recent pygmy owl occurrence," reflecting the "core-corridor" concept of ecological reserve design developed by conservation biologists. The bulk of the critical habitat was located in Pinal County, between Phoenix and Tucson (more than 430,000 acres), and Pima County, home of Tucson (more than 260,000 acres). The agency sought to rely on public lands as much as possible (more than 420,000 acres of state lands and more than 110,000 acres of BLM lands), but found it necessary to designate significant areas of private land as critical habitat (nearly 140,000 acres), especially northwest of Tucson, home to the greatest concentration of pygmy owls in Arizona.[30]

As this process played itself out at the FWS, the SCBD applied pressure locally. In late November 1997, SCBD protestors and other concerned citizens blocked preliminary development work in Tucson until a stop-work order could be delivered, all captured by television news cameras. For its part, the FWS warned Pima County officials that such building permits could violate the Endangered Species Act. Soon after, Pima County Development Services placed a moratorium on new building permits in much of northwest Tucson. It lasted just a few weeks, however, before the county lifted it. Pima County soon responded in another way when the Board of Supervisors approved efforts by local, state, and federal agencies and groups to develop a regional conservation plan. The board also required pygmy owl surveys any time a property owner or developer requested a change in zoning, surveys that could cost up to $2,500 per acre.[31]

The focal point in the battle between pygmy owl habitat and development was a high school proposed by the Amphitheater School District in northwest Tucson. The project would develop more than 70 acres in prime pygmy owl habitat. The local media dubbed the issue "kids versus owls." Using its political venue of choice, the SCBD and Defenders of Wildlife won a temporary restraining order against the school district in March 1998, preventing it from clearing the site. In the end, the court sided with the kids—it ruled in November 1999 that environmental groups had failed to prove that the school would harm the pygmy owl. The court removed its injunction, and the site was cleared by bulldozers in two days.[32]

As these legal battles played out, the Pima County Board of Supervisors voted in May 1998 to adopt the Sonoran Desert Protection Plan, drafted by the SCBD and supported by a coalition of 31 environmental groups. The plan, in its second draft in April 2005, is designed to protect the pygmy owl and 17 other endangered species, covering more than 5 million acres. The plan proposed buying roughly 400,000 acres to protect regional biological diversity and sensitive natural communities at an estimated cost of between $300 million and $500 million. These new directions by the county drew praise from the CBD: "The Board has . . . exhibited a willingness never before shown in the West to examine new methods of regional conservation planning and cooperation." Developers such as Stanley Abrams have bought into the plan in search of certainty: "I do not know a rational builder who does not want to have certainty in knowing where you can and can't go." Secretary of the Interior Bruce Babbitt testified before Congress that the plan "really is the most exciting event of its kind anywhere in the United States." Indeed, it is roughly ten times the size of the San Diego multi-species Habitat Conservation Plan (HCP), held up as the model for allowing development to move ahead while still protecting endangered species. (For more on Habitat Conservation Plans, see chapter 6.) The board also ruled that no new rezoning of land in pygmy owl critical habitat could occur while the plan is being developed, though existing development projects with permits could go forward if they received approval from the FWS. Once the plan is finalized, though, it is likely to redirect development to less ecologically sensitive southeast Tucson. "It is a whole new universe in Northwest Tucson," Suckling claimed. "If there's going to be any development at all, it's going to have to be done in a completely new way to protect the pygmy owl."[33]

Against this backdrop, the FWS issued its final critical habitat rule for the pygmy owl in July 1999. The acreage was adjusted only slightly, increasing to 731,712 acres, approximately 1 percent of Arizona. There were changes to ownership, though, with state lands increasing to 435,000 acres and BLM lands declining to 91,000 acres. Opposition to pygmy owl protection began to increase at the state government level after the critical habitat designation, largely because of the state lands included in the designation. Development forces also went on the offensive, with a development-oriented group filing a lawsuit to de-list the pygmy owl as well as revoke the critical habitat designation.[34]

These countersuits bore fruit for development interests. In September 2001, district court judge Susan Bolton voided critical habitat for the pygmy owl on the grounds that the FWS had not thoroughly investigated the economic impact of the designation, as required by the Endangered Species Act. Bolton rejected developers' argument that the pygmy owl should not even have been listed. That was not the end of the critical habitat story, however. Suckling claimed the CBD would "push [the FWS] to double the area of critical habitat." Suckling was close. In November 2003 the FWS proposed 1.2 million acres as critical habitat for the pygmy owl. Before the agency could issue its final rule, however, the case took another twist. The developers appealed Bolton's decision on ESA listing for the pygmy owl, and the Ninth Circuit Court of Appeals ruled in August 2003 that the FWS had not met its legal burden in listing the pygmy owl as endangered in the first place. It had failed, the court ruled, to demonstrate that the subspecies of pygmy owl in Arizona is genetically unique from the population in Mexico. Despite this setback, Suckling believed the ruling left the FWS plenty of room to meet this requirement—and that the pygmy owl would remain endangered and its critical habitat would exceed a million acres. More bad news for the CBD followed. In April 2006, the FWS—citing the appeals court ruling—dropped the pygmy owl from the endangered list. CBD and other environmental groups soon filed suit to have the pygmy owl returned to the endangered species list.[35]

Despite the seeming ambiguity of the pygmy owl case, the CBD is not yet done with the case and the shape and future of development in metropolitan Tucson has fundamentally changed. The CBD has not—by any means—stopped development. Nor has the group won every battle. Indeed, it lost its most visible battle to prevent the building of a high school in critical pygmy owl habitat in northwest Tucson. Nevertheless, the dynamic of development has changed. Noah Greenwald, a CBD conservation biologist, saw the pygmy owl as a success story, even if de-listed: "It drove Pima County to create the Sonoran Desert Conservation Plan. And that has provided for more orderly development, while protecting sensitive tracts of desert from urban sprawl." The listing of the owl gave the CBD and its allies the power to force developers and county officials to accept a plan drafted by a coalition of environmental groups. The days of freewheeling, unfettered growth and sprawl into the surrounding desert were over. The county would work with the state and federal governments to protect an additional 400,000 acres of land, this in a county where public land ownership already approached 90 percent. This plan, costing between $300 million and $500 million, was based on cutting-edge research in ecological reserve design. Although the CBD did not achieve the sweeping policy disruptions it had achieved in logging and grazing, it had succeeded in shattering the existing political and economic status quo in southern Arizona. This policy change was achieved by using one of the most powerful tools for environmental policy change in American politics: the courts and the Endangered Species Act.[36]

Even as endangered species policy has been pushed onto different pathways—cutting funds for new species listing through appropriations politics, agency decisions to reduce work on listing and critical habitat decisions, and collaborative work through habitat conservation plans— the law has proved invulnerable to significant amendment, despite fervent opposition by many western Republicans. The Endangered Species Act and the courts have been the vehicle for the most dramatic conservation and natural resources policy change since 1990. The previously noted northern spotted owl case led to a nearly 90 percent decline in logging in the Northwest, but ESA-related moratoriums stopped national forest logging in many other parts of the country as well (e.g., the Indiana bat in Vermont and New Hampshire). Grazing, too, has declined substantially across the western public lands—by more than 25 percent on BLM lands during this period. Perhaps most importantly today, the Endangered Species Act and the courts are changing water politics— salmon in the Columbia River system; Rio Grande silvery minnow in New Mexico; the least tern, Great Plains piping plover, and pallid sturgeon in the Missouri River system; and two species of suckerfish in the Klamath Basin in Oregon and California. These are hardly the stories of gridlock or pragmatic environmental policymaking.[37]

Remaking Air Quality Policy through the Courts? *American Trucking Associations v. EPA*

National Ambient Air Quality Standards (NAAQS) have been the foundation of air pollution policy in the United States since passage of the Clean Air Act in 1970. The law charged the Environmental Protection Agency with establishing primary and secondary standards for carbon monoxide, ground-level ozone, hydrocarbons, nitrogen dioxide, particulate matter, and sulfur dioxide. Later, lead was added to the list and hydrocarbons were dropped as redundant with ground-level ozone. The law also directed the EPA to review scientific developments related to these pollutants every five years and, if necessary, adjust the standards to protect public health, allowing for an adequate margin of safety. Clearly these standards have major ramifications on public health and compliance costs for affected businesses. Hence it is not surprising that the

EPA's standards are often challenged in court. Like so much of pollution control policy, court cases are part of the administrative process of establishing regulations. In the late 1990s, however, one such challenge went far beyond the normal channels of administrative law. For a time, the ruling by the U.S. Court of Appeals for the District of Columbia Circuit in *American Trucking Associations v. EPA* (1999) threw into doubt the entire national framework of air pollution policy—and many other regulatory frameworks. Industry, stymied in its efforts to reform the Clean Air Act in Congress, turned to the courts, where it came close to unraveling the entire pollution control system, nearly presenting industry with an opportunity to recreate pollution control in a vision much more to its liking.[38]

The path to the *American Trucking Associations* decision began in the early 1990s when the American Lung Association filed several lawsuits against the Environmental Protection Agency, arguing that the agency had missed its statutory deadline to review new scientific evidence for the ozone and particulate standards, and then, when the EPA declined to change the ozone standards in 1992, the American Lung Association sued the EPA over its decision. In *American Lung Association v. Browner* (1994), regarding the particulate standard, Judge Alfredo Marquez required the EPA to complete its review of the standard by January 31, 1997. The agency decided to revisit the ozone standard at the same time.[39]

As the November 1996 deadline for making the proposed standards public approached, the political debate intensified. EPA Administrator Carol Browner stated: "This is one of the most important decisions I will make to protect public health in this country." The decision engendered fervent debate within the White House, where economic officials argued for less stringent regulations than those being considered by the EPA. Environmentalists, meanwhile, were pressuring Browner and Vice President Al Gore on the Clinton administration's most significant environmental decision to date. When the EPA issued the stringent proposed regulations, it touched off immediate and intense opposition from industry groups. According to a story in the *National Journal*, none of the previous regulations proposed or adopted by the EPA during Browner's term as administrator "sparked the political firestorm that's resulted from the agency's new clean air rules." Although the Clean Air Act requires the standards to be set based only on public health effects—indeed, costs cannot be considered—the standards were put through a benefit-cost analysis by the Clinton administration. The estimated benefits of $120 billion and estimated costs of $8.5 billion were attacked by industry. Opponents also questioned the science underpinning the rule revisions.[40]

Leading the opposition was the Air Quality Standards Coalition, made up of major corporations from the car and trucking, chemical, electric utility, and petroleum industries. The coalition assembled a budget of more than $2 million to oppose the new rules, money that went to hiring such heavyweight lobbyists as C. Boyden Gray, former White House counsel to President George H. W. Bush. The coalition had numerous business allies, including the National Association of Manufacturers, individual corporations, and Citizens for a Sound Economy (a conservative think tank that was spending $5 million on a campaign to convince voters to overhaul the nation's environmental laws). Furthermore, many state and local governments, worried about how the new rules would affect their economies, joined industry in opposition, including the National Association of Counties and the National League of Cities. Among elected officials, support and opposition typically followed regional rather than partisan cleavages. Many Republican governors, especially from the Midwest, attacked the rules, but, as noted below, there was no consensus among Republican governors. Many Democrats, too, opposed the new standards. More than 90 Democratic members of Congress wrote to President Bill Clinton, urging him to block the new standards. The leading Democratic opponent in Congress was Representative John Dingell of Michigan, a longtime leader on air quality policy in the House. Other Democratic opposition came from Midwestern mayors, including Dennis Archer of Detroit and Richard Daley of Chicago.[41]

Environmental groups, including the Clean Air Trust, the NRDC, and U.S. Public Interest Research Groups, coordinated efforts in support of the rules; some groups argued that the Environmental Protection Agency should have made the new standards even stricter. Another crucial actor was the American Lung Association and its allies focused on public health. Since the main health effects of ozone and particulates are respiratory problems for children and the elderly, child welfare and senior citizen groups were also strong supporters of the new standards. Northeastern politicians, including Republican governors William Weld

(Massachusetts) and Christine Todd Whitman (New Jersey), were the final major source of support for the standards. As noted above, the issue was not strictly partisan. While most Democrats supported the new standards, many from the Midwest opposed them.[42]

Although opponents sought to generate enough public and business pressure to convince the Clinton administration to relax the proposed standards, they knew that environmentalists had far better relations with the White House. With the Republican takeover of Congress in 1995, industry sought help there as well. Senator Lauch Faircloth (R-North Carolina), chair of the Subcommittee on Clean Air, Wetlands, Private Property and Nuclear Safety of the Environment and Public Works Committee, introduced a bill in the 104th Congress to dramatically overhaul the entire Clean Air Act. Democrats and moderate Republicans condemned the bill, and it never received serious attention. Industry ran into the legislative gridlock that was stalling virtually all action on the environment in the 1990s. Given this reality, an oil industry lobbyist optimistically speculated "that a local backlash would be corporate America's 'foot in the door to open up the Clean Air Act.'"[43]

Meanwhile, the White House was quiet on the proposed standards. Although Browner continued her very public defense of the standards, she received no support from Clinton, Gore, or other top administration officials. This silence masked an intense debate within the administration. Top economic advisers sought standards much closer to the status quo. They argued the proposed standards came with too high a price. What Clinton would decide did not become clear until late June when Gore publicly endorsed the proposed standards. Clinton broke his silence on June 25, 1997: "We will find a way to do this that grows the American economy. But we have to keep having a clean environment to have healthy children." The final standards, published in the *Federal Register* in July, included new standards for very fine particles (PM2.5) and a new eight-hour standard for ozone: 0.08 parts per million (ppm), replacing the previous 0.12 ppm over one hour.[44]

Opponents quickly considered their options. One option was to block the new standards in Congress. A bill to establish detailed provisions on implementing the standards gained 130 co-sponsors in the House of Representatives. Republican leaders, including Commerce Committee chair Thomas Bliley (Virginia), were circumspect about mounting this attack on the new standards, however. As we described in chapter 3, the party had overreached on environmental issues in the 104th Congress. Pressure on Bliley and the Republicans came from Dingell and fellow Democrats, who made up a third of the co-sponsors. Supporters of the standards in Congress responded quickly. Long-time clean air champion Henry Waxman (D-California) and leading green Republicans Sherwood Boehlert (New York) and Christopher Shays (Connecticut) announced that at least 145 representatives would support the standards, enough to prevent an override of a presidential veto if it should get to that stage. The frontal legislative assault foundered in the congressional bog.[45]

A second option proved more fruitful. A number of industry opponents to the standards, led by the American Trucking Associations, challenged the new standards in the U.S. Court of Appeals for the District of Columbia Circuit, the court of original jurisdiction for Clean Air Act regulations. As noted above, such forays in administrative law have been part of the environmental rulemaking process since the creation of the new environmental laws of the 1970s; but this case went beyond debating the merits of the EPA's standards. One of industry's arguments focused on the constitutionality of the EPA's standard setting authority. In a surprising ruling on a 2–1 vote in May 1999, the court issued a decision that struck at the very heart of the Clean Air Act and beyond. The judges ruled that the standard setting provisions of the 1970 Clean Air Act and its amendments amounted to "an unconstitutional delegation of legislative power" by Congress to the EPA. Based on this reasoning, the EPA's new standards were unlawful. According to dissenting judge David Tatel, the decision contradicted "the last half-century of Supreme Court nondelegation jurisprudence." Tatel further noted that the majority ignored ten decisions by the District of Columbia Appeals Court upholding the EPA's ability to set such standards. While industry groups praised the decision, Browner called it "bizarre and extreme." Environmental groups agreed. "It's an extreme interpretation of the Constitution," claimed NRDC attorney David Hawkins. Georgetown University law professor Richard Lazarus argued that the decision was "the basic challenge to the administrative state." If the *ATA* decision stood, not only would the Clean Air Act be fundamentally undermined, but also so would most other pollution control laws since they too featured broad congressional delegation to the EPA.[46]

The Environmental Protection Agency appealed the decision, and the Supreme Court agreed to take the case. In doing so, the Supreme Court also agreed to revisit an issue that industry had raised unsuccessfully in *ATA*: could the agency consider costs in setting the new ozone and particulate standards? Since the Supreme Court would be addressing two major issues in its decision (delegation and regulatory costs), the legal scholar Cass Sunstein called the decision "the most eagerly anticipated case in administrative law in many years." The decision in *Whitman v. American Trucking Associations* (2001) was a complete victory for the EPA on these two issues. In his opinion for the unanimous Court, Justice Antonin Scalia wrote that the Clean Air Act "unambiguously bars cost consideration from the NAAQS-setting process, and this ends the matter for us as well as the EPA," and that the actions of the EPA fit "comfortably within the scope of discretion permitted by our precedent."[47]

Responding to the remaining aspects of the courts' decisions, the Environmental Protection Agency retained the standards it issued in July 1997. In what appeared to be the final case on the standards, the District of Columbia Court of Appeals ruled in March 2002 in *American Trucking Associations v. EPA* that the agency met all legal requirements and the new standards could be implemented. The long administrative, legal, and political journey to these new standards was hardly over, however. The EPA did not issue its proposed rule to implement the new ozone standard until July 2003. Usually the agency must designate areas of the country that do not meet new standards within two years. The EPA was slowed, however, by the court decisions and also by two actions of Congress: the Transportation Equity Act for the Twenty-first Century (1998) stretched the Clean Air Act deadline for non-attainment from two years to three, and an appropriations rider for fiscal year 2000 prevented the EPA from spending any funds to designate areas in non-attainment until the Supreme Court issued its decision in *ATA* or June 2001, whichever came first. The EPA did not issue its guidance memorandum on particulate matter until April 2003.[48]

The Environmental Protection Agency finalized the standards and designated non-attainment areas in 2004. This, however, did not settle the matter. Health and environmental groups sued the EPA in March 2003, arguing that the agency was overdue to revise the standards for ozone and particulate matter. The court agreed, noting that it had been more than five years since July 1997, when the EPA had issued the latest standards. A court-approved settlement between the EPA and the health and environmental groups required new proposed rules by 2005 for particulate matter and 2006 for ozone. In September 2006, EPA Administrator Stephen Johnson proposed reducing the daily fine particulate standard by nearly half, while keeping the existing annual standard.[49]

Although industry ultimately failed in its effort to fundamentally alter air quality policy in the *ATA* decisions, it came much closer to achieving this goal in the courts than it did in Congress. This underscores a fundamental difference between making environmental policy today and in the 1970s. To be sure, the courts have been deeply involved in air pollution policy since the passage of the Clean Air Act in 1970. But with few exceptions, the judges have served as interpreters of provisions of the statute and referees on new standards and rules. In the first *American Trucking Associations* case, the Court of Appeals ruling struck at the very heart of the Clean Air Act. That industry was having some success against the Clean Air Act in the late 1990s was not surprising; rather it is the venue that was surprising. Republicans had taken control of both the House of Representatives and the Senate in 1994. This was the time for industry to work with its allies in Congress to make the changes it sought, such as weighing costs and benefits in establishing NAAQSs. But such reform efforts got nowhere in Congress. The alternative pathway of the courts, with its rich population of Republican-appointed judges, proved a much better venue to effect policy change. With Congress still gridlocked, and more Republican judges being appointed, it may be only a matter of time before the courts, not Congress, deliver substantial policy change in the realm of air quality.[50]

Administrative Strategies in the Judicial Process

As we noted in chapter 4, presidents face severe constraints on their ability to achieve their policy goals. Terry Moe demonstrated that one result of this was the increasing politicization of administration—presidents use their appointment powers, their ability to centralize decisionmaking in the White House and the Executive Office of the President, and their discretion in the administrative process to advance their agendas.[51] Chapter 4 showed that deadlock in environmental policymaking in Congress, coupled with intensifying partisanship on these issues, has pushed presidents to the increased use of executive powers in this area. Presidents face the same sorts of constraints and incentives in the judicial process. The courts are a readily accessible venue for groups seeking to shape the nation's environmental policies in ways that may or may not reflect the president's objectives. The rigidity of the statutory structure has increased the political stakes in judicial interpretations, and the historic impact of the courts in this field has clarified the stakes. Not surprisingly, we have seen presidential administrations using the appointment power and their control of crucial decisions about what and whether to litigate to shape environmental policy.

Politicizing Appointments

In the same way that judicial activism on civil rights politicized judicial appointments in the 1950s and the 1960s, the increasing significance of the courts as environmental policymakers has led to growing interest in the environmental records of judicial nominees. For environmentalists, the stakes in these appointments have been raised by the increasingly conservative caste of the federal judiciary, shaped as it has been by Republican control of the presidency for all but eight years between 1981 and 2006, and aggressive ideological screening of judicial nominees in much of that period. Both Ronald Reagan and George H. W. Bush gave the conservative wing of their party substantial leverage over judicial appointments; the broader right turn in American politics has begun to have its influence on the prospects for environmental interests in the courts.[52] The limited number of studies of judicial decisionmaking on environmental issues finds that Democrats' appointees are generally more receptive to standing for environmental groups and aggressive agency actions than Republican appointees.[53]

Reagan's Attorney General, Edwin Meese, showed particular interest in the Fifth Amendment's takings clause as a tool for leveraging "a revisiting and restoration of economic liberty." He sought to place conservatives on courts that would play a crucial role on takings issues (e.g., the new Court of Federal Claims, the Federal Circuit Court of Appeals), and pressed for changes to the courts' interpretations of the Fifth Amendment with potentially profound implications for the government's regulatory powers.[54] More recently, during George W. Bush's administration, environmentalists have charged that the president was using his nominating power to stack the lower federal courts with judges hostile to environmental regulation.[55] In 2001 a coalition of environmental groups wrote to members of the Senate urging them to "carefully scrutinize the judicial nominations for the federal courts because the judges appointed to the federal bench over the next few years will dramatically affect the level of public health and environmental protection in this country." These groups have investigated and publicized the environmental records of many nominees (Earthjustice maintains an extensive website devoted to this purpose) and have mobilized opposition on the basis of environmental concerns. For example, environmentalists denounced Bush appeals court nominee Jeffrey Sutton as "one of the country's leading advocates for a new and virulent form of judicial activism that is advancing an anti-environmental agenda." They asserted that another appeals court nominee, Janice Rogers Brown, was "far outside the mainstream of even conservative legal thinking. Her views put in jeopardy our nation's bedrock environmental protections along with many other hallmark legislative achievements of the twentieth century."[56]

Sutton was confirmed; Brown's nomination was blocked at first but was approved in 2005. The larger point, however, is that environmental issues have begun to enter into the politics of judicial nominations— indeed, there is an environmental politics of judicial nominations.[57] As the judicial pathway has increased in importance, the stakes in positions on the federal bench have grown substantially.

Positioning in the Judicial Process and the "Sue and Settle" Strategy

As party polarization on environmental issues intensified and the stakes in judicial interpretations of largely fixed statutory frameworks grew, the legal positions taken by federal agencies in environmental litigation attracted greater scrutiny. Critics of the Clinton administration raised questions about some of its legal positions—for example, its settlement of a lawsuit filed by environmental and animal rights groups concerning snowmobiles in Yellowstone National Park—but, as in the case of judicial appointments, environmental groups highlighted this issue in responding to the legal-political strategies of the Bush administration.[58] Defenders of Wildlife's Judicial Accountability Project focused on the administration's positions in cases involving forest management policies and the National Environmental Policy Act. According to this group, in the first two years of the Bush administration the Forest Service was a defendant in 61 suits challenging forest policy. The administration made arguments on forest management issues in 46 of those cases, and in 31 of them—67 percent of the time—it made arguments hostile to accepted legal interpretations. Despite the increasingly conservative caste of the federal judiciary, and despite the tradition of deference to administrative agencies in the courts, the administration succeeded in only three of these 31 "hostile" arguments. In this same period federal agencies were involved in 172 cases involving the implementation of the NEPA. In 94 of those cases (54 percent) the administration made arguments that would have limited the law's reach, but it won only 21 of those cases (a 22 percent success rate). In the 78 cases in which the administration made NEPA-friendly arguments, it won 75 times—a 96 percent success rate. The studies argued that the Bush administration was willing to push the legal envelope, probing for openings and pushing its environmental policy objectives despite likely defeat in the courts.[59]

The suspicion that the Bush administration had brought administrative strategies to the judicial process came to a head in environmentalists' claims that the administration was pursuing a "sue and settle" strategy of "creative capitulation" to favored interests. That is, in several cases it appeared that the administration failed to appeal rulings by lower courts that weakened environmental laws, did not strongly defend settled laws and rules in court, and chose to settle winnable suits out of court to achieve its policy goals. Critics pointed to a series of cases including a settlement with the snowmobile manufacturers' association on snowmobile access to Yellowstone Park, settlements of legal challenges to the "diesel rule" on air pollution from diesel fuels and the "Tulloch rule" on wetlands protection, and challenges to the Northwest Forest Plan.

The Bush administration denied the charges, but those denials were not always convincing. In responding to charges that its settlements with the timber industry in cases challenging the Northwest Forest Plan came in cases the industry could not have won in court, Agriculture Undersecretary Mark Rey (who at the time of the development of the forest plan was a vice president of the American Forest and Paper Association, which was deeply involved in the struggle) at once denied any sweetheart deals ("No litigation is friendly"), claimed that Bush "officials are doing nothing the Clinton administration didn't do in the 1990s," and pointed to procedural protections: "Each of the settlements the Bush administration agrees to is presented to a judge and will be subject to public comment. . . . Nobody gets frozen out of our actions because the public ultimately is going to get a chance to comment. If they are dissatisfied, they will get their own opportunity to sue."[60] Rey's denial of "sweetheart deals" is questionable, and his assertion that participation in the settlement process ensures that the public interest is represented is equally problematic.[61] It is true, however, that the Clinton administration entered into legal settlements with environmental groups that addressed key forest policy questions and deeply frustrated timber interests. The crucial point is that Democratic and Republican administrations alike are seeking to advance their environmental agendas through the positioning of the federal government in litigation, and through rulemaking settlements.

Cutting Trees and Cutting Deals in the Pacific Northwest In 1991 conflict in the Pacific Northwest over the effect of logging on the endangered northern spotted owl had culminated in an order by Judge William Dwyer restricting old-growth logging and timber sales in the region's federal public lands. In 1992 Dwyer rejected a Bush administration plan that would have resumed logging activity, holding to his position that forest management had long been marked by "a remarkable series of violations of environmental laws" by federal agencies. Environmentalists' success in winning logging restrictions had devastating consequences for timber communities, and tensions between loggers and environmentalists sharpened.[62] During the 1992 presidential campaign Bill Clinton promised a "timber summit" to break the deadlock over forest policy, and soon after the election he convened a conference in Portland at which he heard from those interested in shaping the administration's strategy.

In July 1994 the Clinton administration produced the "Forest Plan for a Sustainable Economy and Sustainable Development," commonly known as the Northwest Forest Plan.[63] The plan outlined an "adaptive management" strategy for 24 million acres of public lands in the Northwest. It would hold timber sales to about 25 percent of the rate seen in the 1980s and protect about 80 percent of the region's old-growth forests from logging. It also called for careful surveys to precede timber sales. These surveys would focus on watersheds and forest ecosystems, not merely the tracts to be logged, and analyze the impact of the sales on 77 plant and animal species. The Clinton administration intended to bring the plan directly to Dwyer's court, seeking no new forest legislation and no changes to the Endangered Species Act. Administration spokesman Tom Tuchmann observed that Congress had been deadlocked on the spotted owl and the Endangered Species Act for many years, and that this was unlikely to change. "Congress represents its constituency very well," he said, "and the people of this region continue to be divided."[64] Legislative gridlock led to a heavy role for the judiciary in the timber wars, and led the Clinton administration to work through the courts, bypassing Congress with a plan that would not have to be vetted by legislators.

The Forest Plan drew fire from all sides. The Sierra Club described it as a "profound disappointment," an AFL-CIO representative said the plan would hit the Northwest "like a battery of misguided Tomahawk missiles," and Mark Rey of the American Forest and Paper Association warned that the plan would yield more "court-ordered gridlock." Logging interests thought the plan would deliver far less than the annual 1.2 billion board feet of timber it promised, and environmentalists feared the plan would fail to hold back pressures on the Forest Service and the Bureau of Land Management for more timber.[65] The logging industry sought to tie up the Forest Plan in the courts, creating a *judicial* gridlock that would invite congressional intervention. Republican victories in the 1994 congressional elections increased the attractiveness of this strategy, but even then timber lobbyists were skeptical that Congress could or would act on this issue.[66]

The Northwest Forest Plan confronted several legal challenges as it worked its way to approval. The timber industry challenged the process by which the plan was developed, filing suit in the District of Columbia District Court, which it saw as a friendlier venue than Judge Dwyer's Seattle court. The industry won its case in the District of Columbia, but Judge Thomas Penfield Jackson refused to block implementation of the Forest Plan and deferred to Judge Dwyer. The timber coalition then dropped its suit in an attempt to avoid a hearing in Dwyer's court, but in an unusual order Dwyer gave the government permission to counter-sue the timber coalition to address the issues raised in the industry's suit. Meanwhile, a coalition of environmental groups also sued, charging that the administration had ignored evidence that all old growth needed to be protected to preserve viable owl populations, and that the plan failed to adequately protect anadromous fish.[67]

In December 1994, Dwyer upheld the Northwest Forest Plan, noting that the implementation of the plan would "mark the first time in several years that the owl habitat forest will be managed by the responsible agencies under a plan found lawful by the courts."[68] Yet the court's initial acceptance of the plan was only the start of an arduous process. Environmentalists attacked the plan's implementation, complaining that required surveys were not being done or were not being done adequately. A coalition of environmental groups sued and Judge Dwyer blocked timber sales pending resolution of the suit, once again severely restricting logging in old-growth forests. Pressing their advantages, 20 environmental groups sent a letter to Clinton calling for a ban on logging in unprotected wilderness as well as protections for roadless areas. Timber interests cried foul. "Every time the environmental community is successful in meeting an objective," Jim Geisinger of the Northwest Forestry Association observed, "they shift the goal posts further."[69] Yet the timber industry had its own angle of attack on the Forest Plan. In 1995 Congress passed the "salvage rider," which blocked citizen groups' challenges to timber sales covered by the Forest Plan until 1997. (See chapter 3.) Senator Slade Gorton's (R-Washington) rider to the fiscal year 2000 Interior Appropriations Bill, which was ultimately dropped from the bill, would have allowed the Forest Service and the Bureau of Land Management to plan timber sales without performing any wildlife surveys.[70]

In November 1999, the Clinton administration entered into a legal settlement with the environmentalists that ended Dwyer's injunction against the timber sales. The environmental groups agreed to drop their suit, to allow the planned timber sales to proceed without further litigation, and to a streamlined survey process in return for an agency commitment to conduct the surveys mandated by the forest plan.[71] The timber industry was frustrated that the settlement did not specify a date for the completion of the surveys. This raised the possibility of long delays in the approval of timber sales and questions about whether tracts designated for logging would ever actually see the ax.[72] The Northwest Forestry Association reacted bitterly to the settlement deal. Spokesman Chris West said "We've been cut out of this process" and argued that the agreement was aimed at helping the Gore campaign for president. "He can't have a failed forest policy hanging over his head. So they cut a sweetheart deal with the plaintiffs." Agriculture Undersecretary Jim Lyons responded: "There is no political agenda here. What this does is get us out of the courts and allows timber to be harvested while following the Northwest Forest Plan."[73]

George W. Bush's victory in the 2000 presidential election brightened prospects for the timber industry, which launched new lawsuits against the implementation of the Forest Plan. In April 2002, the American Forest Resource Council, the Western Council of Industrial Workers, and the Association of O&C Counties proposed "A Global Framework for Settlement of Litigation Challenging Agency Actions Relating to the Northwest Forest Plan."[74] This coalition, frustrated by the failure of the Forest Plan to deliver promised timber cuts and environmentalists' success in blocking logging of old-growth stands through litigation and its legal settlement with the Clinton administration, offered to settle four cases challenging the implementation of the Plan. The coalition presented a set of legal principles "that should not be contested by the federal government" and demanded five agency actions guided by those legal principles. The Bush administration responded favorably and agreed almost point-by-point to the timber coalition's demands. The administration made major concessions, agreeing to review the ESA listings of the spotted owl and the marbled murrelet, rewrite important provisions of the "aquatic strategy" aimed at protecting salmon habitat, modify a program requiring foresters to search for species on their lands before allowing timber cuts to go forward, reexamine critical habitat designations, and examine policies on the proper use and logging of more than 2.2 million acres of federal timberlands in Oregon.[75]

Timber interests applauded the settlement, seeing it as an appropriate effort to rebalance policy in the face of the Northwest Forest Plan's failure to deliver more than half of its promised timber cuts. The Bush administration and timber groups argued that the Clinton administration had failed to implement its own program and that lawsuits from environmentalists had hindered realization of Forest Plan goals. Environmentalists charged that the timber industry's lawsuits could not have prevailed in court, and that Bush's appointees had used the settlement to allow logging interests to rewrite forest management policy.[76] The courts had long been the pivotal battleground in the Northwest's timber wars. Clinton, Bush, and their political allies seem to have found powerful flanking movements in the subtle politics of "sue and settle."

The settlement was not only a significant policy statement—Bush's concessions to the timber industry were also infused by political considerations. The timber coalition highlighted political concerns in its communications with the Justice Department. The coalition argued that the administration should agree to a new economic analysis of the critical habitat designations for the spotted owl and the marbled murrelet, warning that if the administration failed to settle and the litigation proceeded the administration would "find itself in the Supreme Court defending either its shift to the 'full economic analysis' position required by the Tenth Circuit, which will be criticized as another capitulation to economic interests at the expense of the environment, or its adherence to the Clinton Administration's baseline approach, which has been universally denounced by the resource-user community as arrogant disregard for the economic effects of the ESA." The coalition warned that this would leave the administration with "a classic 'lose-lose' outcome that it would be prudent to avoid."[77] Timber interests argued that the Justice Department would be wise to avoid a politically untenable position, and that from a political standpoint settlement negotiations were a better venue for resolving these issues than the courts themselves. Ironically, though, the strategy has proved less than successful. Environmental groups sued the Bush administration over its decision to drop the "survey and manage" rule requiring the government to assess biological diversity in public forests before they are logged. Judge Marsha Pechman overturned the Bush rule and reinstated the Clinton rule in a January 2006 decision. Six months later, the Bureau of Land Management and Forest Service released a draft environmental impact statement in hopes of convincing the judge of the merits of replacing the survey and manage rule, so the process continues.[78]

Settling the Boundaries of Wilderness in Utah   The Federal Land Policy and Management Act of 1976 (FLPMA) required the Secretary of the Interior to review Bureau of Land Management roadless areas of 5,000 acres or more and, within 15 years, to report to the president on the suitability of these areas for preservation as wilderness. The president would then make recommendations for wilderness designations to Congress, which could use its power under the Wilderness Act to protect wild lands.[79]

The Bureau of Land Management initially completed the inventory during the George H. W. Bush administration. It reviewed 22 million acres of federal lands in Utah and concluded that 2.5 million acres deserved designation as "wilderness study areas" (WSAs). President Bush passed along a recommendation to Congress that it designate these lands as wilderness under the Wilderness Act. The Utah congressional delegation backed the proposal for roughly 2 million acres of new wilderness in the state, but environmental groups, suspicious of a Republican-dominated inventory process, sought to protect more lands, almost 6 million acres. At stake were large tracts of the Red Rock region in southeast Utah, greatly valued by environmentalists for its beauty, by some locals for motorized recreation, and by economic interests for its potential as a site for resource extraction. Utah legislators and environmental interests introduced wilderness bills, but these went nowhere between 1991 and 1996. Environmental interests had the muscle to block the more limited proposals (Clinton was sure to veto), and congressional Republicans were well positioned to stop the environmentalists' drive for 6 million new acres of Utah wilderness.[80]

In June 1996, Secretary of the Interior Bruce Babbitt moved to break the stalemate. In a letter to James Hansen (R-Utah), chair of the Public Lands Subcommittee of the House Resources Committee, Babbitt observed that "an important reason for this stalemate is that the various interests involved are so far apart on the threshold, fundamental issue of how much BLM land has wilderness characteristics in the state." He informed Hansen that he was ordering a "reinventory" of Utah lands focused on the disputed tracts identified in the proposals for 6 million acres of wilderness. The review team would use the same legal criteria applied in the original inventory, and Babbitt made clear that this review would not lead directly to recommendations on wilderness designations. He reported to the Senate Appropriations Committee that this was a "narrowly focused exercise directed at a unique problem: the extraordinary 20-year-old Utah wilderness inventory controversy."[81] FLPMA had required the inventories to be completed by 1991, but Babbitt found statutory authority for the reinventory in language directing the department to "prepare and maintain" the inventory "on a continuing basis."[82] Babbitt chose not to allow for public comment on the inventory until the Bureau of Land Management's work on the new survey, described as "fact gathering," was completed.

Utah officials reacted bitterly. Republican Senator Orrin Hatch argued: "The reinventory is a political ploy to try to justify designating BLM land as wilderness that does not meet the requirements of the Wilderness Act. The standards, criteria, and procedures being used in this inventory are biased and indefensible in many instances. . . . It is too bad we cannot trust this administration to deal with us in a fairer and more straightforward manner." State representative Brad Johnson declared himself "ready to fix bayonets."[83] Instead of pursuing civil war, the state challenged Babbitt in federal district court in October 1996, seeking to block the new inventory. The suit charged that the Department of the Interior was inventorying state trust lands without authorization; conducting the inventory without legislative authority because FLPMA required reports on the suitability of roadless areas for wilderness by 1991; creating *de facto* wilderness; arbitrarily interpreting FLPMA and treating Utah in an arbitrary and unequal manner; failing to provide for public input into the inventory and failing to follow other rulemaking procedures; and failing to present an environmental impact statement as required by the National Environmental Policy Act. In November 1996 the court ordered the Department of the Interior to stop work on the inventory pending a decision in the case on the merits. District Judge Dee Benson ruled that the Utah case was likely to succeed because (a) under FLPMA the Bureau of Land Management's authority to conduct the inventory expired in 1991 and (b) even if the law *did* authorize the inventory, the Department of the Interior had failed to provide for public participation.[84]

The Bureau of Land Management stopped its inventory, but the legal struggle moved up to the court of appeals level. In March 1998, the circuit court ruled that the district judge had erred because Utah lacked standing to challenge the inventory. The appeals court sent the case back to the district court with instructions to dismiss Utah's case.[85] The denial of standing was an important setback for Utah. Its case against the reinventory was stymied and would only be renewed with a new filing in the spring of 2003.

The Bureau of Land Management quickly reorganized the reinventory team, focusing its analysis on the 3.1 million acres of federal land that had been deemed unsuitable for wilderness designations in the original inventory but were included in the more expansive proposals for wilderness designations proposed in Congress. The agency's 1999 Utah Wilderness Inventory Report concluded that 2.6 million *additional* acres of federal land (beyond the 2.5 million acres identified as meriting wilderness designation in the 1991 inventory), as well as 443,000 acres of state trust land, warranted consideration for wilderness designations. This land was then to be managed according to the guidelines set in the Bureau of Land Management's wilderness handbook, pending action by Congress.[86] In view of Babbitt's position, the Utah delegation's opposition to a broader wilderness proposal, and the strength of conservative Republicans in Congress, it was unlikely that there would be any congressional action.[87] The continuing stalemate amounted to a tenuous victory for environmentalists because the Bureau of Land Management would treat the land as wilderness.

But the 2000 election brought a new chapter in the struggle over the boundaries of wilderness in Utah. Led by Secretary of the Interior Gale Norton, the Bush administration acted boldly to upend Babbitt's solution. In March 2003 the state of Utah filed a new complaint against the Babbitt reinventory policy. Two weeks later, Norton and Utah Governor Mike Leavitt (R) announced a settlement of the suit. The settlement was approved by the district court shortly thereafter, before environmental groups had an opportunity to make the case that they should be allowed to participate as interveners. Norton's closed door negotiations with

Leavitt were particularly fruitful. Not only did he win a favorable settlement of the reinventory issue; he also won major concessions from the Department of the Interior on the control of roads across public lands in the state.

The settlement was a major victory for Utah and a defeat for advocates of the broader wilderness designations. The Department of the Interior agreed that it had no authority to identify additional wilderness-quality lands above and beyond those included in inventories as of 1991. It dropped the reinventory and declared that the deal with Utah would extend beyond the state's borders to all BLM lands. The Bureau of Land Management would not add any more lands to its wilderness management areas without approval from Congress, it would withdraw the "Wilderness Inventory Handbook" adopted in the Babbitt era, and it would exclude any mention of wilderness designations in ongoing land use planning processes in several Utah field offices.[88] "From a practical standpoint," said Governor Leavitt, "this means that we will have more wildernesses in the state of Utah. But it will be Congress and the law that decides where and how much, not the Department of the Interior and a set of regulations." Secretary of the Interior Norton wrote: "The Department stands firmly committed to the idea that we can and should manage our public lands to provide for multiple use, including protection of those areas that have wilderness characteristics." But, echoing Leavitt, she wrote: "Only Congress can create a wilderness area. We are making that clear by settling the lawsuit."[89]

Critics attacked the settlement on procedural and substantive grounds. Some charged Leavitt with hypocrisy. He had bitterly attacked Clinton for failing to consult adequately before using his powers under the Antiquities Act to create the Grand Staircase-Escalante National Monument, but he had happily engaged in secret negotiations with the Department of the Interior on the wilderness issue.[90] Others found the circumstances of the deal surprising. "Remarkably," the Utah environmentalists Stephen Bloch and Heidi McIntosh wrote, "the vehicle for this settlement was a seven year old lawsuit that had been entirely inactive since 1998, and in which the plaintiffs filed a third amended complaint only days before the settlement agreement was filed and approved by the court."[91] Jeff Widen of the Colorado Environmental Coalition was also concerned about the manner in which the deal was settled: "The timing of the suit is incredible. A number of state-based wilderness groups tried to intervene, and before the judge ever ruled, Interior just came out of the blue and settled this thing."[92] Indeed, the Southern Utah Wilderness Alliance (SUWA), the Wilderness Society, and the Natural Resources Defense Council had sought the right to intervene, but the case was settled and approved by the district court before their status was established.[93]

The substance of the deal also drew fire. Defenders of Babbitt's approach argued that reinventory was intended only to prevent wilderness from being "whittled away" while Congress struggled with the issue. "So," former BLM Director Pat Shea observed, "we are back to the whittlers, who will weasel their way through the wilderness." McIntosh of SUWA said that the settlement "leaves open some of the most spectacular lands in the West to oil and gas company drilling, mining, and off-road vehicle use."[94] New Mexico Governor Bill Richardson (D) complained about the national reach of the Utah deal. He had hoped for a wilderness designation for Otero Mesa, located south of Alamogordo on BLM lands thought to hold potential as a site for gas drilling. "It is disturbing," Richardson declared, "that the department made this significant decision in the context of litigation with the state of Utah without notice, opportunity for comment or participation by all affected states—including New Mexico."[95] Yet, just as with the Northwest Forest Plan, the "sue and settle" strategy has not proved as effective as the Bush administration had hoped. In August 2005, Judge Benson withdrew his support for the "no more wilderness settlement," claiming that he did not intend the settlement to become permanent. The legal language of the settlement was dissolved in September, though both BLM and Utah officials claimed they would continue to honor the agreement. In September 2006, Benson rejected environmentalists' claims to standing to sue to undo the settlement between Utah and the Department of the Interior and asserted that, even if the case were justiciable, the agreement between Utah and the Department of the Interior would stand. Environmentalists plan to appeal the decision.[96]

These cases demonstrate some of the consequences of legislative deadlock on these issues. Faced with a stalemate on wilderness designation in Utah, Babbitt stretched executive power under FLPMA to advance the land-protection goals of environmentalists and the Clinton administration. Babbitt's gambit seemed to prevail in the judicial process, yet his Republican successor at the Department of the Interior engineered a settlement forcing a reversal of the Babbitt policy in Utah and nationwide. Importantly, this entire dispute took place in the context of a larger debate over Clinton's use of executive authority under the Antiquities Act to protect lands, and his larger effort to protect roadless areas from development. (See chapter 4.) In the Northwest Forest Plan case, Clinton's effort to ameliorate conflict over logging fell apart as environmentalists and timber companies sought to exploit advantages under the plan in the courts and administrative agencies. The latest chapter is the Bush administration's decision to concede to the timber industry in the face of lawsuits challenging implementation of the plan, and the trading of charges that Clinton and Bush were making "sweetheart deals" with their political allies.

The settlement cases also illustrate a paradox in environmental policy. While Congress is gridlocked and we see high levels of political mobilization on all sides of these issues, policy is highly unstable, veering sharply depending on the position of the president and decisions taken in the many venues that matter in the judicial process, from the offices of the Department of Justice and the Department of the Interior to the courtrooms of judges with different attitudes toward environmental protection. In the Utah case, being "stuck" might mean either 2 million acres of wilderness or 6 million, and it could mean two on one day and six on another day, depending upon the attitude of a judge or the Department of the Interior. In the Northwest, the range of movement within gridlocked policy was several hundred million board feet of timber annually. The stakes are high, partisanship is intense, and the distance between the politics of settling and unsettling in the judiciary could not be more different than that envisioned by those seeing policy gridlock or the emergence of more collaborative, cooperative, pragmatic, rational environmental policymaking.

Conclusion

There is considerable continuity in the courts' role in environmental policymaking, but these continuities create important barriers to the development of next generation policy. Legislative design, judicial openness to citizen groups, and strong political pressures have made litigation a crucial force in this arena for decades. Agency decisionmakers operate in an environment in which many of their choices are vulnerable to judicial scrutiny. This has had enormous and positive consequences for policymaking, offering formerly powerless groups powerful leverage against established interests—citizen suits have strengthened pluralism and governmental accountability. Yet with increasing group conflict and bureaucratic accountability have come some negative implications attached to the power of the courts in environmental policymaking.[97] In 1983 Melnick wrote skeptically about the capacity of the judiciary for effective participation in regulatory policymaking. He described the courts' effects on the EPA as "neither random nor beneficial," and questioned both the coherence of policies issuing from the courts and whether "courts have helped administrators to design programs that achieve at the lowest possible costs the objectives established by elected officials after enlightened discussion." He observed: "The policymaking system of which the federal courts are now an integral part has produced serious inefficiency and inequities, has made rational debate and conscious political choice difficult, and has added frustration and cynicism among participants of all stripes." Nevertheless, the courts offer perhaps the most popular path into the green state for environmental and business groups frustrated with a gridlocked Congress.[98]

The openness of environmental policy choices to attack in the courts has often upended efforts to collaborate, negotiate, or compromise our way out of environmental policy conflicts. Federal agencies can negotiate management plans for deserts and rivers and forests that use locals' input and economic incentives to achieve policy goals, yet behind those efforts legal mechanisms empower disappointed interests. The CBD has worked through the courts to use the Endangered Species Act as an instrument for institutional disruption, seeking radical ends through fully legal means. It is empowered by the language of the Endangered Species Act and its access to the courts, and as long as the language of the law does not change—and Congress has had no success in significantly reforming the Endangered Species Act in recent years, despite great controversy—the CBD will continue to attack agency actions and development activities. In the Pacific Northwest Clinton attempted an inclusive approach to dealing with a hard policy problem. Environmental groups launched legal challenges grounded in the plan's failure to live up to the requirements of the Endangered Species Act; industry groups sought to bring congressional action against the Northwest Forest Plan by highlighting the chaotic effects of managing public lands through lawsuits, injunctions, and settlements. Kieran Suckling's observation that the Endangered Species Act exists only in the federal courts is crucial. We have built a host of processes (negotiations, collaborations, conservation planning, technical review teams) around the law, but at the core is a clear statute empowering disaffected interests to upend the "workable compromises [that] have been jury-rigged around and within the existing labyrinth of rules."[99]

Furthermore, legislative gridlock has generated significant changes in the role of the courts in environmental policymaking. Although the courts still play a central role in interpreting the meaning of statutes and in overseeing the rulemaking process, courts today are playing a more central role. The cases discussed in this chapter demonstrate how interested parties use the courts to achieve policy goals, goals that they have been unable to achieve in a gridlocked Congress. Despite the furor expressed by many in Congress over the reach of the Endangered Species Act in the cases of the spotted owl and the pygmy owl, Congress has been unable to substantially alter the law. Despite a Republican Congress from 1994 through 2006, and, more recently, Republicans in control of Congress and the White House, advocates of changing air pollution law and public lands law have been unsuccessful through the legislative pathway. So, among other pathways, groups turn to the courts, and Congress has had great difficulty addressing the effect of important judicial decisions with new legislation.

Of course the courts have many weaknesses as policymakers, some noted above. But for those challenging the status quo, creating legal "train wrecks" through the courts and the labyrinth of environmental laws and rules is not as problematic as it might seem to observers of the entire American political system. The chaos created by shutting down all timber harvesting on public lands in Arizona and New Mexico or removing the constitutional foundations of the entire Clean Air Act is clearly problematic, but for the Center for Biological Diversity and for industry the chaos is preferable to the status quo. A more positive view of this might suggest that with Congress deadlocked, the courts offer possibilities for creative environmental policy advances.[100]

Where does this leave us? The courts are likely to remain important environmental policymakers, since it is not likely that congressional gridlock will soon end or that the green state will be substantially reformed. However, one change may significantly limit use of the judicial pathway. The tightening of standing rules would strike a severe political blow to environmentalists. This is particularly true in the era of legislative gridlock, in which the possibilities for congressional action are limited and environmentalists must seek to protect and expand the gains of the 1960s and the 1970s in the courts. During the 1990s, the U.S. Supreme Court appeared to be on course to limit standing for citizen groups claiming environmental harms. In a 1983 law review article, Justice Antonin Scalia denounced "the judiciary's long love affair with environmental litigation" and argued that courts should be more aggressive in using the Constitution's "cases and controversies" requirement to turn away citizen suits. Following Justice Scalia's leadership, in *Lujan v. National Wildlife Federation* (1990) and *Lujan v. Defenders of Wildlife* (1992) the Supreme Court ruled against environmentalists' standing claims, with ominous portents for environmental groups.[101] One commentator saw the Court embarked on the legal "equivalent of Sherman's march through Georgia" with respect to standing law; another commentator, law professor John Echeverria, argued that "In effect, the courts are invalidating congressional provisions granting citizens the right to enforce environmental laws."[102] Environmentalists braced themselves for more limits on their rights to litigate, yet in *Friends of the Earth v. Laidlaw Environmental Services* (2000) the Court allowed a controversial citizen suit under the Clean Water Act to go forward. The *Laidlaw* decision, while welcomed by environmental groups, created significant dissonance in this area.[103] The courts are still open to environmentalists' claims, but the future direction of the law and the composition of the Supreme Court are bound to change. It remains to be seen how the narrowing of the judicial pathway would channel the political pressures still building in the environmental policy arena. A crucial question for the next generation school of environmental governance is whether the tightening of standing rules, which would lessen the role of adversarial legalism in environmental policymaking, would open possibilities for creative, pragmatic solutions to pressing problems or decisively tip the balance of power in favor of economic interests in ways that would cut against hopes for balance, rationality, and pragmatism.

At present, then, the continuing ability of citizen groups to participate in litigation is in some doubt, calling into question a fundamental feature of environmental policymaking since the late 1960s. This alone raises questions about the notion that we are moving in halting steps toward a more pragmatic approach to environmental policymaking. Instead, the courts have opened basic questions about who participates and about who governs, answers to which carry huge and unpredictable consequences for the future direction of policy.

6

The Collaborative Pathway in Environmental Policymaking

Most students of U.S. environmental regulation would agree that the legislative explosion of the 1960s and the 1970s was triggered by enthusiasm for the cause of environmental protection unchained from the practical challenges of policy implementation. Statutory commands such as those to eliminate water pollution or ignore economic costs in species protection were passed easily by Congress but quickly met intense political resistance and ground against economic and technological realities. Just as quickly, the difficulties of risk assessment and measuring the benefits and costs of regulation generated fundamental conflict over exactly what Congress had committed the nation to in its eager embrace of environmentalism.[1]

The environmental laws of the golden era drove a profound expansion of government power in the service of emergent values and newly powerful interests. The green state became a focal point for struggle as the larger political system attempted to come to grips with the laws' enormous economic and social effects. Scholars have noted a loose consensus on the need for strong environmental protections, but for more than 20 years environmental issues have sharply divided Congress and interest groups, and the regulatory process has been marked by partisan maneuvering and frequent recourses to litigation by frustrated groups.[2]

In chapter 1 we outlined the critique of the efficiency and effectiveness of the golden era laws that has emerged since the 1970s, a critique that has underpinned both a conservative assault on the green state and the proposals for reform that have emerged from the "next generation" school. Policymakers have embraced new *tools* like economic incentives and cost-benefit analysis, reflecting movement toward what Marc Eisner called an "efficiency regime" in regulatory affairs.[3] Another movement, the subject of this chapter, involves the embrace of new *processes* aimed at involving interested groups more directly in decisionmaking processes. Standard administrative procedures for public involvement and the environmental laws' invitation to citizen litigation have been deemed inadequate or even counterproductive; reformers have embraced collaborative approaches that they expect will mitigate conflict and lead to more effective, efficient, and flexible policy choices. Negotiated regulation, less formal "reinvention" projects like President Clinton's Common Sense Initiative and Project XL, habitat conservation planning, and collaborative conservation share the goals of managing conflict and addressing endemic inefficiencies by "bringing society back in" to the policymaking process.[4]

The collaborative pathway has developed in part because it follows from the conventional critique of command-and-control policymaking, and in part because it has served a range of political interests. Clinton hoped that his participatory reinvention initiatives would demonstrate the flexibility of beleaguered institutions, fending off crippling attacks on the green state from a hostile Congress. On the other side, the failure of conservative broadsides against the green state in the 104th Congress showed some business and conservative interests the futility of these attacks. Some saw negotiated regulation and collaboration as attractive alternatives that might take the confrontational edge off the laws adopted in the 1960s and the 1970s and yield more flexible and less costly regulations. At the local level, citizens in communities badly divided by environmental conflicts and suffering economic disruptions from new approaches to resource management embraced collaborative conservation models in hopes of increasing the peace and creating some measure of economic stability.[5]

These collaborative efforts seek to renegotiate the relationship between state and society defined in the basic environmental laws, and raise several crucial questions.

First, while some moves down the collaborative path have been sanctioned by statutes, parts of the new agenda test the limits of environmental laws—one critic noted of Clinton's collaborative Project XL, "If it isn't illegal, it isn't XL."[6] The use of administrative action and informal negotiations with affected interests to stretch uncomfortable legal constraints is a serious attack on central premises of the new social regulation, and it is notable that this is the ultimate "policy without law"—the development of fundamentally new approaches to regulation and natural resources policy without statutory changes.[7]

A second, related problem is whether this collaborative approach can truly, in the words of Mary Graham, create "workable compromises . . . jury-rigged around and within the existing labyrinth of rules." If a collaborative group agrees to a proposal for forest management, what's to prevent parties that disagree with the agreement from seeking to block the proposal through a host of laws—the Administrative Procedures Act, the Endangered Species Act, the National Environmental Policy Act, and the National Forest Management Act for starters? Can the collaborative pathway truly flourish without clearing away the multiple layers and paths in the existing green state?[8]

Third, collaborative approaches raise questions about accountability. How can we ensure that negotiated arrangements are consistent with the public interest? Edward Weber, a strong advocate for collaboration, focused on the accountability problem confronting collaborative conservation groups, and argued that well-designed processes can produce accountability. In contrast, Theodore Lowi, who in *The End of Liberalism* attacked the handover of public authority to private interests in the New Deal regulatory system, looked at the collaborative movement skeptically. In the New Deal era, Lowi argued, vague statutory language carried broad delegations of authority to administrative agencies, but provided little guidance to those agencies about how to use that authority. This created opportunities for negotiation over what the statutes would mean in particular cases, and generally worked to the advantage of organized interests at the expense of the public interest. In attacking arguments for flexibility in environmental regulation, Lowi wrote: "This is where I came in 35 years ago in my confrontation with the late New Deal policies. . . . The motivation is the same—to try to finesse the coercive nature of public authority. . . . Again, pretend away public authority."[9] Legislative gridlock has pushed policymaking down an old and well-beaten pathway, one that policymakers in the 1970s thought they had closed off with statutory mandates that are now criticized for being inflexible. The result is an effort to reconstruct "policy without law" in a context in which these efforts will always be highly contentious and open to challenge in the courts.

This chapter explores three areas in which policymakers have sought to integrate private interests in the policymaking process in new (and, as it turns out, old) ways. First, in the 1990s habitat conservation planning under the Endangered Species Act became a crucial part of the Clinton administration's endangered species program. We will review the evolution of habitat conservation planning and focus on Plum Creek Timber's multi-species plan for lands in Washington state. Second, in the regulatory process there has been movement from formal negotiated regulation under the Negotiated Rulemaking Act of 1990 to more flexible, participatory "reinvention" efforts. We will trace the evolution from more to less formal processes, focusing on the Clinton-era reinvention initiatives. Third, through the 1990s local "collaborative conservation" efforts focusing on the management of natural resources proliferated. This section looks briefly at the collaborative conservation movement, comparing the work of two groups, California's Quincy Library Group and the Quivira Coalition in New Mexico, to explore the potential and limitations of this emerging pathway. The conclusion will explore the implications of the movement toward collaboration and negotiation for the green state, and the constraints that settled institutions and the politics of multiple orders places on the possibilities for this emerging pathway.

Habitat Conservation Planning: Collaboration through the Endangered Species Act

In the rare cases in which it has been aggressively implemented, the Endangered Species Act has proved to be an extremely powerful law. From the Tellico Dam in Tennessee to the forests and rivers of the Pacific Northwest, the law has driven significant changes in the practices of federal agencies and disrupted settled patterns of resource exploitation on public lands. The ESA also threatens private property rights. Threatened and endangered species often live on private lands, and the ESA—understood to prohibit all "harms" to listed species, including damage to species habitat—may make many otherwise legitimate private development activities illegal. This has been a source of considerable concern to large and small landowners alike.

In 1982, Congress amended the law to offer relief to those faced with the possibility of ESA-based limits on the use of their private lands. The ESA's new Section 10 would give the Secretary of the Interior "more flexibility in regulating the incidental take of endangered and threatened species" and address "the concerns of private landowners who are faced with having otherwise lawful actions not requiring federal permits prevented by Section 9 prohibitions against taking."[10] The amendment offered non-federal owners a way around the absolute ban on actions that would damage species habitat and "harm" listed species. They could negotiate a relaxation of the ESA's "take" prohibition with the Fish and Wildlife Service or the National Marine Fisheries Service (now called NOAA Fisheries).

The amendment created a process by which non-federal landowners could gain "incidental take permits" (ITPs) that would allow them to alter habitat despite the possibility of harm to listed species. To receive a permit, a landowner must submit a "habitat conservation plan" (HCP) estimating the impact of development activities on listed species and showing how the impact of those activities will be minimized and mitigated. The Secretary of the Interior has authority to issue an ITP if she finds that the HCP will, "to the maximum extent practicable," mitigate the take, and if the resulting harm "will not appreciably reduce the likelihood of the survival and recovery of the species in the wild."[11] HCPs vary in size and scope, from plans submitted by owners of small lots dealing with one species to comprehensive plans covering hundreds of thousands of acres and many species.

Section 10 had roots in landowners' concerns about property rights as well as the growing sense in the ecological community that the ESA's focus on *species* instead of habitat protection limited the law's effectiveness. Yet Congress was also reacting to political developments. Private lands on California's San Bruno Mountain targeted for development held habitat for ESA-protected butterflies. After a decade-long fight, several cities, the Fish and Wildlife Service, the California Department of Fish and Game, San Mateo County, landowners, developers, and environmentalists agreed in 1980 to allow destruction of some butterfly habitat. In return, the deal required developers to preserve and enhance butterfly habitat in other areas. This was an innovative deal, but it appeared to be illegal since the development it allowed would kill listed butterflies—clearly prohibited by the Endangered Species Act. Section 10 amended the 1973 law to allow deals like this, and the San Bruno agreement became the first approved HCP.[12] San Bruno seemed to show that negotiation could lead to reasonable resolutions to classic struggles between environmentalists and developers, and Congress moved "to provide the institutional framework to permit cooperation between the public and private sectors in the interest of endangered species habitat preservation."[13]

What sort of cooperation does Section 10 anticipate? The only formal participants in habitat conservation planning required by the law are landowners and the relevant federal agencies. Landowners may open the process to other groups, such as conservationists, recreation groups, or independent scientists, but this is entirely the choice of the landowner submitting the plan. A study of participation in habitat conservation planning focused on 45 large plans covering more than 1,000 acres found that environmental, tribal, and commodity interests were involved—at varying levels—in 60 percent of the HCPs, meaning that 40 percent were negotiated with no outside participation. Where participation occurred, it was often ineffective—few Fish and Wildlife Service staffers said that public participation yielded substantive changes to plans, and in more than one-third of the cases public participation had no apparent effect on the outcome. Independent scientists played an even smaller role in the development of the HCPs, with active or moderate involvement in 28 percent of the cases.[14]

As exercises in pluralist decisionmaking, HCPs often seem to fall short. A heavy burden falls on federal agencies with limited budgets and limited staffs to represent the public interest in negotiations with private interests over what are, in effect, business plans. Political science highlights the risk of "agency capture" inherent in processes like this, and in the case of HCPs environmentalists have shared this concern. Political pressures on the agencies to produce plans, driving a negotiation process dominated by regulated interests, may produce deals that fail to fulfill the ESA's promises.

The first 12 years after passage of Section 10 saw little action on HCPs. Only 14 plans were approved between 1982 and 1992, and as of 1994 only 39 had been approved. Most of these plans covered only a few acres and focused on individual species. Karin Sheldon showed there were many reasons for the dearth of HCPs in this period, including the costs of developing and implementing plans, which fell heavily on landowners; the high transaction costs involved in negotiating plans; the limited budgets of federal agencies; and landowners' lack of certainty about whether the plans would hold in light of changing science or the discovery of new species on their lands. Moreover, since few landowners actually faced legal action under the Endangered Species Act for illegal takes—federal agencies face staggering problems in monitoring and enforcing the prohibition on takes on private lands, and lack the budgets and will to aggressively enforce the law—they had weak incentives to submit plans.[15]

Yet during the Clinton years habitat conservation planning moved to center stage. By 1997 more than 400 plans covering approximately 19 million acres of land had been approved or were in process. In the Pacific Northwest 27 percent of commercial forestland was covered by HCPs, or was in the process of being covered, and across the country the Fish and Wildlife Service and the National Marine Fisheries Service were encouraging landowners to submit plans.[16]

Why did the HCP program suddenly take off? From a biological perspective, the need to focus on habitat protection generally, and on private lands in particular, was obvious. Ecologists had long thought the Endangered Species Act needed to look beyond species counts to habitat protection, and the HCPs offered a way of addressing habitat degradation and fragmentation. Further, a 1994 report by the General Accounting Office asserted that 90 percent of listed species have some or all of their habitat on non-federal lands, and that nearly 40 percent were present only on non-federal land. If the ESA's goal of preserving species was to be realized, it had to reach privately owned lands. HCPs could influence landowners' choices in ways that would help to fulfill the goals of the ESA.[17]

The political logic was also overwhelming.

First, the approach was consistent with Clinton's commitment to moving beyond a "false choice" between economic prosperity and environmental protection. Thus, the administration acknowledged that landowners had legitimate concerns about the Endangered Species Act and moved to address those concerns. Assistant Secretary of the Interior George Frampton recognized that "from a private landowner's point of view, the Endangered Species Act looks like a nuclear weapon," and the administration declared its intention to improve the efficiency and effectiveness of the law while protecting property owners. It saw Section 10 as a way of drawing landowners into species protection while sheltering them from the ESA "gone nuclear."[18]

Second, Republicans in the 104th Congress were determined to weaken the Endangered Species Act. In the Senate, Slade Gorton's (R-Washington) proposal, deemed the moderate alternative, would have eliminated the threat of fines and imprisonment for landowners who destroyed endangered species habitat, and would have dropped the ESA's objective of protecting "the ecosystems upon which endangered species and threatened species depend." Secretary of the Interior Bruce Babbitt claimed that the Gorton bill would have effectively repealed the ESA. On the House side, conservatives sought to curtail the role of the federal government in species protection on private lands, relying instead on states, voluntary compliance, economic incentives, and "conservation through commerce including the private propagation of animals and plants."[19] The Clinton administration was squeezed between environmentalists seeking more aggressive species protections, the need for greater protections for species on private lands, and ascendant conservatives seeking to gut the Endangered Species Act. Section 10 offered a chance of escape, and the administration took that chance. John Kostyack of the National Wildlife Federation observed that the Clinton administration had "spent six years turning a virtually nonexistent Habitat Conservation Program into a major Endangered Species Act initiative covering more than 11 million acres of land."[20]

The administration adopted two rules to encourage landowners to develop HCPs. First, the "no surprises" rule guaranteed landowners that once a plan was approved, the government could not demand changes to the plan in light of new information, new scientific knowledge, or changes in the condition of a species. "No surprises" gave property owners certainty about management of their lands for the length of the agreement, and in many cases the terms were quite long. Of the 132 plans approved in the Pacific Region, 30 percent were for terms of 50 years or more, and 50 percent were for terms of 30 years or more—three plans were set for 100 years.[21] Second, the "safe harbor" rule encourages voluntary efforts by landowners to manage their lands to support listed species. Landowners receive assurances that if listed species move onto their property or grow in numbers as a result of their efforts to protect habitat, they will not face new restrictions on use of their property.[22] The Clinton administration sought to increase predictability for property owners in ways that would encourage them to submit HCPs. Most observers think that these rules effectively encouraged landowners to participate in the program.

Nevertheless, the rules were controversial. In a letter to Congress, 150 conservation scientists criticized the "no surprises" rule for locking in land-management practices for long periods of time, arguing that this "does not reflect ecological reality and rejects the best scientific judgment of our era. Moreover, it proposes a world of certainty that does not, has not, and will never exist."[23] "No surprises" was, of course, not science policy at all—it was a political necessity designed to increase landowner participation in HCPs. As the National Center for Environmental Decision-making Research (NCEDR) concluded, decisionmakers in environmental policy rarely use "science-centered" models: "They describe themselves as being 'in the middle,' facing the challenge of balancing competing interests and incentives, incorporating multiple perspectives and concerns, and making inevitable tradeoffs. Indeed they use few of the tools and little of the information potentially available to them, partly because they do not think that science provides the answers to their institutional, political, and practical problems."[24] The practical problems confronting the Clinton administration included pressures from environmentalists, the resistance of property owners to potential restrictions on land use, and a Congress in which "moderation" had come to be defined as an effective repeal of the Endangered Species Act.

The stakes in the HCP program grew following the Supreme Court's decision in *Babbitt v. Sweet Home Chapter of Communities for a Greater Oregon* in June 1995. The Court upheld the Fish and Wildlife Service's ruling that the ESA's definition of prohibited "harm" to listed species includes the modification or destruction of species habitat, even on private lands.[25] This removed any ambiguity about the ESA's restrictions on otherwise lawful private development activities, and made it clear that many development activities on lands inhabited by listed species were illegal. This led landowners—particularly large landowners such as timber companies—to the HCP bargaining table.[26]

Plum Creek's Cascades HCP

One such company was Plum Creek Timber, which has major land holdings in the Pacific Northwest's spotted owl country. Plum Creek had logged aggressively in the 1980s, creating highly visible clear cuts—some in patches as large as a square mile—along the Interstate 90 corridor through Washington's Cascade Mountains. A corporate descendant of the Northern Pacific Railroad, its 170,000 acres along Interstate 90 were interspersed with 201,000 acres of Forest Service lands and 41,100 acres of private and state lands in a checkerboard pattern that is the legacy of legislation signed by Abraham Lincoln. The company had a poor reputation as an environmental steward: one Washington congressman dubbed Plum Creek the "Darth Vader" of northwest timber companies.[27]

The spotted owl listings posed major challenges to Plum Creek, particularly given the intermingling of its Cascade lands with federal property. Operating in prime owl habitat, the company found itself compelled to avoid takes inside a series of 2,523-acre "owl circles," habitat around nesting sites on and overlapping Plum Creek lands. Logging was illegal or sharply limited within these 1.8 mile radius circles, whose locations changed with the identification of new nesting sites. Plum Creek representative Lorin Hicks testified to Congress: "The listing of the northern spotted owl and subsequent federal 'guidelines' trapped over 77 percent of Plum Creek's Cascade Region in 108 owl 'circles.' Indeed, with every new listing Plum Creek was skidding closer to becoming the poster child for the taking of private lands."[28]

Plum Creek valued the timber within each circle at $25.2 million and claimed it spent $500,000 annually on surveys of owl nesting sites.[29] The status quo was unacceptable to the company, and Darth Vader was ready to cut a deal with representatives of the republic. "For us," said Lorin Hicks, "the answer came with Habitat Conservation Plans."[30] Discussions of the Plum Creek HCP for the Cascades began in 1994 and took nearly two years, the company spending more than a million dollars developing the plan. Signed on June 27, 1996 at a public ceremony attended by Secretary of the Interior Babbitt and Secretary of Agriculture Dan Glickman, it was seen as a model for future plans. This "multi-species" HCP addressed habitat issues for four listed species—the northern spotted owl, marbled murrelet, gray wolf, and grizzly bear—as well as 281 other species. The company agreed to defer harvests on 2,600 acres of old-growth forest, to leave trees around sensitive habitats, and to increase the size of the young forests owls use for forage and dispersal. To address concerns about salmon habitat, it developed a riparian strategy for the management of 20 watersheds. The plan also anticipated a land swap between the Forest Service and Plum Creek. In return for this, the company got the right to log heavily in other areas, including the right to reduce the percentage of its holdings in old growth from 20 percent (1996 total) to 8 percent by 2025. Under the plan, the total number of owl nesting sites would likely decline, but as Plum Creek biologist Hicks observed: "This is a take mitigation plan, not an owl recovery plan." The HCP was set for 50 years and is renewable for another 50 years. "If we didn't have the opportunity to re-up," Hicks noted, "it would create the perverse incentive to basically provide only what's required and zero out all extra habitat by the end of the permit period."[31]

The Clinton administration and the company celebrated the deal. Fish and Wildlife Service Assistant Regional Director Curt Smitch said: "This is a huge shift in land management. It's finally managing for an entire ecosystem, which is what scientists and environmentalists have been asking for all along." Babbitt saw the Plum Creek Habitat Conservation Plan as the "most innovative and sophisticated" plan yet developed, calling it "another example of President Clinton living up to his commitment to make the ESA work better." He continued: "This Administration has accomplished major strides in making the ESA work better and more flexibly. . . . We have implemented a number of policies that are revolutionizing our capability to work voluntarily with property owners throughout the country. The flexibility in the Act, and this Administration's goal to encourage certainty for landowners through a multi-species approach to conservation, has allowed companies like Plum Creek Timber to look at ecosystems and watersheds on their land and develop a blueprint for long-term protection that we can all be proud of."[32] Plum Creek representative Hicks testified to the Senate as follows: "For Plum Creek and other applicants, the HCP process has been the principal catalyst for private landowners to undertake unprecedented levels of scientific research and public involvement."[33]

Despite this optimism, the Plum Creek deal drew substantial criticism from the environmental and scientific communities, as well as from some interested in the principle of collaborative decisionmaking. Critics attacked the "no surprises" rule, the perceived weakness of the plan's measures for mitigating the impact of harvests on listed species, the number of "takes" allowed, gaps in the science informing the plan, the role played by the company itself in monitoring results, and the peripheral involvement of environmental groups in the process. Tim Cullinan, an Audubon Society biologist, said: "The concern is that the Fish and Wildlife Service is trying so hard to demonstrate the flexibility and adaptability of the ESA that they're willing to compromise too much."[34]

Two issues in the Plum Creek debate reverberated beyond the plan's specifics to a broader critique of Habitat Conservation Plans. First, there was the question whether independent science adequately informed the plan. Hicks addressed this in congressional testimony:

Let's dispel the myth that HCPs are not based on science. When my company, Plum Creek, created its first HCP, we took on a very complex challenge. Not only did we have 4 listed species in our 170,000-acre Cascade project area, but 281 other vertebrate species, some of which would likely be listed in the next few years. Combine this with the challenges of checkerboard ownership . . . and you have a planning challenge of landscape proportions. To meet this challenge, we assembled a team of scientists representing company staff, independent consultants, and academic experts. We authored 13 technical reports covering every scientific aspect from spotted owl biology to watershed analysis. We sought peer reviews of 47 outside scientists as well as state and federal agency inputs. As a result of these inputs, we made technical and tactical changes to the plan.[35]

Plum Creek chose to establish the peer review panel voluntarily, and named the panel members. Agency representatives were satisfied with the company's approach, but others complained about the absence of effective input by independent scientists. One participant at the periphery of the process said: "Plum Creek told the public these [documents] were reviewed from the outside, but really the reviewers were people chosen or hired by Plum Creek or FWS to review these papers." One panel member said that many suggestions from the reviewers were ignored in developing the Habitat Conservation Plan: "Any suggestions on major issues were simply not addressed."[36] A 1999 study of a broad sample of Habitat Conservation Plans found that the plans were generally not well informed by science. Peter Kareiva, the lead investigator on the project, summarized the major findings in testimony to Congress. He observed that planning suffered from a dearth of data about "the most basic biological processes pertaining to endangered species—such as what is the rate of change in their populations locally? Nationally? What is their reproductive schedule? What is happening to their habitats in quantitative terms?" Kareiva asserted that for many plans the data "are so scant that the HCPs should not really be called 'science-based,' since science requires data from which inferences are drawn and tested." Further, he said that few plans include adequate provisions for monitoring affected populations or habitats: "So-called adaptive management may be mentioned in HCPs, but an extremely small percentage of HCPs actually establish any adaptive management procedures."[37] These critical findings spilled over onto the Plum Creek plan, since the Cascades HCP was in the study sample. The study questioned the finding that harvests planned for the Cascades project area would affect owl populations only minimally. One member of the study team asserted that there were "no data available to support this notion." Since this finding was necessary for Secretary Babbitt to have approved the plan, the study raised real questions about the Plum Creek agreement. The Fish and Wildlife Service questioned some of the Kareiva study's findings but acknowledged that HCPs were a "work in progress" and announced several initiatives to strengthen the scientific basis of the plans.[38]

The second crucial issue involved public participation. As we noted above, conservation planning involves the government agency (the FWS or the NMFS) and the landowner; landowners may invite other participants into the process at their own discretion. In practice, the extent of participation of outside groups varies, but the most systematic report on this topic (conducted at the University of Michigan and financed by Defenders of Wildlife) argued that planning processes often do not include extensive or effective outside participation. This makes it easier to come to agreements, but, the study suggested, often substantially weakens the resulting plans in technical and legal-political terms.[39]

Whether the Plum Creek process was appropriately inclusive is a matter of debate. One study of the process identified three "layers" of participants.[40] The primary actors were Plum Creek, the Fish and Wildlife Service, the National Marine Fisheries Service, and consultants hired by the company. The second layer consisted of the Washington State Departments of Fish and Wildlife and Natural Resources, the Environmental Protection Agency, and the tribes. These participants reviewed the plan and offered suggestions. The third layer included some environmental and recreational groups, the Northwest Indian Fisheries Commission, and the city of Tacoma. These participants reviewed the plan and offered comments, with some presenting unofficial reviews of the National Environmental Policy Act reports.

Views of the actual openness of the process varied depending upon the "layer" in which participants found themselves. Company and agency representatives reported that they thought that the process for integrating the views of outside groups was sound, though some acknowledged that they thought that Plum Creek could have tried harder to reach out to the tribes. Plum Creek took a proactive role in informing outside groups about the plan because the lands in question were popular recreational areas, but it also sought a streamlined process that would allow it to move through the planning process quickly. Outside groups complained that there were few opportunities for meaningful public input. "By the time the NEPA process was opened up," one participant observed, "the public was only rubber stamping the plan. The deal had already been done."[41]

Jeremy Anderson and Steven Yaffee found that Plum Creek offered outsiders "numerous opportunities to comment on its plans and created expectations that it would seriously consider those comments." Yet in the final analysis those stakeholders concluded that their comments were ignored and that the plan did not adequately incorporate their views. Despite a public commitment to openness, Anderson and Yaffee found that Plum Creek "tightly controlled the development of the HCP." According to Charlie Raines of the Sierra Club, "as it went farther along you could tell they were smiling and being very pleasant, but they weren't changing the substance. It was sugar krispies: sugar-coated on the outside but no nutritional value." Yakima Nation representative Jim

Matthews asserted: "It was basically a Plum Creek and FWS show. Whatever they came up with is what we got."[42] A Plum Creek representative acknowledged that groups may be frustrated when their participation does not translate into influence. One FWS official took a harder line: "Maybe these groups always feel like they are underrepresented in the process."[43]

As the number of Habitat Conservation Plans grew, the Fish and Wildlife Service and the National Marine Fisheries Service addressed several criticisms of the approach in an addendum to the HCP handbook.[44] Under this "5-point policy," the agencies would (1) require HCPs to include clear statements of biological goals, (2) push for adaptive management to address uncertainties about the plans' effects on listed species, (3) provide for more effective monitoring, (4) clarify the criteria used by the agencies to establish the duration of plans, and (5) provide more opportunities for public participation. Scientists and much of the environmental community warmly received these changes, but it remains to be seen whether the HCP program's scientific integrity and participatory character can be significantly improved.

Habitat conservation plans are a central component of the emerging collaborative regime in environmental policymaking, reflecting many of the strengths of the larger movement. Significantly, habitat conservation planning is grounded in statutory language, Section 10 of the Endangered Species Act. Despite its statutory basis, the program confronts serious questions about its legitimacy and effectiveness. The expansion of HCPs came in the context of severe budgetary and personnel problems in the larger ESA program. The Fish and Wildlife Service and the National Marine Fisheries Service could not effectively process listing petitions, designate critical habitat, or consistently compel other federal agencies to take actions necessary to protect listed species. Critics argued that rather than simply *supplementing* other efforts under the Endangered Species Act, habitat conservation planning *displaced* other legally mandated activities. One vocal critic of HCPs was Kieran Suckling of the Center for Biological Diversity. "As these plans become bigger and bigger," he said "they supersede recovery planning. There are no recovery plans for 70 percent of endangered species. The Fish and Wildlife Service says it has no money to do recovery plans, but it has found money to do more than 400 HCPs. . . . Babbitt has created a shadow ESA. He's saving the ESA by killing endangered species."[45] The ESA's language is clear, and Section 10 did not repeal requirements for listing species or designating critical habitat. Opponents have taken their case to the courts, challenging the "no surprises" rule and dragging HCPs into the labyrinth. Although the rule is technically still intact after years of litigation, challenges to the "no surprises" rule and the related "permit revocation rule" continue. The Clinton Administration used its administrative discretion to alter the priorities of the endangered species program, perhaps to take a broader ecosystem focus, but undoubtedly shifting resources to cutting deals with landowners.[46]

Moreover, there is significant concern about the processes that produce HCPs, the quality of the science upon which they are based, and the weakness of monitoring programs. The extent of participation varies from case to case, depending upon the attitudes of the property owners and the demands of agency officials. There are some legitimate concerns that representation is asymmetric, with property owners exercising considerable influence over the planning process. Property rights are obviously important, but the Endangered Species Act asserts a national interest in species preservation, and planning processes should reflect this reality.

Further, as has been shown, many HCPs lack solid scientific grounding, and outcomes have not been aggressively monitored. HCPs represent a major and continuing federal commitment—for example, roughly one-fourth of the land area of the state of Washington is now managed under HCPs, with more lands to be added to the total soon, and the George W. Bush administration has approved more than 200 plans since it took office in 2001. Not only does it appear that many plans were not well grounded scientifically, but it is also difficult to determine whether they are meeting their goals of protecting species.[47] Supporters of the program see a healthy flexibility, a new kind of environmental policymaking for a new era. Skeptics see old politics—government cutting deals with landowners, hither and yon, with little understanding of the consequences of those choices. The new HCP Handbook provides more guidance for framing and monitoring, in essence acknowledging the weaknesses of

HCPs to date. Still, there has been little systematic monitoring of these plans, there are few resources available to do so, and they are vulnerable to legal challenge.[48]

One premise of the movement for the new social regulation in the 1960s and the 1970s was that agency capture had been problematic for the American regulatory state. Policy would be better and more democratic if we created processes that would invite interest-group conflict in the legislative process and then in the courts, rather than excluding some interests in the name of streamlined processes governed by experts and regulated interests. The conflictual policy environment that resulted creates serious problems, and there is need for creative thinking about ways to escape that trap. The HCP framework appears promising, but it also risks a retreat to decisionmaking involving asymmetric representation, in which property owners drive the process, federal agencies are under mandates to speed through plans satisfactory to those private interests, and the public interest in species preservation is weakly represented.

Reinventing Regulation through Negotiation

The regulatory system that emerged in the late 1960s and the 1970s resulted from values changes, the emergence of the new public interest movement reflecting those values, and concerns about the problem of "agency capture" in the New Deal regulatory regime.[49] Hostility to corporate political power melded with the perception that industries controlled many agencies they were built to regulate, prompting new thinking about institutional design. The reformers of the late 1960s aimed to set things right with the "new social regulation."[50]

The new social regulation simultaneously attacked agency capture and the political influence of business corporations. First, Congress would write more specific legislation holding agencies to clear goals and deadlines. This was particularly important in environmental regulation, where the goals and deadlines were sometimes unrealistic but their impact was profound. Congress would force the EPA's hand, limiting its "discretion while fostering an adversarial relationship between regulators and regulated."[51] Action-forcing statutes would help to ensure that the agency pursued the public interest as defined by Congress, mitigating the threat of agency capture. Second, citizen groups would play a more significant role in rulemaking and policy implementation, balancing the influence of business groups. The courts required agencies to open their decisionmaking processes to greater participation by public-interest groups, while Congress and the courts made it easier for citizen groups to sue to enforce agency accountability. Reformers built a new regulatory regime reflecting concerns about the New Deal system and the new balance of forces in American politics.[52]

Before long, however, resurgent business interests, conservative politicians, and academics attacked environmental regulations for imposing unnecessary expenses and irrational constraints on business operations.[53] Critics found the system plagued by a "malaise" marked by inefficiency, excessive costs, delays, and an entrenched adversarialism that focused debate on procedural questions rather than problem solving.[54] Congress has achieved some reforms—the tradable permit system adopted in the Clean Air Act Amendments of 1990 is the key example, but, for reasons we discussed in chapters 2 and 3, it has been unable to move comprehensive regulatory reforms of pollution control legislation. Despite decades of criticism, and despite considerable and creative thinking about ways to improve the old laws, pollution regulation is still dominated by the "lords of a little while ago"—the laws and institutions that grew out of the public-interest movement of the late 1960s and the 1970s.[55]

In chapter 4 we showed that presidents have wrestled with the green state's regulatory apparatus through administrative centralization, Office of Management and Budget-centered regulatory clearance, cost-benefit analysis requirements, and other mechanisms.[56] This section deals with a different angle of attack: efforts to remake regulation through negotiations with regulated interests and other groups.

The search for more collaborative approaches has been central to the next generation agenda. Marian Chertow and Daniel Esty observed that the old system "compartmentalized problems by media" in complex, rigid, and sometimes internally contradictory statutory and regulatory structures. It created few incentives for exceptional environmental performance, invited litigation, and "implied a level of absolutism in pursuit of environmental purity" that prevented rational tradeoffs between environmental protection and other values. Chertow and Esty called for new "policies that are not confrontational but cooperative, less fragmented and more comprehensive, not inflexible but rather capable of being tailored to fit varying circumstances."[57] This perspective has been influential, culminating in the Clinton administration's 1995 National Performance Review document, "Reinventing Environmental Regulation," which embraced both the conventional critique of command and control regulation and the case for moving beyond adversarialism.[58] There have been many experiments with environmental partnerships, several of them aimed at circumventing constraints imposed by golden era statutes. In these experiments, policymakers seek solutions to particular regulatory problems and a testing ground for approaches that might underpin a transformation of the regulatory system.

In this section of the chapter, we focus on three such experiments: negotiated regulation ("reg-neg") and two Clinton-era initiatives, the sector-level "Common Sense Initiative" and the site-focused "Project XL." We summarize these efforts and show that, despite high hopes and occasional successes, there is little evidence that these experiments have made much progress in either tackling narrow regulatory problems or rebuilding environmental regulation along new lines. We then turn to a broader analysis of collaborative regulation and the prospects for building a next generation green state somewhere along the pathway marked by these experiments. Institution building will be extraordinarily difficult, we conclude, owing to the politics of environmental policy in the era of legislative gridlock and to the complexity of the green state.[59]

One Step Down the Collaborative Path: Negotiated Rulemaking

Under conventional "notice-and-comment" rulemaking, agencies gather information, draft proposed rules, and then publish those proposed rules in the *Federal Register*. Agencies may hold informal meetings with interested groups before the publication of the proposed rule, but formal participation takes place after the draft rule is published. Interested parties then have the right to submit written comments, and the agency may hold public hearings. If the agency chooses to go forward with the rule, it publishes the final version at least 30 days before it becomes effective. The average time for developing rules by the conventional process is approximately three years, and hostile interests regularly challenge rules in court.[60] David Pritzker and Deborah Dalton summarized common concerns:

The adversarial nature of the normal rulemaking process is often criticized as a major contributor to the expense and delay associated with regulatory proceedings. Agency rulemaking may be perceived as merely the first round in a battle that will culminate in a court decision. The need to establish a formal record as a basis for potential litigation sharpens the divisions between parties, and may foreclose any willingness to recognize the legitimate viewpoints of others. In these circumstances, parties often take extreme positions in their written and oral statements. They may choose to withhold information they think is damaging. . . . What is lacking is an opportunity for the parties to exchange views, and to focus on finding constructive, creative solutions to problems.[61]

In 1990, building on experiments from the previous two decades, Congress adopted the Negotiated Rulemaking Act.[62] The law's basic premise is that under certain conditions it may be desirable to bring interested parties together to negotiate the text of a proposed rule before that proposed rule is published in the *Federal Register*. Congress concluded that traditional rulemaking "may discourage parties from meeting and communicating with one another," leading to unnecessary conflict and litigation, and that it "deprives the affected parties and the public of the benefits [of] cooperation" as well as the advantages of "shared information, knowledge, expertise, and technical abilities possessed by the affected parties."[63] The activism of public-interest groups and the openness of the courts to citizen suits exacerbated all of these problems. At its core, negotiated rulemaking ("reg-neg") was a response to problems associated with the new social regulation. Thus, the *solution* to the problem of agency capture— a more adversarial, less flexible rulemaking process—became a *problem* to be solved by a more cooperative approach in which interested parties would participate formally in the earliest stages of rulemaking.

Congress then revived an old and controversial premise of regulatory policymaking: "the parties who will be significantly affected by a rule participate in the development of a rule."[64] It hoped that involving relevant interests early in rulemaking, rather than waiting for the notice-and-comment period, would speed rulemaking and "increase the acceptability and improve the substance of rules, making it less likely that the affected parties will resist enforcement or challenge such rules in court."[65] Critics of this move raised concerns about agency capture and business influence. They worried that flexibility sought by champions of negotiated rulemaking would "subvert the basic, underlying concepts of American administrative law—an agency's pursuit of the public interest through law and reasoned decisionmaking. In its place, negotiated rulemaking would establish privately bargained interests as the source of putative public law."[66]

How does the reg-neg process work? The law does not require agencies to use negotiated regulation, but gives them the option where it appears the approach might yield good results. After determining whether reg-neg is appropriate for a given problem, the agency convenes an advisory committee representing the interests affected most directly by the rule. Agencies usually seek balanced representation, though participants frequently report that some relevant group has been excluded.[67] The objective is to develop consensus on a proposed rule. The agency then uses the consensus agreement as the basis for a draft rule published in the *Federal Register*. Committee meetings are open to the public, and the committees operate under ground rules negotiated in advance. For example, participants may agree not to submit negative comments or litigate on points of consensus. Negotiated rulemaking *supplements* rather than displaces conventional rulemaking. Negotiated rules are still subject to conventional notice-and-comment procedures after the draft rule is published.[68]

The promised benefits of reg-neg go beyond speeding rulemaking and reducing litigation. Advocates see it as a cornerstone of a new regulatory system. Philip Harter, a law professor and a leading advocate for reg-neg, argues that negotiated rules will enjoy greater legitimacy than rules adopted through conventional procedures. Negotiating consensus will, he hopes, yield more satisfying, reasonable decisions reflecting the sound data and the common sense of the parties. Jody Freeman argued that a sustained commitment to reg-neg could transform the regulatory state by challenging "the conceptual constraints of the traditional administrative regime," encouraging broad participation, problem solving, and the erosion of the public-private divide.[69] President Bill Clinton shared these hopes, supporting reg-neg as part of his regulatory reinvention project. The 1993 National Performance Review endorsed reg-neg, and Clinton's Executive Order 12,866 directed federal agencies "to explore and, where appropriate, use consensual mechanisms for developing regulations, including negotiated rulemaking." Clinton also demanded that agencies either identify at least one rulemaking in which they would use reg-neg or explain to the Office of Management and Budget why the approach was not feasible for them.[70]

The Environmental Protection Agency led the way in reg-neg, using the process more frequently than any other agency. Between 1983 (when the first serious experiments took place) and 1996, federal agencies produced 36 final rules linked to reg-negs. The EPA issued twelve of those rules, and no other agency issued more than seven.[71] The agency used the approach to tackle some difficult issues, including developing standards for reformulated gasoline under the 1990 Clean Air Act Amendments, residential woodstove emissions, coke oven emissions, workers' exposure to agricultural pesticides, chemical leaks, and wood furniture manufacturing.

Some EPA cases reveal the potential of reg-neg to resolve problems in the rulemaking process. Freeman found that the chemical equipment leaks rulemaking begun in 1989 pushed the policy debate in creative directions, yielding consensus language that satisfied environmentalists and industry. The reg-neg produced enforceable standards and participants deemed the consensus process successful. She found that the reg-neg developed a new conceptual approach to the control standard and led to discussions of greener production processes and fruitful information sharing among companies seeking best practices. The negotiations revealed that pollution control and production goals could be compatible, an understanding that had not been widely shared in the industry before the reg-neg. Here, negotiated regulation apparently generated innovative solutions to vexing policy problems.[72]

Yet systematic analysis has raised doubts about the general effectiveness of negotiated rulemaking. First, negotiated rulemaking is rare and is likely to remain so because (a) the conditions under which the approach is likely to succeed do not appear very often, and (b) negotiations are time-consuming, straining the resources of all participants. Between 1991 and 1996, 24 of the 20,190 final rules issued by federal agencies (0.1 percent) emerged from reg-negs. In 1996, then the peak year, seven of the 3,762 rules issued by federal agencies were rooted in formal regulatory negotiations.[73] It is unlikely, then, that agencies or stakeholders can sustain a large number of reg-negs on complicated and contentious issues. Second, Cary Coglianese undermined two central claims for the advantages of reg-neg, finding that it neither reduced the amount of time needed to write rules nor reduced litigation rates.[74] Indeed, in the subset of cases he studied it appeared that negotiated rules were more likely to be litigated than rules generated in the traditional notice-and-comment process. Reg-neg participants tend to be more satisfied with the process than participants in conventional rulemaking, but it is unclear that participant satisfaction is related to the quality of policy choices.[75] Coglianese's findings have drawn fire, but the softest version of his conclusion—negotiated rulemaking has not yet delivered on its promise—seems consistent with the evidence.

Coglianese's work challenges the faiths that we can process around the basic conflicts that give rise to struggles over environmental policy and that reg-neg can contain conflict to the negotiating room, preventing it from spilling over into other venues. Further, negotiated regulation highlights at least two critical issues for collaborative approaches: the problem of squaring administrative flexibility with the rule of law and the potential for the development of a clear path through the environmental policy labyrinth to "cleaner, cheaper, smarter" regulation.

Policy without Law, Policy against Law? The new social regulation created inefficiencies and excessive conflict, but reformers took the less flexible, more adversarial course for defensible reasons. In *The End of Liberalism*, Lowi decried "policy without law," or ad hoc choices made by administrative agencies in the absence of clear congressional guidance.[76] The new collaborative approaches present us with another difficulty: the possibility of inconsistency between negotiated agreements and reasonably clear statutory requirements, or policy *against* law. There are two questions here: Can reg-negs consistently serve the public interest and respect the integrity of law? Since they are in part responses to perceived flaws in the existing regulatory structure, can collaborative approaches actually succeed within the constraints of law, without statutory changes that would clear the path toward greater flexibility and efficiency? This section will deal with the first of these questions; the second is treated in light of experiences with the Clinton reinvention project discussed in the following section.

Reg-negs can break through the boundaries set by environmental statutes. This sometimes occurs under traditional rulemaking, but with reg-neg the very value of the approach lies in its flexibility. This can lead to consensus deals that are "better than the law" from the perspective of the parties. William Funk's study of the EPA's 1987 woodstove regulations showed that the reg-neg produced consensus rules that violated parts of the Clean Air Act. Negotiators were aware of these problems but agreed to work around them where they found agreement within the group. Thus, consensus rather than the law became the legitimizing standard for some of the rules. The negotiated rules themselves were credible. They promised to improve air quality, and the reg-neg process may well have produced better results than a conventional rulemaking would have. Yet the parties' agreement on what worked for them overrode statutory limits. Whatever legitimacy the rules might have gained through negotiation was weakened to the extent that those rules set policy against the law. It is significant that there was no legal challenge to the woodstove rules because all of the parties to the agreement had agreed not to sue, and outsiders lacked the resources to challenge the decisions.[77] Funk worried that "the incentives to make negotiated rulemaking succeed . . . undermine and subvert the principles underlying traditional administrative law by elevating the importance of consensus among the parties above the law, the facts, or the public interest."[78] The reality that traditional administrative law, and the environmental statutes, have not always worked well cannot justify simply ignoring those statutes.[79]

This was not the only reg-neg in which participants moved forward despite uncertainty about the legality of their actions. In 1991 negotiations over reformulated gasoline standards, participants agreed on a compliance measure that would focus not on gallon-by-gallon emissions but whether, on average, fuel producers met Clean Air Act standards. EPA officials and some environmentalists charged that averaging was illegal, and "there was no doubt about the intent of environmental advocates and states to litigate the averaging provisions if adopted outside the reg-neg. Yet within the context of the reg-neg, the averaging issue became negotiable."[80] Funk worried that under reg-neg "agencies learn that achieving consensus of the parties is the measure of success. . . . Thus the agencies are likely to see their role not as serving the public interest, but as generating a consensus among the parties to a negotiation."[81]

Negotiating Air Quality: The Reformulated Gasoline Reg-Neg Edward Weber described the reformulated gasoline (RFG) rule adopted in 1991 as a successful application of negotiated regulation.[82] Yet it is also true that, far from offering a clear path through the environmental policy labyrinth, even this successful rulemaking faced difficult twists and turns and treacherous intersections with other policymaking paths. Though the negotiated agreement held against strong political challenges, even the victors seemed discouraged by the process. The RFG fight simultaneously demonstrates some of the strengths of reg-neg and the difficulties of creating any equilibrium out of the complex, contentious stuff of environmental politics since the golden era.

In the Clean Air Act Amendments of 1990, Congress took aim at urban smog with a reformulated gasoline program. Congress required the use of cleaner-burning fuels in nine cities with serious air quality problems and required that the new fuel formula yield no net increase in nitrous oxide emissions and that it be 15 percent lower in volatile organic compounds emissions than standard gasoline. The debate in Congress focused on the definition of clean fuels and led to a compromise embracing methanol, ethanol, natural gas, and reformulated gasoline. The EPA would define a clean-fuels model that would meet the smog-control goals set by Congress.

As Weber noted, this was a major decision: the oil and auto industries, midwestern agricultural interests, environmentalists, and state regulators held huge stakes in the EPA's work. Oil companies worried about the costs of developing and distributing RFG and the impact of new "mixed" formulas on its share of the gasoline market. It faced years of planning and billions in expenditures to retool facilities. Auto manufacturers worried that vehicles using RFGs might not meet federal mileage standards, forcing them to develop new engine designs. Agricultural interests and allied legislators saw the possibility for enormous profits in a rule supporting the use of corn-based ethanol. Environmentalists wanted tough standards, and state regulators wanted a clear, enforceable policy on pollution from vehicles that would reduce pressures on them to bring the anti-smog hammer down on stationary, industrial sources of pollution. The EPA found itself at the center of what promised to be a bitter fight.

The agency turned to negotiated regulation to try to speed the rule-making and avoid future litigation. The parties to the reg-neg and the White House agreed to a formal protocol blocking intervention from the executive branch outside the reg-neg, forbidding participants from lobbying outside the reg-neg, and committing all parties to support the consensus agreement by promising not to sue. This "assurance mechanism" bound the groups, the Environmental Protection Agency, and the White House to honor the results of the negotiations, and was crucial in securing the participation of environmentalists and state regulators in the process.[83] This would ensure that the agreement would stick, giving the negotiated rule safe passage through the environmental policy labyrinth.

After difficult negotiations the parties struck an agreement in August 1991, and in April 1992 the Environmental Protection Agency published a proposed rule based on the consensus language. As the deal took shape, however, ethanol interests grew nervous. The typical ethanol-gasoline blend is more volatile than gasoline itself, meaning that it releases more volatile organic compounds into the air than normal gasoline. The blend's volatility exceeded the standard set in the Clean Air Act Amendments of 1990. Section 211(h) of the amendments provided an "ethanol waiver" allowing the blend to be sold in the "high ozone season" in urban areas, but the law did not include any waiver for ethanol in setting the requirements for reformulated gasoline in section 211(k). The reg-neg agreement did not specifically include the waiver, either, but it did contain an ambiguous provision that might be read to allow the ethanol blends. The EPA did not think that it had legal authority to include an ethanol waiver in the RFG program, however, and the industry was hit hard when the proposed rule did not contain that waiver.[84]

Over the howls of the other parties to the agreement, the ethanol interests broke their promise not to lobby outside the reg-neg and raced to Congress and the White House for help. The industry secured a nonbinding "sense of the Senate" amendment to an appropriation bill calling the proposed rule illegal. It appealed to the White House, and the ethanol waiver became an issue in the 1992 presidential campaign. In October 1992, President George H. W. Bush announced that he would grant the ethanol waiver, upsetting the reg-neg and breaking the administration's commitment to the process. While EPA officials argued that Bush's proposed waiver would have to go through normal rulemaking procedures, Clinton simultaneously dismissed the Bush decision as a campaign ploy and promised the corn growers support for ethanol in a Clinton presidency (though he did not promise the ethanol waiver). Neither campaign could easily ignore the pleas of ethanol interests given the political importance of the corn-growing states.[85]

So the conflict over RFG quickly spread beyond the confines of the negotiating room. In late 1993 the Clinton administration reversed Bush's decision on the ethanol waiver and published a final rule in keeping with the original negotiated agreement. But along with that decision it announced a program to appease ethanol interests that threatened the reg-neg: the EPA adopted a rule requiring that at least 30 percent of the gasoline sold in cities with the worst air quality contain additives from renewable sources, a boon to ethanol. The oil industry challenged the 30 percent rule in the courts and succeeded in blocking it. The oil industry did not charge that the EPA's sop to ethanol had violated the reg-neg. Industry attorneys convinced their clients that the reg-neg was an "unenforceable 'gentlemen's agreement'" rather than a legal contract despite the parties' commitments to the pre-negotiation protocols. Ethanol was dealt a blow and the oil industry won an important victory.[86]

Yet the actions of the White House and the Environmental Protection Agency raised questions about the reg-neg process as a whole, even for the winners. Ellen Siegler, an attorney for the American Petroleum Institute, wrote:

. . . one of the most important benefits API sought in the fuels reg-neg was a degree of certainty that the informal agreement would be implemented without major changes sufficient to allow API members to plan to meet Clean Air Act fuels requirements until at least the year 2000. At the conclusion of the reg-neg, API believed it had achieved this objective. The events that occurred after the completion of the reg-neg—the NOx reduction requirements and the ethanol mandate, including the ensuing litigation over the ethanol mandate and the petition for reconsideration regarding the NOx requirement—taught API that this benefit can be taken away by an agency for political or other reasons. . . . The experience of the fuels reg-neg, in short, left API with the view that the costs of a reg neg can far outweigh its benefits and that the federal government can too easily find ways to walk away from a deal.[87]

The reg-neg delivered on some of its promises. Under difficult circumstances, participants developed a workable solution, on time, that satisfied most of the parties. The agreement held against powerful political pressures as two presidential administrations and powerful legislators sought ways to appease the ethanol interests. Yet the case also highlights the limitations on reg-neg and the difficulties of establishing a policy equilibrium in this field. The ethanol interests and the Bush administration broke the agreement to support the negotiated consensus. The Clinton administration tried to find a middle way but also ended up appeasing the ethanol interests with policies inconsistent with the reg-neg. The dispute landed in the courts—an eventuality that reg-neg was intended to avoid. The agreement held, but the collapse of the pre-negotiation protocols raised doubts about the approach, as evidenced by the comments from the oil industry attorney quoted above. These deals are embedded in a swirling, contentious politics marked by many venues in which they might be undone; the politics of RFG could not be contained by the reg-neg.

Indeed, the reg-neg was quickly overwhelmed by other problems in the RFG program. And of course ethanol politics rolled on, with the industry probing various policy venues and seeking to attach its ambitions for corn-based fuel additives to the tax code, farm bills, and other legislation.[88] The oil companies turned to the gasoline additive MTBE (methyl tertiary butyl ether) to meet the oxygenation standard for cleaner-burning fuels set by the Clean Air Act Amendments of 1990. MTBE was cheaper and arguably more effective than ethanol, but it is a carcinogen and began to turn up in groundwater in various areas around the country. In 2000, as many as 9,000 community water wells in 31 states were contaminated by 250,000 leaking tanks. The Clinton administration proposed a ban on MTBE, but the Bush EPA set aside this proposed ban. With the federal government unable to act, several states prohibited the use of MTBE. All of this boosted the fortunes of ethanol. Finally, the energy legislation adopted in 2005 set aside the oxygenation standard adopted in the 1990 Clean Air Act Amendments and required oil refineries to use increasing amounts of renewable fuels, rising from 4 billion gallons per year in 2006 to 7.5 billion in 2012.[89]

Down the "Alternative Path" to Common Sense and Project XL

As we noted above, the Clinton administration endorsed negotiated rulemaking but also forged beyond it, seeking to develop models for a more collaborative, flexible regulatory system.[90] Unlike reg-neg, though, the Clinton reinvention efforts were not legitimized by statutes. Instead, the administration sought ways around the existing regulatory structure, moving well beyond areas of the map charted by Congress.

The major projects in the reinvention program were the Common Sense Initiative (CSI), launched in 1994, and Project XL (for Excellence in Leadership), launched in 1995. CSI, described by EPA Administrator Carol Browner as "probably the biggest new direction in environmental protection since the founding of the EPA," embraced a sector-level approach to regulatory negotiation and improvement. Project XL, called "one of the most ambitious and potentially consequential U.S. experiments seeking common ground in environmental policymaking," focused largely on controlling emissions at the level of individual plants.[91]

CSI promised "cleaner, cheaper, smarter" regulation and promised to generate legislative proposals for improving environmental policymaking. CSI would enhance environmental protection and lower compliance costs by addressing problems industry by industry rather than by focusing on individual pollutants. The EPA created a CSI Council and six industrial subcommittees: auto manufacturing, computers and electronics, iron and steel, metal finishing, oil refining, and printing.[92] These committees were asked to seek ways to improve environmental protection while reducing compliance costs, develop projects on pollution prevention, streamline permitting and reporting requirements, encourage superior performance and the development of new technologies, and ensure enforcement of chronic violators. Browner said that CSI would "take environmental protection beyond the command-and-control, pollutant-by-pollutant approach [by] developing more integrated, comprehensive strategies for protecting our air, our water, and our land." In assessing CSI, Browner claimed that it "promoted unprecedented levels of cooperation among stakeholders, those most affected by environmental decisions" and that "in this manner, we avoided the old adversarial approach that produced gridlock in the past."[93]

Unfortunately, independent assessments show that CSI had little success. A 1997 report by the General Accounting Office noted that in three years the project generated three formal recommendations to the EPA, none of them major. The GAO criticized the EPA for focusing on CSI's apparent success in generating activities like stakeholder meetings while giving little attention to its lack of effectiveness in generating substantive improvements to regulation. Some of the subcommittees were more successful than others, but CSI participants interviewed for one program assessment reported that they "gradually came to believe that the Initiative would not be the vehicle for gaining far-reaching change to the EPA's rules and regulations."[94] Cary Coglianese and Laurie Allen concluded that the CSI's results were "modest," noting that only five of roughly thirty subcommittee recommendations had led to changes to EPA rules. Few of the projects produced much in the way of substantive policy change or environmental improvements; most led to the generation of some information and educational materials.[95] While CSI was terminated, some projects continued under different auspices and the Bush EPA has pursued a "Sector Strategies Program" that bears some resemblance to CSI.[96] The sector-level approach to negotiating regulations is sensible and it is hard to imagine that the idea will ever be completely abandoned. Yet CSI's problems offer a cautionary note.

Project XL, rooted in the Aspen Institute's discussion of the "alternative path" to environmental regulation, was also ambitious. Administrator Browner said that XL would be "where we will find the next generation of environmental improvement, the next generation of environmental technology."[97] The project promised flexibility, a better fit between regulatory demands and the situations of specific firms, and ongoing communication between regulated firms, regulators, and publics interested in clean plant operations. Movement down the collaborative pathway had finally rolled past the negotiation of general rules and sector-specific plans to the gates of individual firms, where government officials, business representatives, environmentalists, and others might find common ground on "cleaner, cheaper, smarter" rules for governing plant-level operations.

Project XL encouraged site-specific pollution control projects as alternatives to existing command-and-control requirements. When the new approach promised to deliver "superior environmental performance," the EPA would waive constraining regulatory requirements. Companies would submit proposals for projects to the EPA, which would evaluate them on several criteria, including the promise of superior environmental performance, cost savings and efficiency gains, the level of support from parties with stakes in the project, the existence of progress measures, the promise that the program would test new ideas that might eventually inform other EPA programs, and effects on workplace safety and environmental justice. Proposals would identify stakeholders, and the EPA could comment on this or even reject a proposal if the list was inadequate, but it was up to the regulated firm to keep interested parties involved in negotiations. The final project agreement would reflect a consensus of the stakeholders. Bush EPA Administrator Christine Todd Whitman, who would oversee the end of XL, described it as a model of how regulators should work—"building partnerships with stakeholders, focusing on results, and moving away from conventional command and control approaches to more cooperative partnerships."[98]

Project XL had some success, achieving more than 40 final project agreements with firms and some state pollution control agencies.[99] The idea that businesses should be free to seek the most effective means of achieving environmental standards set by regulators remains powerful, and few would challenge the notion that it is important to work with individual plants to achieve flexible, smart regulations. Yet, like the experience with CSI, Project XL's overall performance disappointed most observers and many participants. Environmentalists complained that they were marginalized in technical debates. Businesses complained about the vague standard for the superior environmental performance they would have to deliver in return for regulatory flexibility, and both firms and state agencies chafed against the EPA's caution about stretching existing statutes and rules. The program suffered from a mismatch between the initial promise and what EPA leaders thought they could deliver under the law. Clinton's invitation to businesses to apply for exemptions from regulatory requirements generated requests for broad waivers and big changes to policy. The EPA balked because it lacked clear legal authority to make these changes, and negotiations dragged on.[100] Despite the EPA's efforts to improve Project XL while it was in progress, and the creation of an Office of Reinvention to oversee XL and other reform initiatives, the project continued to disappoint. On average agreements took more than 20 months to negotiate, environmentalists decried XL projects as industry-driven, and businesses thought the whole process was too slow and that the EPA was unnecessarily rigid.[101]

What common problems plagued these collaborative experiments? Both CSI and XL were plagued by uncertainty about whether the EPA had the authority to grant the waivers of statutory and regulatory requirements anticipated by the programs. The regulatory reform initiatives were undertaken in part because Congress had been unable to fix many problems in the regulatory system due to gridlock. Yet the progress of those initiatives was limited by the same legislative gridlock and inflexible statutes that motivated them.

Alfred Marcus and co-authors studied the failure of an XL project at a 3M facility in Hutchinson, Minnesota and found that uncertainty about the legality of the project contributed to its failings:

. . . a troubling issue was whether Project XL-Minnesota could be carried out without violating existing environmental laws and requirements. The project by no means was operating with a clean slate, because it had to contend with the massive structure of environmental laws and regulations created since the birth of the EPA in 1970. If the statutory foundation for the pilot was insufficient, how could EPA proceed? The agency's view was that there was not much leeway in the law. . . . Without additional legal authority, it was unclear if the agency could make the changes that XL required. . . . It was unclear, for instance, if EPA had the authority to grant 3M facility-wide air pollutant emissions standards, waiver of individual emissions source permitting requirements, and reduced reporting of compliance. In comparison with congressional enactments, the Clinton-Gore declaration of XL policy did not have the legal standing to permit exceptions to the law.[102]

"A fundamental problem with Project XL," Charles Caldart and Nicholas Ashford observed, "is that it envisions a kind of regulatory flexibility that has not been granted by Congress." This led the EPA to behave cautiously and firms—fearing being sued by citizen groups—to approach the expensive process of negotiating a consensus warily.[103] The EPA expected hundreds of applications from firms to participate in the program from which it would select 55 for experiments. By the end of 1996 it had received only 45 proposals, in part because it was unclear to businesses what the purchase would be given statutory constraints.[104]

The same problem plagued the Common Sense Initiative, which sought to overcome a fundamental problem in the green state, the media-specific focus of its pollution control institutions, through sector-level deliberation. The major environmental statutes limit the EPA's discretion to waive and trade and bargain across media, and however rational, well intended, and justified the effort it is difficult to turn environmental policymaking into a "grand bazaar."[105] The frustrating statutes and rules that CSI was designed to evade through consensus bargaining cast a long shadow over negotiations.[106] According to a September 1996 industry report on the reinvention program, "there is no short cut, no way around the difficult task of trying to legislate a better system."[107] Yet the legislative pathway appears to be blocked, and experiments like this appeared to be the only way through to a better system for policymakers. In the 1990s Republican legislators had little interest in giving President Clinton a legislative victory on environmental questions, and environmental advocates were terrified of opening up the environmental laws to greater flexibility in the conservative climate of the 104th and 105th Congresses.

These reinvention experiments were also hampered by the commitment to consensus. There are good reasons to pursue consensus. If environmentalists and community representatives participate, consensus decision rules may mitigate concerns that collaborative processes will be dominated by industry. Further, consensus can serve as an alternative source of legitimacy for decisions that may be at odds with the existing legal framework. In view of the vulnerability of these deals to litigation, getting agreement from the interested parties is, if it can be achieved, quite sensible. The consensus approach is also appealing on its face, squaring nicely with the assumption that environmental protection goals are consensual and that modern policymaking needs to focus on sensible means for achieving ends we all agree upon. Finally, consensus processes may yield narrower yet important benefits: better informed policy, less litigation, and improved compliance.

Yet gaining consensus is cumbersome, and there is little evidence that consensus rules reduce conflict and litigation or yield superior policy choices. In fact, Coglianese found that consensus rules create new issues around which conflict can occur (Who will participate? What does the agreement we struck mean? Does the policy eventually adopted reflect the agreement?), that they do not reduce litigation, and that consensus-based decisionmaking does not necessarily lead to better choices. In fact, Coglianese argued, consensus groups tend to focus on areas where there is widespread agreement, giving less energy and attention to more contentious (and perhaps more important) questions. Coglianese found that most CSI projects produced research and education projects, shying away from more difficult issues.[108] More serious issues provoked more serious conflicts of value and interest. Environmentalists' complaints about their lack of influence in a Project XL initiative at an Intel facility in Arizona provoked an outburst by the company's government-affairs director: "People have misconstrued what the stakeholder process is all about. Citizens are going to make decisions . . . that are binding on Fortune 500 companies?"[109] This comment reflects an important issue at stake in these consensus efforts and the larger collaborative enterprise of which they are a part. The collaboration project forces agency officials, firms, and citizen groups to seek the boundaries of public authority case by case. Where should the line be drawn between public authority and private choices? Once negotiations move past easy agreements to produce educational materials and confront harder choices, participants must tackle fundamental questions about the scope of public authority at individual plants, in particular regions, or for specific economic sectors. A consensus that "cleaner, cheaper, smarter" regulation is possible will not help participants to mark the boundaries of public authority case by case, time and again, as these collaborations spread across the landscape of environmental policy. They are unlikely to prove to be a solution to adversarialism. Instead, they are the source of a different kind of adversarialism—perhaps more manageable, perhaps not—in this field.

Reconstructing Environmental Regulation?
The failings of the aforementioned reinvention efforts have not curbed enthusiasm for reform, with advocates seeking lessons that might improve the next generation of next generation ideas.[110] The reform process will be incremental, marked by setbacks and learning that might, advocates hope, inform the development of a new, collaborative regulatory regime. Preconditions for significant changes in the basic structure of regulatory policy seem to be in place: new economic pressures on U.S.

firms; demands from businesses, academics, environmentalists, and others for more efficient and effective policies; and increasing interest in new policy tools and new administrative doctrines emphasizing collaboration over command and control.[111]

Despite decades of criticism and rising pressures for change, though, the basic structures of the green state created in the 1970s to deal with pollution remain firmly in place. As we noted in chapter 1, pollution control is a basic commitment of the American state, embedded in laws, in the institutional structure and organizational commitments of the Environmental Protection Agency, and in public expectations expressed by environmental groups. It is not surprising that the collaborative experiments we have seen thus far have made only limited headway against the "tenacious organization of power" that has grown out of the golden era of environmental legislation. The movement toward collaboration is an effort to reconstruct our basic approaches to pollution regulation, confronting all of the barriers involved in such ambitious projects. [112]

The familiar critiques of command-and-control regulation and the media-specific focus of the Environmental Protection Agency focus on central characteristics of the green state. There are openings for some important changes at the margins, but it will be difficult to address causes of inefficiency built into the very structure of the green state without new laws. The absence of statutory authorization has driven these regulatory reinvention initiatives to the margins; experiments like CSI and Project XL can set the stage for new legislation, just as early reg-negs cleared the way for the Negotiated Rulemaking Act. The political context has changed considerably since 1990, however, and translation of these experiments into statutory changes seems unlikely at best.

The inability of reformers to write these projects into statutes leaves them vulnerable to election results, interfering with the process of institutionalization. Participants in debates over environmental policy are aware that Republican and Democratic administrations will carry different priorities. Firms and environmental groups involved in negotiations over regulation may look beyond the discussions at hand in hopes that the voters will deliver them a friendlier Environmental Protection Agency and a friendlier White House next time around. Why accept a deal now when the EPA might be amenable to one that you would like much better a year or two hence? Can we trust the EPA to hold to this commitment, given that it may soon have different political masters? Beyond this, political instability will slow the process of cultural change at the EPA. It will be difficult to keep up the pressures necessary to move the agency to embrace more flexible, collaborative processes to the extent that the commitment to collaboration (and different types of collaboration) depends on which party controls the White House.

Institutionalizing flexibility will be extraordinarily difficult in any case. In an early assessment of the Clinton reinvention project, Donald Kettl observed that the effort lacked an integrating force, any "glue" that might organize dozens of projects and hundreds of decisions being made across the government into a force for lasting change. Too many "large mandates supported by mushy thinking . . . fueled the sense of adhocracy . . . a sense . . . only increased by the frenzy of accompanying reform."[113] How will policymakers translate "a sense of adhocracy" into a coherent reform program? How will they balance a widely asserted interest in flexibility and reasonableness in regulation with the demands of the golden era environmental laws?

Advocates of next generation environmental policymaking note that their agenda rests on a "firm foundation," a strong public consensus favoring pollution control and the conservation of public lands. This is an important point, yet this public consensus is a weak reed upon which to rest ambitions to "reconfigure and reinvigorate the environmental policy debate in America."[114] This classic "permissive consensus" in public opinion predicts little about environmental politics or policy except that few politicians will risk proclaiming they are anti-green, and although it blocked radical reforms in 1995 and 1996 it has not prevented an increase in partisanship on environmental issues. The commitment to collaboration, if it is to transform the green state, will almost surely have to drive changes in statutes. Further, it will have to confront old questions about appropriate relationships between public authority and private interests in policymaking. Reformers in the 1960s and the 1970s understood the pathologies of "interest-group liberalism" and attacked the "cozy triangles" that marked much of regulatory politics. They advanced a new vision of the way that the boundaries of public authority should be marked and defended. Modern critics of command-and-control, top-down environmental regulation have offered persuasive arguments about the inefficiencies of the green state and the pathologies of command-and-control regulation. Advocates of collaborative approaches confront the challenge of establishing grounds—perhaps statutory grounds—for the legitimacy of their vision of a more flexible, negotiated green state.

Collaborative Conservation: Seeking Common Ground on Management of Public Lands

In the wake of intensifying conflict over public lands management in the West—on issues ranging from grazing to logging to recreation to water to wildlife—there has been a growth of collaborative conservation initiatives throughout the region. Collaborative conservation involves efforts to bring opposing stakeholders together to work towards win-win policy outcomes. These efforts typically center on bringing together commodity interests and environmental groups, though recreation interests often play an important role. Government officials play an ambiguous role in these collaborative efforts. They usually have a seat at the table, but need to be careful due to their roles as enforcers of laws as well as having to be cognizant of federal laws dealing with advisory boards. Nongovernmental stakeholders are often seeking to influence the government officials—in terms of timber harvests, grazing, wilderness designation, and the like. These efforts seek to integrate economic and environmental goals, and in most cases primarily involve local participants. That is, the stakeholders are mainly those who live and work in the area rather than national environmental groups or corporate executives from headquarters. These approaches have generated widespread scholarly, media, political, and foundation interest. Given the often informal and ephemeral nature of these collaborations, no one knows for sure how many groups exist; estimates range from the hundreds to the thousands.

Supporters of collaborative conservation claim that it will not only improve environmental policymaking but also help to revitalize democracy and community in these rural areas by involving local citizens in real governance. They argue for the benefits of decentralization, consensus, and active citizen participation. Critics, including many national environmental groups, have focused on problems of accountability, authority, expertise, and agency capture. These skeptics argue that the integrity of national political authority is at stake. Congress has passed a set of environmental laws that dictate how federal lands must be managed, and allowing local groups—no matter how well intentioned—to have a special role in interpreting these laws and managing these lands is a dangerous precedent.[115]

Most research on collaborative conservation has focused on cases of collaboration centered on public lands issues in the West. Ronald Brunner and co-authors argued that community-based initiatives represent an innovative way to advance the common interest. This new path is a response to the increasing gridlock and citizen disconnect in natural resources policy, a way around a system where "participants of all kinds are trapped to a considerable extent in a complex structure of governance that institutionalizes conflict more than it facilitates the integration or balancing of different interests into consensus on policies that advance the common interest." Brunner et al. then examined the state of collaborative conservation by studying four cases—water management and the Upper Clark Fork Steering Committee in Montana, wolf recovery in the northern Rockies, bison management in the greater Yellowstone ecosystem, and timber management in the Sierra Nevada through the Quincy Library Group. The Upper Clark Fork case represented the clearest success for collaborative conservation; wolf and bison management could not, in any sense, be described as successes for collaborative conservation. The Quincy Library Group, which has received more attention than any other case of collaborative conservation, will be discussed further below.[116]

Another significant recent work on collaborative conservation is by Edward Weber, who argued that grassroots ecosystems management (GREM) is an exciting institutional innovation because "In search of better governance *and* enhanced accountability to a broader array of interests, coalitions of the unalike are creating and choosing alternative institutions for governing public lands and natural resources." Based on case studies of the Applegate Partnership in Oregon, the Henry's Fork Watershed Council in Idaho, and the Willapa Alliance in Washington, Weber found positive results in areas such as habitat protection, invasive species control, timber harvests, and stream flows, and noted that the groups exhibited a complex and holistic accountability. Why did these groups form? According to Weber, "participants in GREM criticize government as inaccessible, biased, inefficient, and ineffective. The perception is that existing participation processes are not fair because they are dominated by organized interests and tend to place too much emphasis on science and expertise and not enough on social/community impacts and needs." In response, "a number of citizens in the Applegate, Henry's Fork, and Willapa areas accepted the challenge offered by reconciliation and the idea that if they could just get the institutions right, they would be better able to discover the common ground necessary for building and sustaining a new community." Yet since Weber completed his research two of his case study groups have collapsed—the Willapa Alliance disbanded in 2000 after eight years because support from foundations had dried up, and the Applegate Partnership suspended its meetings two years later because some participants failed to follow group norms, which made it difficult to reach consensus.[117]

There is no doubt that collaborative conservation is part of a new next generation pathway based on negotiation and consensus, but how significant will it become? Does it represent the future of environmental politics as its most optimistic boosters claim? What of the numerous failures and the limited successes thus far? We turn now to an examination of two collaborative conservation initiatives. In the first of these initiatives, the Quincy Library Group focused on achieving a particular policy outcome; in the second, the Quivira Coalition focused on altering the process of grazing policy and management on public and private lands. After examining these two initiatives, we will return to offer our analysis of the collaborative conservation pathway more generally.

The Quincy Library Group: New Governance in the Old Labyrinth
Plumas County Supervisor Bill Coates, local environmentalist Michael Jackson, and Tom Nelson of the timber company Sierra Pacific founded the Quincy Library Group in December 1992. These individuals began meeting at the town library in Quincy, California to see if they could find any common ground regarding the management of regional national forests, policy that was currently frustrating environmentalists and the timber industry alike. The local environmental group Friends of the

Plumas was frustrated with the Forest Service's Plumas National Forest plan adopted in the late 1980s. The group, with allies among the national environmental groups, unsuccessfully appealed the plan on water and wildlife grounds. Local timber interests were upset because timber sales from Northern California's national forests were declining, from 205 million board feet in 1987 to 120 million feet in 1991, as a result of environmentalists' appeals and lawsuits. To the north, the northern spotted owl was disrupting timber harvests. The possibility of an Endangered Species Act listing for a related subspecies, the California spotted owl, cast a shadow over the northern Sierra Nevada. Coates, Jackson, and Nelson sought a way out of this mess. The QLG developed a Community Stability Proposal for the management of the Lassen National Forest, the Plumas National Forest, and portions of the Tahoe National Forest in summer 1993. The plan proposed some timber harvesting, with a focus on fire and fuel reduction and watershed restoration intended to enhance fisheries and watershed health generally. Loggers would avoid roadless areas, riparian areas, and scenic river corridors.[118]

To the surprise of the QLG, the U.S. Forest Service declined to accept the proposal. The local forest supervisor and the regional forester were uncomfortable with the lack of expert participation in developing the proposal, also noting a need to work in the framework of existing procedural laws. The QLG took its case to Washington, gaining a meeting with Forest Service Chief Jack Ward Thomas and Assistant Secretary of Agriculture Jim Lyons. Lyons and the Clinton administration generally embraced the QLG's proposal and instructed the Forest Service to implement the plan. However, the local Forest Service officials did not embrace the proposal. A version of the proposal was included as an alternative in the environmental impact statement in the California Spotted Owl report, but this process was sidetracked when the agency decided to undertake the Sierra Nevada Conservation Framework. By 1996, the QLG had had enough of the agency's bureaucratic recalcitrance.[119]

The QLG then went to Congress. Representative Wally Herger (R-California) shepherded a bill directing the Forest Service to implement the Community Stability Proposal as a pilot project through the House of Representatives, where it was passed 429–1 in July 1997. National environmental groups, however, opposed the bill; they claimed it violated existing procedures and they disagreed with its logging provisions. This lobbying stalled the bill in the Senate, where it remained for months. Even California's senators were caught up in the morass, Dianne Feinstein (D) supporting the bill and Barbara Boxer (D) opposing it. The bill was eventually passed in the Senate as a rider to an omnibus appropriations bill in October 1998. Despite passage of the Herger-Feinstein Quincy Library Group Forestry Recovery Act, the QLG proposal became enmeshed in further policy problems. By the time the Forest Service completed the final Environmental Impact Statement related to the Quincy plan, the Forest Service had to scale back timber cutting to reduce fire risk because of provisions in the Sierra Nevada Conservation Framework, which covered eleven national forests in the mountain range. The QLG (and other groups) appealed the Forest Service's decision, since by reducing the allowable amount of timber cutting it struck at the heart of the collaborative proposal. The Forest Service rejected all appeals, and it began to implement this variant of the Community Stability Proposal in the spring of 2000, nearly seven years after the QLG developed it. Administrative changes continued, however. The Forest Service finalized the Sierra Nevada Framework in early 2001, further limiting harvesting. QLG members' patience was nearly exhausted. Working with the Forest Service was a "process with no end and no results," according to Bill Coates. In March 2003, after the Bush administration made additional changes to the Sierra plan, the QLG filed a lawsuit against the Forest Service for failure to implement the 1998 congressional act— not enough timber would be harvested, and some of the proposed cutting would occur in roadless areas and would require new roads. The Forest Service responded by stating that it would implement the QLG proposal, after which environmental groups filed a counter-suit.[120]

Although the QLG might represent successful collaborative conservation in developing the Community Stability Proposal, once it entered the labyrinth of the green state it met with frustration, and the process as a whole has hardly been collaborative. Its first barrier was the multi-tiered Forest Service bureaucracy. The QLG failed at the local and regional levels and seemed to achieve success at the national level, gaining the support of the Assistant Secretary of Agriculture. Nevertheless, with Forest Service Chief Thomas opposed to the QLG proposal as well, the agency could prevent implementation of the group's plan by forcing it to conform to a multitude of existing laws (most significantly the ESA and the National Environmental Policy Act), the regional Sierra Nevada initiative, and funding shortfalls—all in the face of a congressional statute. On the legislative track, although its proposal sailed through the House of Representatives, it quickly ran into congressional gridlock on environmental politics in the Senate, from which it could only escape through the stealth technique of appropriations politics. Finally, facing determined resistance from the Forest Service in the Clinton and Bush administrations, the QLG felt it had no alternative but to turn to the courts. Once there, a number of mainstream environmental groups joined it in challenging the Forest Service plan from a different perspective. So what began as a new way to make policy, finding common ground among environmentalists and timber interests, wound its way through the green state labyrinth for several years before emerging at a familiar place in environmental policy—the courts. As this case demonstrates, it is difficult to escape the green state to achieve policy goals, even when many parties agree that it is desirable. We now turn to another type of collaborative conservation, one focused more on process than policy development.[121]

The Quivira Coalition: The "Radical Center"?

The management of grazing on the public lands was of little concern to environmental groups until the 1970s. Since then, this has become one of the most contentious issues in the environmental arena. A number of environmental groups have called for an end to grazing on public lands. Some groups have focused on using existing laws (such as the Endangered Species Act) and the courts to reduce livestock on public lands. More recently, environmentalists have proposed a voluntary program where the federal government would buy ranchers' grazing permits and permanently retire grazing allotments. Legislation to create such a program was introduced in the House of Representatives in 2003. Ranchers, facing declining economic returns, development pressures in many locations, and environmental opposition, have responded strongly—the "wise use" movement and the "county supremacy" movement, for example. They have also relied on powerful political connections in western states. Several ranchers have refused to recognize federal authority over public lands, resulting in long-running criminal cases in Arizona, Nevada, and New Mexico. In response to the increased polarization and the high level of conflict, groups throughout the West have sought to address these grazing issues through collaborative conservation.[122]

Ranchers and conservationists in a number of locales have sought to come together in a middle ground, or what has come to be called the "radical center."

Ranchers feared for their future. As they battled environmentalists and the bureaucracy on a number of fronts, several ranchers sought another way. Some environmentalists sought another approach. Though they often succeeded in court, these environmentalists were not pleased with the quality of watersheds even after the removal of cattle. They sought restoration, not just removal, and they wanted to enlist ranchers to help with this restoration. Furthermore, many environmentalists were concerned that rural residential subdivisions were a far greater threat to the landscape than ranching, and under the motto "cows not condos" they sought ways to connect with ranchers. In this context, the rancher Jim Winder and the conservationists Barbara Johnson and Courtney White founded the Quivira Coalition in 1997 to focus on this radical center, primarily in New Mexico but also in Arizona. The Quivira Coalition's original mission statement read:

The purpose of the Quivira Coalition is to teach ranchers, environmentalists, public land managers, and other members of the public that ecologically healthy rangeland and economically robust ranches can be compatible. Our mission is to define the core issues of the grazing conflict and to articulate a new position based on common interests and common sense. We call this new position the New Ranch. It addresses the ecological and economic needs not only of ranchers and environmentalists, but also of the nation as a whole. In a regular newsletter, in lectures, workshops, site tours, and in research, the Quivira Coalition will facilitate the definition and application of the New Ranch.[123]

Winder sought collaboration and new ideas in the face of increasing economic and legal challenges to his ranching business. White, the executive director of the Quivira Coalition, offered an environmentalist's perspective on the attractiveness of the radical center. Tired of the political and legal approach to environmentalism, which in his view was accomplishing little to improve land health, he hoped to work with ranchers to improve soil, water, and grass quality ("land health"). Central to improving land health are returning certain natural forces (such as fire) to the land, recognizing grazing as a natural form of ecological disturbance, and active and widespread monitoring. "The principal chore ahead is restoration," wrote White. Ranchers could help to achieve this in a way that lawsuits could not.[124]

William de Buys, a member of the Quivira Coalition, described the radical center as "collaborative and interest-based." "When we are smart enough to separate our interests from our political positions," he wrote, "we can do some really good work. Then we can have the flexibility to experiment, to innovate, to make mid-course corrections, to take on partners we never thought we'd be working with, and so on." De Buys put forth these four principal characteristics of the radical center: "It involves a departure from business as usual; it is not bigoted . . . ; [it] involves a commitment to using a diversity of tools . . . ; [and it] is experimental." In early 2003, under the auspices of the Quivira Coalition, 20 environmentalists, ranchers, and scientists wrote and signed an "Invitation to Join the Radical Center" in an effort to move the debate about grazing away from lawsuits and political polarity toward a middle ground. This invitation, addressed to anyone interested, was a way to get the Quivira Coalition's message to a larger audience, especially of ranchers and environmental group members who might not be getting an accurate picture of the debate about grazing from the groups to which they belonged.[125]

The Quivira Coalition does not file lawsuits or lobby for new legislation; rather, it advocates for new ranching methods, for restoration, and for land health through education, outreach, and demonstration projects. Among the techniques the group uses are outdoor classrooms, workshops, newsletters, site tours, and books. It has also established a third-party monitoring and assessment arm under the name Cibola Services. The Quivira Coalition has focused its attention on restoration and management of riparian areas, on herding, on holistic management, on grass banking, on the monitoring of rangelands, on defining and marketing conservation values, and on biodiversity management. Ranchers who have worked with the Quivira Coalition are almost universally enthusiastic about the group. The greatest outputs from its numerous activities are sharing knowledge, building trust, and, in a number of locations, improving land health.[126]

That the Quivira Coalition decided to avoid lawsuits and lobbying is important. This collaboration of environmentalists and ranchers is based on a growing but still fragile sense of trust. Many differences of opinion remain on issues ranging from endangered species to water management. Having to determine a particular policy position could severely strain this collaboration. As for lawsuits, the effort to find common ground was launched, in many ways, in response to the many lawsuits over grazing on public lands throughout the West.

Although the Quivira Coalition has had tremendous influence in New Mexico and beyond, garnering the support of many environmentalists, ranchers, and state and national officials, many other ranchers and environmentalists have opted not to move to the radical center. Eric Ness, spokesperson for the New Mexico Farm and Livestock Association, suggested that the Quivira Coalition was a fine group, but an unnecessary one. "To imply that they're doing a somehow better job than the regular old day-to-day rancher," he said, "I don't think that's right. We've been ranching here for 400 years with no problems." John Horning, executive director of the New Mexico environmental group Forest Guardians, was critical of the Coalition for different reasons: "I think the people at the Quivira Coalition are driven by a cultural imperative to protect and revitalize ranching and the ranching culture. . . . I think they have huge blind spots to the impacts of ranching in the Southwest." Robin Silver of the Center for Biological Diversity is blunter: "The best thing that could happen to the ranchers (in the West) would be that we just shut them all down."[127]

The voices of Ness, Horning, and Silver, especially the latter two, illuminate the greatest challenge that the Quivira Coalition and other collaborative conservation groups face. Ranchers such as Ness simply may not participate in the new ranching without some coercion. Over time, however, the Quivira Coalition thinks that Ness and others like him will move in its direction because it is in their self-interest. This may very well be true; many ranchers around the West are adopting more progressive and sustainable techniques for economic and stewardship reasons. The problem presented by recalcitrant environmentalists is another matter. Dan Dagget, a former Quivira Coalition board member, made exactly this point while describing his frustration when ranchers were trying to have a new, more progressive grazing plan approved for their Forest Service allotment in Arizona: "Finally, with everyone at the end of their patience, one of the Forest Service people said 'You don't seem to get it. Our decision will be made on the basis of process and process only. Results are irrelevant to what we're doing here. Our decisions are based on process because that's what we get sued on.'" For all the progress the Quivira Coalition has made in building trust and in helping ranchers and other landowners improve their management, the green state and its "process" remains. As long as it does, groups such as the Center for Biological Diversity will try to use it to achieve their goals.[128]

Can the Radical Center Hold? Collaboration, Public Lands, and the Green State

Clearly, when we can make policy in an inclusive, collaborative way that leads to win-win outcomes, we should follow this path. Collaborative conservation has achieved results such as stream restoration and habitat improvement, and it has done this in ways that builds trust within communities. The organic growth of such initiatives across the country demonstrates that they are likely here to stay; some communities and interests will venture down this pathway as far as they can. Even the George W. Bush administration has hopped on the collaboration bandwagon, with the president issuing an executive order charging federal agencies to facilitate cooperative conservation. Yet the likelihood that collaborative conservation will become a major new pathway, or (as some optimistic boosters of the "next generation" approach maintain) the new way of making conservation and natural resources policy, is another matter. So far, the successes of groups such as the Quivira Coalition seem to be as far as collaborative conservation can go. The experience of the QLG is perhaps more indicative of what happens when collaborative efforts engage larger policy issues. The QLG is seeking significant policy change, and consensus is highly unlikely in an arena as diverse as public lands policy. Groups outside the collaborative process will turn to alternative pathways to block policy changes they oppose. The outlines of the QLC story are likely to be repeated across the western landscape. By seeking voluntary change from willing partners, the Quivira Coalition presents a less threatening but also a less directly significant policy pathway.[129]

There are a variety of limitations and problems with the collaborative conservation pathway. Much of the criticism thus far has focused on questions of accountability and legitimacy: How are people to collaborate selected? In what sense are they representative of the larger citizenry? What of the rule of law? Collaborative conservation faces three other major challenges. First, can collaboration overcome fundamental value differences? For example, can it work when some parties are opposed to reintroduction of the grizzly bear under any circumstances and other parties have that as their primary goal? Second, can the economic sustainability goals of collaborative conservation—even when agreed upon and implemented—be successful in the rapidly expanding global marketplace? That is, will western agriculture and timber production be economically competitive against beef from Argentina and timber from Chile, even with local support? As land and water values rise, will rural landowners and communities be able to respond financially? Third, and perhaps most important, can collaborative conservation negotiate a path through the labyrinth of the green state—the laws and institutions created over the last 100 years?[130]

Most advocates of collaborative conservation recognize the constraints of the green state. Indeed, in their eyes this green state and congressional gridlock necessitated the innovative approach of collaborative conservation. "By the mid 1980s," Donald Snow observed, "most actors in the nation's and the West's environmental debates came to realize that regardless of their political positions or the constituencies they represented, positive advancement of agendas had become stalled."[131] Collaborative conservation, they argued, is a way to get around the many laws, regulations, agencies, and national groups that block on-the-ground progress. But supporters come in many stripes. Some argue that collaborative conservation is a new way of making policy—one that is part of "a transformation that rivals the movement's shift from protest politics in the 1960s to its institutionalization in American politics in the 1970s and 1980s." Others make far more modest claims, such as this: "The future of public lands management is likely to be much more mundane—it will continue to be characterized by incremental modifications to existing, national policy regimes, but hopefully with a flexibility and creativity that can only come from experimentation on the periphery—from local partnerships."[132] Supporters of collaborative conservation recognize that the green state helped to create the conditions leading to its rise; laws such as the Endangered Species Act and the National Forest Management Act have given environmental groups leverage to force commodity interests to discuss altering their ways of doing business.

Yet for collaborative conservation to succeed broadly, for it to become central to a next generation of environmental policy, these very components of the green state must be bypassed. But how can space and authority for real collaboration be created in the face of the existing, often conflicting, institutional and legal commitments? Jack Ward Thomas, chief of the Forest Service in the mid 1990s, commented: "The combination of laws passed from 1870 to now is a sort of blob. It doesn't work, and we try to go around it to get things done." But Thomas also made use of that blob to block implementation of the QLG plan, despite a law and support for the plan from his superiors in Washington. Kent Connaughton, supervisor of the Lassen National Forest during part of the QLG debate, was not quite so blunt, but he acknowledged the difficulty of navigating through the green state—for the QLG as well as his own agency: "a welter of laws, regulations, court decisions, and microbudgeting from Congress that hinder a forest from moving decisively in any one direction." Another example comes from the Applegate Partnership. One of the first collaborations, a jointly planned timber sale called Partnership One, failed because "the ranger district wrote a sloppy environmental assessment and regional environmentalists successfully appealed the sale." Collaborative conservation gets lost in the labyrinth yet again.[133]

Given the gridlock in Congress that protects the fundamental components of the status quo, it appears unlikely that collaborative conservation can achieve the significant goals its supporters hold out for it. As successful as a local collaboration may be, it still must deal with existing agencies, regulations, laws, and interests. There is nothing to stop the Center for Biological Diversity from filing a lawsuit under the Endangered Species Act that unravels a carefully constructed proposal, or from stopping timber interests from suing an agency for violation of the Federal Advisory Committee Act. We see collaborative conservation, then, as a new pathway for conservation and environmental policy. But we do not think it will become the central component of a next generation of environmental policymaking as long as the existing institutional, legal, and regulatory environmental order—the green state—is still in place. Just getting the institutions right may not sound too difficult, but changing the web of environmental laws, regulations, and institutions created over 100 years for a variety of aims is a gargantuan enterprise. Creating space for the successful proliferation of these groups would require nothing less than re-creating the green state.

Conclusion

In this chapter we have described movements toward collaboration in environmental policymaking in three areas: endangered species, pollution regulation, and conservation and natural resources management. Each of these three movements emerged out of concerns about excessive conflict and policy problems specific to each issue area. Landowners' outrage at the Endangered Species Act, threats to the law in Congress, and a growing recognition of the importance of gaining landowners' cooperation in species protection motivated the expansion of habitat conservation planning. Proponents hoped that the Endangered Species Act could be saved from its critics and that its effectiveness could be improved through cooperative-conservation planning around private lands. Concerns about delay and inefficiency in rulemaking, and the inefficiency of rules themselves, led Congress to embrace negotiated regulation, and then to administrative "reinvention" experiments involving private interests deeply in the process. Advocates hoped that these approaches would bring more pragmatism to the process and help to build a common sense of purpose that would overcome the confrontational politics so often seen in regulatory policymaking. On public lands, intense conflict over emerging, greener management priorities generated enthusiasm for collaborative conservation projects involving locals in shaping those priorities. Proponents hoped that collaborative conservation could end the wars in the woods and on the range, producing mutually beneficial management strategies reflecting both economic realities and good stewardship.

Each of these movements dealt with a crucial issue in the basic architecture of environmental policy, the problem of balancing public authority and private interests, by striking new balances in favor of greater stake-holder participation. The laws of the 1960s and the 1970s were designed, in part, to avoid the pathologies of agency capture and interest-group lib-eralism by imposing action-forcing requirements on bureaucracies and providing for citizen lawsuits to monitor agencies' compliance with the laws. In all three of these areas the embrace of collaboration aimed to alle-viate conflicts endemic to "top-down" decisionmaking and to draw stake-holders together with agency officials for a range of purposes: to open space for discussion about priorities, to avoid "regulatory unreasonable-ness," to use local knowledge and businesses' understandings of their own production processes in crafting public policy, and to engage citizens with diverse interests in building a sustainability ethic.[134]

The dream of collaboration has deep roots in American political cul-ture, where the ideological attractions of pluralism and traditional con-cerns about big government join in the interest-group liberal commitment to self-regulation. It also reflects unique features of the environmental pol-icy arena, where, presumably, the public consensus that environmental protection and conservation are important is shared by environmental lobbyists, polluting industries, logging companies, and all the other par-ticipants in stakeholder bargaining. Within that consensus, and limited by that consensus, new approaches to environmental policy might emerge out of pluralistic bargaining.

The goals of collaboration are worthy, and in some cases these experi-ments have made impressive gains. But there remain substantial account-ability challenges, pressing questions about who should participate and how various demands should be weighed by public officials, and concerns about the legality of some pragmatic, flexible solutions to policy problems given statutes that impose clear requirements on agency officials and pri-vate interests. The collaborative project confronts basic problems of strik-ing appropriate balances between public authority and private interests, of ensuring proper representation and weighing competing demands in bargaining, and of maintaining the integrity of law in a regulatory regime committed to flexibility and negotiation. Moreover, it faces these prob-lems in a thick institutional setting in which many of these problems have been addressed before, with past resolutions embedded in laws, rules, and bureaucratic practices. Advocates for collaboration face the problem of reorienting the green state in opposition to central premises of the new social regulation.

In each of these cases Congress did act in some way to open collaborative policymaking pathways, yet in all cases the legislative action was insufficient to break through the labyrinth. A federal district court decision in *Sierra Club v. Babbitt* (1998) showed that habitat conservation plans are vulnerable to legal claims that the scientific bases of the plans are inadequate and that the mitigation efforts anticipated by the plans are insufficient. The court found no rational basis in the administrative record for incidental take permits granted to an Alabama developer to take listed beach mice, finding that the Department of the Interior's assessment that development would have "no significant impact" on mouse populations had no basis in population inventories, population trend data, or information on the minimum size of a viable population. Indeed, the court concluded, while it was "unclear . . . on what basis the findings of no significant impact were made," it was apparent that the finding was *not* made using sound scientific evidence.[135] In view of findings that the science underpinning many of the plans is weak and that there has been little effective monitoring, there is likely to be legal controversy in this area over the next few years. Further, Section 10 of the Endangered Species Act did not suspend requirements that the appropriate federal agencies list species, designate critical habitat, or develop recovery plans. The HCP project is vulnerable to the extent that it displaces rather than supplements actions required by the law.

Negotiated regulation delivered on some of its promises, but studies of its general effectiveness in speeding rulemaking and heading off litigation indicate that it has fallen short of its proponents' hopes. Even the reformulated gasoline rule, touted with good reason as an important success, appeared to be at best a mixed bag not long after the negotiations were completed. Clinton's administrative "reinvention" experiments made little progress, constrained as they were by conflicts over the appropriate levels of participation and influence by various stakeholders and, of course, the absence of statutory mandates that would have clarified for participants what could and could not be negotiated. Finally, the Quincy case demonstrated that however well intentioned, practical, and satisfying to participants, local experiments in collaborative conservation are, for better and worse, deeply embedded in the green state's layers of institutions, rules, and processes. The collaborative conservation movement represents something important and even admirable in the politics of environmental policymaking, but when they reach beyond highlighting the value of collaboration for good stewardship (the Quivira approach) to rewriting forest management plans and policies (the QLG), collaborative conservation-as-policymaking quickly moves onto difficult and uncertain pathways in the congressional appropriation process, the administrative process, and the courts.

Advocates of next generation reforms have looked to these collaborative initiatives as harbingers of change in the green state, to be joined with tools like the use of economic incentives to reconstruct environmental policy. There is evidence that such experiments can serve as the basis for wide-ranging changes in policy and, ultimately, new statutes initiating a new regulatory regime. Yet the record thus far shows that despite the promise of these efforts, the collaborative impulse faces a "tortuous course" through the green state labyrinth, facing the "tenacious organization of power" embedded in the layers of political development and the multiple pathways that have developed.[136] Furthermore, while critics of top-down regulation have developed a powerful critique of traditional approaches to making regulatory policy, and while they have made a strong case that collaboration can yield both procedural and substantive improvements, they have not yet shown how these approaches—adopted on a broad scale—can successfully address core questions of political architecture or public philosophy—how can private interests and public authority be effectively balanced in a bargaining regime?

7

The States and Environmental Policy: Junior Partner, Next Generation Innovator, Passionate Advocate, or All of the Above?

Concerns about the inefficiency and rigidity of golden era environmental laws has pushed policy initiative out to collaborative projects, in the hope that delegating authority will yield less conflict and more pragmatic policy solutions. These same concerns, deepened by congressional gridlock, have driven reformers to look to the states. There, the argument goes, the greater flexibility of state governments can yield policy innovation, opening the way to the next generation of environmental policy.

Advocates of devolution argue that states have a variety of advantages over the federal government as sites for environmental policymaking, and that the states' already important role should be expanded. State governments are closer to the problems; they tend to be more pragmatic problem solvers. States' experiments with different policies allow us to learn what works best for addressing particular problems. Furthermore, the variety of settings for environmental problems across the nation calls for responses tailored to specific areas. (Something that might be necessary in California might not be a high priority in North Dakota.) Those who see the emergence of a "next generation" environmental policy have seen the rising importance of the states as an important part of this development. "National debate about environmental policy remained polarized," wrote Mary Graham, "but around the country issues were being resolved in ways that seemed strikingly pragmatic."[1]

Many environmental groups, frustrated by congressional gridlock and Republican control of the national government, have also looked to the states hoping to find more receptive officials in state capitals. Given California's significance in the national economy, many environmentalists speak of the "California effect," which they hope will lead to the national adoption of these new California policies. Even Europeans are taking notice: "Together, with our American colleagues, we indeed hope that this [California] is a back door to the Bush Administration," said Karla Schoeters of the Climate Action Network Europe.[2] Yet other environmentalists view state leadership warily, fearing that groups seeking to roll back environmental protections may be more influential in Cheyenne or in Little Rock than in Sacramento or in Washington, DC.

We begin this chapter with a brief review of recent efforts to devolve greater policymaking authority to the states, highlighting the progress and limitations of these efforts. The inability of Congress to offer a "safe legal harbor" for many of these projects complicates the construction of a new environmental federalism; intense partisanship on environmental issues has also hindered a steady flow of power to the states.[3] We then move on to three central points about the current role of the states. First, we focus on innovation, offering a summary of trends in state leadership and focusing on climate change and land protection in New York. Regulatory devolution and innovation are exciting parts of the story of state policymaking in the era of gridlock, yet these movements can run up against the constraints of the green state. Second, we show that states, in addition to being sites of innovation and flexibility and pragmatism, are sites of environmental conflicts quite as intense as those at the federal level. Case studies of environmental policymaking at the polls in Montana and Oregon highlight the depth of such conflicts and the tortuous paths that these struggles take. Finally, we show that states, along with being sites for next generation innovation as well as old style environmental conflict, have become important actors in the green state labyrinth in their own right, with state attorneys general using the courts to challenge federal policies and to find ways around congressional gridlock—and with federal policymakers frequently responding by blocking state initiatives. In the final analysis, we find the situation in the states to be more ambiguous and complex than that presented by those who champion new roles for the states. Looking to the states to address problems offers no easy escape from a bitterly contested environmental politics, or from legislative gridlock at the national level.

The States in the Green State

Before the end of the nineteenth century, conservation and environmental policy were handled entirely at the state level. At first these laws dealt with topics like deer hunting, predator bounties, and setting fires to clear forests. The states continued this leadership role into the late 1800s, when the federal government became deeply involved in conservation and natural resources management and the second layer of the federal green state was established. Indeed, action at the state level largely served as a precursor to what would eventually happen at the national level. New Hampshire, for example, is credited with creating the first permanent government agency to deal with conservation—a Fish Commission in 1864. By 1900, this Commission was joined by a Board of Health (which, in each of the states, was the proto-water-pollution-control agency) and a Forestry Commission, each created several years before its federal counterpart. With the exception of the water projects undertaken by the Army Corps of Engineers and the Bureau of Reclamation, the states continued to be the focal point of conservation and natural resources policy except on the federal public lands following the conservation era of 1890–1920.[4]

During the golden era of environmental policy (1964–1980), however, the states surrendered primary control over a host of issues to the federal government. Washington became supreme policymaker for air pollution, water pollution, hazardous wastes, toxic chemicals, and drinking water safety. Even in policy realms where the states retained supremacy, chiefly the management of fish and wildlife, private land, and solid waste, state authority was eroded by the Endangered Species Act, the Coastal Zone Management Act, the Surface Mining Control and Reclamation Act, and the Resource Conservation and Recovery Act.[5]

The states have maintained three major roles since the creation of the third layer of the national green state.[6] First, states remain the focal point for regulating private land, a power that they frequently share with local governments. This power is most generally used through planning and zoning, though a few states have developed statewide land-management programs. Many states also regulate particular types of private land or land-management activities, including farmland protection, forest practices, wetlands, and, working with the federal government, coastal lands.

Many states also own substantial tracts of land that are managed for a variety of purposes, from grazing to wilderness.

Fish and wildlife management is the second main responsibility of the states. Although the Endangered Species Act has infringed on state authority in this area, the states retain primary authority for species not on the federal threatened or endangered lists. Most states also have endangered species programs of their own (45 as of 1998), as well as sophisticated biodiversity inventories and, increasingly, programs for the management of non-game species (often administered in conjunction with the Nature Conservancy). States regulate hunting, manage game habitat, and stock fish. State wildlife management is not immune to controversy, of course, and hunting and predator issues are especially contentious.[7]

The third main responsibility is working with the federal government to implement national pollution control laws. In the case of air pollution, states must devise and enforce implementation plans to meet national standards. Hence, when car owners get their cars tested for emissions, they are dealing with state—not federal—officials. Similarly, any factory that discharges into a river or lake must get a permit from the relevant state agency, not from the Environmental Protection Agency. In the management of solid waste, states retain a great deal of latitude, but the Resource Conservation and Recovery Act establishes guidelines that each state must follow. Over time, the federal government has further decentralized policy implementation. By the late 1990s, Barry Rabe reported that states "collectively issue more than 90 percent of all environmental permits, complete more than 75 percent of all environmental enforcement actions, and rely on the federal government for less than 25 percent of their total funding." Furthermore, states were increasingly taking the initiative in certain environmental policy areas, such as pollution prevention, regulatory integration, and increased use of market incentives as an environmental policy tool.[8]

Much of the political science scholarship on the states and environmental policy has focused on the implementation of the national pollution control regime. Scholars have found significant differences among the states in fulfilling this role, though most states have made progress in building capacities to protect the environment since the 1960s. DeWitt John reported in the mid 1990s that "Virtually all states have taken some steps to go beyond federally imposed requirements, and some have taken the lead in several areas," yet "activism is concentrated in certain states." Many studies have ranked the states' capacities for environmental protection; for example, in 2001 the Resource Renewal Institute found that the top five states were Oregon, New Jersey, Minnesota, Maine, and Washington, and the bottom five states were Alabama, Wyoming, New Mexico, Arkansas, and Oklahoma.[9]

The persistence of variation in state capacities for environmental protection poses a strong challenge to the devolution idea. "What . . . emerges," Rabe's study of states' use of permitting as a regulatory tool concluded, "is a decidedly mixed picture. . . . Further devolution of authority may be a desirable goal and may indeed foster more innovation. But the ultimate architects of any such strategy will need to consider the wide range of state-level capacity for pursuing such steps rather than blithely assume that the mere delegation of authority from federal to state hands will usher in the next generation of environmental policy so widely desired. . . . Many states . . . appear unprepared to step up to the formidable challenges of integration and prevention."[10]

Two additional problems beyond this uneven state performance are continued state reliance on federal policy designs and funding and the complexity of environmental problems that cross state borders. Although state reliance on federal grants has declined in recent years, in the 1990s many states still relied heavily on federal funds for their environmental and natural resources programs—40 to 50 percent in some cases. Furthermore, many of the most innovative programs in the states have been financed through federal grants. One of the main reasons that the federal government became so deeply involved in pollution control policy in the 1970s was that many of the pollutants crossed state boundaries. This basic fact has not changed for many pollutants, such as ozone and water pollution in major rivers.[11]

"No Easy Task": Reconstructing Environmental Federalism

Arguments for the devolution of federal authority to the states have been on the national agenda for decades, and they have been prominent in the environmental arena. Citing familiar concerns with Washington-centered

command-and-control regulation, and adding concerns about the imposition of "unfunded mandates" on the states, devolution advocates argue
that empowering the states would acknowledge the states' growing
capacities and willingness to protect the environment, reduce tensions
between the Environmental Protection Agency and state agencies, and
give states flexibility to pursue priorities defined using cost-effective
means. State policymakers frustrated with inadequate federal funding
and EPA micromanagement, and in some cases feeling their own new
regulatory muscle, have chafed at federal oversight. Administrative reformers have supported them: in 1995 the National Academy for Public
Administration described the federal-state relationship in environmental
policymaking as broken and argued that EPA should give states more
freedom of action, an "accountable devolution" of federal power to the
states.[12]

Under pressure from frustrated state officials and a Republican Congress
seeking to weaken the EPA, and influenced by next generation ideas
about devolution and efficiency, the Clinton administration sought to
restructure the federal-state relationship in environmental policy. The
administration's approach had several pieces, the most significant of
which was the National Environmental Performance Partnership System
(NEPPS), "the most substantial reform in the EPA-state relationship
since those relationships were first established."[13] NEPPS was formalized
in an agreement negotiated between EPA and state officials in 1995.
Under NEPPS, the EPA could develop "performance agreements" with
states. The EPA would agree to evaluate states' implementation of federal pollution laws in terms of their results—environmental improvements,
levels of compliance—and not measures of agency activity. This would
yield a results-oriented policy, with states given some freedom to choose
the means to achieve environmental gains. NEPPS also provided for
"differential oversight": states with excellent results would be granted
greater freedom of action. Further, NEPPS attempted to address some
funding issues in environmental federalism, providing "performance
partnership grants" allowing states to consolidate various categorical
grants and target resources on what they defined as their most pressing
environmental problems. The program was ambitious: its goal was to
"shift from control of separate media (air, water, waste) . . . to overall

planning for the states' environments. By focusing on environmental improvement . . . NEPPS aim[ed] to ensure progress in pursuit of environmental goals, establish partnerships between states and regional EPA offices, and foster the transition to greater state autonomy."[14]

Devolution is an attractive and generally popular idea, and NEPPS was a serious effort. Yet most analyses of the program concluded that it had only mixed results.[15] Participation in the program expanded rapidly beyond the initial pilots, but on the major measures of success—including the development of appropriate measures of environmental results to use to evaluate state performance, and reductions in EPA oversight of state agency activities—there have been few real gains. Clifford Rechtschaffen and David Markell found that "NEPPS has not lived up to its promise"; Denise Scheberle noted that the restructuring of federal-state relations in environmental policymaking has been "no easy task."[16]

The failures of NEPPS flow from problems common to efforts to reinvent the federal-state relationship in environmental policymaking: established laws, rules, and norms hinder reform. Congress could not provide a "safe legal harbor" for these policy experiments; the General Accounting Office reported that EPA officials worried that "environmental statutes or regulations sometimes prescribe the level of oversight required of EPA, leaving little room for EPA to scale it back."[17] State officials cited the rigidity of rules and laws as a major barrier to reform, as well as "cultural resistance" from EPA officials comfortable with old ways of doing business. Yet federal officials had reasons to be squeamish. They found significant shortcomings in some state enforcement programs and saw notable reductions in enforcement actions in some states, and worried that in some hands NEPPS might be a rollback program rather than a productive reform of the environmental protection system. Scheberle rightly noted that the EPA's discomfort with NEPPS "stemmed in part from their discomfort with court suits that challenged perceived failures in procedural compliance. The EPA can be sued, and has been sued, for failure to perform nondiscretionary duties under U.S. pollution control laws."[18]

The record since the 2000 election shows that partisan interests can also divert the downward flow of authority in environmental policymaking. The Bush administration's rhetorical commitment to devolution has been aggressive, but the record has been mixed. Jan Mazurek, a strong advocate of decentralizing next generation reforms, argued that "on the environment, the White House is highly selective—and often blatantly political—in devolving key environmental decisions to the states."[19] It is no surprise that politics interferes with the principle of devolution—Bush had strong reasons early in his administration to block offshore oil drilling near Florida while pushing it in California, for example. But it is important to note that frustration with the inefficiencies of top-down, command-and-control regulation is just one of many strains shaping environmental policymaking. The intense partisan polarization that has marked Washington politics affects the use and the utility of the state pathway.

Paths around Gridlock: The States as Leaders and Innovators

Despite the limitations of the formal reinvention of environmental federalism, since the mid 1980s states have come to be seen as important environmental policy innovators. As gridlock tied up Washington, states increasingly took the lead where they could. Lynx reintroduction in Colorado is one example. The lynx was listed as endangered in Colorado's endangered species program before it made it onto the federal threatened species list in 2000. While battles on endangered species tore across the West, the Colorado Division of Wildlife decided to deal with the lynx proactively. It quietly began a reintroduction program for the lynx in 1999. As of June 2005, more than 100 transplanted lynx were alive in Colorado, with more than 40 kittens born in the 2005 breeding season. Western state legislatures demonstrated further leadership in 2005, passing a series of new conservation and environmental laws. Washington passed a high performance green building law, granted tax incentives for alternative energy, and adopted energy efficiency standards for several types of appliances. Wyoming established a trust fund to preserve wildlife and habitat. And Idaho passed a law tightening regulation of cyanide-leach mining in the state.[20]

DeWitt John examined the states' role as innovators in his 1994 book *Civic Environmentalism*, in which he "explains how states and localities stepped forward in the 1980s, when federal environmental policy was hampered by stagnant budgets and political gridlock." John saw state policymakers attempting to address pressing problems not reached by federal policy, including non-point pollution, restoring and protecting ecosystems, and preventing pollution. They often chose to do so using non-regulatory tools, namely information and incentives, with a more collaborative and pragmatic focus. "Civic environmentalism" clearly fits the next generation vision of environmental policy. As do most advocates of the next generation approach, John acknowledged the importance of the green state: "Civic environmentalism is not a replacement for traditional regulatory policies; it is rather a complement to those policies. . . . [It] is possible because it is sheltered by a forest of environmental laws and nourished by new values and knowledge." John found that the federal government played important roles even in the three cases he studied in depth. In Iowa's efforts to protect groundwater, the key was federal funding; in Florida, a federal lawsuit and federal funding were key to protecting and restoring the Everglades; and in Colorado, federal funds and information were important catalysts moving energy conservation forward.[21]

In this section, we examine two examples of innovative policymaking at the state level, focusing on actions that have been taken in areas where Congress has been unable to act assertively in recent years: climate change and land protection. In these areas states have taken leadership roles; subsequent sections, however, will show that to understand the broader picture of state environmental policymaking in the era of gridlock it is necessary to look beyond devolution and innovation.

Addressing Climate Change in the States

"While climate change policy appears hopelessly deadlocked in Washington," wrote Barry Rabe in his 2004 book *Statehouse and Greenhouse*, "a set of governments that cuts across partisan and regional lines is demonstrating that it is possible to make some significant inroads on this issue, often through creative initiatives tailored to particular state circumstances and opportunities."[22]

The story of climate change policy at the national level in the United States is familiar. Although the United States was one of the first nations to ratify the United Nations Framework Convention on Climate Change (in 1992), deadlock in Washington soon set in. The Clinton administration supported policy action to reduce greenhouse gases, but after it was forced to abandon its 1993 proposal to tax fossil fuels and the Republicans took control of Congress in 1994, legislative movement on climate change ground to a halt. (The most significant anthropogenic greenhouse gases are carbon dioxide, methane, nitrous oxide, and fluorinated gases.) This gridlock was best illustrated by the Senate's 95–0 resolution in July 1997 rejecting the Kyoto Protocol unless it was amended to include mandatory greenhouse gas reductions by developing countries. In 2000, presidential candidate George W. Bush pledged to work for passage of a law to reduce air pollution from power plants, a proposal that included CO_2, but he abandoned this pledge once elected. He soon went even further, withdrawing the United States from the Kyoto Protocol process entirely.[23]

But Washington's failure is not the only story here. In *Statehouse and Greenhouse*, Rabe documented significant policy action on controlling greenhouse gases at the state level. "[Over] the past decade," Rabe wrote in 2004, "approximately one-third of the American states have created multiple policies that show considerable promise of reducing greenhouse gas." Rabe focused on the activities of twelve states, ranging from major success stories to major failures. Since here we want to demonstrate the potential for the state pathway as a way to make environmental policy when Congress is gridlocked, we will focus our discussion on the successes.[24]

Most state-level successes involved the development of renewable portfolio standards (RPSs), which require state utilities to generate a specific amount or percentage of their electricity from renewable sources. As of November 2006, 23 states had RPSs in place. These states were located throughout the country and were as likely to be governed by Republicans as Democrats. One of the pioneers, surprisingly, was Texas—never known as an environmental policy innovator, home of the U.S. oil and gas industry, and producer of such leading foes of greenhouse-gas-reduction policy as George W. Bush and Tom DeLay. Yet in 1999, Bush, then governor of Texas, signed the Restructuring of Electric Utility Industry Acts into law. This law required Texas utilities to generate an additional 2,880 megawatts of electricity (equivalent to approximately

3 percent of the state's generating capacity) through renewable sources by 2009. Although this may not seem like much, Texas leads all states in generating greenhouse gases (in 1999 it generated 75 percent more than runner-up California), and such a reduction would be significant.[25]

As Rabe pointed out, economic rather than environmental concerns drove the Texas policy: "[It] made economic sense to attempt to diversify the state's sources of electricity. . . . Policy proponents . . . were aware of the greenhouse gas ramifications [but] they consciously decided to play them down." Several factors contributed to the adoption of the RPS in Texas. First, the state's electric grid was largely insulated from those of other states, making it more difficult to import or export electricity. By the early 1990s, Texas began importing electricity for the first time, indicating a need to diversify its sources away from its traditional reliance on oil and gas. Second, the federal Energy Policy Act in 1992 required states to develop long term energy strategies and, importantly, to engage the public in this planning process. Texas officials used an innovative deliberative polling process, through which they discovered significant public interest in developing renewable energy sources. This led to the RPS being included in a larger bill endorsed by agency officials, business interests, and environmental groups that would lead to new competition in electricity, protect the stranded costs of utilities, and improve air quality. Texas's fast start in meeting the RPS was due to wind power. The state ranks second only to North Dakota in wind-power potential.[26]

The other states making use of RPSs are clustered in the Southwest, the upper Midwest, and the Northeast, with leading goals of 30 percent in Maine by 2000 (realistic due to the state's reliance on hydroelectric power), 25 percent in New York by 2013, and 20 percent in California by 2017. But RPSs are not the only story. Rabe reported on several other state initiatives to reduce greenhouse gases: California and CO_2 emission standards for motor vehicles; Georgia and vehicle use reduction; Nebraska and carbon sequestration; New Hampshire and multi-pollutant standards for fossil fuel power plants; Oregon and CO_2 reduction tied to new power plants; Wisconsin and mandatory CO_2 reporting; and New Jersey and a multi-sector strategy to meet a Kyoto Protocol-style reduction goal of a 3.5 percent reduction in emissions of greenhouses gases below 1990 levels by 2005. Furthermore, there are regional efforts to reduce emissions of greenhouse gases, most notably the agreement by the New England governors and Eastern Canadian premiers to achieve 1990 emission levels by 2010 and 10 percent below 1990 levels by 2020. California raised the bar even higher in August 2006, adopting legislation requiring a 25 percent reduction in CO_2 emissions by 2020.[27]

How can we explain these successes, given the tremendous difficulties in moving greenhouse-gas-reduction policy at the national level? Rabe focused on the role of policy entrepreneurs in the different states, people who often have more freedom to maneuver and have contacts across more governmental units than at the federal level. These leaders have taken advantage of federal inaction on climate change, or the "policy room" for state action, and have shown that reducing greenhouse gases can further economic development. The federal government supported state action in important ways though, through the Energy Policy Act and the State and Local Climate Change Program, which provided grants and technical assistance to the states in the early 1990s. From our perspective, two key characteristics of the green state help explain this action on the state pathway. First, as Rabe noted, the lack of current or past federal action in this arena makes it open policy terrain. This is not the case for related air pollution issues, where the federal Clean Air Act can constrain state action. Second, focusing on the success of RPSs, electricity regulation has long been a state responsibility, with state public utility commissions usually regulating electric utilities from their inception. Hence, state governments, utilities, businesses, and environmental groups think first of the states when focusing on issues related to electricity generation.[28]

Protecting Land: New York State's Adirondack Park

Six years before the federal government began to establish forest reserves in 1891, the state of New York started to protect its own forest lands. Although the circumstances were different than at the national level—New York was protecting lands that had already been logged and were privately owned, unlike the public domain lands of the West—New York was at the forefront during the conservation era of green state building. Protection for forests in the Adirondack Mountains first came in 1885, when New York established the Adirondack Forest Preserve. Supporters of watershed protection for consumption and transportation, hunters and fishers, and resort and estate owners favored the reserve, all fearing that continued heavy logging would have dire consequences. The 1885 law dictated that all state-owned land in the preserve "shall be forever kept as wild forest lands." At the time the law was passed, the state owned nearly 700,000 acres in the Adirondacks, primarily tax-forfeit lands abandoned after being logged. Seven years later, the Adirondack Forest Preserve was integrated into the Adirondack Park. More significant, in 1894 constitutional convention delegates added the "forever wild" clause to the New York Constitution. Still part of the state constitution, the clause reads: "The lands of the state, now owned or hereafter acquired, constituting the forest preserve, as now fixed by law, shall be forever kept as wild forest lands. They shall not be leased, sold or exchanged, nor shall the timber thereon be sold, removed or destroyed." As the state continued to acquire land over the next 100 years, this clause came to protect approximately 2.5 million acres of land in the Adirondack Park.[29]

Development pressures accelerated in the Adirondacks in the 1960s, and citizens and state policymakers responded. They rejected a proposal to create a 1.7-million-acre national park in the Adirondacks, believing that New Yorkers could do a better job of protecting these lands than the federal government. The state legislature passed the Adirondack Park Agency Act in 1971, mandating the development of master plans for state and private lands in the park and creating the Adirondack Park Agency to implement the private land use plan. The master plan for state-owned lands engendered little controversy since these state lands were already protected as "forever wild" under the state constitution. The private land plan was controversial, but after much wrangling it was approved in 1973. The goal of this private land regulation has been to protect the wilderness character of state lands and to protect private open space in the park. To help achieve this goal, certain types of development anywhere on private land require a permit from the Adirondack Park Agency. At this time, the Adirondack Park was expanded to its present size of 5,821,183 acres, larger than six states.[30]

In the 1980s, development pressures again rose in the Adirondacks and across northern New England, driven in part by the wave of corporate takeovers in the forest products industry and the resulting increase of land for sale. In 1989, in response, New York's governor, Mario Cuomo (D), established the Commission on the Adirondacks in the Twenty-First Century. Among the commission's recommendations were a one-year moratorium on building outside of villages, stricter controls on shoreline development, and further land acquisition by the state. Many residents of the Adirondacks strongly opposed these and other recommendations. Groups such as the Adirondack Fairness Coalition and the Adirondack Solidarity Alliance mobilized against further development restrictions in the park. Despite significant support for the commission's findings within the park, the political controversy blocked legislative action on the recommendations.[31]

In the early 1990s, the political mood in the Adirondacks and in Albany appeared to mirror that of Washington and that of the nation as a whole. Indeed, the Adirondack region was a hotbed for property rights activists, opposed to the Adirondack Park Agency and its regulation of private lands and the purchase of more lands for the forest preserve. Unlike in Washington, however, this deadlock broke during the governorship of George Pataki (R). As Pataki reached the end of his three terms in office, he met his goal of protecting 1 million acres of land in New York, more than 600,000 acres of which are in the Adirondacks. This was a remarkable achievement during a period (1995–2006) in which most land-protection efforts were going nowhere in a gridlocked Congress and in which President Clinton relied, controversially, on executive powers under the Antiquities Act and rulemaking to protect lands.

Pataki, a strong advocate of land protection in the Adirondacks, used substantial political capital to achieve this protection. Three major deals were central to Pataki's success, and all three shared a major reliance on conservation easements rather than land purchases and a partnership with a private conservation group that either supplied funds or purchased the land to hold for eventual state acquisition, often both. (A conservation easement, negotiated on a case-by-case basis, typically allows the seller to retain ownership and to continue logging the land, but the development of resorts, condominiums, or houses could no longer occur on the lands.)

The first major deal was between the state and Champion International. The forest products company was selling all of its land in New York,

Vermont, and New Hampshire. The Conservation Fund bought all of the lands, intending to hold them until they could be sold to various state and federal agencies, as well as to private landowners with conservation easements. In December 1998, Pataki announced that New York was buying 29,000 acres to be added to the Adirondack Park forest preserve, and purchasing conservation easements on 110,000 more acres in the park. The easements would extinguish development rights on the lands and secure public access for recreation. This deal proved to be a win-win arrangement. Since the state pays property tax on its lands in the Adirondack Park, local communities suffered no loss of tax revenue. The forest products community won since the 110,000 acres covered by the easement could stay in forest management. Property rights advocates were quieted, to some degree, since the 110,000 acres remained in private ownership. And environmental groups were delighted with the 29,000-acre acquisition of the ecologically and recreationally most important lands and the end of development potential on 110,000 additional acres. New York paid $24.5 million for the land and easements, funds that came from the 1996 Environmental Quality Bond Act.[32]

The second deal, announced on Earth Day 2004, was even bigger. New York announced plans to purchase conservation easements on more than 255,000 acres of International Paper forest land in the Adirondack Park, and acquire 2,000 additional acres for the forest preserve. This $25 million purchase was the largest land-protection deal in state history (with funding from the state Environmental Protection Fund and the federal Forest Legacy Program). Again the Conservation Fund helped to structure the easements and provided bridge financing. There were a few new twists to the International Paper deal. The easements were called a working forest easement, essentially requiring a certain amount of timber harvesting on the land. This further placated timber-industry interests. Also, the state purchased different types of easements for the land: development rights would be extinguished on all of the land, but full public recreation rights would be acquired on only 84,000 acres, with hiking and snowmobile trail rights—but not hunting rights—acquired on the other 171,000 acres.[33]

In January 2005, Pataki announced yet another conservation deal involving more than 100,000 acres, this one with the Canadian paper company

Domtar Industries. The state would acquire a working forest easement on 84,000 acres of land purchased by the Lyme Timber Company. The Nature Conservancy acquired the remaining 20,000 acres, which it would eventually sell to the state. With the completion of this deal, the third largest land-protection agreement in state history, New York will have increased its protected open space by nearly 20 percent in ten years. "During the last ten years, New York has led the nation in land conservation efforts," Pataki proclaimed. The contrast with the Republican regime a few hundred miles to the south could hardly be clearer. In the period 1995–2005, after completion of this and other pending deals, New York protected 612,000 acres in the Adirondack Park, 536,000 acres via conservation easements and 76,000 acres through purchase. As of October 2005, of the approximately 5.5 million acres of land in the park, the state owned nearly 2.5 million acres and held conservation easements on another 540,000 acres, for a total of 55 percent of the land in the park protected by the state.[34]

New York's success in conserving more than 600,000 acres of land in the Adirondack Park is a testament to the ability of states to engage in creative conservation and environmental policymaking, in sharp contrast to the congressional gridlock on land protection. Several characteristics help explain this success in New York. First, the state had clear responsibility in this policy area. The Adirondack Forest Preserve was established in 1885, at the beginning of the conservation period of green state building. For more than 100 years, land conservation in the Adirondacks was a state responsibility, not a federal one. A second major characteristic was a policy entrepreneur, in this case the governor. A few years into his first term, Pataki began to use his political capital to broker major conservation deals. A moderate Republican in a state dominated by the Democrats, Pataki needed to appeal to environmentalists and moderate suburban voters. Protecting the Adirondacks proved to be one such issue. He risked alienating the largely Republican voters of the Adirondack region, who, together with a vocal property rights movement, were upset over park management and opposed further state land acquisition. Pataki, working with allies in the conservation movement, made widespread use of conservation easements to ameliorate this risk. By purchasing easements on private lands that would for the most part continue to be managed for forest products, Pataki reduced opposition from the forest products industry and its supporters. Although property rights advocates typically opposed even the conservation easement deals, their opposition was ineffective. The innovative use of large-scale easements, the third major characteristic, risked alienating conservation supporters who might have demanded full fee acquisition of the lands. Conservationists, however, noted that since the state already owned 2.5 million acres protected as "forever wild" in the Adirondack Park, the use of easements was an acceptable way to protect the land from development. The fourth and final major factor in New York's success in land conservation was a ready source of funds. New York created the Environmental Protection Fund in 1993 to provide a source of cash for state and local protection of conservation and historic lands through purchase of the land or protective easements. The fund is financed primarily by real estate transfer fees, and it allocated $40 million for land protection in 2005. In summary, the state of New York undertook a tremendously successful program in land conservation during a period of congressional gridlock on conservation and the environment. The land protection in the Adirondacks is a model of a state-driven next generation approach to conservation.[35]

The two cases considered in this section barely scratch the surface of innovative environmental policy at the state level, but they do illustrate what can be accomplished in the states. The efforts to reduce greenhouse gases and New York's land conservation in the Adirondacks share two central characteristics. First, state leadership came in areas that were traditionally state responsibilities—electric utility regulation and land protection in one of the nation's oldest parks. And second, the states' approaches to the policies reduced significant opposition. Rather than framing the Texas renewable portfolio standard as a way to reduce emissions of greenhouse gases, the RPS was presented as an opportunity for economic development. Environmental advocates still got greenhouse gas reductions out of the policy, but the opposition of business interests was lessened by this alternative framing. In the Adirondacks, opposition by property rights advocates and timber interests to further state land acquisition was circumvented through the use of conservation easements. Another significant point in the greenhouse-gas-reduction case was that the states were working in open policy terrain. Since the federal government has essentially no policy on greenhouse gases, the states had substantial freedom to create new policy. It is this combination of characteristics, some based in the institutions and history of the green state and some in the particular constellation of interests on an issue, that serves as the best indicator of when the states have the potential to be the site of innovative environmental policy.

Environmental Policymaking at the Polls: States as Sites of Bitter Environmental Conflicts

Across the United States, state and local ballot measures have become more important policymaking tools, and this trend has shaped environmental policymaking.[36] Deborah Guber found more than 370 state-level ballot measures on environmental questions between 1964 and 2000, with an erratic upward trend.[37] The Defenders of Wildlife found thirteen environmental policy issues on ballots in ten states in November 2004; the Trust for Public Land reported 217 conservation measures across the country the same year, including county-level and local questions, and that these measures generated $4 billion in new conservation funding.[38]

Many crucial, highly contentions issues have been addressed at the polls, including suburban sprawl and growth management, logging on state and private land, brownfields redevelopment, property rights, product labeling for genetically engineered foods and toxics, water quality, nuclear waste disposal, and wildlife management. One major proposal, California's failed 1990 "Big Green" initiative, would have imposed stricter standards than federal laws in many areas, including emissions of greenhouse gases, the manufacture of chlorofluorocarbons, pesticide and herbicide use, oil drilling, and timber harvesting.[39] Many factors have driven environmental policymaking onto this pathway. For some issues, including greenhouse gases, federal gridlock has led activists and policymakers in the states to try to advance their agendas without congressional action. Other issues, including sprawl and land protection, have been mainly state and local concerns. In some cases, the failure of state legislatures to act, or to satisfy important constituencies, has led advocates to take their concerns to the voters. Like the federal government, state governments have been challenged by deep conflict on environmental policy questions, and some of these highly contentious questions have been presented to voters at the polls.

Commentary on the exploding use of ballot measures has concentrated on the quality of campaigns and the extent to which special interests have taken over the initiative process, the capacity of voters to make sound choices, the quality of the policies that emerge from ballot initiatives and referenda, and the consistency of direct democracy with the republican commitments of the framers of the Constitution.[40] The focus here is narrower, on the ways that states become sites for intense environmental conflicts, and whether the importance of this pathway in environmental policymaking is consistent with the next generation notion that state-level environmental policymaking will bring more pragmatism and a more effective balancing of interests. It appears that environmental policymaking at the polls often represents just another source of instability and unpredictability, rooted in the deep contentiousness of these issues and the availability of numerous points of access to the policymaking process—from the ballot box to the courts and legislatures, and back to the polls again.

It is impossible to represent this broad movement with a few case studies, but the following two cases illustrate both the kinds of deep conflicts states confront and the nature of direct democracy at work in conservation and environmental policymaking. This section presents overviews of two issues, one a victory for environmentalists in Montana banning cyanide-leach gold mining in the state, and the other the success of property rights activists in attacking Oregon's system of land use planning.

Banning Cyanide Heap-Leach Mining in Montana

Cyanide "heap-leach" mining is used to extract trace amounts of gold that cannot be mined profitably using standard technologies. Ore is excavated from huge open pits and dumped into heaps that are flattened by bulldozers. A cyanide solution is then sprayed on the heaps, leaching out the gold, which runs into rubber-lined reservoirs for processing. The technique, developed in the 1980s, involves massive excavations, producing perhaps an ounce of gold from 200 tons of ore. Cyanide leaching enables mining firms to reopen abandoned mines, expand existing mines, and extract gold where they could not have done so profitably without this process.[41]

Cyanide is dangerous, and leach-mining accidents have contaminated ground and surface water. A cyanide spill from Colorado's Summitville Mine in 1992 killed all life on a 17-mile stretch of the Alamosa River. An accident at a Romanian mine in 2000 introduced cyanide and other metals into the Tisza River, with the effects reaching 250 miles downstream and into the Danube. Major incidents like these, coupled with documentation of many smaller accidents in the United States and abroad, raised concerns about the practice.[42] These problems have been exacerbated by the open-pit excavations, which expose tons of sulfur-laden rock to air and water, creating sulfuric acid runoff. These concerns came to a head in Montana, which in 1998 banned cyanide-leach mining when voters passed Initiative 137. Six years later voters faced this issue again and rejected a measure sponsored by mining interests that would have revived cyanide-leach mining. Mining interests framed these votes as referenda on mining's future in Montana, but in 1998 and 2004 voters supported a focused ban on cyanide-leach mining.[43]

Initiative 137 was introduced by a Helena-based environmental group, the Montana Environmental Information Center. The MEIC emphasized the difficulty of using the dangerous chemical safely, documenting many accidents at Montana mines. The MEIC also highlighted two other issues. First, mining companies facing high cleanup costs often declared bankruptcy, leaving taxpayers to pay. In 1982, for instance, a 52,000-gallon spill of cyanide solution at the Zortman-Landusky mine poisoned the town of Zortman's water supply. A mine employee discovered the accident when he noticed the almond smell of cyanide in tap water at his home. The state, several tribes, and the Environmental Protection Agency sued the mine operator, Pegasus Gold Corporation, which agreed to pay for water treatment, studies of water quality, and monitoring. In 1998, however, Pegasus declared bankruptcy, forfeiting its $30 million cleanup bond and leaving the state with $33 million in additional costs and the need to operate water treatment facilities indefinitely.[44] Second, the MEIC argued that when mines contaminate water they infringe upon neighbors' property and water rights. For example, when the Golden Sunlight Mine (near Whitehall) poisoned local water sources, downstream landowners had to sell their property to the mining company. Runoff from the C. R. Kendall mine polluted streams that local ranchers depended on for water, and the ranchers found that cleanup work sharply reduced the amount of water available to them.[45] Water and property rights are taken seriously on the western range, and the MEIC showed that cyanide-leach mining threatened those rights.

Initiative 137 aimed to block permits for any new cyanide-leach mining in Montana, but its main target was the Seven-Up Pete Joint Venture's planned project near Lincoln, close to the Blackfoot River. Canyon Resources applied for a state mining permit in 1994, and claimed to have spent $70 million on project development. It expected a major boon, projecting $1.5 billion in revenues from the operation.[46] Mining interests asserted that with modern technologies the risks of cyanide-leach mining could easily be managed. The concentrations of cyanide in the leaching solution are low, and Canyon Resources spokesman Bill Snoddy asserted that cyanide is "a great chemical. It's unstable; it breaks down quickly." There were no recorded human fatalities in Montana from cyanide-leach mining, but the miners feared that the public would overestimate the risks. Snoddy warned: "The public does not understand mining. It's a very technical issue."[47]

Unsure that it could convince citizens that cyanide could be used safely near water supplies and prized fishing streams, the miners pressed economic and even cultural arguments against the initiative. Snoddy argued that Initiative 137 was "just another attempt by extremist groups to limit opportunities in Montana," contending that "cyanide is not the issue. Jobs are the issue. This is an effort by the MEIC to take jobs away from Montana. . . . It is duplicity at its best." The initiative would not only stop the McDonald project, it would discourage other mining companies from investing in Montana. The loss of jobs would bring "human suffering, the destruction of family life," and speed the transformation of Montana into a "theme park for the wealthy."[48]

Despite the economic stakes, the campaign was quiet.[49] There were two major reasons for this. First, Canyon Resources was weak financially. The company had lost backing from the mining giant Phelps Dodge in 1997 and had laid off all but three employees. It lacked funds even to complete an environmental impact statement required for its state mining permit, and faced a lawsuit from the state for missed payments. Further, the C. R. Kendall Corporation, a Canyon Resources subsidiary, faced cleanup costs it could not meet at its Kendall mine. The company had offered the state mineral rights in lieu of cash to cover its obligations; Montana officials estimated that its $1.9 million bond would fall $4 million short of total cleanup costs. Naturally, the problems at Kendall did not help Canyon's public relations during the Initiative 137 campaign.[50] Second, in 1996 Montana voters had adopted Initiative 125, which banned direct corporate contributions to initiative campaigns. That year the mining industry spent around $2 million fighting a "clean water" initiative, but in 1998, under the constraints of Initiative 125, it spent little. Just two weeks before the Initiative 137 vote, total spending from all groups was only $30,000. At that time, the leading pro-mining group reported receipts of $1,310 and expenditures of less than $400. Mining interests were hamstrung by the ban on corporate spending.[51]

A coalition of groups (including the Montana Mining Association) successfully challenged the ban on corporate contributions in federal court, and it was overturned just a few days before the election.[52] The mining industry then pushed hard against Initiative 137, but despite a last minute flurry of fundraising its spending was minimal and barely matched that of the ban's advocates, with environmentalists spending $79,189 and the mining interests spending $78,975.[53] David Owen, president of the Montana Chamber of Commerce, complained that under Initiative 125 the initiative process was dominated by non-profit groups targeting the business community. Initiative 137 proponents noted the irony in this, citing the mining industry's longstanding influence over state government in Montana and its overwhelming spending advantage in the 1996 clean water campaign.[54]

Initiative 137 was approved 53–47 percent by the voters, but the issue hardly ended there. Mining interests immediately sought to overturn the result in the legislature and the courts. The Montana legislature considered several options, but few legislators wished to challenge the will of the voters, and Governor Marc Racicot (R) shared this concern, so the legislature did not act. Senator Chuck Swysgood (R) concluded: "When you combine the environmental issue with an initiative issue, it's a pretty steep mountain to climb."[55] Opponents of the ban on cyanide-leach mining would need help from the courts or would have to qualify their own initiative to repeal Initiative 137.

Legal challenges centered on two issues. First, the Montana Mining Association and two mining companies argued that the ban on corporate contributions had unfairly limited the industry's ability to make its case, so the initiative should be overturned. This claim failed, with the federal courts unconvinced that Initiative 125 limits had wrecked the industry campaign.[56] Second, Canyon Resources pressed a "takings" claim, asserting that Initiative 137 denied the company the use of its property without compensation. Canyon Resources argued that the state had encouraged it to develop the mine, that permit delays had driven up costs, and that state officials had assured the company that the mining would be legal. Canyon Resources President Richard DeVoto said: "Fundamentally, our contract rights, our property rights, and basic fairness have all been violated by the enactment of I-137."[57] This suit failed; the Montana Supreme Court ruled that the opportunity to develop the mine did not constitute a property right. In applying for its permit the company had agreed to abide by state laws, and the ban on cyanide-leach mining became one of those laws.[58]

Failure in the legislature and in the courts led the Montana Mining Association and Canyon Resources to press for a new initiative to overturn Initiative 137. Initiative 147, which appeared on the ballot in November 2004, promised new safeguards against spills. Mining interests spent heavily on the contest. In mid-October, the miners' campaign organization, Miners, Merchants, and Montanans for Jobs and Economic Opportunity, reported receipts of almost $2.2 million, 97 percent of which came from Canyon Resources. Two groups opposing repeal of the ban, Save the Blackfoot and Montanans for Common Sense Water Laws, had raised around $490,000. Tim Smith, manager of the Helena-area Montana Tunnels mine, said that in the Initiative 137 campaign the mining industry "had its hands tied while environmental groups were playing on emotions about fishing and people." "This time," he continued, "we're coming out like gangbusters."[59]

Despite the intensity of the miners' campaign, Initiative 147 was defeated 58–42 percent. Smith declared: "It's a sad day for the American mining industry and the future economy of Montana. The environmentalists did it again, using scare tactics."[60] Indeed, the public health scare caused by the ominous presence of cyanide in water sources and threats to the fishery on the Blackfoot River put the environmentalists in the driver's seat on this issue. Yet in 1996 the mining industry's campaign against the environmentalists' "clean water" initiative (itself an effort to overturn a law favored by mining interests that had been passed in the state legislature) featured an ad depicting a woman drinking deep from a stream running out of the Beale mine as evidence that there weren't water quality problems associated with mining, as well as what environmentalists described as misleading claims from the industry that the initiative's restrictions would affect citizens' rights to drain dishwater from their sinks. Such messages, along with a few million in spending by the mining industry, sank the clean water initiative.

The Montana case is instructive in several ways. First, it played out against the backdrop of the failure of Congress to reform the Mining Law of 1872 to address the environmental problems caused by mining. In the absence of long-awaited amendments to federal statutes from the first layer of the green state, some of the conflict on these issues has been displaced to the states. Second, the case shows the use of the initiative as a route around state-level legislative gridlock, or (as in the case of the clean water initiative) as an avenue for attacking laws deemed unacceptable. Policy initiative did move beyond the legislative process to new institutions and new venues, yet neither at the polls nor in the courts was there much room for balancing interests on the morning after Earth Day— these were all-or-nothing, no-holds-barred fights. The campaigns themselves, driven by advocates and seeking to mobilize ambivalent and apathetic citizens, are hardly played to the next generation center. [61]

Land Use Planning and Property Rights in Oregon

With the adoption of the Land Use Planning Act of 1973, Oregon became the first state to adopt a statewide system of land use planning. The law required Oregon cities to establish Urban Growth Boundaries based on projections of the amount of land they would need for housing, economic development, and open space. It aimed to concentrate growth in already settled areas, restraining sprawl by sharply restricting rights to convert farm and timber land to residential zoning outside the Urban Growth Boundaries. Governor Barbara Roberts (D) said that "the basic principle that farm and forest land that can be part of commercial operations must be saved for future farm and forest use" was "the cornerstone of Oregon's land use program."[62]

The Oregon system has been widely admired by planners, winning a prize from the American Planning Association in the early 1980s and serving as a model for other states' laws. In 1991 Governor Roberts called her state a "showcase for proving growth and the environment can live harmoniously," and the state's reputation for livability grew apace. Portland was widely praised by planners, and its success was linked to the larger land use program.[63]

On the surface, it appeared that Oregon had cut through conflicts between development and environmental interests to create a model land use program. Yet frustration boiled beneath the surface. Development interests once dismissed by Governor Tom McCall (R) as "wastrels and despoilers" mobilized against the system, supported by rural residents who felt the bite of land use restrictions.[64] The Urban Growth Boundaries slowed sprawl, but they also distorted housing markets and created frustrations for individuals looking to build homes on farmland or to convert their lands to cash. In a next generation world, the next move would be to seek a balance between the state's successful but sometimes painful commitment to land protection and legitimate concerns about property rights and the interests of rural residents. But of course this did not happen. Instead, opponents of the system took their concerns to the polls in efforts to destroy it.

After several failed attempts, critics got their way in 2000, when 54 percent of Oregon voters "detonated" the state's planning system by supporting Measure 7. Measure 7 called for reimbursement to property owners for any loss flowing from most land use regulations adopted, enforced, or applied after the current owner took possession of the property.[65] The state's Supreme Court overturned Measure 7 on technical grounds, but property rights activists reworked their initiative and Oregonians again pushed the plunger. In 2004 they adopted Measure 37 by a vote of 61–39 percent, again exploding the old rules and creating chaos in land use planning. A county judge overturned the new law, and Oregon's property rights activists cried foul. The director of the property rights group Oregonians in Action declared: "If this means a Measure 38, we'll be back with a Measure 38. At some point, the courts will understand that people deserve the right to have their property protected." Oregonians in Action did not have to file a new initiative, however. The Oregon Supreme Court ultimately upheld Measure 37 in early 2006.[66]

Oregonians in Action led the battle for these initiatives. The group derided the state's system of land use planning in language familiar to students of environmental regulation: "too top-down, too complex, too inflexible, and too costly. . . . There are too many state-imposed, one-size-fits-all, inflexible regulations. The system was intended to simplify and expedite land use decisions, but it has become too complex, time-consuming, and costly. . . . Procedures are too cumbersome and too easily used to stop land use decisions of all kinds."[67] The pro-initiative campaigns drew upon powerful symbols (e.g., elderly rural residents disadvantaged by land use planning rules) and values, and these symbols undoubtedly touched many inattentive voters. But Oregonians in Action's commitment to strict limitations against regulatory takings of private lands to provide public benefits was clear to any Oregonian who cared to pay attention.

Opponents of Measure 7 highlighted its radical implications. The environmental group 1000 Friends of Oregon called the proposal "an anarchist's manifesto." Governor John Kitzhaber (D) observed: "It does not overturn our land use laws, but it raises serious questions about the extent to which we can enforce them. . . . Not only does it make Oregonians pay a phenomenal amount, costing taxpayers billions of dollars—at the same time, it would destroy our quality of life, the very soul of our state, what makes us proud to call ourselves Oregonians." Kitzhaber estimated that compliance with Measure 7 would cost the state $1.6 billion and local governments $3.8 billion.[68] He asserted that neither the state nor localities could afford these costs, so Measure 7 would effectively end enforcement of land use regulations: "Beach protection laws would be impossible to enforce; urban growth boundaries would be a thing of the past."[69]

Measure 7's passage generated many new policy questions, and the Oregon Legislature turned to craft a compromise. Lawmakers made some progress, but the effort foundered on such issues as the sources of funds to pay compensation and the retroactivity of the measure.[70] The *Oregonian* (Portland's major daily newspaper) lauded legislators on both sides of the political aisle for their attempt to strike a workable deal, but worried that even good faith compromises "would still saddle Oregon with a clunky, untested land use compensation apparatus that would sap resources and, we're convinced, invite more conflict and litigation than it would ever resolve" because the "starting point for negotiations—and distorting them from the beginning—is the very extremity of Measure 7."[71]

As planning officials wrestled with implementing Measure 7, the issue ended up in state courts. The Oregon Supreme Court invalidated the measure, finding that as a proposed constitutional amendment Measure 7 illegally made multiple, unrelated changes to the state constitution.[72] The *Oregonian* hoped that this might buy time for a next-generation-style resolution, allowing "a year or two to think, to plan, to open a discussion with citizens who may never have given a thought to the ways zoning and land use regulations mostly enhance rather than hurt property values."[73] This was not to be. Property rights activists immediately brought forth the "Son of Measure 7," a new initiative designed to avoid the problems that had led to Measure 7's defeat in the courts.

Measure 37 differed from Measure 7 in two important respects. First, it proposed a statutory change rather than a constitutional amendment, avoiding the technical problems that had killed Measure 7. Second, it made it clear that government could modify or waive land use rules if it did not wish to pay compensation.[74] Since governments would lack the resources to pay compensation for most claims, it was widely expected that planning officials would regularly waive development restrictions. The debate around Measure 37 was similar to the fight over Measure 7, and as was noted earlier property rights activists won a bigger victory at the polls in 2004 than they did in 2000.

Measure 37 created administrative, legislative, and legal chaos. The new law offered planning officials little guidance about implementation, leaving open such basic questions as what materials claimants would have to provide to back their appeals, what sorts of hearings and community meetings were necessary for considering claims, and whether fees could be required. There was wide variation across the state in how compensation claims were handled, with some counties quickly waiving development restrictions and others proceeding slowly. Some planning offices were overwhelmed by the volume of petitions, unable to meet the six month deadline for processing claims and facing lawsuits. Tough substantive questions about the transferability of development rights and the potential impact of Measure 37-driven development on the value of surrounding property were left open.

The state legislature, which typically provides guidance on the implementation of ballot measures, did not come into session until after Measure 37 went into effect, and when it finally met its efforts proved fruitless. The Democratic Senate and the Republican House failed to come to agreement, with the Senate preferring to simply specify procedures for making claims and appealing decisions and the House embracing Oregonians in Action's agenda. The *Oregonian* reported on the legislature's struggles: "Nobody likes the law as written, but nobody will budge to broker sweeping land use reforms. Ending the legislative session without action means that hundreds of disputes will play out one-by-one in local planning offices and courtrooms."[75]

And Measure 37 did find its way into the courtroom. In a suit sponsored by 1000 Friends of Oregon, a county court invalidated the law, holding that it violated the Oregon constitution's "equal protection" provision by treating landowners who had acquired their property at different times differently and that it undermined the state's capacity to regulate for the public health, safety, and welfare by forcing governments to pay to enforce land use regulations. This broad ruling appeared to be devastating to property rights interests, yet it generated more confusion since it was unclear whether it applied only to the four counties that were party to the case or across the whole state. Ultimately the Oregon State Supreme Court heard the case. It rejected all of the trial court's major findings, and in early 2006 it upheld Measure 37.[76]

There are several lessons to draw from the Oregon case. First, while there may have been strong sentiment in the state for striking a better balance between property rights and land protection, the state's institutions have not delivered such a balance. The legislature has been unable to do so, and the initiative process produced extreme measures and then sanctioned them as the expressed will of the people. States may do very well at pragmatic balancing in many areas, but clearly there are other patterns as well. Importantly, perhaps encouraged by the Oregon measure, property rights activists placed regulatory takings measures on the ballots in four western states in 2006. Although Proposition 207 won in Arizona, similar measures lost in California, Idaho, and Washington. The key is that we are likely to see further efforts to make such policy via initiative. Second, as in the Montana case, the ballot pathway is simply a part of a policy labyrinth, at once emerging from the failures of the legislative process and then intersecting legislative, judicial, and administrative paths as the policy questions at issue move from venue to venue.[77]

These cases may lead to unnecessary pessimism about the role of ballot measures in environmental and conservation policymaking. Indeed, it is striking to see citizens going to the polls and voting to tax themselves to conserve lands and to clean up local contaminated sites or to protect themselves against cyanide poisons. Yet, just as recent research has shown that the initiative process deviates significantly from the populist ideal, these cases show that the use of this pathway does not always square with the pragmatic "next generation" vision of the future of environmental policymaking.[78] First, the initiative process is increasingly dominated by activist groups, and is used by those groups to seek substantial changes in policy at the expense of political opponents. Property rights groups, anti-logging activists, and environmental interests can hardly be said to be seeking pragmatic solutions to policy problems—they wish to use the initiative process to further their dearest political goals, and do so in campaigns featuring emotional, mobilizing appeals that are bound to polarize citizens and policy debate. Second, a pragmatic approach to environmental policymaking would rely on learning and incrementalism, and it appears that bypassing legislatures hinders this process. "For all of their failings," Richard Ellis wrote, "legislatures have the singular virtue of being capable of identifying, correcting, and learning from past errors. . . . The real problem of initiatives is not that they are more likely to produce poor public policy than legislatures—though they may—but rather that mistakes made by initiatives are more difficult to correct."[79] Finally, it is too easy to conceive of the states simply as sites of clearer-headed, pragmatic thinking about environmental policy problems. Many of these policy issues are extremely contentious, and changing the venue doesn't much change the stakes or the politics.

The States Enter the Labyrinth

There are clear examples of the states acting as policy innovators, often working in a pragmatic, flexible manner central to the next generation vision. Such next generation attributes, however, are not typical of the initiative and referendum pathway, as just discussed. In this final section, we see policymaking that is far removed from the next generation vision. Rather, it is based on policy advocates venue shopping for favorable settings, probing the green state for pathways that might deliver policy outcomes unavailable in Congress. The central characteristic of this arena is conflict and opportunism rather pragmatism and collaboration. We begin with a discussion of the efforts of several states and their allies to seek new federal policies through lawsuits. With activist attorneys general leading the way, the states have been most forceful in their efforts to have the U.S. Environmental Protection Agency regulate emissions of greenhouse gases. These attorneys general have moved into a policy void on this issue, with Congress gridlocked and the executive branch disinclined to act. We then turn to a discussion of the sometime federal response to state policy initiatives. Even when states make environmental policy, some federal actors and their allies may be unwilling to let those state policies move forward. Both of these discussions illustrate that often the states are simply new venues for interest-based, conflict-oriented environmental policymaking, rather than a center for collaborative, next generation policymaking.[80]

The States Turn to the Courts to Advance Policy Goals

At the same time that the states were adopting innovative policies such as the renewable portfolio standards to reduce global greenhouse gases, several states were using another approach, one far removed from next generation pragmatism and collaboration yet familiar to students of environmental policy—the courts. A group of primarily Northeast and West Coast states initiated two major lawsuits seeking to force reductions in greenhouse gases. One case sought to have the EPA regulate emissions from motor vehicles as greenhouse gases under the Clean Air Act; the second sought to find several electric utilities guilty for their emissions of greenhouses gases under public-nuisance law. The states, like virtually every other actor in the environmental policy process, have been probing the green state for opportunities to advance their policy goals. Blocked in Congress, they have not only acted on their own, but have also sought to use existing laws to achieve their goals.[81]

The first case has its roots in the late 1990s. In 1998 and 1999 two different EPA general counsels concluded that CO_2 qualified as an air pollutant under the Clean Air Act, the latter confirming the EPA's interpretation in a letter to a House committee. Later that year, in testimony to Congress, EPA Administrator Carol Browner claimed that the EPA had authority to regulate emissions of greenhouse gases under the Clean Air Act. Shortly thereafter, in October 1999, Greenpeace, the International Center for Technology Assessment, and the Sierra Club petitioned the EPA to regulate emissions of four greenhouse gases (carbon dioxide, methane, nitrous oxide, and hydrofluorocarbon) from new motor vehicles. The Clinton administration delayed action on the petition for more than a year, finally beginning a 90 day public comment period just before it left office in January 2001.[82]

The Bush EPA rejected the petition in September 2003, citing a memo from EPA General Counsel Robert Fabricant dated August 29, 2003. Fabricant contradicted the Clinton-era opinions and concluded that the Clean Air Act does not authorize the EPA to regulate emissions of greenhouse gases. He withdrew the agency's previous statements on this matter because they no longer represented the EPA's stance. Furthermore, the EPA determined that greenhouse gases were not air pollutants under the Clean Air Act, and even if they were air pollutants, the EPA had the discretion to decide not to regulate these gases, which the EPA would exercise in support of President Bush's current approach to global climate change (relying on further research and voluntary reductions).[83] Between the EPA's announcement of this finding and its publication in the *Federal Register*, the International Center for Technology Assessment announced that it would sue the EPA. Several states joined this lawsuit, becoming the principal plaintiffs in the case. In announcing California's intent to sue, Governor Gray Davis (D) stated "This issue is vital to the future of our states." By the time the case was decided, twelve states, the District of Columbia, American Samoa, Baltimore, New York City, and several environmental groups were on one side, while eleven states, industry, and the Washington Legal Foundation joined the EPA on the other side.[84]

The Court of Appeals for the District of Columbia issued a complex split decision supporting the EPA in *Commonwealth of Massachusetts v. Environmental Protection Agency* in July 2005. The majority ruled that the EPA Administrator "properly exercised his discretion . . . in denying the petition for rulemaking." In a spirited dissent, Judge David Tatel came to a different conclusion. "EPA has failed to offer a lawful explanation for its decision," he wrote. He asserted that greenhouse gases "plainly fall within the meaning of 'air pollutant'" and if the administrator judges that such pollutants will endanger public health or welfare "then EPA has authority—indeed, the obligation—to regulate their emissions from motor vehicles." Furthermore, in response to the EPA's argument that the agency is not required to regulate greenhouse gases even if they are air pollutants, Tatel concluded that "EPA's reasoning is simply wrong."[85]

Tatel wrote in dissent, but it is important to underscore that the arguments made by these states found significant support within the Court of Appeals. The lack of a strong, clear decision in the case meant that the judicial pathway was not closed to those seeking to force the federal government to reduce greenhouse gases under the Clean Air Act. The states lost their request for a rehearing of the case, but the Supreme Court accepted the case and heard oral arguments in November 2006.[86]

Eight states and New York City filed the second lawsuit in July 2004. Basing their case on a common-law public-nuisance claim, the states' attorneys general sought to have the five largest electric utilities in the country, responsible for 10 percent of the nation's annual CO_2 emissions, reduce these emissions by 3 percent annually for the next decade. In unveiling the lawsuit, New York Attorney General Eliot Spitzer (D) commented: "The science underlying our lawsuit is universally accepted. The law is clear. All that is now lacking is action." That action would come through nuisance law, "the traditional law governments use to make polluters clean up." Attorney General Richard Blumenthal (D) of Connecticut noted that the lawsuit was an effort to break the gridlock on climate change. The case represented "an opportunity to shake up and reshape the way an industry does business," he said, comparing the case to previous state action against the tobacco companies.[87] This legal strategy failed in the first round as well. In September 2005, federal District Court Judge Loretta Preska dismissed the case. Preska ruled that "these actions present non-justiciable political questions that are consigned to the political branches, not the Judiciary." The following month, the states appealed the decision.[88]

A third lawsuit was launched in June 2003. Connecticut, Maine, and Massachusetts sued the EPA to compel the agency to classify CO_2 as a "criteria pollutant" under the Clean Air Act. If successful, the lawsuit would have required the EPA to issue National Ambient Air Quality Standards for CO_2, as it currently does for six other wide-ranging pollutants such as ozone and sulfur dioxide. The lawsuit was withdrawn, however, when the Bush administration altered the previous opinion that CO_2 was a pollutant in the Fabricant memo discussed above.[89]

State lawsuits against the federal government are widespread beyond the arena of climate change. Such cases have been discussed in earlier chapters dealing with the roadless rule (on both sides of the issue), New Source Review and other air quality regulations, and public lands cases relating to the Antiquities Act and wilderness study areas. More recent state lawsuits have spanned the spectrum of conservation and environmental policy. In the arena of public lands policy, in February 2004, California sued the Forest Service for approving a plan dramatically increasing logging on the eleven national forests in the Sierra Nevada; New Mexico filed suit against the Bureau of Land Management to prevent oil and gas development on the Otero Mesa in April 2005; and in September 2005 Utah celebrated an appeals court victory on the definition of a road on federal lands. On other fronts, New York and three other states sued the EPA over pesticide safety for children in September 2003, and in September 2005 fifteen states sued the Energy Department for failing to adopt energy efficiency standards for more than twenty appliances. Such lawsuits are part of a larger trend of activist state attorneys general. "Our action is the result of federal inaction," claimed Connecticut Attorney General Richard Blumenthal. "The [Bush] administration has not just failed to enforce the law, it has sought to undercut it and gut it. . . . States are filling the vacuum." Attorney General Elliot Spitzer of New York concurred: "We are right on the facts. This isn't new regulation. It's enforcement of existing statutes." Business and industry often disagree with these suits. "The overreaching of the state attorneys general is a problem that is growing," said Lisa Rickard of the U.S. Chamber of Commerce. "They're trying to regulate through litigation."[90]

Although the states have not yet been successful in their legal efforts to force the federal government to regulate CO_2 emissions, these cases and the others mentioned above demonstrate that the states, like other actors in the arena of conservation and environmental policy, are actively using a variety of policy pathways to achieve their goals. At a time when advocates of less regulation and more unbridled economic development gained the upper hand in Washington, many states, frequently joined by environmental groups, probed the green state to find a way to use existing laws to achieve their policy goals. That this is occurring does not seem surprising, but it is certainly a far cry from next generation devolution, pragmatism, or collaboration.

Forget States' Rights, Washington is in Charge

While several states have pursued their policy interests through the courts, other interests have sought to use federal power to block state policies they opposed. An excellent example of this sparring took place in 2003. The California Air Resources Board, building on regulatory actions taken in 1990 and 1996, adopted rules to reduce air pollution from small engines used in lawnmowers, leaf blowers, and other nonroad equipment. Opponents turned to the appropriations pathway. Although the regulations would only apply to such engines in California, Senator Christopher Bond (R-Missouri) took immediate interest. Briggs & Stratton, a major manufacturer of such engines, had two plants in Missouri—plants the company indicated it might close if the new regulations went into effect. Rather than re-tool its production lines, the company would shut the plants and build new ones outside of the country, leading to the loss of 2,000 manufacturing jobs. Bond, chair of the Veterans Affairs, Housing and Urban Development, and Independent Agencies Subcommittee of the Appropriations Committee, offered an amendment to the 2004 Fiscal Year bill blocking the California regulation. States around the country were upset with this challenge to their regulatory authority. Indeed, the Environmental Council of the States sent a letter in support of California to the committee, but for naught. The amendment was passed 17–12. California and its two Democratic senators, Barbara Boxer and Dianne Feinstein, lost in the committee but vowed to continue their fight.[91]

The debate intensified, but Bond's amendment survived on the Senate floor. Feinstein blocked Senate business for more than three hours in an effort to force a vote on Bond's amendment, but without success. "If the California rule was allowed," said Tom Savage of Briggs & Stratton, "it would have cost Americans 22,000 manufacturing jobs in 23 states." Alan Lloyd, chair of the California Air Resources Board, countered: "It's outrageous that California is held hostage by special interests in Washington, DC. It is very sad. To jeopardize children's health in California, it's a terrible precedent." Although Bond's amendment required the EPA to develop national regulations for these small engines within a year, Lloyd was unimpressed. "The track record at the EPA has not been a good one. Relying on the EPA has never worked in the past. It is unconscionable that progress in California is being jeopardized."[92]

California had one last chance: the conference committee. The House appropriations bill did not include the rider, and it was opposed by California's new governor, Arnold Schwarzenegger (R), and by that state's large House delegation. Indeed, Schwarzenegger himself lobbied the conference committee to drop Bond's amendment. Governor George Pataki of New York also lobbied against the Bond amendment. Senator Dianne Feinstein called the amendment "the mother and father of all environmental riders," since it would make significant changes to the Clean Air Act without any hearings in Congress. In the end, the conference dropped the rider, allowing the regulation to proceed.[93]

The federal government has also sought to block other states' efforts in conservation and environmental policy. Wyoming passed a law in 2005 giving surface property owners more control over energy development when another party owns the mineral rights to the property (split estate ownership). Bureau of Land Management Director Kathleen Clarke concluded that the law imposed "inappropriate . . . economic burdens" and hence did not apply to cases where the Bureau of Land Management controlled mineral rights. Congress has also passed an appropriations rider to trump state laws on the siting of liquid natural gas terminals and preempt certain state energy efficiency standards. The federal government is also suing Massachusetts to overturn that state's oil-spill law. Steve Hinchman, of the Conservation Law Foundation, claimed these federal actions were "the 1970s in reverse. Then, the feds stepped in with more stringent standards than the states to ensure that the environment was protected. Now, as states get ahead of the federal government, they're stepping in to protect industry. . . ." A final example is the Gasoline for America's Security Act, passed by the House of Representatives in October 2005 in the wake of Hurricane Katrina. Among other things, the bill would relax air pollution standards at thousands of industrial facilities. "It is the most blatant attack on state and local environmental authority that I've ever seen," claimed William Becker, executive director of the State and Territorial Air Pollution Program Administrators and the Association of Local Air Pollution Control Officials.[94]

We should not be surprised to see at least some actors at the state level pursuing their interests along policy pathways in a manner that resembles a miniature version of Washington. Many of the same forces creating gridlock in Washington are also at work in the states. Robert Duffy noted an increase in activity by environmental interest groups in the states during the 1990s, focusing especially on elections.[95] These groups have become increasingly sophisticated, frequently connected to national groups. By 2002, 30 states featured their own League of Conservation Voters, connected through the Federation of State Conservation Voter Leagues. Although business representatives often champion the next generation approach, especially the goals of collaboration and flexible, negotiated regulation, they do not hesitate to follow other pathways to protect their interests when necessary. For example, the chemical industry fought New Jersey's extraordinarily innovative pollution-prevention-and-control program in the courts for years. The state pathway is a complicated one. In addition to the innovations and commitments to collaboration and pragmatism that have received so much attention, there is also intense conflict and considerable instability, with actors probing the green state and exploring a variety of policy pathways in pursuit of their interests.[96]

Conclusion

As we noted at the beginning of this chapter, the states are not strangers to a leading role in conservation and environmental policymaking. It wasn't until the 1960s and the 1970s that the federal government nationalized pollution control policy and made inroads into land and wildlife policy. As gridlock has solidified in Congress, the states have re-emerged as leaders in making environmental policy. In addition to the possibility of bypassing the federal green state and the gridlock in Congress, the states have several general advantages as policymakers. These advantages include the ability to customize policy to particular conditions, the ability to better engage citizens in policymaking, and the ability to better work across agency and professional boundaries, all of which the states can do better now than in 1960 because institutional capacity has improved. Yet another layer has been added to the green state—a layer that significantly shapes what the states can and cannot do.[97]

States have been at their innovative best in addressing the challenge of climate change. Beyond the use of renewable portfolio standards discussed above, the most impressive actions have been the adoption of the Regional Greenhouse Gas Initiative by seven northeastern states in December 2005, the nation's first mandatory regional pact for the reduction of greenhouse gases, and the adoption of California's CO_2 emission standards for motor vehicles by ten additional states, constituting roughly one-third of the U.S. auto market. As the case of the Adirondacks shows, the states have been quite effective in land protection.[98]

There are, of course, limits to this state pathway.

One potential limit is the unevenness or patchiness of state policy. Some would celebrate these differences across the states as evidence that they offer some relief from "one size fits all" federal regulation. Advocates of more uniform environmental policy argue, however, that issues such as clean drinking water are of such fundamental importance, comparable to civil rights, that citizens should have the same level of protection throughout the nation. Others focus on the problematic nature of different state policies for business. It is instructive to consider the different stories that emerged from neighboring western states since 2000. California has become the leader of new environmental policymaking in the nation.

"As California goes, so goes the nation," wrote Donald Kettl. "American policy for auto emissions is subtly shifting course," he continued, "driven by activities at the state and international levels. It's not that EPA doesn't matter. It's just that the Washington political battles that consume EPA aren't really central to the shaping of long-term environmental policy." Next door, however, the Arizona Senate voted to end funding for the state Department of Environmental Quality in March 2005. Although the agency was eventually reauthorized, State Senator Jack Harper (R) spoke for many when he claimed that the "DEQ has become a vindictive, threatening organization." Furthermore, despite the tremendous successes in several states in crafting policy to reduce greenhouse gases, numerous states have passed legislation blocking any action on climate change or have taken no action at all.[99]

Another limit is funding. Innovative policies often cost money, and states are frequently short of funds. In June 2003, for example, 46 states were about to begin new fiscal years without budgets in place, "after a spring in which states have made record tax increases and spending cuts."[100] States frequently remain dependent on the federal government for funding, whether to undertake pioneering programs (such as New Jersey's comprehensive efforts to reduce emissions of greenhouses gases) or to implement existing ones. An increased reliance on states for environmental policymaking will favor states with access to more dollars— states that are larger or wealthier, states that are less tax averse or willing to issue bonds to fund their programs, or states with substantial energy funds (such as Wyoming).[101]

Third, states face some of the same challenges as Congress and the federal government. Even several states noted for their leadership on environmental issues face challenges similar to those at the national level. In Oregon, environmental groups have lost much of their clout in the state legislature, beyond their failures on Measures 7 and 37. In California, Governor Schwarzenegger's nominee to head the Air Resources Board was rejected by the state senate in September 2005 on a party-line vote. Even former Utah governor Mike Leavitt's (R) much-touted Enlibra initiative, which sought a collaborative approach to environmental policymaking in the West, has been criticized by environmental groups. Heidi McIntosh, issues coordinator for the Southern Utah Wilderness Alliance, said: "The governor has never called us once to talk about how Enlibra could be implemented. I think that's pretty telling." Insofar as the Southern Utah Wilderness Alliance is one of the leading conservation groups in Utah, and that the state has not hesitated to turn to the courts to achieve its goals (see chapter 5), it would appear that environmental politics in Utah remains sharply divided, hardly moving toward a pragmatic, collaborative future. The examples of states suing the federal government and the federal government seeking to block state actions discussed above underscore the conflict inherent in much state environmental policymaking.[102]

A fourth challenge is impossible for states to solve. Certain problems cross state borders, and without the cooperation of other states there is nothing that the most innovative and effective state policy can do to change that. These issues are most difficult in the cases of air pollution, climate change, and certain cases of water pollution.[103]

Perhaps most problematic of all is that actors using the state pathway cannot escape the green state. As the federal green state has developed, more and more laws, policies, and regulations have been created at the national level. As this green state has expanded, the room for states to make environmental policy has shrunk. This is true in nearly every area of conservation and environmental policy. Such innovative efforts to alter pollution control policy as the Common Sense Initiative and Project XL (see chapter 6) failed largely because the states and other policy advocates could not escape existing federal law. The National Environmental Performance Partnership System has foundered for the same reasons. California's effort to regulate emissions of greenhouses gases from automobiles is being challenged in court on the grounds that it violates federal law.[104]

What, then, can we say about the state policy pathway? Clearly, most state policymaking scores highly, at least compared to other pathways, in terms of accountability, legitimacy, and rationality. States appear able to serve as policy innovators when two conditions hold. First, they have greater opportunities to innovate when they are acting on open policy terrain. This is the case with greenhouse-gas-reduction policy, where there is no federal law analogous to the Clean Air Act. Second, state policymaking is likely to succeed in areas where the states have existing, secure policy responsibilities. Regulation of public utilities and protection of land within a state are excellent examples of this. These conditions, of course, do not guarantee state action. There is also tremendous potential for contingency and conflict on the state pathway. Contingency arises when state policymaking intersects with federal policymaking and when actors turn to the courts or to initiatives and referenda to make policy. Furthermore, the state pathway does not lead away from or around fundamental conflicts or the larger constraints of the green state. Policy advocates will pursue other venues, such as the courts and Congress—thereby dragging opponents into the green state labyrinth—when such a course furthers their interests. Those seeking to alter existing environmental policy—business interests, mainstream environmentalists, or advocates of next generation reform—are likely to find the state pathway intriguing, but they should understand that it is still affected by the federal green state.

8

Gridlock, Green Drift, and the Future of Environmental Politics

The world of environmental policy changes every day, but the basic forces yielding legislative gridlock on the environment remain in place. The policymaking environment is thick with contending interests, and their battles take place in a public opinion environment that, in the main, supports the policy status quo. Partisanship remains strong, heightening mobilization on all sides of environmental issues and limiting prospects for compromise that might yield movement toward meaningful reform. Big environmental battles like the struggle over drilling in the Arctic National Wildlife Refuge still receive considerable media attention, making environmentally moderate Republicans and conservative Democrats squeamish about angering their constituents on highly visible votes. And, as we have noted, the presence of a variety of non-legislative pathways along which environmental policies can be effectively and less visibly shaped and reshaped diminishes the political imperative for legislative reform on many issues.

Moreover, for the top leadership of the parties the environment remains a second-tier concern. Some Republican legislators like former Representative Richard Pombo of California and Don Young of Alaska burn for radical statutory changes, but the core Republican leadership has higher priorities, ranging from domestic and international security to budgetary issues and social security reform. The party's leadership created a debacle for itself in trying to reshape environmental laws in 1995 and 1996, and since that time it has not made these issues a major legislative priority and instead has pushed for change along other paths. Likewise, the low priority given environmental issues in the 2004 presidential contest by John

Kerry shows how Democratic leaders have subordinated those issues to other, higher priority policy concerns. Kerry's environmental record differed sharply from Bush's, but—as evidenced by the limited attention given to the environment in the presidential debates or in campaign statements—he did little public work to highlight those differences. His campaign focused on the Bush administration's conduct of the Iraq war, its handling of budgets, and its stewardship of the economy. Democratic strategists calculated that a loud and proud campaign on environmental issues would alienate voters in the swing states of Ohio, Michigan, and West Virginia. A late September *New York Times* editorial lamented Kerry's reticence to speak out on climate change: "It would help, too, if . . . Kerry, whose record on this issue has been strong, sent the . . . message in a more public and compelling venue than his campaign Web site."[1] Had he been elected, Kerry would have had no strong mandate to push ahead with a legislative program on the environment.

This is not to say that Republican control of the national government has not generated legislative pressures on the green state. Bush won passage of healthy forest legislation and a major energy bill, and conservative legislators have continued to push for major policy changes through normal legislative channels and in budget politics.[2] Revisions of the Endangered Species Act and even the National Environmental Policy Act have moved ahead on the congressional agenda, though they were not enacted. Republican budgetary priorities had important influence on policy and policy implementation in some areas, and in 2005 advocates of drilling in the Arctic National Wildlife Refuge nearly won their objective using budget rules.[3] Still, the conservatives' central legislative goals on air pollution have been stymied, the anti-green firebrands are deeply frustrated, and it would be hard to argue that the Republican Party's electoral triumphs broke open the legislative logjam on the environment.[4]

Environmentalists were certainly delighted with the outcome of the November 2006 congressional elections. Not only did Democrats take control of both the House of Representatives and the Senate, but longtime foes such as Richard Pombo and Charles Taylor (R-North Carolina, chair of the House Appropriations Subcommittee on Interior, Environment, and Related Agencies) lost their seats. But how will this change environmental policymaking in Washington? The biggest change is that environmentalists will need to play less defense to protect the green state status quo. It is extremely unlikely that Democrats will push for oil drilling in the Arctic National Wildlife Refuge or to gut the National Environmental Policy Act. However, those seeking to strengthen environmental protections still face a closely divided Congress and a Republican president. Furthermore, the environment is not uniformly a high priority among the Democrats. While Senator Barbara Boxer (California), new chair of the Environment and Public Works Committee, has called for quick action on climate change, her counterpart in the House of Representatives, John Dingell (Michigan), chair of the House Energy and Commerce Committee, is in less of a rush. In sum, it is unlikely that Congress is on the verge of breaking its environmental gridlock.[5]

Despite all the barriers to legislative change—and perhaps because of these barriers to legislative change—struggles over environmental policy continue on other pathways. Presidential leadership has been crucial in this. The layered statutory commitments that comprise the green state are difficult to change, but presidents are well positioned to exploit many of the paths through the labyrinth explored in this book, and presidential leadership energizes action along many of the pathways we have described. The use of appointments and administrative centralization to attempt to redirect agency priorities, the exercise of unilateral authority under laws like the Antiquities Act, and the assertive use of rulemaking— all in part reactions to congressional gridlock as well as the opportunities afforded by the complexity of the green state—have been important engines of policy disruption and policy change. Presidential administrations have responded to the politicization of the judicial process with a bit of politicization of their own, with evidence of a growth of strategic behavior in litigation and the development of an environmental policy angle to judicial appointments. Presidents are better positioned than any other actors in the system to operate across the depth and breadth of the green state, and while they meet many barriers they can and do constantly disrupt the status quo, generating considerable instability if not lasting policy change.

The presidency, as the main source of comprehensive direction and leadership in the American political system, tilts the contours of the landscape on which virtually all of these policymaking pathways run.[6] Bill Clinton achieved little of consequence for the environment in the legislative process in the 1990s, yet he brought significant new directions to environmental policy. He shifted the ground toward greater land protection with his use of the Antiquities Act, the roadless rule, and the Northwest Forest Plan. His regulatory reinvention initiatives and commitment to a third way in regulatory policy energized collaborative efforts and shaped the institutional context in which those efforts would proceed. The administration's commitment to habitat conservation plans pushed policymaking on endangered species far down the collaborative path. Clinton's major political appointments in this field opened new access to the green state for environmentalists, with Carol Browner working on Environmental Protection Agency reinvention and Bruce Babbitt spearheading the unsuccessful legislative and administrative attacks on the dominant policy regimes in mining and grazing. Clinton's defense of the basic environmental laws against conservative attacks highlighted the public's general commitment to environmental protection, countering the Republicans' efforts to tilt the field radically, and the administration managed to push debates over air quality in new directions in the New Source Review debate. His major legislative initiatives failed, and he frustrated the environmental community on salvage logging and other issues. Yet he fought a successful holding action on the environment in Congress for much of his presidency, and Democratic control of the White House clearly tilted the pathways on which environmental policy choices were and are made, sometimes just slightly but sometimes decisively, in directions favored by greens.

The Bush administration has, of course, shifted this ground in a different direction. The struggle over snowmobiles in Yellowstone National Park is instructive. In complicated legal and administrative maneuvering, the Clinton administration moved toward a ban on private, individual snowmobile use in the park that was announced in 2001; through equally complicated maneuvering, the Bush administration found new administrative and judicial paths to guide the machines back into Yellowstone. In late 2003, federal district judge Emmet Smith wrote:

The gap between the decision made in 2001 and the decision made in 2003 is stark. In 2001, the rulemaking process culminated in a finding that snowmobiling so adversely impacted the wildlife and resources of the park that all snowmobile use must be halted. A scant three years later, the rulemaking process culminated in the conclusion that nearly 1,000 snowmobiles will be allowed in the park each day. (The latter decision) was completely politically-driven and result-oriented.[7]

Smith surely overlooked the political nature of the Clinton administration's move, but the key point is that under Bush the snowmobiles' path into Yellowstone now runs downhill rather than up the steep grade created by Clinton's opposition. Secretary of the Interior Gale Norton's well-publicized ride on the paths blazed by the Bush administration ("We have a better understanding of . . . why people are so excited about the opportunity to snowmobile here") symbolized the tilt in the policy terrain created by Bush's election.

The Bush experience illustrates three crucial characteristics of environmental policymaking in the era of gridlock.

First, the policy status quo, supported generally by public opinion and aggressively and specifically by the advocacy community, is formidable. Recognizing ecological reality and political necessity, the Bush administration accepted and advanced green goals in some areas, as when it adopted a rule for diesel engine emissions affecting emissions from non-road diesel equipment (e.g., bulldozers, tractors, and generators). In this same vein it ratified some important Clinton-era decisions favored by environmentalists, including another "diesel rule" affecting emissions from trucks and buses. When it has challenged the status quo its efforts have often met resistance that has forced it to back off. This was the case with the administration's flirtation with a wetlands policy that held out the possibility of removing millions of acres from federal regulation; by Earth Day 2004, Bush had abandoned this and was offering up a "no net loss of wetlands" policy aimed at defusing sharp criticism of the wetlands proposal and the administration's larger environmental stance.[8]

Second, the Bush administration, like its predecessor, has pushed hard along non-legislative pathways. Clinton tried to cut through gridlock on public lands protection using executive authority and rulemaking; Bush has offered no significant land-protection initiatives, reversed course on the roadless rule, floated plans for selling off parts of the public domain, and dramatically eased access to the public lands for mining and energy interests.[9] The administration has carried along the Clinton-era commitment to collaborative regulation and resource protection, though, as one observer put it, "programs conceived in the Clinton administration as a form of alternative dispute resolution are valued by the Bush administration as potentially less restrictive alternatives to existing environmental laws and regulations."[10] On endangered species, for example, the Clinton administration sought to save the Endangered Species Act through the elaboration of habitat conservation plans (HCPs). The Bush administration has continued to approve HCPs, but it also reduced efforts to list species, limited and reduced critical habitat designations, and ignored growing evidence of problems in the habitat conservation planning program itself.[11] As we showed in chapter 4, much of the Bush agenda on pollution issues has been fought in the rulemaking process and through implementation and enforcement, such as on New Source Review. In another visible case, both the EPA inspector general and the Government Accountability Office found that political concerns distorted the EPA's rulemaking process on mercury emissions from power plants, with Bush officials rigging the analysis to prove—contrary to much evidence—that the administration's favored cap-and-trade proposal was superior to other options for controlling mercury emissions.[12] Given a gridlocked Congress and controversial policy goals, presidents seek their advantages where they can find them, and the rulemaking process is crucial. And of course, like all presidents, Bush attempted to shape policymaking generally and environmental policymaking specifically through administrative politicization, including the aggressive use of the Office of Management and Budget to rein in regulators, political pressures within agencies and on scientific matters (see the mercury example above, and criticisms of the administration's position on global warming), and political appointments that placed ideological firebrands in positions of responsibility for making crucial environmental policy choices. Appointments to positions in the natural resource field were particularly controversial, beginning with Gale Norton replacing Bruce Babbitt at Interior, but continuing to many lower-level appointments. Bush placed Mark Rey, once a leading lobbyist for the timber industry, in charge of forest policy at the Agriculture Department, and Steven Griles, a lobbyist for coal and oil interests, in charge of Bureau of Land Management lands, wildlife refuges, national monuments, and national parks at the Department of the Interior. Bush's first appointment to head the Environmental Protection Agency was environmental moderate

Christine Todd Whitman, in a gesture clearly intended to signal the Bush administration's acceptance of the basic commitments to environmental protection rooted in the golden era environmental laws. Whitman's tenure was brief, in large part because she was uncomfortable with the administration's path in pollution control policymaking.

Third, even as the Bush experience demonstrates the ways that the green state at once constrains and opens opportunities for policy change, it also reveals a key weakness of the "next generation" vision of the future of environmental policy. Quite simply, it is not clear that "politicizing presidents" will see benefits in pursuing the pragmatic agenda. It is true that Clinton found that the green position on mining and grazing overlapped with arguments for more economically efficient mining and grazing policies, and that he saw policy and political advantages in collaborative experiments. Yet he learned that the political costs of attempting reform on these resource issues were high. On pollution control policy he pressed ahead with various reinvention experiments, but the scope of this experimentation was limited by his unwillingness—as a defender of the central policy commitments of the 1960s and the 1970s—to open up the basic laws to amendment. Bush's commitment to the next generation approach was weaker. Jan Mazurek of the Progressive Policy Institute observed that when Bush came to office he found "a growing, bipartisan consensus around the need to update antiquated environmental laws and regulations with more market-based, information-driven, and community-friendly ways to protect the environment . . . eighteen reports that squarely endorsed modernization, a legislative proposal to modernize environmental laws, and a policy community poised to champion its passage and implementation."[13] Yet Bush allowed progress toward the next generation vision "grind to a halt," rejecting market-based approaches to dealing with global warming, pursuing a selective, politicized approach to devolving authority in environmental regulation to states, and failing to invest in the information technology infrastructure necessary for a more flexible, results-oriented pollution control regime. On mining and grazing, similarly, Bush refused to confront the inefficiencies of federal policies governing these activities, instead acting as a defender of those embattled yet still formidable policy regimes. Further, in areas such as mercury where the Bush administration moved toward market-based solutions, or in its advocacy of collaborative approaches to wetlands protection and regulatory enforcement, attentive advocacy groups in the environmental community challenged the strategies and raised doubts about the intentions of the administration. Mazurek complained that Bush "squandered an historic opportunity" to restructure pollution regulation along next generation lines, but obviously Bush viewed his political and policy opportunities differently.[14]

We should not expect that presidents—whose efforts will be crucial in the era of gridlock—will be interested in restructuring environmental policy along next generation lines. Indeed, the possibilities of a substantial reconstruction of environmental policy in the United States seem remote as presidents, to use Stephen Skowronek's term, confront a reasonably stable policy regime. On mining and grazing and timber, Clinton found himself to be what Skowronek called a "preemptive" president, at odds with established regimes and trying to draw together coalitions across partisan and ideological lines to attack wasteful, environmentally destructive policies and practices. Yet on pollution policy Clinton was the classic "faithful son," a defender of the established regime interested in modernizing the old regime to preserve it even while defending it from sharp attacks. Where the new and old regimes ground together, as in endangered species issues on timberlands or pollution issues surrounding mining and grazing, Clinton pressed green concerns on old systems, but—as in the Northwest Forest Plan—could hardly break with old commitments to resource extraction. Bush's position is different. He governs as a defender of the "lords of yesterday" in timber, mining, and grazing, forced to recognize new realities but struggling to preserve the old order. His partisan commitments and political alliances tie him to the mining, grazing, and timber regimes. On pollution issues he is a classic pre-emptive leader, seeking changes in a stable order, using tactics like issue framing ("Clear Skies") to express fealty toward the old regime while seeking to push policy in more conservative directions.[15] Clinton and Bush found themselves oriented quite differently toward the various layers of the green state, but both found their leadership possibilities shaped by the apparent stability of the many layers of the green state and the crashing and grinding of those layers.

Although congressional gridlock remains in place and presidents will continue to serve as the catalysts for action on the different policy pathways, it is also the case that over time, regardless of which party has been in the White House, environmental policy is likely to haltingly move in the direction favored by environmentalists. We examine this phenomenon in the next section.

Green Drift in a Conservative Time

Despite the strained conditions for most Americans [since 1973], there was no broad progressive political reaction, as there had been during the Depression. On the contrary, the social programs and regulations of the New Deal and Lyndon Johnson's Great Society were increasingly attacked, pared down, and eliminated. Government regulation of airlines, truckers, and communications became more permissive under Presidents Jimmy Carter and Ronald Reagan. The regulation of banks, brokers, and other financial services was relaxed under Bill Clinton. Laws protecting organized labor were weakened or poorly enforced. Besides cutting income taxes sharply and making them more regressive, Reagan reduced the proportion of people covered by unemployment insurance, Federal support of education fell as a percentage of Gross Domestic Product as well. Affirmative action programs were circumscribed by the courts, and Clinton limited the scope of federal welfare programs.[16]

This passage from Jeff Madrick's article "The Way to a Fair Deal" in the *New York Review of Books* summarizes a familiar account of American politics since the mid 1970s—the nation has moved to the right and so have many of the public policies of the "right nation."[17] This shift, rooted in the 1960s, gained momentum with the election of Ronald Reagan in 1980, was strengthened by Republican control of Congress after 1994, and was consolidated by George W. Bush's presidential victories in 2000 and 2004. The Republican vision on taxes and welfare has helped to transform public policy, and, as evidenced by the fact that some version of Social Security privatization is now an agenda item if not yet a political reality, it has reshaped political possibility in the country.

Some observers see that there has been a right turn in environmental policy reflecting this larger shift in policy and the public agenda. In their influential essay "The Death of Environmentalism," Michael Shellenberger and Ted Nordhaus argued (without citing any specific examples), that it had been "easy for anti-environmental interests to gut 30 years of environmental protections." Richard Lazarus noted that the repudiation of the Gingrich agenda on environmental policy showed the depth of environmental policy commitments in the country, and observed that in the immediate aftermath of the failure of the Contract with America there was a tightening of standards and an extension of environmental concerns to reach issues of environmental justice. Yet Lazarus found that Bush's election held dark portents for environmentalists:

. . . the emergence in 2003 of this new "Republican" moment in environmental law may have enormous portent. For the first time ever, since the beginning of the modern environmental law era, the political appointees and nominees to all three branches of the federal government are effectively controlled by one political party that seems largely united in its willingness to question and fundamentally reform existing pollution control and resource conservation laws.[18]

Our view is considerably different. We have argued that, despite legislative gridlock, the environmental policy arena has been dynamic, as struggles over policy have moved onto non-legislative paths. One of the hallmarks of this policymaking has been instability, with constant twists and turns as issues drift across institutional venues and up and through layers of the green state. Yet we think that far from a "right turn" in environmental policymaking, there's a great puzzle here. We see a slow and even halting general movement in policy directions favored by environmentalists, a "green drift" in environmental policymaking discernible despite the increasing conservatism of American politics, despite the Republicans' political strength, and despite the defeats environmentalists have suffered on major issues such as global warming.

Two examples help to illustrate this green drift. Environmental groups and several states have harshly criticized the Bush administration's decision in March 2004 to reject a Clinton administration finding to regulate mercury emissions from coal burning utilities as a hazardous air pollutant. In its place, the Environmental Protection Agency issued a final mercury rule in March 2005 that would use a less stringent cap-and-trade program to reduce these emissions. Several states and environmental groups sued the Bush administration in an effort to force the EPA to implement stricter pollution control provisions. It is useful, however, to understand why it is that the Bush administration was issuing new rules to regulate mercury emissions to begin with. The 1990 Clean Air Act

Amendments required the EPA to regulate numerous toxic air pollutants, including mercury. When the EPA missed several deadlines, the Natural Resources Defense Council and the Sierra Club sued the agency. The EPA settled these suits in the mid 1990s, agreeing to a timetable for the release of a rule to regulate mercury. The Bush administration had no choice about whether it would or would not issue new regulations limiting mercury emissions. The combination of the existing green state (the 1990 Clean Air Act Amendments) and mobilized environmental groups and states forced the Bush administration to issue such rules. While we may debate whether or not the Bush rules are as strong as they could be, it is clear that the new rules will lead to less mercury emissions than in the past—green drift. A second example is the reduction of timber harvesting on national forests. In the period 1980–1989, companies harvested an average of 10.3 million MBF (thousand board feet) per year from the national forests. In the period 1995–2005, that annual average dropped to 4.1 million MBF—a 60 percent decline. Much of the decline can be attributed to environmental groups making use of the green state (laws such as the Endangered Species Act and the National Forest Management Act) and the courts, acting against the backdrop of a Republican Congress for the entire period and a Republican president for half of it. This illustrates another case of green drift at work.[19]

The keys to explaining this green drift are many of the same forces contributing to policy gridlock—the tremendous mobilization of interest groups and public support of environmental protection and the accumulated weight of the green state that makes retreat on environmental matters a tremendous political undertaking—one that conservatives have yet been unable or unwilling to mount. These factors have not only frequently blocked conservative change, but also have tilted politics and policy toward the agendas of environmentalists. When the recent layer of the green state was laid down in the years 1964–1980, it was accompanied by fundamental changes in society that continue—namely the development of a highly professional and relatively well-funded issue advocacy community and widespread—though admittedly shallow—public support. This combination of strong interest groups and broad public support has helped prevent the kind of rollbacks that occurred in other liberal and progressive policy realms. One major difference between environmental and many other liberal/progressive policy areas is that virtually all citizens benefit from a reduction in pollution and a widespread, diverse population benefits from outdoor recreation and wildlife protection—including many traditionally Republican supporters like hunters and fishers. On natural resources and endangered species issues, opposition is concentrated on those few whose property rights are affected by laws like the ESA or wetlands protection, and those engaged in commodity production (e.g., logging, mining, and ranching)—a rapidly declining portion of the population, even in the rural West. On pollution issues, where business interests sometimes oppose the green agenda, environmentalists frequently enjoy significant advantages as protectors of public health. They can easily mobilize a public highly sensitive to environmental health risks, advancing a kind of populism with broad resonance in the population. These characteristics are very different from welfare benefits, for instance, which are delivered to relatively few citizens.

The top layer of the green state sets the basic topography of modern environmental policymaking. It lays over the old regimes governing management of the public lands, imposing legal mandates for conservation and pollution concerns on those pursuing the old ways. The result is a constant grinding of the new against the old, and the result is less the "moving stalemate" between environmentalism and business interests described by Karen Orren and Skowronek in their sketch of the development of federal public lands policy, than constant, if halting, abrasion of the old order by the harder realities of the Clean Water Act, the Endangered Species Act, and other golden era laws.[20] In pollution control policy the golden era statutes—inefficient, bitterly contested, frustrating, begging for next generation reform—remain the law, the policy status quo. This policy regime held back the Reagan revolution and helped to break the Gingrich charge on the policy legacies of the 1960s and the 1970s. It has frustrated the George W. Bush administration, with the president paying fealty to the policy regime even while trying to make conservative changes at the margins. The statutory frameworks governing pollution control institutionalize the position of the political forces that carried the day in the golden era, and carry the effects of that mobilization forward despite conservative criticism and larger concerns about the inefficiencies of the old order.

Thus, we think that portents of the "death of environmentalism" and of a sharp right turn in environmental policymaking are unduly pessimistic. It is certainly right for environmentalists to be alarmed at any weakening of the existing environmental policies and we agree with Shellenberger and Nordhaus that "people in the environmental movement today find themselves politically less powerful than we were one and a half decades ago," and that "the greatest achievements to reduce global warming are today happening in Europe." Although the essay was certainly accurate in its take on the current problems of the mainstream environmental movement to get climate change policy passed in Washington, we find the argument that the trajectory of the environmental movement has exhausted itself and the overall reasoning of the essay to have several major shortcomings.[21]

Most significantly, Shellenberger and Nordhaus don't acknowledge the existence and significance of the green state. This green state creates opportunities for environmentalists to move their agenda ahead through other pathways, around a gridlocked Congress and a currently recalcitrant president. Laws such as the Clean Air Act and Endangered Species Act have led to significant environmental advances since 1990, and considerable progress has been made on climate change at the state level through public utility commissions and legislatures. In policy areas where laws were adopted in the golden era of environmentalism, U.S. policy is often the strongest in the world (again, for example, on clean air and endangered species protection). Furthermore, this green state has been strikingly resistant to rollback, unlike most other progressive policy arenas. This is not to say there have been no rollbacks; certainly the Bush administration has used its discretionary power to alter public lands management—especially to greatly expand energy development on public lands—and to alter the implementation of pollution control laws. It has also had some limited success in Congress, most notably the Healthy Forests Restoration Act. But no major environmental law has been substantially weakened. In sum, environmental groups have been able to play extremely good defense, based on the green state and public opinion, better defense than any other liberal or progressive policy advocates. Lastly, in their sketch of an invigorated environmental movement, they do not discuss how it would interact with the intercurrence of the existing green state, layers of policies adopted over more than 100 years. In sum, it is not at all surprising that given the constellation of political forces since 1995 that the United States has not adopted a comprehensive policy for reducing green gases, a policy that would be perhaps the most far-reaching environmental policy in the nation's history. But this hardly means environmentalism is dead.[22]

Green Drift and Private Pathways

Further evidence of green drift comes in exploring another set of pathways not yet discussed in this book: private paths around gridlock. As gridlock ossified in Congress, societal interests sought their goals through a series of private or civil society pathways that bypassed the green state altogether. As was the case of the five pathways previously discussed, the use of these private pathways increased significantly during the 1990s. While limited in their reach and ultimate prospects, each path leads, in a meandering way, in the direction of greater environmental protection. The three main private pathways are land protection via land trusts, altering business behavior through consumer purchasing decisions, and voluntary business moves toward superior environmental performance.

Private land-protection efforts have grown tremendously since the mid 1980s, undertaken primarily by regional and local land trusts. Such private land protection began with the Trustees of Reservations in 1891 in Massachusetts, but it wasn't until the mid 1960s that the number of land trusts really began to grow. The growth reached its peak in the 1990s, when the number of land trusts doubled nationally. In 1985 there were 535 land trusts; by 2003 there were more than 1,500. Roughly two-thirds of these land trusts belong to the national umbrella organization, the Land Trust Alliance.[23]

At first, land trusts protected land in two basic ways. They purchased the land and either maintained ownership or transferred the land to a government agency for management. Beginning in the 1980s, land trusts started to make more use of conservation easements. As we discussed in chapter 7, a conservation easement is a right to property owned by a non-profit group or government agency. Such easements generally prohibit any development on the property and may include additional restrictions (e.g., guaranteed public access, forest management prescriptions). Land trusts purchase or accept as gifts such easements; landowners receive a tax benefit due to the reduced value of their land. According to Richard Brewer, "local land trusts had protected a total of about 6.5 million acres as of the year 2000. More than 80 percent, 5.6 million acres, had been protected since 1990, a decade in which, federally and in most states, very little new land was being preserved by government." Protected acreage by regional and local land trusts reached 9.4 million acres in 2003 (this figure did not include national land trusts such as The Nature Conservancy, which combined have protected an additional 25 million acres). More than half of this land has been protected through conservation easements.[24]

The Nature Conservancy, one of the largest environmental groups in the United States, operates differently than the Natural Resources Defense Council or the Sierra Club. Rather than lobby or file lawsuits, The Nature Conservancy conserves land it identifies as valuable— through purchase and retention, purchase and transfer to a government agency, or purchase of conservation easements. As of 2003, The Nature Conservancy had protected 15 million acres in the United States.[25]

Clearly, land trusts have been tremendously successful, with advocates bypassing a gridlocked Congress and a labyrinthine green state to conserve land. Nevertheless, this private pathway faces a number of challenges.

First and foremost, much of the funding to purchase land or easements comes from governments. And of course, land trusts that sell property to government agencies rely on government funds and willing government partners. In this sense, land trust activities have not bypassed the green state; rather, they are working along another pathway. Since these land trust actions involve willing sellers, perhaps this aspect of land trust action is best considered part of the collaborative pathway. There are two other significant challenges for land trusts: monitoring and enforcing conservation easements, and challenges to certain land deals that critics argue are merely tax dodges for the wealthy. The nature of easements and how they are taxed bring land trusts right back to the green state, since this is the purview of legislatures and judges. Indeed, in 2005 Congress held hearings on taxation and conservation easements, sending a shiver down the spine of the land trust community.

A second major private pathway is the use of consumer purchasing power to achieve desired environmental and sustainability goals. Rather than seeking legislation to improve farm and forest management or reduce emissions of greenhouse gases, consumers use their purchases to further these goals. One major approach to green consuming focuses on third-party certification of superior environmental performance by producers. In order of significance, this includes organic food, forest certification, and building certification. Until 1990, when Congress passed the Organic Foods Production Act and the federal government became significantly involved in establishing national standards, organic agriculture functioned through a system whereby farmers met a set of management standards—namely not using synthetic fertilizers and pesticides, a third-party organization verified that the farmers were doing what they said they were doing, and consumers who purchased organic food for health and/or environmental reasons. There was no government regulation. Farmers willingly decided to use an organic approach and consumers willingly purchased organic foods, usually paying a premium. Organic food sales grew dramatically over the period 1995–2005, with annual increases between 17 and 21 percent during the period. Sales totaled $10.4 billion in 2003, approximately 2 percent of food sales in the United States.[26]

Forest certification got off to a later start and has not achieved anywhere near the success of organic agriculture. In the early 1990s environmentalists, foresters, loggers, and sociologists came together to seek a common definition for sustainable forestry. Out of this conversation, the Forest Stewardship Council (FSC) was born, with the U.S. branch created in 1995. Landowners meet a set of sustainable forest standards as determined by the FSC. A party approved by the FSC then certifies that the landowner is following these management standards, and the consumer purchasing green-certified forest products rewards this sustainable management. As of January 2006, 22 million acres of public and private forestland were certified through the FSC process in the United States. The forest products industry established a second certification regime, the Sustainable Forestry Initiative, in 1994. Approximately 150 million acres are enrolled in the SFI program, though critics argue that SFI lacks a true independent third-party certification process analogous to the FSC program. Although the forest certification process has enrolled millions of acres, it has been less successful in the marketplace thus far, for a variety of reasons.[27]

A final example of the third-party certification process is green buildings. The U.S. Green Building Council created the Leadership in Energy and Environmental Design (LEED) program as "a voluntary, consensus-based national standard for developing high-performance, sustainable buildings." Since its launch in 2000, nearly 300 buildings have been LEED certified and more than 2000 additional projects are underway.[28]

Purchasing environmentally superior products is another consumer approach to achieving environmental goals. Labeling of products to demonstrate their environmental superiority over other products is one such tactic. Examples of these practices include labeling canned tuna as dolphin-safe, including the percentage of recycled material in paper products, and marketing "green" investment portfolios (approximately $151 billion was invested in socially screened mutual funds in 2003, roughly 2 percent of the overall market share, though these figures include more than simply green investing). In many ways this labeling approach is a lesser version of third-party certification. The producer of the good or service makes an environmental claim, typically one that is not verified by an independent party, and consumers can spend their money on products meeting environmental goals that they support. Although such labeling clearly makes a difference for some consumers, the overall effects of this approach have been limited so far. Consumers, for instance, like dolphin-safe tuna, but they are unwilling to pay more for it. Other green consuming can focus on products that are widely known to have superior environmental performance. Perhaps the best examples of this are hybrid vehicles and compact fluorescent light bulbs. For both of these products, consumers who purchase them can reduce their use of energy, thereby reducing emissions of greenhouse gases and other air pollutants that come from burning coal or gasoline. Some environmental groups are also bypassing the green state to directly compel corporations to achieve environmental goals, such as pressuring Dell to begin recycling its computers.[29]

In sum, all these components of the private consumer pathway rely on the basic foundation of the free market system; consumers use their purchases to reward firms engaged in behavior that furthers their perspectives on the environment. In this most basic sense, this pathway does not rely on government action in any way. Yet public policy is often involved in shaping these market exchanges. For example, dolphin-safe tuna was largely a result of disputes over administration of the Marine Mammal Protection Act, and the purchasing of compact fluorescent light bulbs may be a part of a public utility commission's conservation mandate. This green consuming approach raises three fundamental questions. First, can we trust business claims to superior environmental performance, especially without third-party certification? And even with such certification, can we trust the certifiers? There has been some dispute, for instance, in the FSC certification process that the FSC was certifying unworthy forestland in order to increase the number of certified acres as quickly as possible. The second question comes from environmental advocates who argue that U.S. citizens already consume too much and the nation cannot buy its way to a sustainable future. And third, will significant green consumption take place? Findings so far indicate that "green marketing has not lived up to the hopes and dreams of many managers and activists. . . . Most consumers simply will not sacrifice their needs or desires just to be green."[30]

The third and final pathway around the public green state is the other side of the consumer purchasing transaction—business actions to achieve sustainability. There are many reasons why businesses might move in this direction, including a response to consumers and shareholders as discussed above. Other reasons for businesses to alter their operations to become more sustainable include basic economic incentives, the growth of the corporate responsibility movement, and in response to actions taking place outside of the United States. Many of these rationales overlap, making it difficult to determine why a business behaves in a particular way. Clearly, if a business perceives a market advantage to green behavior, it will pursue this. The advantage may come from cutting costs, such as through energy conservation, or through increasing market share. Wal-Mart, for example, announced a wide-ranging set of environmental initiatives in fall 2005 aimed at improving energy efficiency and reducing packaging. These goals can both cut Wal-Mart's costs and improve its image. The public response to these efforts varies, depending on what a company proposes to do and how it behaves overall. If the green action is minor, it is often branded as greenwashing by environmental critics.[31]

Although there is much dispute over what "corporate social responsibility" (CSR) actually means, there is no denying that the practice has grown tremendously since 1990. David Vogel reported that more than 2,000 firms throughout the world issued reports on their CSR practices. The rise in CSR can be traced, Vogel argued, to its use as an alternative to government action:

Virtually every NGO demand, ranging from reducing carbon emissions to protecting forests to reducing the use of antibiotics in beef and chicken, could in principle be addressed through additional government regulation. But because the increased political influence of business has made the enactment of such regulations more difficult, many activists have chosen to lobby executives instead of politicians. Getting some large corporations to change their policies is often easier than changing public policy.

Nevertheless, "the most important driver of corporate interest in CSR is the argument that good corporate citizenship is also good business," although the relationship between CSR and profitability is inconclusive.[32]

There are numerous examples of environmental CSR in the U.S, perhaps most significantly the more than 100 corporations that have achieved or set voluntary targets to reduce emissions of greenhouse gases. Many corporations have turned to the International Organization for Standardization (ISO) to demonstrate their commitment to sound environmental practices. ISO 14001 is a voluntary environmental management system based on industry best practices. In 2002, nearly 40,000 firms were ISO certified, yet fewer than 3,000 of these were U.S. firms. It is also unclear if these ISO-certified firms have superior environmental performance. Vogel concluded that "government regulation and the threat of litigation, along with the cost savings associated with many environmental programs, make it difficult to assess the *net* impact of corporate virtue on environmental quality in the United States or Europe." Nevertheless, "CSR may frequently be a second-best alternative [to government regulation], but second-best is still better than nothing at all."[33]

Since most major American corporations operate in an increasingly global marketplace, these corporations often need to respond to policies made in other nations in order to access those markets and to maintain integrated corporate operations. Currently it is the European Union that is the pacesetter of such new environmental regulations. For example, General Electric's chief executive officer, Jeffrey Immelt, argued that "99 percent of all new regulations the company faces are . . . going to come not from the federal government but from the EU." Of course, globalization can also limit environmental policy made in the United States, such as in the dolphin-tuna case under the General Agreement on Tariffs and Trade in 1991 and the turtle-shrimp dispute under the World Trade Organization in 1998.[34]

These three pathways all seek to bypass the green state, and each demonstrates that real policy change has occurred along these private or civil society pathways. But it is also clear these pathways cannot entirely escape the green state and its shadow. Whether it is a land trust obtaining funds from a government to protect lands or a business engaging in socially responsible behavior to forestall government regulation, the green state clearly influences these seemingly nongovernmental pathways. Furthermore, despite significant successes, especially in private land protection, the effectiveness of these private pathways pales in comparison to the effects of national conservation and environmental policies. The Clean Air Act and the Endangered Species Act apply to all of the country. As successful as the organic food movement has been, it makes up only 2 percent of food sales. Although laudatory, only a handful of corporations have announced firm goals for reducing greenhouse gases. In sum, these private pathways can play a major role in prodding the federal government to act and in supplementing the green state, but they can in no way replace it.

One issue here echoes points raised in chapter 6 about the limits of collaboration as a tool for making fundamental environmental policy choices. The private paths are important, and various voluntary conservation and pollution reduction programs will play a role in the future. But the values and interests at stake in this policy area are so important and various, and the economic stakes are so high, that we should recognize that despite the environment's position as a "motherhood issue" there is no escape from politics, from instability and unpredictability, and perhaps the green drift. Legislative gridlock on some issues may break, but for the most part the future of environmental policy in America will be crafted not in public administration tracts on good government, not in the meeting rooms of local public libraries, and probably not so much even in the halls of Congress. Perhaps it is more accurate to say it will in fact be crafted in all of these places, on all of these pathways and more, undone, remade, and on into a future marked by conflict over these most basic questions about the nature of our common life and our relationship to the natural environment.

Environmental Politics and the Green State Labyrinth

Given the likelihood of continuing legislative gridlock on the environment, the primary movements in policy will take place along the pathways described in this book. And if our analysis of the environmental politics in the years 1990–2006 sheds any light on the future, there is likely to be considerable movement. Legislative gridlock has not created policy gridlock. Instead, environmental policy in many areas has been remarkably unstable despite the stability of the basic statutory frameworks governing pollution, conservation, and natural resources. The green state offers many points of access for interested actors, and the many crossings of the resulting pathways yield frequent collisions and sharp changes of policy direction. Further, despite the institutionalization of past environmental policy commitments, and despite the green drift, changes in partisan control of the White House and Congress have tilted and turned the contours of the policy landscape, redirecting priorities— at least for a moment, until some new direction takes hold along some new path—on issues from air pollution to species protection to land preservation.

The American green state's top layer may bias policy choice in favor of environmentalists, but this is complex and changeable terrain. As we have argued, the green state consists of layers of expectations, statutes, bureaucracies and bureaucratic norms, and administrative and judicial decisions laid down in different eras and reflecting different values and policy concerns. This area is marked by a classic politics of "multiple orders" or "intercurrence," where—as Orren and Skowronek put it— the basic patterns of policymaking are marked by the "dissonance, asymmetry, incongruity" of successive policy commitments, and the resulting "crashing and grinding" of these incongruous orders.[35] More simply, sharply conflicting environmental claims draw legitimacy and even legal standing from different layers of the green state, and the resulting struggles play out in a complex institutional system that may privilege competing claims simultaneously, or successively, leading to a situation in which policy choices are contingent and struggles are open-ended.

Our institutions struggle with these claims as interests spread along the many pathways across the green state. The policy conflicts that we have described have often rapidly shifted from path to path and venue to venue. Congress, for the most part unable to address major environmental issues in the traditional lawmaking process, turned to appropriation riders. These riders typically hold for only short periods of time, such as the 18 month salvage rider or the moratorium on endangered species listings. These represent short term victories for some interest or interests, but no resolution of the challenges of intercurrence. The salvage rider quickly moved into other institutional venues where its meaning and reach were challenged and ultimately modified. Judges have long been wild cards in environmental policymaking; environmentalists' appeals to the courts regularly upend rules, administrative decisions, and collaborative agreements, sending policymaking spinning off in new directions. Clinton and Bush attempted major policy initiatives in the rulemaking process, but the dizzying courses of the roadless rule and New Source Review proposals provide more evidence of the contingency and open-endedness of policy choice in the modern green state. Many collaborative conservation and regulation efforts are informal and therefore hardly stable, changing when groups enter or leave or when dissidents decide to challenge a "consensus" agreement through other channels. John Tavaglione, a Riverside County (California) Supervisor, made this point regarding his experience with HCPs: "I can't tell you how many times our officials traveled to Washington, D.C. to meet with congressional staffs and agencies on this. What was always the challenge to us is that every time you think you have an agreement in place, then someone else, an outside environmental group, finds a way, legally, or otherwise, to put a wrench in the spokes of the wheel."[36]

This returns us to a consideration of the next generation of environmental policy. The Clean Air Act Amendments that created the SO_2 trading system are a signal achievement for those seeking to make our environmental policies more efficient; next generation ideas are powerful and important, and they are shaping policy debate across many areas. Yet in the politics of multiple orders, next generation ideas are simply one more strain in the mix, and the pragmatic accommodations celebrated by champions of this policy paradigm are often fleeting. To date, most next generation innovations—the Clinton reinvention projects, collaborative conservation, efforts at private land protection—have been layered atop existing laws and institutions, and are frequently in tension with past policy commitments and vulnerable to challenge. Congress *could* break down the major barriers to next generation reform and bring more order to pollution, conservation, and natural resources policy, yet the sort of legislative breakthrough necessary to clear the lords of yesterday and the lords of a little while ago from the field seems highly unlikely. In areas where these innovations have had legislative grounding—habitat conservation planning, for example—they have taken deep root, but in many others legislative gridlock crimped prospects for lasting and effective innovation.

Stephen Skowronek's observations on the resilience of the nineteenth-century American state in the face of strong challenges illuminate the politics of reconstructing the green state today. Even in the face of widespread concerns about its effectiveness, "the institutional forms through which American government had been working for decades would not simply give way once their limitations became apparent . . . the governmental order . . . was exposed for the tenacious organization of power that it was," and reform "had to be negotiated through an already highly developed democratic politics."[37]

As we head deeper into the twenty-first century, conservation and environmental policy in the United States will likely continue to be a mix of train wrecks and next generation success stories, of conflict and collaboration. The policy future cannot escape the policy past, so the next generation of environmental policy must be built on past generations, and these past generations are embedded in the often contradictory layers and labyrinth that constitute the green state. The same policy pressures will remain—from environmental groups and businesses, local communities and property owners—and these pressures will continue to find pathways through and around the green state. Even if gridlock eases, real differences of interest and opinion stand in the way of some—but not all—collaboration. In closing, we envision a future of more of the same, with some collaboration and pragmatism, but with plenty of lawsuits and riders and instability too, green drift amid seeming chaos.

Notes

Articles from *Energy and Environment Daily*, *Greenwire*, and *Land Letter* were retrieved through http://www.eenews.net/. Unless otherwise noted, articles in newspapers and law reviews were retrieved through Lexis-Nexis.

Chapter 1

1. Shannon Petersen, *Acting for Endangered Species: The Statutory Ark* (University Press of Kansas, 2002), pp. 27–30.

2. John H. Cushman, "Congressional Republicans Take Aim at an Extensive List of Environmental Statutes," *New York Times*, February 22, 1995; Allan Freedman, "Republicans Concede Missteps in Effort to Rewrite Rules," *Congressional Quarterly Weekly Report*, December 2, 1995, pp. 3645–3647; Jeffrey A. Katz, "GOP Moderates Join Democrats to Keep EPA Intact," *Congressional Quarterly Weekly Report*, November 4, 1995, p. 3383; David Maraniss and Michael Weisskopf, *"Tell Newt to Shut Up!"* (Touchstone, 1996), p. 14.

3. Felicity Barringer and Michael Janofsky, "Republicans Plan to Give Environmental Rules a Free Market Tilt," *New York Times*, November 8, 2004; Michael Janofsky, "Climate Debate Threatens a Republican Clean Air Bill," *New York Times*, January 27, 2005; Darren Samuelsohn and Colin Sullivan, "Deadlocked Panel Defeats 'Clear Skies,'" *Greenwire*, March 9, 2005.

4. See Philip Brick, Donald Snow, and Sarah Van de Wetering, eds., *Across the Great Divide: Explorations in Collaborative Conservation and the American West* (Island, 2001); Ronald D. Brunner, Christine H. Colburn, Christina M. Cromley, Roberta A. Klein, and Elizabeth A. Olson, *Finding Common Ground: Governance and Natural Resources in the American West* (Yale University Press, 2002); Marian R. Chertow and Daniel C. Esty, eds., *Thinking Ecologically: The Next Generation of Environmental Policy* (Yale University Press, 1997); Robert F. Durant, Daniel J. Fiorino, and Rosemary O'Leary, eds., *Environmental Governance Reconsidered: Challenges, Choices, and Opportunities* (MIT Press, 2004); Mary Graham, *The Morning after Earth Day: Practical Environmental Politics* (Brookings Institution, 1999); Donald F. Kettl, ed., *Environmental*

Governance: A Report on the Next Generation of Environmental Policy (Brookings Institution, 2002); Edward P. Weber, *Pluralism by the Rules* (Georgetown University Press, 1998); Edward P. Weber, *Bringing Society Back In: Grassroots Ecosystem Management, Accountability, and Sustainable Communities* (MIT Press, 2003).

5. Weber, *Pluralism by the Rules*, pp. 5–12, 30–50.

6. Kettl, *Environmental Governance*, p. 6.

7. See Daniel A. Farber, *Eco-pragmatism* (University of Chicago Press, 1999); Grant McConnell, *Private Power and American Democracy* (Knopf, 1966).

8. Next generation approaches have been more successful at the state level, yet even there they are not the dominant tendency. We will discuss this in chapter 7.

9. Graham, *The Morning after Earth Day*, p. 112.

10. Christopher McGrory Klyza and David Sousa, "Creating Chaos: The Endangered Species Act as an Instrument for Institutional Disruption," presented at the Annual Meeting of the Western Political Science Association, Las Vegas, March 2001; Jan Mazurek, "Back to the Future: How to Put Environmental Modernization Back on Track," *PPI Policy Report*, April 2003; Craig Welch, "Feds Losing Grip on Species Act: Many Protection Decisions Now Flow from Group's Suits," *Seattle Times*, December 28, 2003.

11. Michael Sherwood, "Court Rules Feds Violated the Law in Failing to Protect Coho Salmon," *Earthjustice*, June 2, 1998, http://www.earthjustice.org.

12. For a lengthy discussion of the green state, see chapter 2.

13. We recognize that during the first 100 years of U.S. history this green state was hardly green in the way we accept that term's meaning today. Early laws and institutions were designed almost exclusively to further economic development. That past—and present—action of entities such as the General Land Office or the Army Corps of Engineers are not considered environmentally oriented does not remove them from being integral parts of the historically constructed green state, and in fact it is difficult to understand the politics of environmental policy in the present without coming to grips with the embedded actions and commitments of the past. We should also note that, despite the existence of a set of 50 green states at the state level, our focus in this book is on the national green state.

14. Karen Orren and Stephen Skowronek, *The Search for American Political Development* (Cambridge University Press, 2004), pp. 17, 86, 108–188.

15. Charles F. Wilkinson, *Crossing the Next Meridian: Land, Water, and the Future of the West* (Island, 1992).

16. Norman J. Vig and Michael E. Kraft, "Toward Sustainable Development," in *Environmental Policy: New Directions for the Twenty-First Century*, sixth edition, ed. N. Vig and M. Kraft (CQ Press, 2006), p. 388.

17. See, for example, Frank R. Baumgartner and Bryan D. Jones, *Agendas and Instability in American Politics* (University of Chicago Press, 1993); Frank R. Baumgartner and Bryan D. Jones, eds., *Policy Dynamics* (University of Chicago

Press, 2002); Sarah Binder, *Stalemate: Causes and Consequences of Legislative Gridlock* (Brookings Institution, 2003); David W. Brady and Craig Volden, *Revolving Gridlock: Politics and Policy from Jimmy Carter to George W. Bush* (Westview, 2006).

18. Jonathan Rauch, *Government's End: Why Washington Stopped Working* (Public Affairs Press, 1999).

19. Eric Schickler, *Disjointed Pluralism: Institutional Innovation and the Development of the U.S. Congress* (Princeton University Press, 2001), p. 267; Orren and Skowronek, *The Search for American Political Development*, p. 108.

20. Stephen Skowronek, *The Politics Presidents Make: Leadership from John Adams to Bill Clinton*, revised edition (Harvard University Press, 1997).

21. Theodore Lowi, *The End of Liberalism* (Norton, 1969); Theodore Lowi, 1999, "Frontyard Propaganda: A Response to 'Beyond Backyard Environmentalism,'" *Boston Review* 24, 1999, no. 5: 17–18.

22. Richard Ellis, *Democratic Delusions: The Initiative Process in America* (University Press of Kansas, 2002).

23. Dennis D. Hirsch, "Bill and Al's XL-ent Adventure: An Analysis of the EPA's Legal Authority to Implement the Clinton Administration's Project XL," *University of Illinois Law Review*, 1998: 129–172; Bradford C. Mank, "The Environmental Protection Agency's Project XL and Other Regulatory Reform Initiatives: The Need for Legislative Reauthorization," *Ecology Law Quarterly*, 25, 1998: 1–89; Alfred A. Marcus, Donald A. Geffen, and Ken Sexton, *Reinventing Environmental Regulation: Lessons from Project XL* (Resources for the Future, 2002); Rena I. Steinzor, "Reinventing Environmental Regulation: The Dangerous Journey from Command to Self-Control," *Harvard Environmental Law Review* 22, 1998: 103–203.

Chapter 2

1. Baumgarter and Jones, *Agendas and Instability in American Politics*, p. 240. On conceiving of legislative stalemate as policy stalemate, see Binder, *Stalemate* and Brady and Volden, *Revolving Gridlock*.

2. Karen Orren and Stephen Skowronek, "The Study of American Political Development," in *Political Science: The State of the Discipline*, ed. I. Katznelson and H. Miner (Norton, 2002), p. 751.

3. Stephen Skowronek, *Building a New American State: The Expansion of National Administrative Capacities, 1877–1920* (Cambridge University Press, 1982); Wilkinson, *Crossing the Next Meridian*.

4. Orren and Skowronek, *The Search for American Political Development*, pp. 113, 166.

5. "Clean Water: Congress Overrides Presidential Veto," *CQ Weekly Report*, October 21, 1972: 274; "Congress Clears Major Water Pollution Control Bill,"

CQ Weekly Report, October 14, 1972, p. 2692; Shannon Petersen, *Acting for Endangered Species: The Statutory Ark*, pp. 27–30.

6. David R. Mayhew, *Divided We Govern: Party Control, Lawmaking, and Investigations, 1946–1990* (Yale University Press, 1991), pp. 34–50. Note that Mayhew's list excludes several key environmental laws, including the Endangered Species Act.

7. Schumer, quoted in E. J. Dionne, "Greening of Democrats: An 80s Mix of Idealism and Shrewd Politics," *New York Times*, June 14, 1989.

8. On the intensification of partisan divisions in Congress and its consequences, see John H. Aldrich and David W. Rohde, "The Transition to Republican Rule in the House: Implications for Theories of Congressional Politics," *Political Science Quarterly* 112, 1997–98: 541–567; Binder, *Stalemate*; John J. Coleman, "The Decline and Resurgence of Congressional Party Conflict," *Journal of Politics* 59, 1997: 165–184; Gary C. Jacobson, "A House and Senate Divided: The Clinton Legacy and the Elections of 2000," *Political Science Quarterly* 116, 2001: 5–28; David W. Rohde, *Parties and Leaders in the Postreform House* (University of Chicago Press, 1991); Barbara Sinclair, "Partisanship and Lawmaking in the 1990s," paper prepared for annual meeting of the Western Political Science Association, Seattle, 1999; Barbara Sinclair, *Unorthodox Lawmaking: New Legislative Processes in the U.S. Congress* (CQ Press, 1997), pp. 81, 82, 227, 228. On increased partisanship in voting behavior, see Larry M. Bartels, "Partisanship and Voting Behavior, 1952–1996," *American Journal of Political Science* 44, 2000: 35–50. On the movement of Republicans to the right on environmental policy, see Jacob S. Hacker and Paul Pierson, *Off Center: The Republican Revolution and the Erosion of American Democracy* (Yale University Press, 2005), pp. 82–85, 97–99.

9. Charles R. Shipan and William R. Lowry, "Environmental Policy and Party Divergence in Congress," *Political Research Quarterly* 54, 2001: 245–263. See also Richard J. Lazarus, *The Making of Environmental Law* (University of Chicago Press, 2004), pp. 150–156, 237–250.

10. James Gerstenzang, "Book Offers Rare Look into Bush Presidency," *Los Angeles Times*, January 7, 2003.

11. Gingrich, quoted in John H. Cushman, "Congressional Republicans Take Aim at an Extensive List of Environmental Statutes," *New York Times*, February 22, 1995.

12. On the weakening of the Democratic Party and the "New Deal political order," see Thomas B. Edsall and Mary Edsall, *Chain Reaction: The Impact of Race, Rights, and Taxes on American Politics* (Norton, 1991); Steve Fraser and Gary Gerstle, eds., *The Rise and Fall of the New Deal Order* (Princeton University Press, 1989); Gary C. Jacobson, "The 1994 House Elections in Perspective," *Political Science Quarterly* 111, 1996: 203–223. On the emerging shape of the party and the new liberalism, see Jeffrey M. Berry, *The New Liberalism: The Rising Power of Citizens Groups* (Brookings Institution, 1999); John B. Judis and Ruy Texeira, *The Emerging Democratic Majority* (Scribner, 2002).

13. Todd Gitlin, *The Twilight of Common Dreams: Why America Is Wracked by Culture Wars* (Holt, 1995); Peter B. Levy, *The New Left and Labor in the 1960s* (University of Illinois Press, 1994); Richard Rorty, *Achieving Our Country: Leftist Thought in Twentieth-Century America* (Harvard University Press, 1998). On liberalism and environmentalism, see Adam Rome, "'Give Earth a Chance': The Environmental Movement and the Sixties," *Journal of American History* 90, 2003: 525–554.

14. Jeff Johnson, "Critics Doubt Clinton's Second Term Will Advance Reg Reforms," *Environmental Science and Technology* 30, December 1996: 524A–525A, http://www.pubs.acs.org.

15. R. Shep Melnick, "Risky Business: Government and the Environment after Earth Day," in *Taking Stock: American Government in the Twentieth Century*, ed. M. Keller and R. Melnick (Cambridge University Press, 1999), pp. 162, 163.

16. Deborah L. Guber, *The Grassroots of a Green Revolution: Polling America on the Environment* (MIT Press, 2003); Harris Poll, "Three-Quarters of U.S. Adults Agree Environmental Standards Cannot Be Too High and Continuing Improvements Must Be Made Regardless of Cost," Harris Interactive, September 13, 2005.

17. John H. Cushman, "House GOP, Softening Stance, Issues Manifesto on the Environment," *New York Times*, May 15, 1996; Timothy Egan, "Look Who's Hugging Trees Now," *New York Times*, July 7, 1996.

18. David Truman, *The Governmental Process* (Knopf, 1951).

19. See Berry, *The New Liberalism*; Christopher J. Bosso, *Environment, Inc.: From Grassroots to Beltway* (University Press of Kansas, 2005); Robert J. Duffy, *The Green Agenda in American Politics: New Strategies for the Twenty-first Century* (University Press of Kansas, 2003); Ronald G. Shaiko, *Voices and Echoes for the Environment: Public Interest Representation in the 1990s and Beyond* (Columbia University Press, 1999).

20. Baumgartner and Jones, *Agendas and Instability in American Politics*, pp. 184–189; Bosso 2005, pp. 7, 82; Robert J. Brulle, *Agency, Democracy, and Nature: The U.S. Environmental Movement from a Critical Theory Perspective* (MIT Press, 2000), pp. 102–105; Michael P. Cohen, *The History of the Sierra Club, 1892–1970* (Sierra Club Books, 1988), p. 275.

21. Bosso, *Environment, Inc.*, p. 76; Mark Dowie, *Losing Ground: American Environmentalism at the Close of the Twentieth Century* (MIT Press, 1995); Robert Gottlieb, *Forcing the Spring: The Transformation of the American Environmental Movement* (Island, 1993); Michael Shellenberger and Ted Nordhaus, "The Death of Environmentalism: Global Warming Politics in a Post-Environmental World," http://www.grist.org.

22. Curtis Moore, "Rethinking the Think Tanks: How Industry-funded 'Experts' Twist the Environmental Debate," *Sierra Magazine*, July/August, 2002: 56–59; Michael Pertschuk, *Revolt against Regulation* (University of California Press, 1982); Kay Lehman Schlozman and John T. Tierney, *Organized Interests*

and American Democracy (Harper and Row, 1986); Mark A. Smith, *American Business and Political Power: Public Opinion, Elections, and Democracy* (University of Chicago Press, 2000); Jacqueline Vaughn Switzer, *Green Backlash: The History and Politics of Environmental Opposition in the U.S.* (Lynne Rienner, 1997); David Vogel, *Fluctuating Fortunes: The Political Power of Business in America* (Basic Books, 1989).

23. Center for Responsive Politics, "Business-Labor-Ideology Split in PAC, Soft Money, and Individual Donations to Candidates and Parties" (2004) and "Business-Labor-Ideology Split in PAC, Soft Money, and Individual Donations to Candidates and Parties" (2002). "Soft money" is the term for political spending related to federal election campaigns that is not regulated by federal election laws. Before the passage of the Bipartisan Campaign Reform Act of 2002, political parties raised tens of millions of dollars in unregulated "soft money" contributions, which they could use to support their candidates in general elections. Since the passage of the Bipartisan Campaign Reform Act, also known as the McCain-Feingold law, parties have been forbidden from taking these contributions. Other, non-party organizations have become the prime recipients and spenders of "soft money."

24. David Helvarg, *The War against the Greens* (Sierra Club Books, 1994); Switzer, *Green Backlash*.

25. Jonathan Rauch, *Government's End: Why Washington Stopped Working* (Public Affairs Press, 1999).

26. On environmental groups and the new media, see Duffy, *The Green Agenda*. On the new media generally, see Richard Davis and Diana Owen, *New Media and American Politics* (Oxford University Press, 1998).

27. Jennifer Lee, "A Call for Softer, Greener Language," *New York Times*, March 2, 2003.

28. Chertow and Esty, *Thinking Ecologically*; Graham, *The Morning after Earth Day*; Kettl, *Environmental Governance*.

29. Baumgartner and Jones, *Agendas and Instability in American Politics*; Robert Repetto, ed., *Punctuated Equilibrium and the Dynamics of U.S. Environmental Policy* (Yale University Press, 2006).

30. Orren and Skowronek, *The Search for American Political Development*, p. 11.

31. Ibid., pp. 128, 112, pp. 156–171 generally.

32. James Willard Hurst, *Law and the Conditions of Freedom in the Nineteenth-Century United States* (University of Wisconsin Press, 1964).

33. Christopher McGrory Klyza, "The United States Army, Natural Resources, and Political Development in the Nineteenth Century," *Polity* 35, 2002: 1–28.

34. Christopher McGrory Klyza, *Who Controls Public Lands? Mining, Forestry, and Grazing Policies, 1870–1990* (University of North Carolina Press, 1996), pp. 11–15, 27–37; Tim Westby, "The Road to Nowhere," *High Country News*, December 20, 2004.

35. Daniel P. Carpenter, *The Forging of Bureaucratic Autonomy: Reputations, Networks, and Policy Innovation in Executive Agencies, 1862–1928* (Princeton University Press, 2001); Klyza, *Who Controls Public Lands?* pp. 15–26; Wilkinson, *Crossing the Next Meridian.*

36. Richard N. L. Andrews, *Managing the Environment, Managing Ourselves: A History of American Environmental Policy* (Yale University Press, 1999), pp. 109–153; Samuel P. Hays, *Conservation and the Gospel of Efficiency: The Progressive Conservation Movement, 1890–1920* (Atheneum, 1975 [1959]); Klyza, *Who Controls Public Lands?* pp. 67–76.

37. Andrews, *Managing the Environment*, pp. 154–200; Klyza, *Who Controls Public Lands?* pp. 109–116.

38. Orren and Skowronek, *The Search for American Political Development*, pp. 161, 162.

39. Andrews, *Managing the Environment*, pp. 201–318; Samuel P. Hays, *Beauty, Health, and Permanence: Environmental Politics in the United States, 1955–1985* (Cambridge University Press, 1987); Klyza, *Who Controls Public Lands?* pp. 37–66, 76–107, 116–140; Lazarus, *The Making of Environmental Law*, pp. 47–97; Wilkinson, *Crossing the Next Meridian.* On emerging conflicts within the Fish and Wildlife Service, see Petersen, *Acting for Endangered Species*, pp. 18–20.

40. Andrews, *Managing the Environment*, pp. 201–283; Lazarus, *The Making of Environmental Law*, pp. 47–97.

41. Andrews, *Managing the Environment*, pp. 255–283; Lazarus, *The Making of Environmental Law*, pp. 98–124.

42. Lazarus, *The Making of Environmental Law*, pp. 125–165. Aside from the Clean Air Act Amendments, the only environmental legislation Congress passed during Bush's administration were the Oil Pollution Act (1990) and the Pollution Prevention Act (1990). Our examination of congressional environmental activity since 1990 in the *CQ Almanac* suggested only five laws that could possibly be considered major environmental legislation during this period beyond the three laws mentioned in the text: the 1992 omnibus water projects law, the Safe Drinking Water Act Reauthorization (1996), the National Wildlife Refuge Organic Act (1997), the Everglades restoration (2000), and the Healthy Forests Restoration Act (2003). The water projects bill is best considered as election year distributive politics rather than major environmental legislation. The reauthorization of the Safe Drinking Water Act did not represent any major changes to the law. The wildlife refuge organic act altered little in how the refuges had been traditionally managed. The Everglades restoration act authorized significant funds to restore the region, but most in Congress viewed it as a local or regional initiative. Lastly, the healthy forests legislation that passed did not include many of the Bush administration's original proposals, and it is also dependent on substantial federal funding, little of which has materialized.

43. Orren and Skowronek, *The Search for American Political Development*, p. 166, pp. 156–171 generally; Klyza, *Who Controls Public Lands?* pp. 1–10, 141–160.

44. Orren and Skowronek, *The Search for American Political Development*, pp. 170, 171.

45. George Hoberg, "The Emerging Triumph of Ecosystem Management: The Transformation of Federal Forest Policy," in *Western Public Lands and Environmental Politics*, second edition, ed. C. Davis (Westview, 2001). On the halting move of environmental policy in the direction favored by environmentalists, we share the view presented by Robert B. Keiter in *Keeping Faith with Nature: Ecosystems, Democracy, and America's Public Lands* (Yale University Press, 2003).

46. Orren and Skowronek, *The Search for American Political Development*, p. 116.

Chapter 3

1. Barbara Sinclair, *Unconventional Lawmaking: New Legislative Processes in the U.S. Congress*, second edition (CQ Press, 2000), pp. 7, 8; Binder, *Stalemate*.

2. "Environmental Impasse," *Washington Post*, March 21, 2005.

3. Johnson, quoted in "Fragile California Desert Bill Blooms Late in Session," 1994, *CQ Almanac* 50: 227, 227–231; Patricia Byrnes, "Wilderness Watch: Congressional Roundup, 1993–1994: Victory for the Desert," *Wilderness*, winter 1994, p. 4; Christopher McGrory Klyza, "Land Protection in the United States, 1864–1997," *Wild Earth*, summer 1998, pp. 41, 42.

4. "Pesticide Rewrite Draws Wide Support," *CQ Almanac* 52, 1996: 3-27–3-28.

5. *Les v. Reilly*, 968 F.2d 985 (*Ninth Circuit Court of Appeals*, 1992); "Pesticide Rewrite Draws Wide Support" 1996, pp. 3-28, 3-29.

6. "Pesticide Rewrite Draws Wide Support," *CQ Almanac* 52, 1996: 3-29–3-34.

7. Gary C. Bryner, *Blue Skies, Green Politics: The Clean Air Act of 1990 and Its Implementation*, second edition (CQ Press, 1995), pp. 114–117; Richard E. Cohen, *Washington at Work: Back Rooms and Clean Air*, second edition (Allyn and Bacon, 1995), pp. 49–69.

8. Bryner, *Blue Skies*, pp. 119–126; Cohen, *Washington at Work*, direct quotations from pp. 92, 93, 96; pp. 86–112 generally; Sinclair, *Unconventional Lawmaking*, pp. 2, 3.

9. Bryner, *Blue Skies*, pp. 117–119, 126–135, 146–152; Cohen, *Washington at Work*, pp. 70–86, 129–152.

10. Charles O. Jones, *The Presidency in a Separated System* (Brookings Institution, 1994), pp. 201–207.

11. Jessica Matthews, "Scorched Earth: Why the Hill Has Become an Environmental Disaster Area," *Washington Post*, October 18, 1994.

12. Catalina Camia, "Poor, Minorities Want Voice in Environmental Choices," *Congressional Quarterly Weekly Report*, August 21, 1993: 2257–2260; Camia, "Controversy, Neglect Bog Down a Bill That Had a Quick Start," *Congressional Quarterly Weekly Report*, August 21, 1993: 2258–2259; Camia, "Bill Elevating EPA to Cabinet Finally Heads for the Floor," *Congressional Quarterly Weekly Report*, November 6, 1993: 3044, 3045; Mike Mills, "EPA Cabinet Measure Hits Snag Over Amendment," *Congressional Quarterly Weekly Report*, February 5, 1994, p. 241.

13. David S. Cloud, "Clinton's Energy Tax Plan Hit by Blast of Cold Air," *Congressional Quarterly Weekly Report*, February 27, 1993, pp. 450–451; Cloud, "Clinton Revises Energy Tax in Bid for Support," *Congressional Quarterly Weekly Report*, April 10, 1993, pp. 910–912; David S. Cloud and Alissa J. Rubin, "Energy Tax, Medicare Focus of Senate Battle," *Congressional Quarterly Weekly Report*, June 12, 1993, pp. 1458–1463; Jon Healey, "Energy Taxes Offer Clinton a Choice of Enemies," *Congressional Quarterly Weekly Report*, January 30, 1993, pp. 214, 215; Healey, "Measuring the BTU Tax," *Congressional Quarterly Weekly Report*, June 12, 1993, p. 1462; League of Conservation Voters, "National Environmental Scorecard, 103rd Congress, First Session" (1994), http://www.lcv.org.

14. Babbitt, quoted in Tom Kenworthy, "Interior Chief Pledges to Overhaul U.S. Policies on Natural Resources," *Washington Post*, April 28, 1993; Kenworthy, "Ranchers and Loggers Fear Landlord Clinton Will Raise the Rent; Pressure Building to Overhaul the 1872 Mining Law," *Washington Post*, November 29, 1992; Kenworthy, "Natural Resources Users Facing Cuts in Subsidies," *Washington Post*, February 18, 1993; Kenworthy, "Mining Law: Benign and Benighted," *Washington Post*, October 23, 1993.

15. Tom Kenworthy, "Babbitt Drops Increase in Grazing Fees," *Washington Post*, December 22, 1994; Kenworthy, "Proposal to Raise Grazing Fees Is Slowly Sinking in the West," *Washington Post*, January 19, 1995; Kenworthy, "Treasury Gets Sheared under New Grazing Fee," *Washington Post*, January 22, 1996.

16. Kenworthy, "Mining Law."

17. Babbitt, quoted in Tom Kenworthy, "A Court Ordered 'Gold Heist,'" *Washington Post*, May 17, 1994.

18. Matthews, "Scorched Earth."

19. Allan Freedman, "The 104th and the Environment," *Congressional Quarterly Weekly Report*, October 12, 1996, p. 2919.

20. Bliley, quoted in Bob Benenson, "GOP Sets the 104th Congress on a New Regulatory Course," *Congressional Quarterly Weekly Report*, June 17, 1995, p. 1693.

21. For example, in 1994 Senator Judd Gregg (R-NH) sought an amendment to the Safe Drinking Water Act that would have barred the EPA from enforcing clean drinking water standards unless the federal government paid all compliance costs. The theory was that the federal government should not direct the states to act and then force states to pay to meet federal requirements.

22. Oxley, quoted in "No Progress on Superfund Overhaul," *CQ Almanac* 51, 1995: 5–11.

23. "Foes Agree on Fishery Act Rewrite," *CQ Almanac* 52, 1996: 4-23–4-25.

24. Marc Allen Eisner, *Regulatory Politics in Transition*, second edition (Johns Hopkins University Press, 2000).

25. Solomon, quoted in Bob Benenson, "House Easily Passes Bills to Limit Regulations," *Congressional Quarterly Weekly Report*, March 4, 1995: 679–682; "Senate Filibuster Derails Efforts to Limit Federal Regulations," *CQ Almanac* 51, 1995: 3-3–3-15.

26. Office of the Vice President, National Performance Review, "From Red Tape to Results: Creating a Government That Works Better and Costs Less," September, 1993.

27. "Senate Filibuster Derails Efforts to Limit Federal Regulations."

28. William D. Ruckelshaus, n.d., "Stepping Stones," http://www.csis.org. The exception was legislation enabling the EPA's National Environmental Performance Partnership System with the states.

29. Tom Kenworthy and Dan Morgan, "Environmental Laws under Budget Ax," *Washington Post*, March 16, 1995.

30. Clinton, quoted in John H. Cushman, "The Environment: Democrats Fight to Restore Curbed Programs," *New York Times*, March 13, 1996; Eric Pianin and John F. Harris, "Clinton, Congress Reach '96 Budget Agreement," *Washington Post*, April 25, 1996; Todd S. Purdum, "Two More Spending Bills Vetoed, But Clinton Offers to Negotiate," *New York Times*, December 18, 1995; Jonathan Weisman, "Pressure to Curtail EPA Boomeranged . . . But GOP Can Claim Some Influence," *Congressional Quarterly Weekly Report*, September 7, 1996, p. 2518.

31. Environmental Working Group, "Congress, We Have a Problem," http://www.ewg.org; Allan Freedman, 1996, "The Environmental Trump Card," *Congressional Quarterly Weekly Report*, April 27, 1996, p. 1518; Barbara Sinclair, "Partisan Imperatives and Institutional Constraints: Republican Party Leadership in the House and Senate," in *New Majority or Old Minority? The Impact of the Republicans on Congress*, ed. N. Rae and C. Campbell (Rowman and Littlefield, 1999), pp. 39–41.

32. The data are from the University of Washington's Policy Agendas Project (http://www.policyagendas.org).

33. "No Winners in Budget Showdown," *CQ Almanac* 51, 1995: 2-44–2-46; Walter Oleszek, *Congressional Procedures and the Policy Process*, sixth edition (CQ Press, 2004), pp. 63–67; Roger H. Davidson and Walter Oleszek, *Congress and Its Members*, tenth edition (CQ Press, 2006), pp. 446–447.

34. Bruce Babbitt, "Springtime for Polluters," *Washington Post*, October 22, 1995.

35. "Alaskan Refuge Bill Stalled," *CQ Almanac* 44, 1988: 173–174; "Arctic Refuge Battle," *CQ Almanac* 43, 1987: 298.

36. Hughes, quoted in "Arctic Refuge Bill Stalls Once Again," *CQ Almanac* 46, 1990: 315.

37. "Budget Veto Kills Arctic Drilling Plan," *CQ Almanac* 51, 1995: 5-22–5-23; Allan Freedman, "Supporters of Drilling See an Opening," *Congressional Quarterly Weekly Report*, August 12, 1995: 2440–2441.

38. Freedman, "Supporters of Drilling See an Opening," p. 2440.

39. "Budget Veto Kills Arctic Drilling Plan"; Ann DeVroy, "Veto Threatened over Arctic Drilling," *Washington Post*, September 22, 1995.

40. President William J. Clinton, "Seven Year Balanced Budget Reconciliation Act of 1995—Veto Message from the President of the United States" (December 6, 1995), http://thomas.loc.gov.

41. M. Lynne Corn and Bernard A. Gelb, "Arctic National Wildlife Refuge: Legislative Issues," issue brief for Congress, October 22, 2002 (Congressional Research Service).

42. Quoted in Eric Pianin, "GOP Targets Spending Bills as Battleground; Election-Year Riders Proliferate as Political and Social Agendas Are Promoted," *Washington Post*, June 28, 1998.

43. Oleszek, *Congressional Procedures*, pp. 53–56; Sandy Streeter, "The Congressional Appropriations Process: An Introduction," in CRS Report for Congress (97-684 GOV), 2004.

44. Sinclair, *Unconventional Lawmaking*, pp. 7, 8.

45. "Scaled-Back Interior Funding Zips Through," *CQ Almanac* 48, 1992: 691. Indeed, riders have occasionally played a major role in natural resources policy, such as the Forest Service organic act in 1897 and regarding public lands grazing in the 1940s.

46. Jane Braxton, "A Quiet Victory in Quincy," *High Country News*, November 9, 1998.

47. John H. Aldrich and David W. Rohde, "The Republican Revolution and the House Appropriations Committee," *Journal of Politics* 62, 2000: 9; Bryan W. Marshall, Brandon C. Prins, and David W. Rohde, "Majority Party Leadership, Strategic Choice, and Committee Power: Appropriations in the House," in *Congress on Display, Congress at Work*, ed. W. Bianco (University of Michigan Press, 2000), p. 72; Sinclair, "Partisan Imperatives and Institutional Constraints," pp. 26–28.

48. George Hager, "As They Cut, Appropriators Add a Stiff Dose of Policy," *Congressional Quarterly Weekly Report*, July 29, 1995: 2245–2248.

49. The description of the riders draws from Congressional Research Service, "Environmental Protection Agency FY 1996 Appropriations: Analyses of House-Passed Riders," *CRS Report for Congress*, 95-966, 1996.

50. Dingell, Lewis, and Obey, quoted in "Cuts Prompt Veto of VA-HUD Bill," *CQ Almanac* 51, 1995: 11-83–11-91; Livingston, quoted in Hager, "As They Cut," p. 2247.

51. Clinton, quoted in Dan Morgan, "Panetta Warns GOP on Spending Bills," *Washington Post*, July 12, 1995.

52. Boehlert, quoted in Jeffrey L. Katz, "GOP Moderates Join Democrats to Keep EPA Intact," *Congressional Quarterly Weekly Report*, November 4, 1995, p. 3383.

53. Dan Morgan, "House Reverses EPA Stance," *Washington Post*, August 1, 1995.

54. Boehlert, quoted in Dan Morgan, "Bid to Curb EPA Fails in House," *Washington Post*, November 3, 1995; Gingrich, quoted in Allan Freedman, "Republicans Concede Missteps in Effort to Rewrite Rules," *Congressional Quarterly Weekly Report*, December 2, 1995: 3645–3647.

55. Babbitt, "Springtime for Polluters."

56. Freedman, "The Environmental Trump Card"; "Interior Bill Sidesteps Controversy," *CQ Almanac* 52, 1996: 10–54.

57. "$16.3 Billion Cut from 1995 Spending," *CQ Almanac* 51, 1995: 11-96–11-105.

58. John Kingdon, *Agendas, Alternatives, and Public Policy*, second edition (Harper Collins, 1995), pp. 165–195.

59. Craig, quoted in *Congressional Record*, 104th Congress, 1st Session, 141, S 8468, March 30, 1995.

60. *Seattle Audubon Society v. Robertson*, 914 F.2d 1311 (Ninth Circuit Court of Appeals, 1990). This rider survived a constitutional challenge that reached the Supreme Court. Environmental groups complained that Congress had essentially directed the courts to resolve the cases leading to the injunctions against logging in specific ways, violating the separation of powers. The Court rejected this argument, finding that Section 318 actually changed the law rather than compelling particular judicial findings under the old law (*Robertson, et al., v. Seattle Audubon Society*, 502 U.S. 429, 1992). See also Keiter, *Keeping Faith with Nature*, pp. 105–108; Alyson Pytte, "Timber, Spotted Owl Interests Find Middle Ground Elusive," *Congressional Quarterly Weekly Report*, September 29, 1990, pp. 3104–3107.

61. *Seattle Audubon Society v. Robertson*, 1989, 1989 U.S. Dist. LEXIS 15005.

62. Patti A. Goldman and Kristen L. Boyles, "Forsaking the Rule of Law: The 1995 Logging without Laws Rider and Its Legacy," *Environmental Law* 27, 1997: 1070–1082; Kevin Kirchner, "Logging without Laws: How the Timber Rider Passed Congress," *Environmental Review Newsletter* 3, September 1996.

63. Michael C. Blumm, "Twenty Years of Environmental Law," *Virginia Environmental Law Journal* 20, 2001: 9.

64. Ross W. Gorte, "The Clinton Administration's Northwest Forest Plan," *CRS Report for Congress*, 93-664 ENR, 1993; "Record of Decision for Amendments to Forest Service and Bureau of Land Management Planning Documents within the Range of the Northern Spotted Owl,"April 13, 1994; Lauren M. Rule, "Enforcing Ecosystem Management under the Northwest Forest Plan," *Fordham Environmental Law Journal* 12, 2000: 211–252.

65. Eric Pryne, "Clinton Forest Plan Upheld," *Seattle Times*, December 21, 1994.

66. Gorton, quoted in *Congressional Record*, 104th Congress, 1st Session, 141, S4868, March 30, 1995.

67. Gorton, quoted in *Congressional Record*, 104th Congress, 2nd Session, 142, S1613, March 7, 1996.

68. Taylor, quoted in Goldman and Boyles, "Forsaking the Rule of Law."

69. Skaggs and Yates, quoted in Goldman and Boyles, "Forsaking the Rule of Law."

70. Murray, quoted in *Congressional Record*, 104th Congress, 1st Session, 141, S4868, March 30, 1995.

71. Slade Gorton and Larry E. Craig, "Congress's Call to Accounting: Riders Rein in the Worse Excesses of an Administration," *Washington Post*, July 27, 1998.

72. Clinton, quoted in Steven T. Taylor, "If a Tree Is Stolen from the Woods . . . Would the Clinton Administration Make Any Noise?" *Washington Post*, October 29, 1995.

73. "Message from the President of the United States Transmitting His Veto of H.R. 1158, A Bill Making Emergency Supplemental Appropriations for Additional Disaster Assistance, for Antiterrorism Initiatives, for Assistance in the Recovery From the Tragedy That Occurred at Oklahoma City, and Making Rescissions for the Fiscal Year Ending September 30, 1995 and for Other Purposes," 104th Congress, 1st Session, 104 H. Doc. 83, June 7, 1995.

74. Gorton, quoted in *Congressional Record*, Senate, 104th Congress, 1st Session, 141, S9480, June 30, 1995.

75. "$16.3 Billion Cut from 1995 Spending."

76. Goldman and Boyles, "Forsaking the Rule of Law."

77. Pope, quoted in Trilby C. E. Dorn, "Logging without Laws: The 1995 Salvage Logging Rider Radically Changes Policy and the Rule of Law in the Forests," *Tulane Environmental Law Journal* 9, 1996: 465.

78. Terry Tang, "A Clear-Cut Case of Slipping a Fast One Through Congress," *Seattle Times*, December 15, 1995.

79. Gorton, quoted in "Timber Salvage Bill Was Clear Bait 'N' Switch," *Seattle Times*, February 28, 1996. Clear cutting is the cutting and removal of all trees from an area of forest.

80. Public Law 104-19 [H.R. 1944], "Emergency Supplemental Appropriations for Additional Disaster Assistance, for Anti-Terrorism Initiatives, for Assistance in the Recovery From the Tragedy That Occurred at Oklahoma City, and Rescissions Act" (Rescissions Act), July 27, 1995, Title II; Pamela Baldwin, "The 'Timber Rider': Section 2001 of the Rescissions Act," CRS Report for Congress 96-163, 1996; Ross W. Gorte, "The Salvage Timber Sale Rider: Overview and Policy Issues," CRS Report for Congress 96-569 ENR, 1996.

81. Bradley, quoted in Terry Tang, "Salvaging the Sad Legacy of the 'Rider from Hell,'" *Seattle Times*, March 15, 1996.

82. Rescissions Act, Section 2001(3).

83. U.S. General Accounting Office, "Emergency Salvage Sale Program," GAO/RCED 97-53, 1997.

84. Baldwin, "The 'Timber Rider.'"

85. Kirchner, "Logging without Laws."

86. Fish and Wildlife Service official, quoted in Goldman and Boyles, "Forsaking the Rule of Law."

87. *Northwest Forest Council v. Glickman*, 82 F.3d 825 (Ninth Circuit, 1996); Goldman and Boyles, "Forsaking the Rule of Law."

88. *Northwest Forest Council v. Glickman*, 1996.

89. Jason M. Patlis, "The Endangered Species Act: Thirty years of Money, Politics, and Science," *Tulane Environmental Law Journal* 16, 2000: 283.

90. Dicks, quoted in Tang, "A Clear-Cut Case."

91. Danny Westneat, "War of the Woods, Cont.," *Seattle Times*, January 31, 1996.

92. Joel Connelly, "Timber Rider 'A Mistake': Clinton Wants to Repeal Law on Old-Growth Cuts," *Seattle Post-Intelligencer*, February 26, 1996; Scott Sonner, "Gore: Salvage Logging Was 'Biggest Mistake,'" *The Columbian*, September 27, 1996.

93. Court decisions, quoted in Wilderness Society, 2002, "Bush's Forest Plan: Salvage Rider Resurrected," http://www.wilderness.org.

94. GAO, "Emergency Salvage Sale Program: Forest Service Met Its Target, But More Timber Could Have Been Offered for Sale," GAO/RCED-97-53, 1997.

95. *Northwest Forest Resource Council v. Pilchuck Audubon Society*, 97 F.3d 1161 (Ninth Circuit, 1996).

96. Phillips, quoted in Danny Westneat, "Hew and Cry Put on Hold—Court Cancels Old-Growth Stands," *Seattle Times*, June 15, 1996.

97. Tom Kenworthy, "U.S., Timber Firms Agree to Save Old-Growth Trees," *Washington Post*, September 19, 1996.

98. Craig, quoted in Charles Pope, "Environmental Bills Hitch a Ride through the Legislative Gantlet," *CQ Weekly*, April 4, 1998; Margaret Kriz, "A Sneak Attack on the Greens," *National Journal*, April 12, 1997, p. 728; Kriz, "Rough Riders," *National Journal*, September 5, 1998, pp. 2022–2025.

99. University of Washington Policy Agendas Project (2006), http://www.policyagendas.org.

100. Rebecca Adams, "Democrats Decry Bush's Clean Air Plan as Favoring Industry over the Environment," *CQ Weekly*, August 3, 2002: 2119–2120. Cap-and-trade is a market-based policy tool to reduce pollution. An administrative agency (such as the EPA) sets a cap, or maximum limit, of a certain pollutant. Firms are allowed to emit a certain level of pollutant, and they receive allowances or permits equaling this level. The total pollution from all firms must be no more than that set by the cap. If a firm emits less than its allowable

level, it may sell its allowance on the market to firms that need additional allowances.

101. Jeffords and Voinovich, quoted in Shankar Vedantam, "Senate Impasse Stops 'Clear Skies' Measure," *Washington Post*, March 10, 2005.

102. Felicity Barringer, "EPA Accused of Predetermined Finding on Mercury," *New York Times*, February 4, 2005; Shankar Vedantam, "Mercury Emissions to Be Traded," *Washington Post*, March 15, 2005.

103. "House Passes Bush Energy Plan," *CQ Almanac* 57, 2001: 9-3–9-9; "Stakes Too High on Energy Bill," *CQ Almanac* 57, 2001: 8-3–8-8.

104. Joseph Anselmo, "MTBE Plan Incites Democrats, Six Republicans to Nix Energy Bill," *CQ Weekly*, November 29, 2003: 2968–2969; Joseph Anselmo, "The Failure of the Omnibus Energy Bill May Lead to Smaller Measures," *CQ Weekly*, December 6, 2003: 3032–3033.

105. Ben Evans, "Details of New Energy Policy Law," *CQ Weekly*, September 5, 2005: 2337.

106. Ibid.

107. Dingell, Markey, and Pope, quoted in Rebecca Adams, "Hard Fought Energy Bill Clears," *CQ Weekly*, July 29, 2005: 2108.

108. Members also sought legislative success by tailoring bills to local needs (e.g., the Clark County Public Lands and Natural Resources Act of 2002, designating nearly a half million acres of wilderness in southern Nevada while also moving thousands of acres of land out of federal ownership). Such bills sought to by-pass gridlock by focusing on more manageable issues. Yet even this approach has run into trouble in Idaho and Utah.

109. EPA, "Brownfields Cleanup and Redevelopment," http://www.epa.gov.

110. "Congress Clears Brownfields Bill," *CQ Almanac* 57, 2001: 9-11–9-12. The Davis-Bacon Act requires workers to receive prevailing local wages on federal projects, a provision strongly backed by unions.

111. Loni Radmall, "President George W. Bush's Forest Policy: Healthy Forest Restoration Act of 2003," *Journal of Land Resources and Environmental Law* 24, 2004: 528–536; Jacqueline Vaughn and Hanna Cortner, "Using Parallel Strategies to Promote Change: Forest Policymaking under George W. Bush," *Review of Policy Research* 21, 2004: 767–768.

112. Cat Lazaroff, "Sparks Fly at Hearing on Bush Fire Plan," Environmental News Service, September 6, 2002.

113. Rebecca Adams, "Rival Plans for Clearing Deadwood Roil Senate Debate on Interior Bill," *CQ Weekly*, September 14, 2002: 2381–2382; Mary Clare Jalonick, "Senate Looks to Interior Bill as Timely Vehicle for Debate on Forest Management Policy," *CQ Weekly*, June 28, 2003: 1623.

114. "Bush Wins Forest Thinning Law," *CQ Almanac* 59, 2003: 9-11–9-13; "Healthy Forests: An Initiative for Wildfire Prevention and Stronger Communities," http://www.whitehouse.gov; Mary Clare Jalonick, "House Take in Thinning Bill

Has No Chance, Say Senate Foes," *CQ Weekly*, May 24, 2003: 1259–1260; Jalonick, "Forest Thinning Bill Is Cleared after Negotiators Resolve Issues Outside of Blocked Conference," *CQ Weekly*, November 22, 2003: 2901; Margaret Kriz, "Bush's Quiet Plan," *National Journal*, November 23, 2002, pp. 3472–3477; Radmall, "President George W. Bush's Forest Policy"; Vaughn and Cortner, "Using Parallel Strategies."

115. Justin Blum, "Another Energy Push Planned," *Washington Post*, February 13, 2005; Justin Blum and Jim VandeHei, "Bush Steps Up Pitch for Drilling in the Refuge," *Washington Post*, March 10, 2005.

116. "Budget Politics," *Washington Post*, March 15, 2005.

117. Stevens, quoted in Justin Blum, "Close Senate Vote Shapes Up on Drilling in Wildlife Refuge," *Washington Post*, March 16, 2005.

118. Cantwell and Gregg, quoted in *Congressional Record*, 109th Congress, 1st Session, 151, S 2759, March 16, 2005.

119. Pombo, quoted in Jonathan Weisman, "Budget Deal Sets Stage for Arctic Drilling and Tax Cuts," *Washington Post*, April 29, 2005; Ben Evans, "The Long Road to ANWR Exploration," *CQ Weekly*, March 21, 2005: 723.

120. Stevens, quoted in Ann Plummer, "ANWR: Oil Drilling," *CQ Weekly*, January 9, 2006: 118; Juliet Eilperin, "And the Saga on Arctic Oil Drilling Continues," *Washington Post*, December 22, 2005; Ben German, "ANWR, Offshore Drilling Jettisoned in House," *Environment and Energy Daily*, November 10, 2005.

121. Ben Evans, "ANWR Still Divides Lawmakers," *CQ Weekly*, March 17, 2006: 764; Jeff Tollefson, "House Again OKs ANWR Drilling," *CQ Weekly*, May 26, 2006: 1474.

122. Lilly, quoted in Andrew Taylor, "Appropriators' Crunch Month Tests GOP Resolve, Unity," *CQ Weekly*, July 5, 2003: 1683–1685.

123. Rebecca Adams, "Bush Attack on Regulations for Arsenic, Surface Mining Has Democrats Vowing Action," *CQ Weekly*, March 24, 2001: 670; "VA-HUD Funds Grow $4.4 Billion," *CQ Almanac* 57, 2001: 2–54.

124. Rebecca Adams, "Democrats Vow to Block Interior Rider," *CQ Weekly*, April 14, 2002: 846–848; "Interior Request Tops $1 Billion," *CQ Almanac* 57, 2001: 2–30.

125. "Interior Request Tops $1 Billion," p. 2–33.

126. On the use of a rider to compel the Forest Service to implement the local collaborative conservation plan developed by the Quincy Library Group, see chapter 6.

127. E. J. Dionne, *Why Americans Hate Politics* (Touchstone, 1991), pp. 9–28.

128. Orren and Skowronek, *The Search for American Political Development*; Weber, *Pluralism by the Rules*.

129. Michael J. Crozier, Samuel P. Huntington, and JoJi Watanuki, *Crisis of Democracy: Report on the Governability of Democracies to the Trilateral Commission* (New York University Press, 1975).

Chapter 4

1. Hays, *Conservation and the Gospel of Efficiency*; Theodore Roosevelt Association, "Conservationist: Life of Theodore Roosevelt," http://www.theodoreroosevelt.org.

2. Terry M. Moe, "The Politicized Presidency," in *The New Directions in American Politics*, ed. J. Chubb and P. Peterson (Brookings Institution, 1985), pp. 235–271; Stephen Skowronek, *The Politics Presidents Make: Leadership from John Adams to George Bush* (Harvard University Press, 1993), pp. 29–32.

3. On the challenges of controlling specific conservation policies through the administrative presidency, see Robert F. Durant, *The Administrative Presidency Revisited: Public Lands, the BLM, and the Reagan Revolution* (SUNY Press, 1992). On the administrative presidency and the environment more generally, see Robert A. Shanley, *Presidential Influence and Environmental Policy* (Greenwood, 1992); Dennis L. Soden, ed., *The Environmental Presidency* (SUNY Press, 1999). For recent works on executive power generally, see Phillip J. Cooper, *By Order of the President: The Use and Abuse of Executive Direct Action* (University Press of Kansas, 2002); William G. Howell, *Power without Persuasion: The Politics of Direct Presidential Action* (Princeton University Press, 2003); Kenneth R. Mayer, *With the Stroke of a Pen: Executive Orders and Presidential Power* (Princeton University Press, 2001).

4. Jonathan P. West and Glen Sussman, "Implementation of Environmental Policy: The Chief Executive," in *The Environmental Presidency*, ed. D. Soden (SUNY Press, 1999), p. 80; Shanley, *Presidential Influence*, pp. 49–89.

5. U.S. National Archives and Records Administration, "Executive Orders Disposition Tables: Administration of William J. Clinton (1993–2001)," http://www.archives.gov; U.S. National Archives and Records Administration, "Executive Orders Disposition Tables: Administration of George W. Bush (2001–Present)," http://www.archives.gov.

6. Shanley, *Presidential Influence*, pp. 27–48, 61–78; West and Sussman, "Implementation of Environmental Policy," p. 87.

7. John D. Leshy, "The Babbitt Legacy at the Department of the Interior: A Preliminary View," *Environmental Law* 31, 2001: 213–219.

8. U.S Forest Service and Bureau of Land Management, "Record of Decision for Amendments to Forest Service and Bureau of Land Management Planning Documents within the Range of the Northern Spotted Owl," April 13, 1994.

9. Ullrich, quoted in Joel A. Mintz, "Treading Water: A Preliminary Assessment of EPA Enforcement during the Bush II Administration," *ELR News and Analysis* 34, 2004, p. 10935.

10. Seth Borenstein, "Pollution Enforcement Off Under Bush, Files Show," *Pittsburgh Post-Gazette*, December 9, 2003. The study compared the Clinton administration monthly average to the Bush administration's record through December 2003.

11. Mintz, "Treading Water," pp. 10937–10940.

12. Matthew Daley, "Getting His Way by Settling Lawsuits," *Detroit News*, April 19, 2003.

13. Senator Charles E. Schumer, n.d., "The Environmental Record of the Ashcroft Department of Justice," http://schumer.senate.gov.

14. Daley, "Getting His Way."

15. APA, quoted in Martin Nie, "Administrative Rulemaking and Public Lands Conflict: The Forest Service's Roadless Rule," *Natural Resources Journal* 44, 2004: 687–742.

16. Sheila M. Cavanagh, Robert W. Hahn, and Robert N. Stavins, "National Environmental Policy during the Clinton Years," paper presented at Economic Policy during the 1990s Conference, Harvard University, 2001, p. 2; Leshy, "The Babbitt Legacy," p. 212; William Booth, "A Slow Start Built to an Environmental End-Run; President Went around Congress to Build Green Legacy," *Washington Post*, January 13, 2001; Keiter, *Keeping Faith with Nature*, pp. 113–117. The ESA rules dealt with safe harbor, no surprises, and candidate conservation agreements. (See chapter 6.)

17. Felicity Barringer, "Bush's Record: New Priorities in Environment," *New York Times*, September 14, 2004; Environment 2004, "Putting Polluters First: The Bush Administration's Environmental Record," http://www.environment2004.org; Juliet Eilperin, "Standoff in Congress Blocks Action on Environmental Bills," *Washington Post*, October 18, 2004.

18. Barringer, "Bush's Record"; Environment 2004, "Putting Polluters First"; Blaine Harden, "Proposal Restricts Appeals on Dams," *Washington Post*, October 28, 2004; Douglas Jehl, "On Rules for Environment, Bush Sees a Balance, Critics a Threat," *New York Times*, February 23, 2003; White House, "Key Bush Environmental Accomplishments," http://www.whitehouse.gov. For other overviews of the Bush environmental record, with a clearly partisan perspective, see Robert S. Devine, *Bush Versus the Environment* (Anchor, 2004); Carl Pope and Paul Rauber, *Strategic Ignorance: Why the Bush Administration Is Recklessly Destroying a Century of Environmental Progress* (Sierra Club Books, 2004).

19. Pope, quoted in Joel Brinkley, "Out of Spotlight, Bush Overhauls U.S. Regulations," *New York Times*, August 14, 2004.

20. Paul Larmer, "A Bold Stroke: Clinton Takes a 1.7 Million Acre Stand in Utah," *High Country News*, September 30, 1996.

21. Carol Hardy Vincent and Pamela Baldwin, "National Monuments and the Antiquities Act," RL30528, *CRS Report for Congress*, April 17, 2000.

22. Keiter, *Keeping Faith with Nature*, pp. 169–218; Sanjay Ranchod, "The Clinton National Monuments: Protecting Ecosystems with the Antiquities Act," *Harvard Environmental Law Review* 25, 2001: 535–589; Andrew C. Revkin, "Bush Plans Vast Protected Sea Area in Hawaii," *New York Times*, June 15, 2006.

George W. Bush's first national monument covered less than an acre; his second—the Northwestern Hawaiian Islands Marine National Monument—covered over 89 million acres, primarily of ocean. This national monument largely codified action taken by Clinton via executive order.

23. Ann E. Halden, "The Grand Staircase-Escalante National Monument and the Antiquities Act," *Fordham Environmental Law Journal* 8, 1997: 713–739; Mark Squillace, "The Monumental Legacy of the Antiquities Act of 1906," *Georgia Law Review* 37, 2003: 473–610.

24. American Antiquities Act of 1906, 16 U.S.C. Sections 431–433.

25. Ranchod, "The Clinton National Monuments," p. 585; U.S. National Park Service, "National Monument Proclamations under the Antiquities Act," http://www.cr.nps.gov.

26. Christine A. Klein, "Preserving Monumental Landscapes under the Antiquities Act," *Cornell Law Review* 87, 2002: 1333–1404.

27. Loretta Tofani, "Fallback Methods Studied for Saving Alaska Lands," *Washington Post*, August 1, 1978.

28. Andrus, quoted in Ward Sinclair, "Carter Aides Hit Alaska Lands Bill as 'Unacceptable,'" *Washington Post*, April 26, 1979; Margot Hornblower, "US Moves to Protect Alaska Land: Andrus Sets Aside 100 Million Acres Pending Hill Action," *Washington Post*, November 17, 1978.

29. G. Frank Williss, "Do Things Right the First Time: Administrative History of the National Park Service and the Alaska National Interest Lands Act of 1980," U.S. National Park Service, 1985.

30. Hammond, quoted in Kathy Koch, "Senate Alaska Lands Debate Underscores Political Split between Gravel and Stevens," *Congressional Quarterly Weekly Report*, July 19, 1980, p. 2016.

31. Timothy Egan, "Alaska Changes Its View on Carter after 20 Years," *New York Times*, August 25, 2000; Williss, "Do Things Right."

32. Squillace, "The Monumental Legacy."

33. Udall, quoted in Williss, "Do Things Right"; Klein, "Preserving Monumental Landscapes."

34. Babbitt, quoted in Lee Davidson, "Babbitt Talks of Three New Monuments," *Salt Lake City Deseret News*, October 20, 1999.

35. Leshy, quoted in Klein, "Preserving Monumental Landscapes."

36. Keiter, *Keeping Faith with Nature*, pp. 180–186; Tom Kenworthy, "President Considers Carving National Monument Out of Utah Land," *Washington Post*, September 7, 1996; Larmer, "A Bold Stroke."

37. Hatch, quoted in Tom Kenworthy, "Conservation Debate Rages over Much of Utah's Grand Staircase," *Washington Post*, June 17, 1995.

38. Bob Benenson, "Utah Wilderness Designation Approved by House Panel," *Congressional Quarterly Weekly Report*, August 5, 1995, p. 2359; "The

Congressional Land Grab," *New York Times*, November 15, 1995; Timothy Egan, "In Utah, a Pitched Battle over Public Lands," *New York Times*, November 13, 1995; Allan Freedman, "Amid Criticism, Panel Approves Utah Wilderness Legislation," *Congressional Quarterly Weekly Report*, December 9, 1995, p. 3737; Testimony of Sylvia Baca, Deputy Assistant Secretary, Department of the Interior, 1995, House Committee on Resources, Subcommittee on National Parks, Forests, and Lands, regarding H.R. 1745 and H.R. 1500, Utah Wilderness Hearing, June 29, retrieved through Lexis-Nexis.

39. Helen Dewar, "Senate Passes Parklands Bill after Dropping Utah Wilderness Proposal," *Washington Post*, May 3, 1996.

40. Testimony of Michael Leavitt, Governor of the State of Utah, House Committee on Resources, Subcommittee on National Parks, Forests, and Lands, regarding H.R. 1745 and H.R. 1500, Utah Wilderness Hearing, June 29, 1995, retrieved through Lexis-Nexis.

41. Kenworthy, "President Considers Carving National Monument Out of Utah Land."

42. Lee Davidson, "Utah Delegates Vow to Block It—If It Happens," *Salt Lake City Deseret News*, September 10, 1996.

43. Lee Davidson, "Republicans Leave No Hearing Unheld in Seeking Culprit," *Salt Lake City Deseret News*, September 27, 1996.

44. Larmer, "A Bold Stroke."

45. Hatch, quoted in Heidi Biasi, "The Antiquities Act of 1906 and Presidential Proclamations: A Retrospective and Prospective Analysis of President William J. Clinton's Quest to 'Win the West,'" *Buffalo Environmental Law Journal* 9, 2002: 189–244; Bennett, quoted in Larmer, "A Bold Stroke"; Murkowski, quoted in Lee Davidson, "GOP Aims to Head off Monument 'End Runs,'" *Salt Lake City Deseret News*, September 30, 1996; Peterson, quoted in Lee Spangler, "Lawmakers Fear Trust Is Broken on Federal Lands," *Salt Lake City Deseret News*, February 12, 1997; Chenoweth, quoted in Al Kamen, "Switching Power: Easier to Pull the Plug," *Washington Post*, June 28, 2000; Lee Davidson, "Green Light for Monument Has Utahns Seeing Red," *Salt Lake City Deseret News*, September 18, 1996; Davidson, "Republicans Leave No Hearing Unheld."

46. *Utah Association of Counties v. Bush*, 316 F. Supp. 2d 1172 (C.D. Utah, 2004); Eric Rusnak, "The Straw that Broke the Camel's Back? Grand Staircase Escalante National Monument Antiquates the Antiquities Act," *Ohio State Law Journal* 64, 2003: 669–730.

47. Lee Davidson, "Surprise! Some Say Monument Wasn't," *Salt Lake City Deseret News*, October 2, 1997.

48. Hedden, quoted in Larmer, "A Bold Stroke."

49. Adam Graham-Silverstein, "Panel Votes to Curb President's Power to Designate Monuments," *CQ Weekly*, August 4, 2001: 1929; Klein, "Preserving Monumental Landscapes"; Rusnak, "The Straw that Broke the Camel's Back?"

50. *Utah Association of Counties v. Bush*, 2004.

51. Squillace, "The Monumental Legacy."

52. Testimony of Bruce Babbitt, Secretary of the Interior, House Committee on Resources, Subcommittee on National Parks and Public Lands, regarding H.R. 2795, Shivwits Plateau National Conservation Area, October 19, 1999, retrieved through Lexis-Nexis.

53. Jana Prewitt and Victoria Voytko, "A History of the U.S. Department of Interior during the Clinton Administration: 1993–2001," Clinton Administration History Project, Washington (2000), http://library.doi.gov. These congressionally protected areas were the Colorado Canyons National Conservation Area, the Las Cienegas National Conservation Area in Arizona, the Santa Rosa and San Jacinto Mountains National Monument in California, and the Steens Mountain Cooperative Management and Protection Area in Oregon.

54. James B. Rasband, "Moving Forward: The Future of the Antiquities Act," *Journal of Land Resources and Environmental Law* 21, 2001: 619–634.

55. Timothy Egan, "The Land Rush: Putting Some Space between His Presidency and His History," *New York Times*, January 16, 2000; Ranchod, "The Clinton National Monuments."

56. Pope, quoted in Douglas Jehl, "The Environment: How an Interior Secretary Helped to Encourage a Presidential 'Legacy,'" *New York Times*, January 19, 2001.

57. Babbitt, quoted in Len Iwanski, 2000, "Congressional Action Best for Missouri Breaks, Babbitt Says," Associated Press, May 3; "Interior Secretary Says He'll Use Sen. Baucus' Suggestions about 'Breaks,'" 2000, Associated Press, April 25; "400 Rally to Oppose National Monument Designation for Missouri Breaks," 2000, Associated Press, April 14.

58. *Tulare County v. Bush*, 540 U.S. 813 (2003); *Tulare County v. Bush*, 306 F.3d 1138 (D.C. Cir., 2002); *Tulare County v. Bush*, 185 F. Supp. 2d 18 (D.D.C., 2001).

59. Lockhart, quoted in Ranchod, "The Clinton National Monuments."

60. Rebecca Adams, "Environmentalists Question Norton's Conciliatory Stands, But Confirmation Expected," *CQ Weekly*, January 20, 2001: 191–192; Eric Pianin, "White House Won't Fight Monument Designations; Norton Says Boundaries, Land Use Rules May Be Amended," *Washington Post*, February 21, 2001.

61. Graham, *The Morning after Earth Day*.

62. Craig W. Allin, *The Politics of Wilderness Preservation* (Greenwood, 1982); Michael P. Dombeck, Christopher A. Wood, and Jack E. Williams, *From Conquest to Conservation: Our Public Lands Legacy* (Island, 2003), pp. 93–116; "The National Wilderness Preservation System," http://www.wilderness.net. The Federal Land Policy and Management Act in 1976 made Bureau of Land Management holdings eligible for Wilderness Act protection.

63. Keiter, *Keeping Faith with Nature*, pp. 198–203; Nie, "Administrative Rulemaking."

64. Dombeck et al., *From Conquest to Conservation*, pp. 95, 96, 103–106; Charles Pope, "A Little Compromise Goes a Long Way in Interior Spending Debate," *CQ Weekly*, July 25, 1998: 2012.

65. Quotes from Forest Service, "Special Areas; Roadless Area Conservation; Final Rule," January 12, 2001 (66 *Federal Register* 3245, generally pp. 3246–3247); Dombeck et al., *From Conquest to Conservation*, pp. 94–104; Ross W. Gorte, "Forest Roads: Construction and Financing," CRS Report for Congress 97–706 ENR, 1997. See also David G. Havlick, *No Place Distant: Roads and Motorized Recreation on America's Public Lands* (Island, 2002), pp. 36–58; U.S. General Accounting Office (GAO), "Forest Service Roadless Areas: Potential Impact of Proposed Regulations on Ecological Sustainability," Report to Congressional Requesters, GAO-01-47, 2000.

66. American Forest & Paper Association, "Inventoried Roadless Areas," http://www.afandpa.org.

67. Craig, quoted in John H. Cushman, "Administration Proposes Moratorium on New Logging Roads," *New York Times*, January 23, 1998; Dombeck et al., *From Conquest to Conservation*, quote p. 107, pp. 106–107; Pamela Baldwin, "The National Forest System Roadless Areas Initiative," *CRS Report for Congress*, RL 30647, 2003, pp. 2–3; John H. Cushman, "Forest Workers Protest Logging," *New York Times*, January 22, 1999; Ross W. Gorte, "Roadless Areas: The Administration's Moratorium," *CRS Report for Congress*, RS 20150, 1999. "Inventoried roadless" refers to areas of national forests identified as roadless during various inventories the Forest Service has undertaken pursuant to the Wilderness Act and forest planning provisions. Some inventoried roadless areas contained roads at the time of the inventory, and in others roads were built following the inventory.

68. Clinton, quoted in Dombeck et al., *From Conquest to Conservation*, p. 110; ibid., quote p. 110, pp. 110–111; Baldwin, "The National Forest System Roadless Areas Initiative," pp. 3, 4, 8, 9. A final rule dealing with the entire national forest road system focusing on existing road maintenance and road decommissioning, rather than building new roads, was finalized on January 12, 2001 (36 C.F.R. Section 212). Forest planning regulations adopted in November 2000 required that roadless areas be explicitly discussed in the revision of forest plans. Revisions to these regulations proposed in December 2002 and finalized in January 2005 eliminated any special consideration for roadless lands in forest plan revisions (36 C.F.R. Section 219).

69. Klein, quoted in Tom Kenworthy, "Clinton Readies Forest Protection Initiative; Directive Would Shield 40 Million Acres," *Washington Post*, October 8, 1999; Rait, quoted in Charles Babington, "Forest Protection Plan Is Unveiled; Clinton Initiative Aims to Ban Road-Building, Logging on 40 Million Acres," *Washington Post*, October 14, 1999. The Heritage Forest Campaign is an alliance of regional and national environmental groups focused on protecting public lands forests.

70. Hamilton, quoted in Douglas Jehl, "In Idaho, a Howl against Roadless Forests," *New York Times*, July 5, 2000; James Dao, "Gore Expands on Clinton's

Forest Protection Plan," *New York Times*, May 31, 2000; Dombeck et al., *From Conquest to Conservation*, pp. 93, 94, 110–112; *Kootenai Tribe of Idaho v. Veneman*, 313 F.3d 1105 (Ninth Circuit, 2002); GAO 2000, p. 9. The process leading to adoption of the final roadless rule in January 2001 included more than 600 public meetings and generated 1.6 million public comments.

71. Dombeck et al., *From Conquest to Conservation*, quotes pp. 113, 114, generally pp. 112–114.

72. Rait, quoted in Douglas Jehl, "Road Ban Set for One-Third of U.S. Forests," *New York Times*, January 5, 2001; Baldwin, "The National Forest System Roadless Areas Initiative," pp. 6–8; Forest Service, "Special Areas," pp. 3243–3273; 36 C.F.R. Part 294; *Kootenai Tribe of Idaho v. Veneman* (2002), p. 1105.

73. Baldwin, "The National Forest System Roadless Areas Initiative," pp. 12–15.

74. *Kootenai Tribe of Idaho v. Veneman*, 142 F. Supp 2d 1231 (D. Idaho, 2001), quotes from pp. 1244, 1247; *Idaho ex rel. Kempthorne v. U.S. Forest Service*, 142 F. Supp 2d 1248 (D. Idaho, 2001). The Kootenai Tribe and the state of Idaho were joined in these challenges by two Idaho counties, a timber company, livestock companies, and motorized recreation groups. Several environmental groups, ranging from the Idaho Conservation League to the Wilderness Society, intervened on behalf of the Forest Service. The injunction also applied to the relevant provisions of the new planning regulations. Legal challenges began even before the roadless rule was finalized. For example, a lawsuit to block the rule over violations of NEPA and NFMA was dismissed as premature in 2000 (*State of Idaho, et al. v. United States Forest Service*). Additional legal challenges were filed in Alaska, the District of Columbia, North Dakota, Utah, and Wyoming.

75. Baldwin, "The National Forest System Roadless Areas Initiative," pp. 16–21.

76. *Kootenai Tribe of Idaho v. Veneman* (2002); Mike Soraghan, "Judge Blocks Ban on Logging, Drilling; Administration Set Stage, Critics Charge," *Denver Post*, May 11, 2001.

77. Baldwin, "The National Forest System Roadless Areas Initiative," p. 24; Forest Service, "Final Rule, Special Areas; Roadless Area Conservation; Applicability to the Tongass National Forest, Alaska," December 30, 2003 (68 *Federal Register* 75136); Katharine Q. Seelye, "Bush to Prohibit Building Roads inside Forests," *New York Times*, June 10, 2003.

78. *State of Wyoming v. United States Department of Agriculture*, 277 F. Supp. 2d 1197 (D. Wyo., 2003); *State of Wyoming v. United States Department of Agriculture*, 414 F.3d 1207 (10th Cir., 2005); Associated Press, "U.S. Fights Roadless Appeal Case," November 14, 2003. The Brimmer decision is illustrative of both the political perspectives and activism that is found in the judicial pathway. Judge Brimmer's political perspective is made clear in a number of places, including the first sentence of his opinion: "Today, the Court considers the legality of 58.5 million acres of roadless area that the United States Forest Service drove through the administrative process in a vehicle smelling of political prestidigitation" (p. 1203), as well as "In its rush to give President Clinton lasting

notoriety in the annals of environmentalism . . ." (p. 1232) and "The Court cannot condone what the Forest Service has done in its rush to provide environmental fame for a President in the last days of his term" (p. 1238). Examples of judicial activism include Judge Brimmer finding Forest Service actions that are legally discretionary—extending comment periods beyond legal minimums and granting cooperative agency status to states—to be arbitrary and capricious.

79. Veneman, quoted in "Veneman Acts to Conserve Roadless Areas in National Forests," 2004, USDA News Release 0283.04; Kempthorne, quoted in Felicity Barringer, "Bush Seeks Shift in Logging Rules," *New York Times*, July 13, 2004; Pombo, quoted in Theo Stein, "Proposal to Put Forests on the Table; States Would Get Say on Projects," *Denver Post*, July 13, 2004.

80. Clapp, quoted in Stein, "Proposal to Put Forests on the Table"; Sittenfeld, quoted in Dan Berman, "Plan Allowing States to Apply for Roadless Rule Exemption to Proceed," *Greenwire*, July 2, 2004; Bill Clinton, "Our Forests May Be on a Road to Ruin," *Los Angeles Times*, August 4, 2004; Felicity Barringer, "Bush Administration Rolls Back Rule on Building Forest Roads," *New York Times*, May 6, 2005; Forest Service, "Special Areas; State Petitions for Inventoried Roadless Area Management; Roadless Area Conservation National Advisory Committee; Final Rule and Notice," May 13, 2005 (70 *Federal Register* 25653–25662).

81. Crapo, quoted in Greg Stahl, "Roadless Areas Rule Could Be Overturned," *Idaho Mountain Express*, July 14, 2004.

82. *People of the State of California v. United States Department of Agriculture* 459 F. Supp. 2d 874 (N.D. Cal., 2006); Dan Berman, "20 Enviro Groups Ask Court to Restore Clinton Roadless Rule," *Greenwire*, October 7, 2005; Bettina Boxall, "Repeal of Road Ban Challenged," *Los Angeles Times*, August 31, 2005; Evan Tea, "Clinton-era Roadless Rule Is Back . . . for Now," *High Country News*, October 16, 2006.

83. Dombeck et al., *From Conquest to Conservation*, quote pp. 94, 95.

84. Keiter, *Keeping Faith with Nature*, p. 121.

85. "A Chronology of the Roadless Area Conservation Policy," Wilderness Society, http://www.wilderness.org; Dombeck et al., *From Conquest to Conservation*, p. 200; Dan Berman, "Appropriations: House Votes to Limit Tongass Roads as Part of Interior Spending Bill," *Environment & Energy Daily*, May 19, 2006. An effort by Senator Craig to block the roadless rule via a rider in 2000 was scuttled by Senate colleagues still smarting over losses to Clinton on such riders and his decision to let the court cases play out first.

86. Arnold W. Reitze, "State and Federal Command-and-Control Regulation of Emissions from Fossil-Fuel Electric Power Generating Plants," *Environmental Law* 32, 2002: 369–433. The emissions data are from 1998.

87. Andrews, *Managing the Environment, Managing Ourselves*, pp. 232–236. In some places where air pollution was especially bad, new pollution control equipment would need to be employed at existing factories. In such cases,

Congress reasoned, it was better to let states require such controls as part of their SIPs.

88. R. Shep Melnick, *Regulation and the Courts: The Case of the Clean Air Act* (Brookings Institution, 1983), pp. 71–112; Reitze, "State and Federal Command-and-Control Regulation," pp. 385, 386; Matthew C. Stephenson, "A Tale of Two Theories: The Legal Basis for EPA's Proposed Revision to the Routine Maintenance, Repair, and Replacement Exception, and the Implications for Administrative Law," *Environmental Law Reporter* 33, 2003: 10791–10792.

89. Reitze, "State and Federal Command-and-Control Regulation," pp. 385, 386; Stephenson, "A Tale of Two Theories," pp. 10791, 10792.

90. CAA, quoted in Stephenson, "A Tale of Two Theories," p. 10792, pp. 10790–10793 generally; *Alabama Power Co. v. Costle*, 636 F.2d 323 (D.C. Cir., 1979); National Academy of Public Administration, *A Breath of Fresh Air: Reviving the New Source Review Program* (National Academy of Public Administration, 2003), pp. 34, 35, 39–41.

91. Reitze, "State and Federal Command-and-Control Regulation," pp. 410–416.

92. *Wisconsin Electric Power Company v. Reilly*, 893 F.2d 901 (7th Cir., 1990); Stephenson, "A Tale of Two Theories," p. 10793.

93. National Academy of Public Administration, *A Breath of Fresh Air*, pp. 37–40, 59–60; Larry B. Parker and John E. Blodgett, "Air Quality and Electricity: Enforcing New Source Review," *CRS Report for Congress*, RL 30432, 2000.

94. Bruce Barcott, "Changing All the Rules," *New York Times Magazine*, April 4, 2004; Parker and Blodgett, "Air Quality and Electricity"; Reitze, "State and Federal Command-and-Control Regulation," pp. 389–392.

95. Browner, quoted in Parker and Blodgett, "Air Quality and Electricity," and generally; Riedinger and Lawrence, quoted in Barcott, "Changing All the Rules," and generally; Edison Electric Institute, 2001, "Straight Talk about Electric Utilities and New Source Review," http://www.eei.org. A report by the Congressional Research Service came to ambiguous conclusions about reductions, depending on complex interactions among NSR and acid rain reduction programs, new source performance standards, and fuel source.

96. National Energy Policy Development Group, *National Energy Policy: Report of the National Energy Policy Development Group* (Government Printing Office, 2001), p. 7–14; Neela Banerjee, "Energy Giants Push to Weaken a Pollution Rule," *New York Times*, April 12, 2002; Barcott, "Changing All the Rules"; Juliet Eilperin, "Standoff in Congress Blocks Action on Environmental Bills," *Washington Post*, October 18, 2004; Reitze, "State and Federal Command-and-Control Regulation," pp. 391–395; Darren Samuelsohn and Colin Sullivan, "Deadlocked Panel Defeats 'Clear Skies,'" *Greenwire*, March 9, 2005.

97. King, quoted in Joseph Kahn, "Criticism and Support for Rules on Clean Air," *New York Times*, July 11, 2001; U.S. Environmental Protection Agency, "New Source Review: Report to the President," 2002, p. 1; U.S. EPA, "NSR 90-Day Review Background Paper," 2001.

98. Barcott, "Changing All the Rules"; Christopher Drew and Richard A. Oppel, "How Industry Won the Battle of Pollution Control at E.P.A.," *New York Times*, March 6, 2004.

99. American Lung Association, quoted in Barcott, "Changing All the Rules," and generally; EPA, "Prevention of Significant Deterioration (PSD) and Nonattainment New Source Review (NSR), Final Rule and Proposed Rule," December 31, 2002 (67 *Federal Register* 80186–80289); EPA, "Prevention of Significant Deterioration (PSD) and Non-attainment New Source Review (NSR): Routine Maintenance, Repair and Replacement, Proposed Rule," December 31, 2002 (67 *Federal Register* 80290–80314); National Academy of Public Administration, *A Breath of Fresh Air*, pp. 66–76; Stephenson, "A Tale of Two Theories," pp. 10790–10798. The D.C. Court of Appeals ruling on the first NSR rule came in June 2005. The court upheld the emission rate and plantwide applicability provisions, but rejected the clean units, pollution prevention, and control project provisions (*State of New York v. U.S. Environmental Protection Agency*, 413 F.3d 3 (D.C. Cir., 2005); Darren Samuelsohn, "Interpretations of NSR Ruling Vary Widely," *Greenwire*, June 24, 2005).

100. Jeffords and Spitzer, quoted in Katharine Q. Seelye, "Draft of Air Rule Is Said to Exempt Many Old Plants," *New York Times*, August 22, 2003; Schaeffer, quoted in Barcott, "Changing All the Rules," and generally; EPA, "Prevention of Significant Deterioration (PSD) and Non-Attainment New Source Review (NSR): Equipment Replacement Provision of the Routine Maintenance, Repair and Replacement Exclusion; Final Rule," October 27, 2003 (68 *Federal Register* 61248–61280); GAO, "Clean Air Act: Key Stakeholders' Views on Revisions to the New Source Review Program," GAO-04-274, 2004; Stephenson, "A Tale of Two Theories," p. 10794.

101. Bush, quoted in Barcott, "Changing All the Rules," and generally; Kuhn, quoted in Eric Pianin, "EPA Eases Clean Air Rule on Power Plants," *Washington Post*, August 28, 2003; GAO, "Clean Air Act."

102. Spitzer, quoted in Terence Neilan, "14 States File Suit in Attempt to Block New E.P.A. Rules," *New York Times*, November 17, 2003; Stephenson, "A Tale of Two Theories," pp. 10795–10807. The 14 states were California, Connecticut, Illinois, Maine, Maryland, Massachusetts, New Hampshire, New Jersey, New Mexico, New York, Pennsylvania, Rhode Island, Vermont, and Wisconsin.

103. *Chevron U.S.A., Inc. v. Natural Resources Defense Council*, 467 U.S. 837 (1984); Stephenson, "A Tale of Two Theories."

104. Spitzer, quoted in Darren Samuelsohn, "Court Blocks Implementation of Bush NSR Reforms," *Greenwire*, December 26, 2003; *State of New York, et al. v. United States Environmental Protection Agency*, Emergency Motion for Stay, November 14, 2003 (D.C. Cir., Docket 03-1380), pp. 1, 7, and generally.

105. Anthony DePalma, "4 Northeast States Join against Pollution," *New York Times*, May 21, 2004; Christopher Drew and Richard A. Oppel, "Lawyers at E.P.A. Say It Will Drop Pollution Cases," *New York Times*, November 6, 2003; Juliet Eilperin, "EPA Issues Draft Rules on Plants' Emissions," *Washington Post*,

October 14, 2005; Michael Janofsky, "Inspector General Says E.P.A. Rule Aids Polluters," *New York Times*, October 1, 2004; Jerry Markon, "Duke Energy Did Not Break Law, Court Says," *Washington Post*, June 16, 2005; Darren Samuelsohn, "Second Wave of NSR Cases Await Bush Administration Action," *Greenwire*, July 14, 2004; Samuelsohn, "Ohio Edison Reaches $1.1 Billion NSR Settlement," *Greenwire*, March 18, 2005; Samuelsohn, "After Nine Years, NSR Battle Lands in Supreme Court," *Greenwire*, October 31, 2006; *United States of America v. Duke Energy Corporation*, 411 F.3d 539 (4th Cir., 2005); *United States of America v. Cinergy Corporation*, 458 F.3d 705 (7th Cir., 2006).

106. *State of New York, et al. v. Environmental Protection Agency*, 443 F.3d 880 (D.C. Cir., 2006); Darren Samuelsohn, "Bush Admin Seeks Supreme Court Review on NSR Rule," *Greenwire*, November 28, 2006.

107. Barcott, "Changing All the Rules"; Tom Hamburger and Alan C. Miller, "EPA Targets Mercury 'Hot Spots' at Power Plants," *Los Angeles Times*, March 16, 2005; Mary Clare Jalonick, "Clean Air: Going the Regulatory Route," *CQ Weekly*, June 7, 2003: 1383; Michael Janofsky, "E.P.A. Sets Rules to Cut Power Plant Pollution," *New York Times*, March 11, 2005.

Chapter 5

1. *Tennessee Valley Authority v. Hill*, 437 U.S. 153 (1978).

2. Oliver S. Houck, "Unfinished Stories," *University of Colorado Law Review* 73, 2002: 867–943; Melnick, *Regulation and the Courts*; Lettie Wenner, *The Environmental Decade in Court* (University of Indiana Press, 1982).

3. Suckling, quoted in Kathie Durbin, "Timber's Bad Boy Comes to the Table," *High Country News*, August 4, 1997; Craig Welch, "Feds Losing Grip on Species Act," *Seattle Times*, December 28, 2003.

4. Douglas Jehl, "Moratorium Asked on Suits That Seek to Protect Species," *New York Times*, April 12, 2001.

5. Melnick, *Regulation and the Courts*, pp. 71, 72, 96, and 71–112 generally; Rosemary O'Leary, *Environmental Change: Federal Courts and the EPA* (Temple University Press, 1993).

6. Baumgartner and Jones, *Agendas and Instability in American Politics*.

7. *Scenic Hudson Preservation Conference v. Federal Power Commission*, 354 F.2d 608 (2nd Cir., 1965); Houck, "Unfinished Stories."

8. *Sierra Club v. Morton*, 404 U.S. 727 (1972).

9. Melnick, *Regulation and the Courts*, p. 9.

10. *Calvert Cliffs Coordinating Committee v. Atomic Energy Commission*, 449 F.2d 1109 (D.C. Cir., 1971); Oliver S. Houck, "The Secret Opinions of the United States Supreme Court on Leading Cases in Environmental Law, Never Before Published!," *University of Colorado Law Review* 65, 1994: 459–517.

11. Wright, quoted in Houck, "Secret Opinions."

12. Gottlieb, *Forcing the Spring*, p. 138; Welch, "Feds Losing Grip."

13. Ray Ring, "Tipping the Scales," *High Country News*, February 16, 2004.

14. Douglas T. Kendall and Charles P. Lord, "The Takings Project: A Critical Analysis and Assessment of the Progress So Far," *Boston College Environmental Affairs Law Review* 25, 1998: 509–588.

15. Robert A. Kagan, *Adversarial Legalism: The American Way of Law* (Harvard University Press, 2001).

16. *Tennessee Valley Authority v. Hill*; George Hoberg, "The Emerging Triumph of Ecosystem Management: The Transformation of Federal Forest Policy," in *Western Public Lands and Environmental Politics*, second edition, ed. C. Davis (Westview, 2001); Petersen, *Acting for Endangered Species*; Steven L. Yaffee, *The Wisdom of the Spotted Owl: Policy Lessons for a New Century* (Island, 1994).

17. Nicholas Lemann, "No People Allowed," *New Yorker*, November 22, 1999, p. 113.

18. Peter Aleshire, "A Bare-Knuckled Trio Goes After the Forest Service," *High Country News*, March 30, 1998; Keith Bagwell, "Pygmy Owl Champions Crusade for Humanity: Environmental Group Winning War in Court," *Arizona Daily Star*, December 7, 1997; Lemann, "No People Allowed," pp. 96–113.

19. Suckling, quoted in Aleshire, "Bare-Knuckled Trio," p. 8; Orna Izakson, "Animal Rights Legal Activists Fight for Endangered Species," *EMagazine*, May-June, 2002, http://www.emagazine.com; Art Rothstein, "Arizona Environmental Group a Trend-Setter in Court Battles," Associated Press, September 8, 1998.

20. Bagwell, "Pygmy Owl"; Pat Brennan, "A Rep for Playing Hardball," *Orange County Register*, October 12, 2000; Center for Biological Diversity, "2005 Annual Report"; Lemann, "No People Allowed," p. 112.

21. Aleshire, "Bare-Knuckled Trio"; Bagwell, "Pygmy Owl"; Tom Kenworthy, "In Desert Southwest, Vigorous Species Act Endangers a Way of Life," *Washington Post*, February 1, 1988; Lemann, "No People Allowed," p. 98.

22. Cowan, quoted in Lemann, "No People Allowed," p. 104; Lane, quoted in Rothstein, "Arizona Environmental Group"; Suckling, quoted in Tom Kenworthy, "Grazing Laws Feed Demise of Ranchers' Way of Life," *Washington Post*, November 29, 1998; Kenworthy, "In Desert Southwest."

23. Tony Davis, "Desert Sprawl: Tucson Paves Its Way across a Fragile Landscape," *High Country News*, January 18, 1999, pp. 1, 6–12; U.S. Fish and Wildlife Service, "Final Rule: Determination of Endangered Status for the Cactus Ferruginous Pygmy-Owl in Arizona," 62 *Federal Register* 10730, 1997 [hereafter cited as USFWS 1997], pp. 3–5, 23, 24.

24. U.S. Fish and Wildlife Service, "Proposed Rule to List the Cactus Ferruginous Pygmy-Owl as Endangered with Critical Habitat in Arizona and Threatened in Texas," 59 *Federal Register* 63975, 1994 [hereafter cited as USFWS 1994], p. 4. The FWS discontinued the Category 2 list in 1996.

25. Joy Nicholopoulos, "The Endangered Species Listing Program," *Endangered Species Bulletin* 24, 1999, November/December: 6–9; USFWS 1994, p. 5.

26. USFWS 1997, quoted on p. 38.

27. "Notice Given of Suit to List Salamander, Wetlands Plants, Riparian Bird, Jaguar as Endangered," http://www.biologicaldiversity.org, posted May 19, 1996; "Suit Filed to List Five Riparian Species as Endangered," http://www.biologicaldiversity.org, posted August 23, 1996; USFWS 1997, pp. 51–52, 60–61.

28. Tony Davis, "Owl Protection Won't Halt Growth, Just Lessen Scale, Officials Say," *Arizona Daily Star*, April 6, 1997; Tony Davis, "Owls and Subdivisions Clash Near Tucson," *High Country News*, March 31, 1997.

29. FWS, "Proposed Determination of Critical Habitat for the Cactus Ferruginous Pygmy-Owl," 63 *Federal Register* 71820, 1998 [hereafter cited as USFWS 1998], p. 3 and generally; *Southwest Center for Biological Diversity v. Bruce Babbitt*, CIV 97–704 TUC ACM (D. Ariz., 1998).

30. USFWS 1998, p. 5, pp. 5–9 generally.

31. "County OKs Regional Pygmy Owl Conservation Plan to Control Growth," http://www.biologicaldiversity.org, posted January 26, 1998; "Pima County Lifts Ban on Building Permits," http://www.biologicaldiversity.org, posted December 15, 1997; "Protestors Block Destruction of Pygmy Owl Habitat," http://www.biologicaldiversity.org, posted December 2, 1997.

32. "Appeals Court Protects Pygmy Owl," http://www.biologicaldiversity.org, posted July 8, 1998; Tony Davis, "Bulldozers Roll in Tucson," *High Country News*, December 20, 1999; *Defenders of Wildlife v. Bernal* (1998).

33. Abrams, Babbitt, and Suckling, quoted in Tony Davis, "A Pocket-sized Bird Takes on Sunbelt Subdivisions," *High Country News*, August 30, 1999; CBD, quoted in "Historic Moment for Endangered Species," http://www.biologicaldiversity.org, posted May 21, 1998; Tony Davis, "Arizona: Tucson Acts to Stall Sprawl," *High Country News*, August 3, 1998; April Reese, "Tucson Area Nears Completion of Ambitious Conservation Plan," *Land Letter*, April 14, 2005.

34. "Enviros Defend Owl Protections Against Developers," http://www.biologicaldiversity.org, posted September 1, 2000; "ESA's Critical Habitat under Fire from Arizona Game and Fish Department," http://www.biologicaldiversity.org, posted September 9, 1999; FWS, "Final Rule: Designation of Critical Habitat for the Cactus Ferruginous Pygmy-Owl," 64 *Federal Register* 37419, 1999.

35. Suckling, quoted in Tim Steller, "Owl's 'Critical Habitat' Voided," *Arizona Daily Star*, September 25, 2001; *National Association of Home Builders v. Norton*, 340 F.3d 835 (Ninth Circuit, 2003); Tony Davis, "Tiny Owl May Lose U.S. Protection," *Arizona Daily Star*, December 16, 2003; Davis, "How a Tiny Owl Changed Tucson," *High Country News*, June 26, 2006; Howard Fischer, "Pygmy Owl Ruling Aids Homebuilders," *Arizona Daily Sun*, August 20, 2003; Douglas Jehl, "Rare Arizona Owl (All 7 Inches of It) Is in Habitat Furor," *New York Times*, March 17, 2003.

36. Greenwald, quoted in Mary Jo Pitzl, "Endangered Species Act Turns 30, Faces Challenges," *Arizona Republic*, December 30, 2003. As noted above, working primarily through the courts and the ESA, the CBD was largely responsible for reducing timber harvests on national forests in Arizona and New Mexico by over 75 percent, and grazing on Bureau of Land Management lands has declined by over 25 percent and by over 20 percent on national forests in the two states. U.S. Department of Agriculture, Forest Service, *Grazing Statistical Summary FY 1988*, 1989, p. 20; U.S. Department of Agriculture, Forest Service, *Grazing Statistical Summary FY 2002*, 2003, p. 25; U.S. Department of the Interior, Bureau of Land Management, *Public Land Statistics 1990*, 1991, pp. 24, 25; U.S. Department of the Interior, Bureau of Land Management, *Public Land Statistics 2002*, http://www.blm.gov, table 3-8c. For a programmatic evaluation of the ESA, see M. F. J. Taylor, K. F. Suckling, and J. J. Rachlinsk, "The Effectiveness of the Endangered Species Act: A Quantitative Analysis," *BioScience 55*, 2005: 360–367.

37. Jehl, "Rare Arizona Owl"; U.S. Department of the Interior, Bureau of Land Management, 1991, pp. 24, 25; U.S. Department of the Interior, Bureau of Land Management, 2003, Table 3-8c. The ESA was significantly amended in 1978, 1982, and 1988.

38. Gary C. Bryner, *Blue Skies, Green Politics: The Clean Air Act of 1990 and Its Implementation*, second edition (CQ Press, 1995), p. 52; 42 U.S.C. Section 7409.

39. *American Lung Association v. Reilly*, 962 F.2d 258 (2nd Cir., 1992); *American Lung Association v. Browner*, 854 F. Supp. 345 (D. Ariz., 1994).

40. Browner, quoted in John H. Cushman, "E.P.A. Advocating Higher Standards to Clean the Air," *New York Times*, November 25, 1996; Cushman, "Stricter Air Rules Could Place Focus on the Midwest," *New York Times*, December 1, 1996; Margaret Kriz, "Heavy Breathing," *National Journal*, January 4, 1997, p. 11.

41. Margaret Kriz, "Business Lobby Divides Democrats," *National Journal*, May 17, 1997, pp. 987–988; Kriz, "Heavy Breathing," pp. 8–12; Peter H. Stone, "From the K Street Corridor," *National Journal*, March 22, 1997, p. 575.

42. Matthew R. Baker, "From the K Street Corridor," *National Journal*, February 22, 1997, p. 376; Kriz, "Heavy Breathing," pp. 9–12.

43. Lobbyist, quoted in Kriz, "Heavy Breathing," p. 12.

44. Clinton, quoted in "White House Endorses EPA's Clean Air Rules," American Association for the Advancement of Science, 1997; John H. Cushman, "Clinton Sharply Tightens Air Pollution Regulations Despite Concern Over Costs," *New York Times*, June 26, 1997; Cushman, "On Clean Air, Environmental Chief Fought Doggedly, and Won," *New York Times*, July 5, 1997; Cushman, "Top E.P.A. Official Not Backing Down on Air Standards," *New York Times*, June 1, 1997; Cass R. Sunstein, "Is the Clean Air Act Unconstitutional?" *Michigan Law Review 98*, 1999: 325. The very fine particles (PM2.5) standards were set at 65 micrograms per cubic meter (mg/m^3) (24 hours), up from the proposed 50 mg/m^3, and 15 mg/m^3 (annual).

45. Richard E. Cohen, "Two Dems Are on Familiar Battleground," *National Journal*, September 6, 1997, p. 1742; "Environmental Agency Tightens Clean Air Rules," *CQ Almanac 1997* 53, 1998: 4–13.

46. *American Trucking Associations v. EPA*, 175 F.3d 1027 (D.C. Cir., 1999), pp. 1033, 1057; Browner and Hawkins, quoted in Margaret Kriz, "Why the EPA's Wheezing a Bit," *National Journal*, July 24, 1999, pp. 2166–2167; Lazarus, quoted in Linda Greenhouse, "Court Question: Is Congress Forsaking Authority?" *New York Times*, May 14, 2000; Allen Schaeffer, 1999, "ATA Victorious in Challenging EPA Clean Air Rules," American Trucking Associations website. The EPA petitioned the D.C. Circuit Court of Appeals for a rehearing, but the court rejected this for the delegation portion of the decision (*American Trucking Associations v. EPA*, 195 F.3d 4 (D.C. Cir., 1999)).

47. *Whitman v. American Trucking Associations*, 531 U.S. 457 (2001), pp. 471, 476; Cass Sunstein, "Regulating Risks after *ATA*," *Supreme Court Review: 2001*, 2002, p. 2.

48. *American Trucking Associations v. EPA*, 283 F.3d 355 (D.C. Cir., 2002); EPA Office of Air and Radiation, "EPA Requests Public Comment on Draft Regulatory Text for the Proposed 8-Hour Ozone Implementation Rule," 2003; EPA Office of Air and Radiation, "Guidance for Determining Boundaries of PM 2.5 Attainment and Nonattainment Areas," 2003.

49. American Lung Association, "Court Settlement Puts EPA on a Schedule to Complete NAAQS Reviews," 2003; "EPA Designates 474 Counties as Failing Air Quality Standards," *New York Times*, April 15, 2004; Felicity Barringer, "E.P.A. Chief Rejects Recommendations on Soot," *New York Times*, September 22, 2006; Darren Samuelsohn, "EPA Targets 243 Counties that May Fail to Meet PM Standards," *Greenwire*, June 30, 2004.

50. Of course, the executive branch has played a major role in air quality policy over the last decade. See the case on New Source Review in chapter 4.

51. Moe, "The Politicized Presidency."

52. Houck, "Secret Opinions."

53. Richard J. Lazarus, "A Different Kind of 'Republican Moment' in Environmental Law," *University of Minnesota Law Review* 97, 2003: 999–1036.

54. Kendall and Lord, "The Takings Project."

55. Ring, "Tipping the Scales."

56. Doug Kendall and Glenn Sugameli, "Sixth Circuit Nominee Jeffrey S. Sutton: A Threat to the Constitution and Fundamental Environmental Protections," http://www.earthjustice.org; Earthjustice, "35 Environmental Groups Oppose Nomination of Janice Rogers Brown," http://www.earthjustice.org.

57. At the state level, John Echeverria observed, "the environment has become a pervasive issue . . . and, in several states has emerged as one of the most prominent, if not the most prominent issue" in judicial elections ("Changing the Rules by Changing the Players: The Environmental Issue in State Judicial

Elections," *New York University Environmental Law Journal* 9, 2001: 217–304).

58. "Parks to Study Snowmobiles' Effect on Bison," *New York Times*, September 28, 1997.

59. John M. Carter, Mike Leahy, and William J. Snape, "Cutting Science, Ecology, and the Transparency Out of National Forest Management: How the Bush Administration Uses the Judicial System to Weaken Environmental Laws," *ELR News & Analysis*, 2003; William Snape and John M. Carter, "Weakening the National Environmental Policy Act: How the Bush Administration Uses the Judicial System to Weaken Environmental Protections," http://www.defenders.org.

60. Rey, quoted in Associated Press, "White House Settles Suits, Reshapes Environmental Policy," April 13, 2003; Associated Press, "Timber Industry Wins Settlement in Case Challenging Northwest Forest Plan," August 8, 2003; Robert McClure, "Bush to Stay Out of Forest Fracas in Visit to State," *Seattle Post-Intelligencer*, August 21, 2003; Senator Charles Schumer, "Environmental Report: The Environmental Record of the Ashcroft Justice Department," press release, 2003. On the Clinton administration's settlements, see Lynda Mapes, "Settlement Would Clear Logjam—Environmentalists' Suit Blocked Timber Sales," *Seattle Times*, November 19, 1999.

61. Jim Rossi, "Bargaining in the Shadow of Administrative Procedure: The Public Interest in Rulemaking Settlement," *Duke Law Journal* 51, 2001: 1015–1059.

62. Dwyer, quoted in Eric Pryne, "Dwyer Lifts Logging Ban in Northwest's Forests, But Lawsuits Still Loom," *Seattle Times*, June 6, 1994.

63. Bureau of Land Management and U.S. Forest Service, "Record of Decision for Amendments to Forest Service and Bureau of Land Management Planning Documents within the Range of the Northern Spotted Owl," 1993.

64. Tuchmann, quoted in Eric Pryne, "Logging Plan Faces Tough Industry Crowd in Northwest," *Seattle Times*, April 12, 1994.

65. AFL-CIO, Rey, and Sierra Club, quoted in Robert Nelson, "Few Surprises or Friends—Clinton Rejects 'Failed Policies of the Past,'" *Seattle Times*, July 1, 1993; Eric Pryne, "Clinton Forest Plan Full of Rules But Not Final Answers," *Seattle Times*, April 11, 1994; Marla Williams, "Reaction Mixed on Clinton's Forest Plan," *Seattle Times*, July 2, 1993.

66. Eric Pryne, "Congress Not Likely to Fight Forest Plan," *Seattle Times*, November 18, 1994.

67. Christopher Hanson, "An Effort to Break Owl-Timber Logjam," *Seattle Post-Intelligencer*, July 2, 1993; Eric Pryne, "Environmental Groups Sue Over Forest Plan," *Seattle Times*, May 20, 1994; Pryne, "Forest Plan Debatable for Environmentalists," *Seattle Times*, April 15, 1994; Pryne, "Tactical Maneuverings in Northwest Timber War," *Seattle Times*, July 22, 1994; Pryne, "Timber Industry Takes Loss in Court," *Seattle Times*, July 1, 1994; Eric Pryne and Bill Dietrich,

"Neither Side Elated with Latest Clinton Forest Plan," *Seattle Times*, February 24, 1994.

68. Dwyer, quoted in Rob Taylor, "Judge OK's Northwest Forest Plan," *Seattle Post-Intelligencer*, December 22, 1994.

69. Geisinger, quoted in Lynda Mapes, "Revamp Forest Plan, Groups Urge Clinton," *Seattle Times*, September 2, 1999.

70. Oregon Natural Resources Council, "'Broken Promises' Lawsuit Chronology," http://www.onrc.org.

71. Mapes, "Settlement Would Clear Logjam."

72. Western Environmental Law Update, "Lawsuit Over Forest Plan Halts Timber Sales in the Pacific Northwest," http://www.pielc.edu.

73. West and Lyons, quoted in Western Environmental Law Update 2000.

74. American Forest Resource Council, Western Council of Industrial Workers, and Association of O&C Counties, "A Global Framework for Settlement of Litigation Challenging Federal Agency Actions Relating to the Northwest Forest Plan," 2002.

75. McClure, "Bush to Stay Out of Forest Fracas."

76. Earthjustice, "Documents Show Timber Industry Driving White House Action," 2003.

77. The coalition, quoted in American Forest Resource Council et al., "Response to Settlement Offer of August 1, 2002."

78. *Northwest Ecosystem Alliance v. Mark E. Rey*, 2006, 2006 U.S. Dist. LEXIS 1846; Dan Berman, "Bush Admin Renews Effort to Replace Survey-and-Manage in Pacific Northwest," *Greenwire*, July 7, 2006.

79. *Utah v. Babbitt*, 137 F.3d 1193 (10th Cir., 1998).

80. Jim Wolff, "Wilderness Impasse Likely to Continue," *Salt Lake City Tribune*, December 10, 1996. As noted in chapter 3, since the late 1970s the norm in wilderness designation policy is that Congress will create new wilderness in a state only if both senators and a majority of representatives from the state support it.

81. Babbitt, quoted in Bureau of Land Management, "Utah Wilderness Inventory," April 7, 1999.

82. *Utah v. Babbitt* 1998; Bureau of Land Management, "Utah Wilderness Inventory."

83. Hatch, quoted in Lee Davidson, "Hatch Calls Babbitt's Vow Misleading," *Salt Lake City Deseret News*, October 9, 1996; Johnson, quoted in Mike Gorell, "Lawmakers Have Tough Words for BLM," *Salt Lake City Tribune*, October 17, 1996.

84. Joe Costanzo, "Babbitt Lacks Authority, Judge Rules," *Salt Lake City Deseret News*, November 21, 1996; "State Suit Accuses Washington of Political Move on Wilderness," *New York Times*, October 15, 1996; *Utah v. Babbitt* 1998.

85. *Utah v. Babbitt* 1998.

86. Bureau of Land Management, "Utah Wilderness Inventory"; Department of the Interior, 2003, "Utah Wilderness Settlement Fact Sheet," http://www.doi.gov.

87. Bureau of Land Management, "Utah Wilderness Inventory."

88. *Utah v. Norton*, 2:96CV0870B (D. Utah, 2003), "Stipulation and Joint Motion to Enter Order Approving Settlement and to Dismiss the Third Amended and Supplemented Complaint."

89. Leavitt and Norton, quoted in Judy Fahys, "Deal Tosses Land Preserve," *Salt Lake City Tribune*, April 12, 2003; Tom Wharton, "Norton Defends Settlement to Roll Back Land Protection," *Salt Lake City Tribune*, June 18, 2003.

90. Wharton, "Norton Defends Settlement."

91. Stephen H. M. Bloch and Heidi J. McIntosh, "A View from the Front Lines: The Fate of Utah's Redrock Wilderness under the George W. Bush Administration," *Golden Gate Law Review* 33, 2003: 473–502.

92. Widen, quoted in Matt Jenkins, "Wilderness Takes a Massive Hit," *High Country News*, April 28, 2003, p. 3.

93. Donna Spangler, "Environmentalists Fighting Utah Wilderness Settlement," *Salt Lake City Deseret News*, May 6, 2003.

94. Shea and McIntosh, quoted in Fahys, "Deal Tosses Land Preserve."

95. Richardson, quoted in Associated Press State and Local Wire, "Richardson Requests Halt of Plan for BLM Lands," May 10, 2003.

96. Joe Baird, "Language of 'No More Wilderness' Pact Is Undone," *Salt Lake City Tribune*, September 16, 2005; Joe Baird, "Judge Upholds Controversial 'No More Wilderness' Settlement," *Salt Lake City Tribune*, September 22, 2006; *Utah v. Norton*, 2006 U.S. Dist LEXIS 73480 (C.D. Utah, 2006).

97. On the general virtues and pathologies of adversarial legalism, see Kagan, *Adversarial Legalism*, pp. 22–33.

98. Melnick, *Regulation and the Courts*, p. 344. On environmentalists and the courts during the presidency of George W. Bush, see Eric Pianin, "For Environmentalists, Victories in the Courts," *Washington Post*, January 27, 2003; Ray Ring, "Shooting Spree," *High Country News*, May 10, 2004. On Wise Use and industry challenges during the Clinton administration, see Keiter, *Keeping Faith with Nature*, pp. 237–239.

99. Graham, *The Morning after Earth Day*, p. 112.

100. See Melnick, *Regulation and the Courts*, pp. 383–393; O'Leary, *Environmental Change*, pp. 168–173.

101. Scalia, quoted in William Glaberson, "Novel Antipollution Tool Is Being Upset by Courts," *New York Times*, June 5, 1999; *Lujan v. Defenders of Wildlife*, 504 U.S. 555 (1992); *Lujan v. National Wildlife Federation*, 497 U.S. 871 (1990).

102. Commentator and Echeverria, quoted in Eacata Desiree Gregory, "No Time Is the Right Time: The Supreme Court's Use of Ripeness to Block Judicial

Review of Forest Plans for Environmental Plaintiffs in *Ohio Forestry Association v. Sierra Club*," *Chicago-Kent Law Review* 75, 2000: 613–639.

103. *Friends of the Earth v. Laidlaw Environmental Services*, 528 U.S. 167 (2000); Linda Greenhouse, "Court Backs 'Citizen Suit' to Clean Up Ailing River," *New York Times*, January 19, 2000.

Chapter 6

1. For a discussion of an early encounter with the complexities flowing from risk assessment, see Farber, *Eco-pragmatism*.

2. Richard J. Lazarus, "A Different Kind of 'Republican Moment' in Environmental Law," *Minnesota Law Review* 97, 2003: 999–1036.

3. Marc Allen Eisner, *Regulatory Politics in Transition*, second edition (Johns Hopkins University Press, 2000), pp. 170–201.

4. Philip J. Harter, "Negotiating Regulations: A Cure for Malaise," *Georgetown Law Journal* 71, 1982: 1–119; Kagan, *Adversarial Legalism*; Weber, *Bringing Society Back In*.

5. Brick et al., eds., *Across the Great Divide*; Brunner et al., *Finding Common Ground*; Weber, *Pluralism by the Rules*.

6. Critic, quoted in Rena L. Steinzor, "Reinventing Environmental Regulation: The Dangerous Journey from Command to Self-Control," *Harvard Environmental Law Review* 22, 1998: 147.

7. Lowi, *The End of Liberalism*.

8. Graham, *The Morning after Earth Day*, p. 112.

9. Theodore Lowi, "Frontyard Propaganda: A Response to 'Beyond Backyard Environmentalism,'" *Boston Review* 24, 1999: 17–18; Lowi, *The End of Liberalism*; Weber, *Bringing Society Back In*.

10. H.R. Conference Report 97-385, quoted in Karin P. Sheldon, "Habitat Conservation Planning: Addressing the Achilles Heel of the Endangered Species Act," *New York University Environmental Law Journal* 6, 1998: 279–340.

11. Marj Nelson, "Habitat Conservation Planning" (1999), http://endangered.fws.gov; Sheldon, "Habitat Conservation Planning."

12. Nelson, "Habitat Conservation Planning"; Sheldon, "Habitat Conservation Planning."

13. H.R. Conference Report, quoted in Sheldon, "Habitat Conservation Planning"; Thomas Reid Associates, "San Bruno Mountain: Preservation of an Ecological Island," http://thecity.sfsu.edu; U.S. Fish and Wildlife Service, "Nation's First Formal Plan to Save Endangered Species Set for Update," news release, July 22, 2004.

14. Jeremy Anderson and Steven Yaffee, "Balancing Public Trust and Private Interest: Public Participation in Habitat Conservation Planning," University of Michigan School of Natural Resources and Environment, 1998, pp. 17–18.

Anderson and Yaffee noted that the ESA, the NEPA, and many state environmental statutes require agencies and applicants to make public notices of proposed activities and their effects. With respect to HCPs, "The (Fish and Wildlife) Service typically notices receipt of an HCP application in the *Federal Register* and then conducts a 30 to 45 day comment period. . . . The law does not require the FWS to incorporate public comments into an HCP or make decisions based on public comments. . . . The law provides the FWS with significant discretion to shape its own public participation policy. However, rather than using the law's flexibility to craft effective public participation the FWS interprets the law narrowly and focuses on explicit disclosure and comment period requirements. The Service encourages applicants to pursue the bare minimum in NEPA documentation and comment periods. . . ." (ibid., p. 22)

15. Sheldon, "Habitat Conservation Planning," p. 292.

16. National Center for Environmental Decisionmaking Research, *Understanding and Improving Habitat Conservation Plans* (1998), http://www.ncedr.org.

17. U.S. General Accounting Office (GAO), "Endangered Species Act: Information on Species Protection on Nonfederal Lands," GAO/RCED-95-16, 1994.

18. Clinton Administration History Project 2000, "A History of the U.S. Department of the Interior during the Clinton Administration, 1993–2001," http://library.ios.doi.gov.

19. John H. Cushman, "Conservatives Tug at Endangered Species Act," *New York Times*, May 28, 1995; William K. Stevens, "Future of Endangered Species Act in Doubt as Law Is Debated," *New York Times*, May 16, 1995.

20. John Kostyack, "The Need for HCP Reform: Five Points of Consensus," 1999.

21. Sheldon, "Habitat Conservation Planning"; FWS, "'No Surprises' Questions and Answers," http://endangered.fws.gov.

22. FWS, "Safe Harbor Agreements for Private Landowners," http://endangered.fws.gov.

23. As quoted in Gregory A. Thomas, "Where Property Rights and Biodiversity Converge, Part I: Conservation Planning at the Regional Scale," *Endangered Species Update* 17, 2000: 141.

24. National Center for Environmental Decisionmaking Research, *Understanding and Improving Habitat Conservation Plans*.

25. *Babbitt v. Sweet Home Chapter of Communities for a Greater Oregon*, 515 U.S. 687 (1995); Kevin Batt, "Above All, Do No Harm: *Sweet Home* and Section Nine of the Endangered Species Act," *Boston University Law Review* 75, 1995: 1177–1231; Tom Kenworthy, "Justices Affirm Wide Power to Protect Wildlife Habitat," *Washington Post*, June 30, 1995.

26. Eric Pryne, "Decision May Nudge Landowners into Action," *Seattle Times*, June 30, 1995. For an examination of another major HCP, see Tony Davis, "San Diego's Habitat Triage," *High Country News*, November 10, 2003.

27. Kathie Durbin, "Timber's Bad Boy Comes to the Table," *High Country News*, August 4, 1997; Eric Pryne, "The Checkerboard Legacy," *Seattle Times*, November 13, 1994; Plum Creek Timber Company and D.R. Systems, n.d, "Plum Creek Timber Co.'s Cascades Habitat Conservation Plan," http://www. for.gov.bc.ca.

28. Testimony by Lorin Hicks, Plum Creek Timber Company, U.S. Senate Committee on Environment and Public Works, Subcommittee on Fisheries, Wildlife, and Drinking Water, July 21, 1999.

29. Durbin, "Timber's Bad Boy"; "Plum Creek Timber Co.'s Cascades Habitat Conservation Plan."

30. Durbin, "Timber's Bad Boy."

31. Hicks, quoted in Durbin, "Timber's Bad Boy"; Susan Jane M. Brown, "David and Goliath: Reformulating the Definition of 'The Public Interest' and the Future of Land Swaps after the Interstate 90 Land Exchange," *Journal of Environmental Law and Litigation* 15, 2000: 235–293; George R. Slingerland, The Effect of the 'No Surprises' Policy on Habitat Conservation Planning and the Endangered Species Act, M.A. thesis, Virginia Polytechnic and State University, 1999; Rob Taylor, "A Timber Plan That's Wrapped in Green," *Seattle Post-Intelligencer*, June 25, 1996.

32. Smitch, quoted in Danny Westneat, "Logging That Will Protect Wildlife?" *Seattle Times*, June 26, 1996; Babbitt, quoted in U.S. Department of the Interior, "Secretaries Babbitt and Glickman Sign Agreements with Plum Creek Timber to Improve Habitat Conservation for Wildlife and Fish," 1996.

33. Testimony by Lorin Hicks, 1999.

34. Cullinan, quoted in Taylor, "A Timber Plan."

35. Testimony by Lorin Hicks, 1999.

36. Mark Miller, "Plum Creek Habitat Conservation Plan," National Center for Environmental Decision-Making Research, 1999.

37. Peter Kareiva et al., "Using Science in Habitat Conservation Plans," National Center for Ecological Analysis and Synthesis and American Institute of Biological Sciences, 1999; Testimony of Peter Kareiva, Northwest Region of the National Marine Fisheries Service, On the National Study of HCPs on Habitat Conservation Science, Senate Committee on Environment and Public Works, July 20, 1999.

38. Rob Taylor, "State Is 'Proving Ground' for Habitat Plan, Babbitt Says," *Seattle Post-Intelligencer*, July 11, 1998; FWS, "Response to AIBS/NCEAS's Study, *Using Science in Habitat Conservation Plans*," 1999. See also Laura Stiffler and Robert McClure, "Too Often, Inadequate Science Hampers Habitat Planning," *Seattle Post Intelligencer*, May 4, 2005; Stiffler and McClure, "Flaws in Habitat Conservation Plans Threaten Scores of Species," *Seattle Post Intelligencer*, May 3, 2005.

39. Anderson and Yaffee, "Balancing Public Trust and Private Interest."

40. Miller, "Plum Creek Habitat Conservation Plan."

41. Ibid.

42. Raines and Matthews, quoted in Anderson and Yaffee, "Balancing Public Trust and Private Interest," pp. 17, 14; ibid., p. 14.

43. FWS official, quoted in Miller, "Plum Creek Habitat Conservation Plan"; Anderson and Yaffee, "Balancing Public Trust and Private Interest," p. 18.

44. Department of the Interior and Department of Commerce, "Notice of Availability of a Final Addendum to the Handbook for Habitat Conservation Planning and Incidental Take Permitting Process," *Federal Register*, 65, June 1, 2000, Docket 981208299-0429-02, RIN:1018-AG06,0648-XA14; Environmental News Network, "U.S. Fine-Tunes Habitat Conservation Plans," March 10, 1999; FWS/National Oceanic and Atmospheric Administration, "Addendum to the HCP Handbook: Executive Summary," May 2000.

45. Suckling, quoted in Durbin, "Timber's Bad Boy."

46. *Spirit of the Sage Council v. Norton*, 294 F. Supp 2d 67 (D.D.C., 2003); Daniel Cusick, "Court Dismisses FWS Appeal Over 'No Surprises,'" *Greenwire*, May 31, 2005.

47. Robert McClure and Lisa Stiffler, "License to Kill: Habitat Conservation Plans Threaten the Survival of Scores of Species," *Seattle Post-Intelligencer*, May 3, 2005; FWS, "Conservation Plans and Agreements Database" (November 30, 2006), http://ecos.fws.gov.

48. Lisa Stiffler and Rob McClure, "Area Under Habitat Conservation Plans Could Soar," *Seattle Post-Intelligencer*, September 26, 2005.

49. Eisner, *Regulatory Politics in Transition*, pp. 118–169.

50. Lowi, *The End of Liberalism*.

51. Eisner, *Regulatory Politics in Transition*, p. 128.

52. Andrews, *Managing the Environment, Managing Ourselves*, pp. 239–242; Eisner, *Regulatory Politics in Transition*, pp. 128–129.

53. David Vogel, *Fluctuating Fortunes: The Political Power of Business in America* (Basic Books, 1989).

54. Harter, "Negotiating Regulations."

55. This borrows from Wilkinson's discussion of the "lords of yesterday" in *Crossing the Next Meridian*.

56. Robert J. Duffy, "Divided Government and Institutional Combat: The Case of the Quayle Council on Competitiveness," *Polity* 18, 1996: 379–399.

57. Daniel C. Esty and Marian R. Chertow, "Thinking Ecologically: An Introduction," in *Thinking Ecologically: The Next Generation of Environmental Policy*, ed. M. Chertow and D. Esty (Yale University Press, 1997), p. 4.

58. President Bill Clinton and Vice-President Al Gore, "Reinventing Environmental Regulation," National Performance Review, March 16, 1995.

59. Eisner, *Regulatory Politics in Transition*, pp. 1–26.

60. Cornelius M. Kerwin and Scott R. Furlong, "Time and Rulemaking: An Empirical Test of the Theory," *Journal of Public Administration Research and*

Theory 2, 1992: 113; Clare M. Ryan, "Regulatory Negotiation: Learning from Experiences at the U.S. Environmental Protection Agency," in *Mediating Environmental Conflicts*, ed. J. Blackburn and W. Bruce (Quorum Books, 1995), pp. 203–209. Some sources assert that 80 percent of EPA rules are litigated, but Cary Coglianese found that the number is much lower, around 26 percent (Cary Coglianese, "Assessing Consensus: The Promise and Performance of Negotiated Rulemaking," working paper, John F. Kennedy School of Government, 1997).

61. David M. Pritzker and Deborah S. Dalton, eds., *Negotiated Rulemaking Sourcebook* (Administrative Conference of the United States, 1995), pp. 2–3.

62. On negotiations in the 1970s and the 1980s, see Coglianese, "Assessing Consensus"; Daniel Fiorino, "Regulatory Negotiation as a Policy Process," in *Negotiated Rulemaking Sourcebook*, ed. Pritzker and Dalton, pp. 849–857; Lawrence Susskind and Gerard McMahon, 1995, "The Theory and Practice of Negotiated Rulemaking," in ibid., pp. 704–736.

63. U.S. House of Representatives, 1990, "Negotiated Rulemaking Act of 1990," 101st Congress, 2nd Session, Report 101-461, April 25, pp. 1–2.

64. Ibid.

65. Ibid.

66. William Funk, "Bargaining toward the New Millennium: Regulatory Negotiation and the Subversion of the Public Interest," *Duke Law Journal* 46, 1997: 1351–1388.

67. For example, a reg-neg committee to develop woodstove emissions standards included representatives from industry, four states, and the Natural Resources Defense Council (William H. Funk, "When the Smoke Gets in Your Eyes: Regulatory Negotiation and the Public Interest—EPA's Woodstove Standards," *Environmental Law* 18, 1987: 61; Susan L. Podziba, "Final Convening Assessment Report on the Feasibility of a Negotiated Rulemaking Process to Develop the All Appropriate Inquiry Standard under the Small Business Liability Relief and Brownfields Revitalization Act," EPA Office of Solid Waste and Emergency Response, Office of Brownfields Cleanup and Redevelopment, December 17, 2002). See also Laura I. Langbein and Cornelius M. Kerwin, "Regulatory Negotiation Versus Conventional Rulemaking: Claims, Counterclaims, and Empirical Evidence," *Journal of Public Administration Research and Theory* 10, 2000: 599–633.

68. EPA Negotiated Rulemaking Fact Sheet, n.d.

69. Jody Freeman, "Collaborative Governance and the Administrative State," *UCLA Law Review* 45, 1997: 35–36; Harter, "Negotiating Regulations." See also Jody Freeman and Laura I. Langbein, "Regulatory Negotiation and the Legitimacy Benefit," *New York University Environmental Law Journal* 9, 2000: 60–139.

70. White House, Executive Order 12,866, "Regulatory Planning and Review," September 30, 1993; White House, Presidential Memorandum, "Negotiated Rulemaking," September 30, 1993.

71. Coglianese, "Assessing Consensus."

72. Freeman, "Collaborative Governance." See also Edward P. Weber and Ann Khademian, "From Agitation to Collaboration: Clearing the Air through Negotiation," *Public Administration Review* 57, 1997: 396–410; Weber, *Pluralism by the Rules*, pp. 120–147.

73. Harter, "Negotiating Regulations"; Weber, *Pluralism by the Rules*. A 1987 EPA assessment found that negotiated regulation placed a heavy burden on both the agency and participants (Funk, "Bargaining toward the New Millennium").

74. Coglianese, "Assessing Consensus"; Mark Seidenfeld, "Empowering Stakeholders: Limits on Collaboration as the Basis for Flexible Regulation," *William and Mary Law Review* 41, 2000: 411–501.

75. Cary Coglianese, "Is Satisfaction Success? Evaluating Public Participation in Regulatory Rulemaking," Faculty Research Working Paper RWP02-038, John F. Kennedy School of Government, 2002; Freeman and Langbein, "Regulatory Negotiation and the Legitimacy Benefit."

76. Lowi, *The End of Liberalism*, pp. 92–107.

77. Robert Choo, "Judicial Review of Negotiated Rulemaking: Should Chevron Deference Apply?" *Rutgers Law Review* 52, 2000: 1069–1120; Funk, "When the Smoke Gets in Your Eyes."

78. Funk, "Bargaining toward the New Millennium," p. 1356.

79. Donald F. Kettl, *Reinventing Government? Appraising the National Performance Review* (Brookings Institution, 1994), pp. 27–30.

80. Weber and Khademian, "From Agitation to Collaboration," pp. 402–403.

81. Funk, "Bargaining toward the New Millennium," p. 1386.

82. Weber, *Pluralism by the Rules*, pp. 120–142. This account of the RFG reg-neg relies heavily on Weber's work. See also Susan L. Meyer, Lawrence Kumins, and Migdon Segal, "Implementation of the Reformulated Gasoline Program," *CRS Report for Congress*, August 1, 1995; Migdon Segal, "Ethanol and Clean Air: The Reg-Neg Controversy and Subsequent Events," *CRS Report for Congress*, June 22, 1993; Ellen Siegler, "Regulatory Negotiations and Other Rulemaking Processes: Strengths and Weaknesses from an Industry Viewpoint," *Duke Law Journal* 46, 1997: 1429–1443; Michael Weisskopf, "Rare Pact Reached to Fight Smog," *Washington Post*, August 16, 1991.

83. Weber, *Pluralism by the Rules*, pp. 130–131.

84. Meyer, Kumins, and Segal, "Implementation of the Reformulated Gasoline Program"; Segal, "Ethanol and Clean Air."

85. Meyer, Kumins, and Segal, "Implementation of the Reformulated Gasoline Program."

86. Siegler, "Regulatory Negotiations."

87. Ibid.

88. David Gushee, "Alternative Transportation Fuels and Clean Gasoline: Background and Regulatory Issues," *CRS Issue Brief for Congress*, January 17, 1996;

Gary Lee, "EPA Backs Ethanol for Fuel," *Washington Post*, July 1, 1994; Cindy Skrzycki, "EPA Finds Rewriting a Rule Is No Barrel of Laughs," *Washington Post*, May 12, 1995; Weber and Khademian, "From Agitation to Collaboration."

89. Alex Canizares and Roger Runninger, "EPA Won't Exempt California from Fuel Rules," *Washington Post*, June 13, 2001; Steven Cohen, Sheldon Kamieniecki, and Matthew A. Cahn, *Strategic Planning in Environmental Regulation: A Policy Approach That Works* (MIT Press, 2005), pp. 101–151; EPA, "State Actions Banning MTBE (Statewide)," June 2004; Renewable Fuels Association, "2005 Energy Bill Sparked Growth in Renewable Fuels," August 6, 2006; "Washington in Brief," *Washington Post*, June 22, 2001; Rick Weiss, "EPA Seeks to End Use of Additive in Gasoline," *Washington Post*, March 21, 2000.

90. Claudia Copeland, "Reinventing the Environmental Protection Agency and EPA's Water Programs," *Congressional Research Service*, March 22, 1996; James E. McCarthy, "Voluntary Efforts to Reduce Pollution," *CRS Report for Congress* 950817, July 13, 1995.

91. Browner, quoted in Cary Coglianese and Laurie K. Allen, "Building Sector-Based Consensus: A Review of the EPA's Common Sense Initiative," Faculty Research Working Paper RWP03-037, John F. Kennedy School of Government, 2003; Marcus, Geffen, and Sexton, *Reinventing Environmental Regulation*.

92. Coglianese and Allen, "Building Sector-Based Consensus"; EPA, "The Common Sense Initiative: Lessons Learned about Protecting the Environment in Common Sense, Cost Effective Ways," EPA 100-R-98-011, 1998, p. 3; GAO, "Regulatory Reinvention: EPA's Common Sense Initiative Needs an Improved Operating Framework and Progress Measures," GAO/RCED-97-164, 1997, p. 17.

93. Browner, quoted in EPA, "The Common Sense Initiative," p. 3.

94. Kerr, Greiner, Andersen, and April, "Analysis and Evaluation of the EPA Common Sense Initiative," prepared for the EPA by Kerr, Greiner, Andersen, and April, Inc., 1999; Martin R. Lee, "The Environmental Protection Agency's FY 2003 Budget," Congressional Research Service, December 16, 2002, p. 6.

95. Cary Coglianese and Laurie K. Allen, "Does Consensus Make Common Sense? An Analysis of the EPA's Common Sense Initiative," *Environment*, January–February 2004, p. 12; GAO, "Regulatory Reinvention," pp. 5, 6.

96. EPA, "Sector Strategies," http://www.epa.gov/sectors/, 2006.

97. Browner, quoted in Hirsch, "Bill and Al's XL-ent Adventure," p. 131.

98. Whitman, quoted in Marcus, Geffen, and Sexton, *Reinventing Environmental Regulation*, p. 2; Seidenfeld, "Empowering Stakeholders."

99. EPA, "Project XL: Implementation and Evaluation," http://www.epa.gov.

100. GAO, "Environmental Protection: Overcoming Obstacles to Innovative State Regulatory Programs," Report to Congressional Requestors, January 2002, pp. 5–8; Rena Steinzor, "Testimony before the House Subcommittee on Water Resources and the Environment, Committee on Transportation and

Infrastructure, on Water Quality Trading: An Innovative Approach to Achieving Water Quality Goals," June 13, 2002.

101. Marcus, Geffen, and Sexton, *Reinventing Environmental Regulation*, pp. 180–181.

102. Ibid., pp. 52–53. See also Carol Wiessner, "Regulatory Innovation: Lessons Learned from the EPA's Project XL and Three Minnesota Project XL Pilots," *Environmental Law Reporter* 32, 2002: 10075–10120.

103. Charles C. Caldart and Nicholas A. Ashford, "Negotiation as a Means of Developing and Implementing Environmental and Occupational Safety and Health Policy," *Harvard Environmental Law Journal* 23, 1999: 183. On the legal problems confronting Project XL, see Hirsch, "Bill and Al's XL-ent Adventure"; Bradford C. Mank, "The Environmental Protection Agency's Project XL and Other Regulatory Reform Initiatives: The Need for Legislative Reauthorization," *Ecology Law Quarterly* 25, 1998: 1–88; Steinzor, "Reinventing Environmental Regulation."

104. David W. Case, "The EPA's Environmental Stewardship Initiative: Attempting to Revitalize a Floundering Regulatory Reform Agenda," *Emory Law Journal* 50, 2001: 44.

105. William Greider, *Who Will Tell the People?* (Simon and Shuster, 1993), p. 105.

106. Coglianese and Allen, "Building Sector-Based Consensus," p. 21.

107. As quoted in GAO, "Environmental Protection: Challenges Facing EPA's Efforts to Reinvent Environmental Regulation," Report to Congressional Requestors, GAO/RCED-97-155, 1997.

108. Cary Coglianese, "Does Consensus Work? A Pragmatic Approach to Public Participation in the Regulatory Process," in *Evaluating Environmental and Public Policy Resolution Programs and Politics*, ed. R. O'Leary and L. Binham (Resources for the Future, 2003); Coglianese and Allen, "Building Sector-Based Consensus."

109. As quoted in Cindy Skrzycki, "Critics See a Playground for Polluters in EPA's XL Plan," *Washington Post*, January 24, 1997; John H. Cushman, "EPA and Arizona Factory Agree on Innovative Regulatory Plan," *New York Times*, November 20, 1996; Silicon Valley Toxics Coalition, "'Project XL' Translates into 'EXtra Lenient' Deregulation," December 20, 2004.

110. Marcus, Geffen, and Sexton (*Reinventing Environmental Regulation*, (pp. 179–196) conclude that these experiments should continue as "opportunities for learning" how to improve regulatory policymaking. See also Cohen, Kamieniecki, and Cahn, *Strategic Planning in Environmental Regulation*.

111. E. Donald Elliot, "Toward Ecological Law and Policy," in *Thinking Ecologically: The Next Generation of Environmental Policy*, ed. M. Chertow and D. Esty (Yale University Press, 1997); Eisner, *Regulatory Politics in Transition*, p. 4; Robert Stavins and Bradley Whitehead, "Market-Based Environmental Policies," in *Thinking Ecologically*, ed. Chertow and Esty.

112. See Skowronek, *Building a New American State.*

113. Kettl, *Reinventing Government?* p. 28.

114. Esty and Chertow, "Thinking Ecologically," p. 1.

115. Among the variety of names this pathway goes by are collaborative conservation, community conservation, community-based conservation, cooperative ecosystem management, grassroots ecosystem management, watershed democracy, and the watershed movement. See Weber, *Bringing Society Back In,* pp. xiii, 3.

116. Brunner et al., *Finding Common Ground,* p. 29 and generally. Other recent significant works include Brick et al., eds., *Across the Great Divide;* Ronald D. Brunner, Toddi A. Steelman, Lindy Coe-Juell, Christina M. Cromley, Christine M. Edwards, and Donna W. Tucker, *Adaptive Governance: Integrating Science, Policy and Decision Making* (Columbia University Press, 2005); Keiter, *Keeping Faith with Nature,* pp. 219–272; Tomas M. Koontz, Toddi A. Steelman, JoAnn Carmin, Katrina Smith Korfmacher, Cassandra Moseley, and Craig W. Thomas, *Collaborative Environmental Management: What Roles for Government?* (Resources for the Future, 2004); Cassandra Moseley, New Ideas, Old Institutions: Environment, Community, and State in the Pacific Northwest, Ph.D. dissertation, Yale University, 1999; Weber, *Bringing Society Back In;* Julia M. Wondolleck and Steven L. Yaffee, *Making Collaboration Work: Lessons from Innovation in Natural Resource Management* (Island, 2000).

117. Kathleen Sayce, former botanist for the Willapa Alliance, personal communication, April 2005; Weber, *Bringing Society Back In,* pp. 3, 52, 61, 254, and generally.

118. Brunner et al., *Finding Common Ground,* pp. 159–170; Keiter, *Keeping Faith with Nature,* pp. 273–278; Ed Marston, "The Quincy Library Group: A Divisive Attempt at Peace," in *Across the Great Divide,* ed. Brick et al., pp. 79–85.

119. Brunner et al., *Finding Common Ground,* pp. 170–173; Keiter, *Keeping Faith with Nature,* pp. 277–278; Marston, "The Quincy Library Group," pp. 85, 86.

120. Coates, quoted in Jane Braxton Little, "Quincy Collaboration Heads to Court," *High Country News,* December 17, 2001; Brunner et al., *Finding Common Ground,* pp. 173–200; Keiter, *Keeping Faith with Nature,* pp. 278–281; Jane Braxton Little, "Motion Filed to Defend Forest Plan," *Sacramento Bee,* April 25, 2003; Marston, "The Quincy Library Group," pp. 86–88.

121. Keiter, *Keeping Faith with Nature,* pp. 281–299; Marston, "The Quincy Library Group," pp. 85, 88–90.

122. Charles Davis, "Politics and Public Rangeland Policy," in *Western Public Lands and Environmental Politics,* second edition, ed. C. Davis (Westview, 2001); Christopher McGrory Klyza, *Who Controls Public Lands? Mining, Forestry, and Grazing Policies, 1870–1990* (University of North Carolina Press, 1996); April Reese, "The Big Buyout," *High Country News,* April 4, 2005.

123. This profile of the Quivira Coalition is based on Barbara H. Johnson, ed., *Forging a West That Works: An Invitation to the Radical Center* (Quivira Coalition, 2003), a compilation of articles from the group's newsletter, as well as all of the Quivira Coalition's newsletters, available at the group's website: http://www.quiviracoalition.org. Mission statement quoted from Quivira Coalition Newsletter, June 1997. 'Quivira' is a Spanish word referring to a fabulous realm just beyond the horizon. The Malapi Borderlands Group, another leading collaborative conservation group, first coined the phrase "radical center."

124. Courtney White, 2003, "A New Environmentalism," in *Forging a West That Works*, ed. Johnson, p. 61, pp. 53–70 generally.

125. William de Buys, "Looking for the 'Radical Center,'" in *Forging a West That Works*, ed. Johnson, pp. 49–52; "An Invitation to the Radical Center," in *Forging a West That Works*, pp. vi–viii.

126. See Tony Davis, 2005, "Rangeland Revival," *High Country News*, September 5; Johnson, *Forging a West That Works*; Quivira Coalition newsletter.

127. Ness and Horning quoted in April Reese, "Quivira Coalition Charts Middle Ground in Ranching Debate," *Land Letter*, January 22, 2004; Silver quoted in Heather Clark, "Group Urges Ranchers, Conservationists Bridge Ideological Divide," Associated Press, July 23, 2001; Davis, "Rangeland Revival."

128. Dan Dagget, "The New Environmentalism: It's about Results," *Quivira Coalition Newsletter*, October, 2001, p. 2.

129. For arguments supporting collaborative conservation, see Philip Brick and Edward Weber, "Will Rain Follow the Plow? Unearthing a New Environmental Movement," in *Across the Great Divide*, ed. Brick et al., pp. 15–24; Philip Brick, "Of Impostors, Optimists, and Kings: Finding a Political Niche for Collaborative Conservation," in *Across the Great Divide*, pp. 172–179. On Bush's cooperative conservation initiative, see Russell J. Dinnage, "First of 24 Public Meetings on Bush Enviro Proposals Solicits Mixed Opinions," *Greenwire*, August 11, 2006.

130. For critiques of collaborative conservation, see George Cameron Coggins, "Of Californicators, Quislings, and Crazies: Some Perils of Devolved Collaboration," in *Across the Great Divide*, ed. Brick et al., pp. 163–171; Davis, "Rangeland Revival"; Keiter, *Keeping Faith with Nature*, pp. 251–258; Lowi, "Frontyard Propaganda."

131. Donald Snow, "Coming Home: An Introduction to Collaborative Conservation," in *Across the Great Divide*, ed. Brick et al., p. 4.

132. Brick et al., *Across the Great Divide*, p. 13; Brick, "Of Impostors," p. 173.

133. Thomas, quoted in Brunner et al., *Finding Common Ground*, p. 218; Marston, "The Quincy Library Group," quote paraphrasing Connaughton p. 88, p. 85; Cassandra Moseley, 2001, "The Applegate Partnership: Innovation in Crisis," in *Across the Great Divide*, ed. Brick et al., p. 106.

134. Eugene Bardach and Robert Kagan, *Going by the Book: The Problem of Regulatory Unreasonableness* (Transaction, 2002).

135. *Sierra Club v. Babbitt*, 15 F. Supp. 2d 1274 (S. D. Ala., 1998). See also *Sierra Club v. Norton*, 207 F. Supp. 2d 1310 (S.D. Ala., 2002).

136. Skowronek, *Building a New American State*, p. 9.

Chapter 7

1. Graham, *The Morning after Earth Day*, p. ix; Donald F. Kettl, "Introduction," in *Environmental Governance*, ed. D. Kettl (Brookings Institution, 2002). There is much policymaking at the local level as well, much of it of real significance. The logic of the movement to local pathways, however, is quite similar to the logic of moving to the state pathway. And since the states are bigger actors on a wider ranger of issues, we focus only on the states in this chapter. On local initiatives, see Kent E. Portney, *Taking Sustainable Cities Seriously: Economic Development, the Environment, and Quality of Life in American Cities* (MIT Press, 2003); Daniel Press, *Saving Open Space: The Politics of Local Preservation in California* (University of California Press, 2002).

2. Schoeters, quoted in Jim Wasserman, "California Becoming Nation's New Gateway for European Enviro Laws," *San Jose Mercury News*, July 25, 2003; Danny Hakim, "California Is Moving to Guide U.S. Policy on Pollution," *New York Times*, July 3, 2002; John Holusha, "States Lead on Environment and Industries Complain," *New York Times*, April 1, 1991; Donald F. Kettl, "Sacramento Rules," *Governing*, December 2002, retrieved through Lexis-Nexis; Matthew L. Wald, "Environmentalists Head for the States," *New York Times*, February 1, 2004.

3. General Accounting Office, "Environmental Protection: Overcoming Obstacles to Innovative State Regulatory Programs," GAO-02-268, 2002, p. 17.

4. Petersen, *Acting for Endangered Species*, pp. 3–20. The information on New Hampshire is part of a dataset collected by one of the authors for a project on the development of state government institutions dealing with conservation and the environment.

5. Andrews, *Managing the Environment, Managing Ourselves*, pp. 201–318; Hays, *Beauty, Health, and Permanence*; Lazarus, *The Making of Environmental Law*, pp. 47–97.

6. States play other roles, often under federal guidelines or with federal support, including supplying water, disposing of solid waste, and overseeing environmental impacts through environmental impact statement requirements for projects like factories and new shopping malls.

7. Susan George, William J. Snape, and Michael Senatore, "State Endangered Species Acts: Past, Present and Future," Defenders for Wildlife, February 1998; Martin Nie, "State Wildlife Policy and Management: The Scope and Bias of Political Conflict," *Public Administration Review* 64, 2004: 221–233.

8. Barry G. Rabe, "Power to the States: The Promise and Pitfalls of Decentralization," in *Environmental Policy: New Directions for the Twenty-First Century*, 6th edition, ed. N. Vig and M. Kraft (CQ Press, 2006), pp. 35–36, and pp. 34–56

generally; Paul Teske, *Regulation in the States* (Brookings Institution, 2004), pp. 15–21, 171–181.

9. DeWitt John, *Civic Environmentalism: Alternatives to Regulation in States and Communities* (CQ Press, 1994), pp. 80, 79, and pp. 51–83 generally; Barry G. Rabe, "Permitting, Prevention, and Integration: Lessons from the States," in *Environmental Governance: A Report on the Next Generation of Environmental Policy*, ed. D. Kettl (Brookings Institution, 2002), pp. 14–57; Eric Siy, Leo Koziol, and Darcy Rollins, *The State of the States: Assessing the Capacity of States to Achieve Sustainable Development through Green Planning* (Resource Renewal Institute, 2001). See also William R. Lowry, *The Dimensions of Federalism: State Governments and Pollution Control Policies* (Duke University Press, 1992); Barry G. Rabe, *Fragmentation and Integration in State Environmental Management* (Conservation Foundation, 1986); Evan J. Ringquist, *Environmental Protection at the State Level: Politics and Progress in Controlling Pollution* (M. E. Sharpe, 1993); Denise Scheberle, *Federalism and Environmental Policy: Trust and the Politics of Implementation*, second edition (Georgetown University Press, 2004). For other examples of state ranking and categorizing, see A. Hunter Bacot and Roy A. Dawes, "State Expenditures and Policy Outcomes in Environmental Program Management," *Policy Studies Journal* 25, 1997: 355–370; Scott P. Hays, Michael Esler, and Carol E. Hays, "Environmental Commitment among the States: Integrating Approaches to State Environmental Policy," *Publius* 26, 1996: 41–58.

10. Rabe, "Permitting, Prevention, and Integration," pp. 17, 51.

11. Rabe, "Power to the States," pp. 34–56.

12. Claudia Copeland, "Environmental Policy: Issues in Federal State Relations," CRS Report for Congress 97-689, 1997; National Academy of Public Administration, *Setting Priorities, Getting Results: A New Direction for the Environmental Protection Agency* (NAPA, 1995), p. 2; Denise Scheberle, "Devolution," in *Environmental Governance Reconsidered*, ed. R. Durant, D. Fiorino, and R. O'Leary (MIT Press, 2004).

13. Clifford Rechtschaffen and David L. Markell, *Reinventing Environmental Enforcement* (Environmental Law Institute, 2003), p. 363.

14. Joyce M. Martin and Kristina Kern, "The Seesaw of Environmental Power from EPA to the States: National Environmental Performance Plans," *Villanova Environmental Law Journal* 9, 1998: 21; Rechtschaffen and Markell, *Reinventing Environmental Enforcement*, pp. 363–364; Scheberle, "Devolution," pp. 371–372.

15. GAO, "Environmental Protection"; GAO, "More Consistency Needed among EPA Regions in Approach to Enforcement," GAO/RCED-00-108, 2000; GAO, "Collaborative EPA-State Effort Needed to Improve New Performance Partnership System," GAO/RCED-99-171, 1999; GAO, "Challenges Facing EPA's Efforts to Reinvent Environmental Regulation," GAO/RECED-97-155, 1997; Rechtschaffen and Markell, *Reinventing Environmental Enforcement*, p. 364; Ross & Associates Environmental Consulting, "How Well Is NEPPS

Working? A Summary Comparison of Several Recent Evaluations of the National Environmental Performance Partnership System," prepared for 1999 ECOS/EPA NEPPS Workshop; Scheberle, "Devolution," pp. 371–373.

16. Rechtschaffen and Markell, *Reinventing Environmental Enforcement*, p. 364; Scheberle, "Devolution," p. 371.

17. GAO, "Collaborative EPA-State Effort Needed."

18. Scheberle, "Devolution," p. 372.

19. Jan Mazurek, "Back to the Future: How to Put Environmental Modernization Back on Track," Progressive Policy Institute, 2003.

20. Colorado Division of Wildlife, "Colorado Lynx Reintroduction and Augmentation Program," December 2002; Colorado Division of Wildlife, "Lynx Update," August 15, 2005; Ray Ring, "As Washington Waffles, Western States Go Green," *High Country News*, July 25, 2005.

21. John, *Civic Environmentalism*, pp. xiv, 14, 15.

22. Barry G. Rabe, *Statehouse and Greenhouse: The Emerging Politics of American Climate Change Policy* (Brookings Institution, 2004), p. 4.

23. Rabe, *Statehouse and Greenhouse*, pp. 8–15.

24. Rabe, *Statehouse and Greenhouse*, pp. xi–xii, and generally.

25. Pew Center on Global Climate Change, "States with Renewable Portfolio Standards"; Rabe, *Statehouse and Greenhouse*, pp. 2, 49–62.

26. Rabe, *Statehouse and Greenhouse*, quote pp. 50–51, pp. 49–62.

27. Felicity Barringer, "Officials Reach California Deal to Cut Emissions," *New York Times*, August 31, 2006; Pew Center on Global Climate Change; Rabe, *Statehouse and Greenhouse*, pp. 53, 62–145; Laura Paskus, "The Winds of Change," *High Country News*, May 2, 2005.

28. Rabe, *Statehouse and Greenhouse*, pp. 9, 21–37.

29. Christopher McGrory Klyza, "Public Lands and Wild Lands in the Northeast," in *Wilderness Comes Home*, ed. C. Klyza (University Press of New England, 2001).

30. *State of New York Adirondack Park State Land Master Plan* (State of New York, 1997); Frank Graham, *The Adirondack Park: A Political History* (Syracuse University Press, 1984 [1978]); Elaine Moss, ed., *Land Use Controls in New York State: A Handbook on the Legal Rights of Citizens* (Dial, 1975); Philip G. Terrie, *Contested Terrain: A New History of Nature and People in the Adirondacks* (Syracuse University Press, 1997), pp. 166–175. All acreage figures for the Adirondack Park are state-supplied estimates.

31. *The Adirondack Park in the Twenty First Century* (State of New York, 1990); Terrie, *Contested Terrain*, pp. 176–183.

32. "Adirondack Park Report," *Northern Forest Forum*, mid-winter 1999, pp. 20–21. A number of smaller acquisitions were also of tremendous importance during this period, including the Whitney Estate and the Tahawus Tract (Peter Bauer, "Adirondack Park Report," *Northern Forest Forum*, mid-winter

1998, p. 12; Phil Brown, "Pataki Isn't Finished Yet; Governor Still Hopes to Reach Million-Acre Goal," *Adirondack Explorer*, September/October 2005, p. 59).

33. Phil Brown, "Pataki Forging Legacy in Land," *Adirondack Explorer*, July/August 2004, pp. 32–33; The Conservation Fund, "The Conservation Fund Joins Governor Pataki and International Paper to Announce the Largest Land Conservation Deal in New York's History," press release, April 22, 2004; New York State Governor's Office, "Governor Pataki Announces Largest Land Preservation in State History," press release, April 22, 2004. Forest Legacy is a federal Forest Service program that distributes funds to the states to protect private forest land through conservation easements.

34. Pataki, quoted in "Governor Pataki Announces"; Brown, "Pataki Isn't Finished Yet."

35. Adirondack Park Agency, "Acreage by County and Land Use Classification," http://www.apa.state.ny.us; Brown, "Pataki Forging Legacy," p. 32; Brown, "Pataki Isn't Finished Yet," p. 5; New York State Department of Environmental Conservation, "Environmental Protection Fund," http://www.dec.state.ny.us.

36. Richard J. Ellis, *Democratic Delusions: The Initiative Process in America* (University Press of Kansas, 2002), pp. 35–42. Ellis reported that 458 initiatives appeared on ballots between 1990 and 2000, tripling the numbers seen in the 1940s, the 1950s, and the 1960s.

37. Guber, *The Grassroots of a Green Revolution*, pp. 130–131.

38. Defenders of Wildlife State Biodiversity Clearinghouse, "2004 Ballot Measures Pre-Election Report," http://www.defenders.org; Trust for Public Land, "LandVote 2004," http://www.tpl.org. See also Jeffrey D. Kline, "Public Demand for Preserving Local Open Space," *Society and Natural Resources* 19, 2006: 645–659; Daniel Press, "Who Votes for Natural Resources in California?" *Society and Natural Resources* 16, 2003: 835–846.

39. Duffy, *The Green Agenda in American Politics*, pp. 172–182; Deborah Lynn Guber, "Environmental Voting in the American States: A Tale of Two Initiatives," *State and Local Government Review* 33, 2001: 120–132; Nie, "Administrative Rulemaking"; Robert Reinhold, "Once Considered a Sure Thing, California's Environmental Package Falters," *New York Times*, September 16, 1990.

40. Shaun Bowler, Todd Donovan, and Caroline J. Tolbert, eds., *Citizens as Legislators: Direct Democracy in the United States* (Ohio State University Press, 1998); David S. Broder, *Democracy Derailed: Initiative Campaigns and the Power of Money* (Harcourt, 2000); Ellis, *Democratic Delusions*.

41. Christina Nicholas, 2004, "Dirty Gold: The Toxic Legacy of Cyanide-Leach Mining," *Mining Australia 2004*; State Environmental Resource Center, 2004, "Banning Cyanide Use in Mining."

42. Nicholas, "Dirty Gold."

43. Susan Gallagher, "Ballot Measure Would Undo Ban on Cyanide in Mining," *Associated Press*, October 18, 2004.

44. Gallagher, "Ballot Measure Would Undo Ban"; Westerners for Responsible Mining, "Zortman-Landusky Gold Mine, Montana," http://www.bettermines.org.

45. "Ballot Measure Would Restrict Use of Cyanide in Mining," Associated Press, October 19, 1998.

46. "Both Sides Debate Initiative that Would End Cyanide Leach Gold Mines," Associated Press, October 13, 1998; "Mining Company Will Ask for Millions in Damages from Montana," Associated Press, March 3, 2000; "Mining Executive on Law: This Is War," *Helena Independent Record*, December 9, 2000.

47. Snoddy, quoted in "Advocates Debate Cyanide Initiative," Associated Press, October 24, 1998.

48. Snoddy, quoted in "Ballot Measure Would Restrict Use of Cyanide in Mining"; Snoddy, quoted in "Both Sides Debate Initiative That Would End Cyanide Leach Gold Mines"; Snoddy, quoted in "Advocates Debate Cyanide Initiative."

49. "I-125 Limits Have Resulted in Quiet Campaign," Associated Press, September 21, 1998; "Judge Will Rule Quickly on Ban on Corporate Spending for Ballot Issues," Associated Press, October 21, 1998.

50. "Challenge to Cyanide Ban Dismissed," Associated Press, October 26, 1999; Mark Matthews, "Voters to Decide Mining's Future," *High Country News*, September 28, 1998; "Mining Company Promises Lawsuits Over Stymied Gold Mine," Associated Press, September 30, 1999.

51. "Initiative Campaigns Report Contributions, Expenditures," Associated Press, October 21, 1998.

52. "Judge Overturns Ban on Corporate Spending for Ballot Issues," Associated Press, October 22, 1998.

53. "Big Spending Didn't Guarantee Success for Ballot Issues," Associated Press, November 24, 1998.

54. Heather Abel, "Has Big Money Doomed Direct Democracy?" *High Country News*, October 28, 1996; "Big Spending Didn't Guarantee Success for Ballot Issues"; "I-125 Limits Have Resulted in Quiet Campaign."

55. Swysgood, quoted in "Odds Were Against Revote on Mining Cyanide Initiative," Associated Press, April 1, 1999; "Arguing Voters Were Uninformed, Senator Wants another Try at Cyanide Ban," Associated Press, December 1, 1998; "I-137 Likely to Dominate Environmental Debate during Session," Associated Press, January 3, 1999; "Racicot Wary of Overturning Voter Initiatives," Associated Press, January 9, 1999.

56. *Montana Chamber of Commerce, et al. v. Argenbright*, 226 F.3d 1049 (Ninth Circuit, 2000).

57. DeVoto, quoted in "Mining Company Sues over Law Stopping Its Proposed Mine," Associated Press, April 11, 2000.

58. *Seven-Up Pete Joint Venture, et al. v. Montana*, 327 Mont. 306 (2005); Bob Anez, "Supreme Court: Cyanide Ban Not Unconstitutional," Associated Press, June 8, 2005.

59. Smith, quoted in Gallagher, "Ballot Measure Would Undo Ban"; Bob Anez, "Company's Support for Mining Measure Tops $2 Million," Associated Press, October 18, 2004; Anez, "Value of Mining Safeguards in I-147 Stirs Argument," Associated Press, October 21, 2004.

60. Smith, quoted in Susan Gallagher, "Voters Refuse to Relax Mining Restriction," Associated Press, November 3, 2004.

61. Tom Kenworthy, "Mining Industry Labors to Drown Montana Water Quality Initiative," *Washington Post*, October 30, 1996; John Zaller, *The Nature and Origins of Mass Opinion* (Cambridge University Press, 1992).

62. Roberts, quoted in "Quotations about Oregon's Land Use Planning Program," 1995, http://darkwing.uoregon.edu; "Oregon: Key Laws/Administrative Actions/Court Decisions/Organizations," http://www.sprawlwatch.org.

63. Roberts, quoted in "Quotations about Oregon's Land Use Planning Program" 1995; John C. Ryan, "Oregon Gets Taken," *American Prospect*, October 21, 2002.

64. McCall, quoted in "Quotations about Oregon's Land Use Planning Program."

65. Randy Gragg, "Measure 7 Detonates Land Use Planning," *Portland Oregonian*, December 3, 2000.

66. OIA director, quoted in Laura Oppenheimer, "Judge Razes Measure 37 Land Law," *Portland Oregonian*, October 15, 2005; *MacPherson, et al. v. Department of Administrative Services, et al.*, 34 Ore. 117 (2006).

67. OIA, "Land Use/Property Rights Concerns of the Oregonians in Action Organization," http://oia.org.

68. Kitzhaber, quoted in Jennifer Anderson, "Kitzhaber, Conservation Groups Say 'No' on Measure 7," Associated Press, November 1, 2000.

69. Kitzhaber, quoted in R. Gregory Nokes, "Opponents Call Measure 7 Threat to Land, McCall Legacy," *Portland Oregonian*, November 2, 2000.

70. "Measure 7 Rewrite Likely Dies in the Legislature," Associated Press, July 5, 2001.

71. "Last Minute Mania on Measure 7," *Portland Oregonian*, June 22, 2001.

72. Dave Hogan, "Court Rejects Property Rights Measure," *Portland Oregonian*, October 5, 2002.

73. "A Reprieve from Measure 7," *Portland Oregonian*, February 23, 2001.

74. Felicity Barringer, "Property Rights Law May Alter Oregon Landscape," *New York Times*, November 26, 2004; Charles E. Beggs, "Voters Again Face Property Compensation Issue," Associated Press, September 25, 2004; Oregon Secretary of State, Elections Division, "Measure 37," November 2, 2004.

75. "House Tries to Rewrite Measure 37," *Portland Oregonian*, June 7, 2005; "Measure 37 Stuck in a Circle of Chambers," *Portland Oregonian*, June 21, 2005; Laura Oppenheimer, "Mild Measure 37 Bill Passes," *Portland Oregonian*, July 8, 2005.

76. Laura Oppenheimer, "Oregon Supreme Court Will Hear Measure 37 Appeal in January," *Portland Oregonian*, November 9, 2005; Peter Sleeth, "Land Use Ruling Puts Issue Back at Square One," *Portland Oregonian*, October 16, 2005; *MacPherson, et al.* v. *Department of Administrative Services*, 2006.

77. Dan Berman, "Regulatory Takings Measures Fail in Calif., Idaho and Wash.," *Greenwire*, November 8, 2006.

78. Ellis, *Democratic Delusions*.

79. Ibid, pp. 201–202.

80. Teske, *Regulation in the States*, pp. 15–21, 225–235.

81. Additionally, the automobile industry challenged California rules requiring automakers to reduce CO_2 emissions from new cars sold in California beginning in 2009 (Tasha Eichenseher, "Industry Sues Calif. to Block GHG Emissions Law," *Greenwire*, December 8, 2004). Since this case was not initiated by the states—as the other two cases were—we will not discuss it here.

82. Darren Samuelsohn, "Northeast AGs Sue Bush Admin over CO_2 Emissions," *Greenwire*, June 4, 2003; Darren Samuelsohn, "Enviros to Sue EPA in Wake of Motor Vehicle Petition Rejection," *Greenwire*, September 2, 2003.

83. EPA, "Control of Emissions from New Highway Vehicles and Engines," September 8, 2003 (68 *Federal Register* 52922–52933).

84. Davis, quoted in Danny Hakim, "States Plan Suit to Prod U.S. on Global Warming," *New York Times*, October 4, 2003; Samuelsohn, "Enviros to Sue EPA." The states suing the EPA were California, Connecticut, Illinois, Maine, Massachusetts, New Jersey, New Mexico, New York, Oregon, Rhode Island, Vermont, and Washington. The states supporting the EPA in the lawsuit were Alaska, Idaho, Indiana, Kansas, Michigan, Nebraska, North Dakota, Ohio, South Dakota, Texas, and Utah.

85. *Commonwealth of Massachusetts v. Environmental Protection Agency*, 415 F.3d 50 (D.C. Cir., 2005).

86. Darren Samuelsohn, "Supreme Court Takes Up Greenhouse Gas Case," *Greenwire*, November 29, 2006.

87. Spitzer and Blumenthal, quoted in Brian Stempeck, "States' Lawsuit Demands Utilities Reduce CO_2 Emissions 3 Percent per Year," *Greenwire*, July 22, 2004. The eight states filing suit were California, Connecticut, Iowa, New Jersey, New York, Rhode Island, Vermont, and Wisconsin.

88. *State of Connecticut v. American Electric Power Company*, 406 F. Supp. 2d 265 (S.D.N.Y., 2005); Pamela Najor, "States, Enviros Appeal 'Public Nuisance' Case against Utilities," *Greenwire*, October 3, 2005.

89. Kirk Johnson, "3 States Sue E.P.A. to Regulate Emissions of Carbon Dioxide," *New York Times*, June 2, 2003; Samuelsohn, "Northeast AGs Sue Bush Admin."

90. Blumenthal, Rickard, and Spitzer, quoted in Brooke A. Masters, "States Flex Prosecutorial Muscle," *Washington Post*, January 12, 2005; Dan Berman, "Calif., Enviros Challenge Sierra Nevada Plan," *Greenwire*, February 2, 2005;

Julie Cart, "New Mexico Won't Go Down without a Fight Over Drilling," *Los Angeles Times*, April 23, 2005; Erin Duggan, "Spitzer Accuses EPA of Safety Risks," *Albany Times Union*, September 16, 2003; Judy Fahys, "Wilderness in Limbo as 'Roads' Are Redefined," *Salt Lake City Tribune*, September 9, 2005; Alex Kaplun, "NYC, 15 States Sue DOE for Failure to Update Appliance Standards," *Greenwire*, September 7, 2005.

91. David Whitney, "Guarding His Turf, Senator Fights Mower Emission Curbs," *Sacramento Bee*, September 5, 2003.

92. Lloyd and Savage, quoted in David Whitney, "State's Small-Engine Pollution Curb Foiled," *Sacramento Bee*, November 13, 2005; Carolyn Lochhead, "GOP Blocks Feinstein's Bid to Save State's Pollution Rule," *San Francisco Chronicle*, November 18, 2003.

93. Feinstein, quoted in Carolyn Lochhead, "Governor Pressures GOP on Lawnmowers," *San Francisco Chronicle*, November 20, 2003; Nick Anderson, "Panel Kills Bid to Curb State Pollution Law," *Los Angeles Times*, November 20, 2003; Felicity Barringer, "A Greener Way to Cut the Grass Runs Afoul of a Powerful Lobby," *New York Times*, April 24, 2006.

94. Becker, quoted in Juliet Eilperin, "Clean-Air Advocates Criticize GOP Gas Bill," *Washington Post*, October 6, 2005; Clarke, quoted in Kerry Brophy, "Hotlines: Wyoming: Feds Oppose State's Effort to Empower Landowners," *High Country News*, August 22, 2005, p. 6; Hinchman, quoted in Susan Milligan, "GOP Gives More Power to Federal Government," *Boston Globe*, May 1, 2005.

95. Duffy, *The Green Agenda*, pp. 163–195.

96. Rabe, "Permitting, Prevention, and Integration," p. 41.

97. John, *Civic Environmentalism*, pp. 271–282; Rabe, "Power to the States," pp. 34–43.

98. Danny Hakim, "Battle Lines Set as New York Acts to Cut Emissions," *New York Times*, November 26, 2005; Darren Samuelsohn, "Northeastern States Sign Regional Global Warming Pact," *Greenwire*, December 20, 2005.

99. Kettl, "Sacramento Rules"; "In Reversal, State Senate Saves Enviro Agency from Sunset," *Greenwire*, March 25, 2005; Rabe, "Power to the States," pp. 43–45; Rabe, *Statehouse and Greenhouse*.

100. Jodi Wilgoren, "With Deadline Near, States Are in Budget Discord," *New York Times*, June 27, 2003.

101. Rabe, "Power to the States," pp. 45–46, 50–51; Rabe, *Statehouse and Greenhouse*, pp. 129–130, 156–158.

102. McIntosh, quoted in Donna K. Spangler, "Leavitt's Enlibra Is Called Hot Air," *Salt Lake City Deseret News*, April 23, 2002; "Environmental Clout in Salem All but Extinct," *Portland Oregonian*, September 29, 2005; Rachel L. Gould, "Senate Rejects Gov. Schwarzenegger Nominee for Air Board," *Greenwire*, September 6, 2005.

103. Rabe, "Power to the States," pp. 46–48.

104. Marcus, Geffen, and Sexton, *Reinventing Environmental Regulation*; Rabe, *Statehouse and Greenhouse*, pp. 102–104, 130, 161–166.

Chapter 8

1. R. W. Apple, "College Students Tune in to Debate but Are Left Wanting Clear Answers," *New York Times*, October 15, 2004; "Warnings on Warming," *New York Times*, September 29, 2004.

2. Jim VandeHei and Justin Blum, "Bush Signs Energy Bill, Cheers Steps towards Self-Sufficiency," *Washington Post*, August 9, 2005.

3. Les Blumenthal, "Task Force Proposes Updates to Old Law," *Tacoma News Tribune*, February 21, 2006; "Endangering Species," *Washington Post*, October 10, 2005; Mike Lee, "Spurred to Action," *San Diego Union Tribune*, February 19, 2006; "Legislative Legacy of 2003: Congress Hands Bush Big Wins," *CQ Weekly*, December 13, 2003: 3094.

4. John Heilprin, "EPA Budget Cuts Trouble Environmental Groups," Associated Press, February 10, 2006; Carl Hulse, "Senate Rejects Bid for Drilling in Arctic Area," *New York Times*, December 22, 2005; Mary Clare Jalonick, "Cuts Hit Conservation, Research," *CQ Weekly*, December 6, 2003: 3014.

5. Felicity Barringer, "Environmentalists, Though Winners in the Election, Warn against Expecting Vast Changes," *New York Times*, November 14, 2006.

6. Moe, "The Politicized Presidency"; Moe, "The Politics of Bureaucratic Structure," in *Can the Government Govern?* ed. J. Chubb and P. Peterson (Brookings Institution, 1989).

7. Smith, quoted in Felicity Barringer, "Plan for Snowmobiles in Two Parks Is Voided," *New York Times*, December 16, 2003.

8. Amanda Griscom, "Syzygy Whiz," *Grist Magazine*, May 13, 2004, http://www.grist.org; Douglas Jehl, "U.S. Plan Could Ease Limits on Wetlands Development," *New York Times*, January 11, 2003; David E. Sanger and David Halbfinger, "For Earth Day, Bush and Kerry Vie on the Environment," *New York Times*, April 22, 2004; Katherine Q. Seelye, "Political Memo: Environment Fits in Political Strategy," *New York Times*, February 1, 2003.

9. Felicity Barringer, "Energy Exploration," *New York Times*, March 5, 2006. In 2006, Bush did designate the 89-million-acre Northwestern Hawaiian Islands Marine National Monument, protecting a large expanse of ocean. This followed Clinton's use of an executive order in 2000 to designate waters in the same area a coral reef reserve to be managed by the National Oceanic and Atmospheric Administration (Andrew C. Revkin, "Bush Plans Vast Protected Sea Area in Hawaii," *New York Times*, June 15, 2006).

10. James McCarthy, "Community-Based Forestry in the United States: Antecedents and New Directions," Ford Foundation Community-Based Forestry

Demonstration Project, 2002; Gale Norton and Ann Veneman, "There's More Than One Way to Protect Wetlands," *New York Times*, March 12, 2003.

11. Tony Davis, "Critical Habitat: The Inside Story," *High Country News*, February 20, 2006, p. 13; Robert McClure and Lisa Stiffler, "License to Kill: Flaws in Habitat Conservation Plans Threaten the Survival of Scores of Species," *Seattle Post-Intelligencer*, May 3, 2005; Craig Welch, "Feds Losing Grip on Species Act," *Seattle Times*, December 28, 2003; Craig Welch, "Bush Switches Nation's Tack on Protecting Species," *Seattle Times*, September 27, 2004.

12. Eric Schaeffer, "Clearing the Air," *Washington Monthly*, July/August 2002; Shankar Vedantam, "EPA Inspector Finds Mercury Proposal Biased," *Washington Post*, February 4, 2005; Vedantam, "EPA Distorted Mercury Analysis, GAO Says," *Washington Post*, March 8, 2005; Vedantam, "New Mercury Rule Omits Conflicting Data," *Washington Post*, March 22, 2005.

13. Jan Mazurek, "Back to the Future: How to Put Environmental Modernization Back on Track," Progressive Policy Institute, April 23, 2003.

14. Ibid.

15. Skowronek, *The Politics Presidents Make*.

16. Jeff Madrick, "The Way to a Fair Deal," *New York Review of Books*, January 12, 2006, p. 37.

17. John Micklethwait and Adrian Wooldridge, *The Right Nation: Conservative Power in America* (Penguin, 2004). For an alternative view, see Jacob S. Hacker and Paul Pierson, *Off Center: The Republican Revolution and the Erosion of American Democracy* (Yale University Press, 2006).

18. Michael Shellenberger and Ted Nordhaus, "The Death of Environmentalism: Global Warming Politics in a Post-Environmental World," 2004; Richard J. Lazarus, "A Different Kind of 'Republican Moment' in Environmental Law," *Minnesota Law Review* 97, 2003: 999–1036.

19. EPA, "Mercury: Controlling Power Plant Emissions: Decision Process and Chronology," http://www.epa.gov; USDA Forest Service, "FY 1905–2005 Annual National Sold and Harvest Summary," http://www.fs.fed.us.

20. Orren and Skowronek, *The Search for American Political Development*, p. 171. On green drift in conservation and natural resources policy, also see Keiter, *Keeping Faith with Nature*. We share Keiter's view on "the ongoing transition toward an ecosystem management policy regime" (p. 318), although not for entirely the same reasons—a concurring opinion of sorts. Most clearly, we disagree with his statement that "as the new age of ecology takes hold, it is forcing us to surmount the dead weight of tradition that has long pervaded public land policy" (p. 326). As we have argued throughout this book, we don't think it is possible to simply surmount the dead weight of the green state; the green state is the foundation to understanding conservation and environmental policy.

21. Shellenberger and Nordhaus, "The Death of Environmentalism," pp. 6, 7. See also Richard W. Behan, *Plundered Promise: Capitalism, Politics, and the Fate*

of the Federal Lands (Island, 2001); Dowie, *Losing Ground*; Gottlieb, *Forcing the Spring*.

22. Shellenberger and Nordhaus, "The Death of Environmentalism." For a recent analysis suggesting that the Healthy Forests Restoration Act has not escaped the green state labyrinth, see Kathie Durbin, "The War on Wildfire," *High Country News*, April 17, 2006.

23. Richard Brewer, *Conservancy: The Land Trust Movement in America* (University Press of New England, 2003), pp. 10–40, 176–184; Land Trust Alliance, "National Land Trust Census," 2006, http://www.lta.org.

24. Brewer, *Conservancy*, p. 11; Land Trust Alliance, "National Land Trust Census."

25. Brewer, *Conservancy*, pp. 183–215; The Nature Conservancy, "How We Work: Conservation Methods: Private Land Conservation," http://nature.org.

26. Organic Trade Association, "Organic Food Facts," http://www.ota.com; USDA, "The National Organic Program: Background Information," http://www.ams.usda.gov.

27. American Forest & Paper Association, "Sustainable Forestry Initiative," http://www.afandpa.org; Forest Stewardship Council, "The History of FSC-US," http://www.fscus.org; Forest Stewardship Council, "Total Certified Area in U.S. Reaches 22 Million Acres," http://www.fscus.org.

28. U.S. Green Building Council, "Resources: USGBC Introductory PowerPoint Presentation," http://www.usgbc.org.

29. Joan Lowy, "Environmentalists Bypass Washington to Pressure Corporations," Scripps News Service, May 25, 2005; David Vogel, *The Market for Virtue: The Potential and Limits of Corporate Social Responsibility* (Brookings Institution, 2005), pp. 60, 135.

30. Vogel, *The Market for Virtue*, quote p. 135, pp. 110–138 generally.

31. Michael Barbaro and Felicity Barringer, "Wal-Mart to Seek Savings in Energy," *New York Times*, October 25, 2005; Claudia Deutsch, "It's Getting Crowded on the Environmental Bandwagon," *New York Times*, December 22, 2005. For a recent treatment on the role of business in U.S. environmental policy, see Sheldon Kamieniecki, *Corporate America and Environmental Policy: How Often Does Business Get Its Way?* (Stanford University Press, 2006).

32. Vogel, *The Market for Virtue*, quotes pp. 9–10, 11, pp. 1–45 generally.

33. Vogel, *The Market for Virtue*, quotes pp. 133, 163, pp. 128, 136–138; Graham Wilson, "Regulatory Reform on the World Stage," in *Environmental Governance*, ed. D. Kettl (Brookings Institution, 2002).

34. John Elkington and Mark Lee, "WEEE Are the World: New E.U. Environmental Standards Are Changing the Global Marketplace," *Grist Magazine*, September 20, 2005, http://www.grist.org; Donald F. Kettl, "Sacramento Rules," *Governing*, December 2002; David Vogel, *Trading Up: Consumer and Environmental Regulation in a Global Economy* (Harvard University Press, 1995);

David Vogel, "The Hare and the Tortoise Revisited: The New Politics of Consumer and Environmental Regulation in Europe," in *Environmental Policy in the European Union*, second edition, ed. A. Jordan (Earthscan, 2005 [2003]), pp. 225–252; Wilson, "Regulatory Reform on the World Stage."

35. Karen Orren and Stephen Skowronek, "Beyond the Iconography of Order: Notes for a 'New Institutionalism,'" in *The Dynamics of American Politics*, ed. L. Dodd and C. Jillson (Westview, 1994), p. 322.

36. Tavaglione, quoted in Tony Davis, "High Noon for Habitat," *High Country News*, February 20, 2006. For other illustrations of the complexities of current environmental policy, see Paul W. Hirt, "A Case Study of Political Influence on Forest Management Decisions, Coronado National Forest, Arizona, 1980s-1990s," in *Forests under Fire*, ed. C. Haggard and A. Gomez (University of Arizona Press, 2001); Martin Nie, "Governing the Tongass: National Forest Conflict and Political Decision Making," *Environmental Law* 36, 2006: 385–480; Nie, "Drivers of Natural Resource-based Conflict," *Policy Sciences* 36, 2003: 307–341; Jacqueline Vaughn and Hanna Cortner, "Using Parallel Strategies to Promote Change: Forest Policymaking under George W. Bush," *Review of Policy Research* 21, 2004: 767–782.

37. Skowronek, *Building a New American State*, p. 9.

Selected References

Aldrich, John H., and David W. Rohde. 1997–1998. "The Transition to Republican Rule in the House: Implications for Theories of Congressional Politics." *Political Science Quarterly* 112: 541–567.

Aldrich, John H., and David W. Rohde. 2000. "The Republican Revolution and the House Appropriations Committee." *Journal of Politics* 62: 1–33.

Allin, Craig W. 1982. *The Politics of Wilderness Preservation*. Greenwood.

Andrews, Richard N. L. 1999. *Managing the Environment, Managing Ourselves: A History of American Environmental Policy*. Yale University Press.

Bacot, A. Hunter, and Roy A. Dawes. 1997. "State Expenditures and Policy Outcomes in Environmental Program Management." *Policy Studies Journal* 25: 355–370.

Bardach, Eugene, and Robert Kagan. 2002. *Going by the Book: The Problem of Regulatory Unreasonableness*. Transaction.

Bartels, Larry M. 2000. "Partisanship and Voting Behavior, 1952–1996." *American Journal of Political Science* 44: 35–50.

Batt, Kevin. 1995. "Above All, Do No Harm: *Sweet Home* and Section Nine of the Endangered Species Act." *Boston University Law Review* 75: 1177–1231.

Baumgartner, Frank R., and Bryan D. Jones. 1993. *Agendas and Instability in American Politics*. University of Chicago Press.

Baumgartner, Frank R., and Bryan D. Jones, eds. 2002. *Policy Dynamics*. University of Chicago Press.

Behan, Richard W. 2001. *Plundered Promise: Capitalism, Politics, and the Fate of the Federal Lands*. Island.

Berry, Jeffrey M. 1999. *The New Liberalism: The Rising Power of Citizens Groups*. Brookings Institution.

Biasi, Heidi. 2002. "The Antiquities Act of 1906 and Presidential Proclamations: A Retrospective and Prospective Analysis of President William J. Clinton's Quest to 'Win the West.'" *Buffalo Environmental Law Journal* 9: 189–244.

Binder, Sarah. 2003. *Stalemate: Causes and Consequences of Legislative Gridlock.* Brookings Institution.

Bloch, Stephen H. M., and Heidi J. McIntosh. 2003. "A View from the Front Lines: The Fate of Utah's Redrock Wilderness under the George W. Bush Administration." *Golden Gate Law Review* 33: 473–502.

Blumm, Michael C. 2001. "Twenty Years of Environmental Law." *Virginia Environmental Law Journal* 20: 5–16.

Bosso, Christopher J. 2005. *Environment, Inc.: From Grassroots to Beltway.* University Press of Kansas.

Bowler, Shaun, Todd Donovan, and Caroline J. Tolbert, eds. 1998. *Citizens as Legislators: Direct Democracy in the United States.* Ohio State University Press.

Brady, David W., and Craig Volden. 2006. *Revolving Gridlock: Politics and Policy from Jimmy Carter to George W. Bush.* Westview.

Brewer, Richard. 2003. *Conservancy: The Land Trust Movement in America.* University Press of New England.

Brick, Philip, Donald Snow, and Sarah Van de Wetering, eds. 2001. *Across the Great Divide: Explorations in Collaborative Conservation and the American West.* Island.

Broder, David S. 2000. *Democracy Derailed: Initiative Campaigns and the Power of Money.* Harcourt.

Brown, Susan Jane M. 2000. "David and Goliath: Reformulating the Definition of 'The Public Interest' and the Future of Land Swaps after the Interstate 90 Land Exchange." *Journal of Environmental Law and Litigation* 15: 235–293.

Brulle, Robert J. 2000. *Agency, Democracy, and Nature: The U.S. Environmental Movement from a Critical Theory Perspective.* MIT Press.

Brunner, Ronald D., Christine H. Colburn, Christina M. Cromley, Roberta A. Klein, and Elizabeth A. Olson. 2002. *Finding Common Ground: Governance and Natural Resources in the American West.* Yale University Press.

Brunner, Ronald D., Toddi A. Steelman, Lindy Coe-Juell, Christina M. Cromley, Christine M. Edwards, and Donna W. Tucker. 2005. *Adaptive Governance: Integrating Science, Policy and Decision Making.* Columbia University Press.

Bryner, Gary C. 1995. *Blue Skies, Green Politics: The Clean Air Act of 1990 and Its Implementation*, second edition. CQ Press.

Caldart, Charles C., and Nicholas A. Ashford. 1999. "Negotiation as a Means of Developing and Implementing Environmental and Occupational Safety and Health Policy." *Harvard Environmental Law Journal* 23: 141–202.

Carpenter, Daniel P. 2001. *The Forging of Bureaucratic Autonomy: Reputations, Networks, and Policy Innovation in Executive Agencies, 1862–1928.* Princeton University Press.

Case, David W. 2001. "The EPA's Environmental Stewardship Initiative: Attempting to Revitalize a Floundering Regulatory Reform Agenda." *Emory Law Journal* 50: 1–100.

Chertow, Marian R., and Daniel C. Esty, eds. 1997. *Thinking Ecologically: The Next Generation of Environmental Policy*. Yale University Press.

Choo, Robert. 2000. "Judicial Review of Negotiated Rulemaking: Should Chevron Deference Apply?" *Rutgers Law Review* 52: 1069–1120.

Coglianese, Cary. 1997. Assessing Consensus: The Promise and Performance of Negotiated Rulemaking. Working paper, John F. Kennedy School of Government.

Coglianese, Cary. 2002. Is Satisfaction Success? Evaluating Public Participation in Regulatory Rulemaking. Faculty Research Working Paper RWP02-038, John F. Kennedy School of Government.

Coglianese, Cary. 2003. "Does Consensus Work? A Pragmatic Approach to Public Participation in the Regulatory Process." In *Evaluating Environmental and Public Policy Resolution Programs and Politics*, ed. R. O'Leary and L. Binham. Resources for the Future.

Coglianese, Cary, and Laurie K. Allen. 2004. "Does Consensus Make Common Sense? An Analysis of the EPA's Common Sense Initiative." *Environment* 46: 10–25.

Coglianese, Cary, and Laurie K. Allen. 2003. Building Sector-Based Consensus: A Review of the EPA's Common Sense Initiative. Faculty Research Working Paper RWP03-037, John F. Kennedy School of Government.

Cohen, Michael P. 1988. *The History of the Sierra Club, 1892–1970*. Sierra Club Books.

Cohen, Richard E. 1995. *Washington at Work: Back Rooms and Clean Air*, second edition. Allyn and Bacon.

Cohen, Steven, Sheldon Kamieniecki, and Matthew A. Cahn. 2005. *Strategic Planning in Environmental Regulation: A Policy Approach That Works*. MIT Press.

Coleman, John J. 1997. "The Decline and Resurgence of Congressional Party Conflict." *Journal of Politics* 59: 165–184.

Cooper, Phillip J. 2002. *By Order of the President: The Use and Abuse of Executive Direct Action*. University Press of Kansas.

Crozier, Michael J., Samuel P. Huntington, and Joji Watanuki. 1975. *Crisis of Democracy: Report on the Governability of Democracies to the Trilateral Commission*. New York University Press.

Davidson, Roger H., and Walter Oleszek. 2006. *Congress and Its Members*, tenth edition. CQ Press.

Davis, Charles. 2001. "Politics and Public Rangeland Policy." In *Western Public Lands and Environmental Politics*, second edition, ed. C. Davis. Westview.

Davis, Richard, and Diana Owen. 1998. *New Media and American Politics*. Oxford University Press.

Devine, Robert S. 2004. *Bush Versus the Environment*. Anchor.

Dionne, E. J. 1991. *Why Americans Hate Politics*. Touchstone.

Dombeck, Michael P., Christopher A. Wood, and Jack E. Williams. 2003. *From Conquest to Conservation: Our Public Lands Legacy*. Island.

Dorn, Trilby C.E. 1996. "Logging without Laws: The 1995 Salvage Logging Rider Radically Changes Policy and the Rule of Law in the Forests." *Tulane Environmental Law Journal* 9: 447–482.

Dowie, Mark. 1995. *Losing Ground: American Environmentalism at the Close of the Twentieth Century*. MIT Press.

Duffy, Robert J. 1996. "Divided Government and Institutional Combat: The Case of the Quayle Council on Competitiveness." *Polity* 18: 379–399.

Duffy, Robert J. 2003. *The Green Agenda in American Politics: New Strategies for the Twenty-first Century*. University Press of Kansas.

Durant, Robert F. 1992. *The Administrative Presidency Revisited: Public Lands, the BLM, and the Reagan Revolution*. SUNY Press.

Durant, Robert F., Daniel J. Fiorino, and Rosemary O'Leary, eds. 2004. *Environmental Governance Reconsidered: Challenges, Choices, and Opportunities*. MIT Press.

Echeverria, John D. 2001. "Changing the Rules by Changing the Players: The Environmental Issue in State Judicial Elections." *New York University Environmental Law Journal* 9: 217–304.

Edsall, Thomas B., and Mary Edsall. 1991. *Chain Reaction: The Impact of Race, Rights, and Taxes on American Politics*. Norton.

Eisner, Marc Allen. 2000. *Regulatory Politics in Transition*, second edition. Johns Hopkins University Press.

Ellis, Richard. 2002. *Democratic Delusions: The Initiative Process in America*. University Press of Kansas.

Farber, Daniel A. 1999. *Eco-pragmatism*. University of Chicago Press.

Fraser, Steve, and Gary Gerstle, eds. 1989. *The Rise and Fall of the New Deal Order*. Princeton University Press.

Freeman, Jody. 1997. "Collaborative Governance and the Administrative State." *UCLA Law Review* 45: 1–98.

Freeman, Jody, and Laura I. Langbein. 2000. "Regulatory Negotiation and the Legitimacy Benefit." *New York University Environmental Law Journal* 9: 60–139.

Funk, William H. 1987. "When the Smoke Gets in Your Eyes: Regulatory Negotiation and the Public Interest—EPA's Woodstove Standards." *Environmental Law* 18: 55–98.

Funk, William H. 1997. "Bargaining toward the New Millennium: Regulatory Negotiation and the Subversion of the Public Interest." *Duke Law Journal* 46: 1351–1388.

Gitlin, Todd. 1995. *The Twilight of Common Dreams: Why America Is Wracked by Culture Wars*. Henry Holt.

Goldman, Patti A., and Kristen L. Boyles. 1997. "Forsaking the Rule of Law: The 1995 Logging without Laws Rider and Its Legacy." *Environmental Law* 27: 1035–1089.

Gottlieb, Robert. 1993. *Forcing the Spring: The Transformation of the American Environmental Movement*. Island.

Graham, Frank. 1984 [1978]. *The Adirondack Park: A Political History*. Syracuse University Press.

Graham, Mary. 1999. *The Morning after Earth Day: Practical Environmental Politics*. Brookings Institution.

Gregory, Eacata Desiree. 2000. "No Time Is the Right Time: The Supreme Court's Use of Ripeness to Block Judicial Review of Forest Plans for Environmental Plaintiffs in *Ohio Forestry Association v. Sierra Club*." *Chicago-Kent Law Review* 75: 613–639.

Greider, William. 1993. *Who Will Tell the People?* Simon and Schuster.

Guber, Deborah L. 2001. "Environmental Voting in the American States: A Tale of Two Initiatives." *State and Local Government Review* 33: 120–132.

Guber, Deborah L. 2003. *The Grassroots of a Green Revolution: Polling America on the Environment*. MIT Press.

Hacker, Jacob S., and Paul Pierson. 2005. *Off Center: The Republican Revolution and the Erosion of American Democracy*. Yale University Press.

Halden, Ann E. 1997. "The Grand Staircase-Escalante National Monument and the Antiquities Act." *Fordham Environmental Law Journal* 8: 713–739.

Harter, Philip J. 1982. "Negotiating Regulations: A Cure for Malaise." *Georgetown Law Journal* 71: 1–119.

Havlick, David G. 2002. *No Place Distant: Roads and Motorized Recreation on America's Public Lands*. Island.

Hays, Samuel P. 1975 [1959]. *Conservation and the Gospel of Efficiency: The Progressive Conservation Movement, 1890–1920*. Atheneum.

Hays, Samuel P. 1987. *Beauty, Health, and Permanence: Environmental Politics in the United States, 1955–1985*. Cambridge University Press.

Hays, Scott P., Michael Esler, Carol E. Hays. 1996. "Environmental Commitment among the States: Integrating Approaches to State Environmental Policy." *Publius* 26: 41–58.

Helvarg, David. 1994. *The War against the Greens*. Sierra Club Books.

Hirsch, Dennis D. 1998. "Bill and Al's XL-ent Adventure: An Analysis of the EPA's Legal Authority to Implement the Clinton Administration's Project XL." *University of Illinois Law Review* 1998: 129–172.

Hirt, Paul W. 2001. "A Case Study of Political Influence on Forest Management Decisions, Coronado National Forest, Arizona, 1980s–1990s." In *Forests Under Fire: A Century of Ecosystem Mismanagement in the Southwest*, ed. C. Haggard and A. Gomez. University of Arizona Press.

Hoberg, George. 2001. "The Emerging Triumph of Ecosystem Management: The Transformation of Federal Forest Policy." In *Western Public Lands and Environmental Politics*, second edition, ed. C. Davis. Westview.

Houck, Oliver S. 1994. "The Secret Opinions of the United States Supreme Court on Leading Cases in Environmental Law, Never Before Published!" *University of Colorado Law Review* 65: 459–517.

Houck, Oliver S. 2002. "Unfinished Stories." *University of Colorado Law Review* 73: 867–943.

Howell, William G. 2003. *Power without Persuasion: The Politics of Direct Presidential Action*. Princeton University Press.

Hurst, James Willard. 1964. *Law and the Conditions of Freedom in the Nineteenth-Century United States*. University of Wisconsin Press.

Jacobson, Gary C. 1996. "The 1994 House Elections in Perspective." *Political Science Quarterly* 111: 203–223.

Jacobson, Gary C. 2001. "A House and Senate Divided: The Clinton Legacy and the Elections of 2000." *Political Science Quarterly* 116: 5–28.

John, DeWitt. 1994. *Civic Environmentalism: Alternatives to Regulation in States and Communities*. CQ Press.

Johnson, Barbara H., ed. 2003. *Forging a West That Works: An Invitation to the Radical Center*. Quivira Coalition.

Jones, Charles O. 1994. *The Presidency in a Separated System*. Brookings Institution.

Judis, John B., and Ruy Texeira. 2002. *The Emerging Democratic Majority*. Scribner.

Kagan, Robert. 2001. *Adversarial Legalism*. Harvard University Press.

Kamieniecki, Sheldon. 2006. *Corporate America and Environmental Policy: How Often Does Business Get Its Way?* Stanford University Press.

Kareiva, Peter, et al. 1999. Using Science in Habitat Conservation Plans. National Center for Ecological Analysis and Synthesis and American Institute of Biological Sciences.

Keiter, Robert B. 2003. *Keeping Faith with Nature: Ecosystems, Democracy, and America's Public Lands*. Yale University Press.

Kendall, Douglas T., and Charles P. Lord. 1998. "The Takings Project: A Critical Analysis and Assessment of the Progress So Far." *Boston College Environmental Affairs Law Review* 25: 509–588.

Kerwin, Cornelius M., and Scott R. Furlong. 1992. "Time and Rulemaking: An Empirical Test of the Theory." *Journal of Public Administration Research and Theory* 2: 113–138.

Kettl, Donald F. 1994. *Reinventing Government? Appraising the National Performance Review*. Brookings Institution.

Kettl, Donald F. 2002. "Sacramento Rules." *Governing*. December.

Kettl, Donald F., ed. 2002. *Environmental Governance: A Report on the Next Generation of Environmental Policy*. Brookings Institution.

Kingdon, John. 1995. *Agendas, Alternatives, and Public Policy*, second edition. Harper Collins.

Klein, Christine A. 2002. "Preserving Monumental Landscapes under the Antiquities Act." *Cornell Law Review* 87: 1333–1404.

Kline, Jeffrey D. 2006. "Public Demand for Preserving Local Open Space." *Society and Natural Resources* 19: 645–659.

Klyza, Christopher McGrory. 1996. *Who Controls Public Lands? Mining, Forestry, and Grazing Policies, 1870–1990*. University of North Carolina Press.

Klyza, Christopher McGrory. 2001. "Public Lands and Wild Lands in the Northeast." In *Wilderness Comes Home: Rewilding the Northeast*. Christopher McGrory Klyza, ed. University Press of New England.

Klyza, Christopher McGrory. 2002. "The United States Army, Natural Resources, and Political Development in the Nineteenth Century." *Polity* 35: 1–28.

Koontz, Tomas M., Toddi A. Steelman, JoAnn Carmin, Katrina Smith Korfmacher, Cassandra Moseley, and Craig W. Thomas. 2004. *Collaborative Environmental Management: What Roles for Government?* Resources for the Future.

Langbein, Laura I., and Cornelius M. Kerwin. 2000. "Regulatory Negotiation Versus Conventional Rulemaking: Claims, Counterclaims, and Empirical Evidence." *Journal of Public Administration Research and Theory* 10: 599–633.

Lazarus, Richard J. 2003. "A Different Kind of 'Republican Moment' in Environmental Law." *Minnesota Law Review* 97: 999–1036.

Lazarus, Richard J. 2004. *The Making of Environmental Law*. University of Chicago Press.

Lemann, Nicholas. 1999. "No People Allowed." *New Yorker*. November 22, pp. 96–113.

Leshy, John D. 2001. "The Babbitt Legacy at the Department of the Interior: A Preliminary View." *Environmental Law* 31: 199–227.

Levy, Peter B. 1994. *The New Left and Labor in the 1960s*. University of Illinois Press.

Lowi, Theodore. 1969. *The End of Liberalism*. Norton.

Lowi, Theodore. 1999. "Frontyard Propaganda: A Response to 'Beyond Backyard Environmentalism.'" *Boston Review*, October: 17–18.

Lowry, William R. 1992. *The Dimensions of Federalism: State Governments and Pollution Control Policies*. Duke University Press.

Mank, Bradford C. 1998. "The Environmental Protection Agency's Project XL and Other Regulatory Reform Initiatives: The Need for Legislative Reauthorization." *Ecology Law Quarterly* 25: 1–89.

Maraniss, David, and Michael Weisskopf. 1996. *"Tell Newt to Shut Up!"* Touchstone.

Marcus, Alfred A., Donald A. Geffen, and Ken Sexton. 2002. *Reinventing Environmental Regulation: Lessons from Project XL*. Resources for the Future.

Marshall, Bryan W., Brandon C. Prins, and David W. Rohde. 2000. "Majority Party Leadership, Strategic Choice, and Committee Power: Appropriations in the House." In *Congress on Display, Congress at Work*, ed. W. Bianco. University of Michigan Press.

Martin, Joyce M., and Kristina Kern. 1998. "The Seesaw of Environmental Power from EPA to the States: National Environmental Performance Plans." *Villanova Environmental Law Journal* 9: 1–29.

Mayer, Kenneth R. 2001. *With the Stroke of a Pen: Executive Orders and Presidential Power*. Princeton University Press.

Mayhew, David R. 1991. *Divided We Govern: Party Control, Lawmaking, and Investigations, 1946–1990*. Yale University Press.

Mazurek, Jan. 2003. Back to the Future: How to Put Environmental Modernization Back on Track. Progressive Policy Institute.

McConnell, Grant. 1966. *Private Power and American Democracy*. Knopf.

Melnick, R. Shep. 1983. *Regulation and the Courts: The Case of the Clean Air Act*. Brookings Institution.

Melnick, R. Shep. 1999. "Risky Business: Government and the Environment after Earth Day." In *Taking Stock: American Government in the Twentieth Century*, ed. M. Keller and R. Melnick. Cambridge University Press.

Miller, Mark. 1999. Plum Creek Habitat Conservation Plan. National Center for Environmental Decision-Making Research.

Mintz, Joel A. 2004. "Treading Water: A Preliminary Assessment of EPA Enforcement during the Bush II Administration." *ELR News and Analysis* 34: 10933–10953.

Moe, Terry M. 1985. "The Politicized Presidency." In *The New Directions in American Politics*, ed. J. Chubb and P. Peterson. Brookings Institution.

Moe, Terry M. 1989. "The Politics of Bureaucratic Structure." In *Can the Government Govern?* ed. J. Chubb and P. Peterson. Brookings Institution.

Moseley, Cassandra. 1999. New Ideas, Old Institutions: Environment, Community, and State in the Pacific Northwest. Ph.D. dissertation, Yale University.

Moss, Elaine, ed. 1975. *Land Use Controls in New York State: A Handbook on the Legal Rights of Citizens*. Dial Press.

National Academy of Public Administration. 1995. *Setting Priorities, Getting Results: A New Direction for the Environmental Protection Agency*. National Academy of Public Administration.

National Academy of Public Administration. 2003. *A Breath of Fresh Air: Reviving the New Source Review Program*. National Academy of Public Administration.

National Center for Environmental Decisionmaking Research. 1998. Understanding and Improving Habitat Conservation Plans.

Nie, Martin. 2003. "Drivers of Natural Resource-Based Conflict." *Policy Sciences* 36: 307–341.

Nie, Martin. 2004. "Administrative Rulemaking and Public Lands Conflict: The Forest Service's Roadless Rule." *Natural Resources Journal* 31: 687–742.

Nie, Martin. 2004. "State Wildlife Policy and Management: The Scope and Bias of Political Conflict." *Public Administration Review* 64: 221–233.

Nie, Martin. 2006. "Governing the Tongass: National Forest Conflict and Political Decision Making." *Environmental Law* 36: 385–480.

O'Leary, Rosemary. 1993. *Environmental Change: Federal Courts and the EPA.* Temple University Press.

Oleszek, Walter. 2004. *Congressional Procedures and the Policy Process*, sixth edition. CQ Press.

Orren, Karen, and Stephen Skowronek. 1994. "Beyond the Iconography of Order: Notes for a 'New Institutionalism.'" In *The Dynamics of American Politics: Approaches and Interpretations*, ed. L. Dodd and C. Jillson. Westview.

Orren, Karen, and Stephen Skowronek. 2002. "The Study of American Political Development." In *Political Science: The State of the Discipline*, ed. I. Katznelson and H. Miner. Norton.

Orren, Karen, and Stephen Skowronek. 2004. *The Search for American Political Development.* Cambridge University Press.

Patlis, Jason M. 2000. "The Endangered Species Act: Thirty Years of Money, Politics, and Science." *Tulane Environmental Law Journal* 16: 257–329.

Pertschuck, Michael. 1982. *Revolt against Regulation.* Berkeley and Los Angeles: University of California Press.

Petersen, Shannon. 2002. *Acting for Endangered Species: The Statutory Ark.* University Press of Kansas.

Pope, Carl, and Paul Rauber. 2004. *Strategic Ignorance: Why the Bush Administration Is Recklessly Destroying a Century of Environmental Progress.* Sierra Club Books.

Portney, Kent E. 2003. *Taking Sustainable Cities Seriously: Economic Development, the Environment, and Quality of Life in American Cities.* MIT Press.

Press, Daniel. 2002. *Saving Open Space: The Politics of Local Preservation in California.* University of California Press.

Press, Daniel. 2003. "Who Votes for Natural Resources in California?" *Society and Natural Resources* 16: 835–846.

Pritzker, David M., and Deborah S. Dalton, eds. 1995. *Negotiated Rulemaking Sourcebook.* Administrative Conference of the United States.

Rabe, Barry G. 1986. *Fragmentation and Integration in State Environmental Management.* Conservation Foundation.

Rabe, Barry G. 2004. *Statehouse and Greenhouse: The Emerging Politics of American Climate Change Policy.* Brookings Institution.

Radmall, Lori. 2004. "President George W. Bush's Forest Policy: Healthy Forest Restoration Act of 2003." *Journal of Land Resources and Environmental Law* 24: 511–536.

Ranchod, Sanjay. 2001. "The Clinton National Monuments: Protecting Ecosystems with the Antiquities Act." *Harvard Environmental Law Review* 25: 535–589.

Rasband, James B. 2001. "Moving Forward: The Future of the Antiquities Act." *Journal of Land Resources and Environmental Law* 21: 619–634.

Rauch, Jonathan. 1999. *Government's End: Why Washington Stopped Working*. Public Affairs.

Rechtschaffen, Clifford, and David L. Markell. 2003. *Reinventing Environmental Enforcement*. Environmental Law Institute.

Reitze, Arnold W. 2002. "State and Federal Command-and-Control Regulation of Emissions from Fossil-Fuel Electric Power Generating Plants." *Environmental Law* 32: 369–433.

Repetto, Robert, ed. 2006. *Punctuated Equilibrium and the Dynamics of U.S. Environmental Policy*. Yale University Press.

Ringquist, Evan J. 1993. *Environmental Protection at the State Level: Politics and Progress in Controlling Pollution*. M. E. Sharpe.

Rohde, David W. 1991. *Parties and Leaders in the Postreform House*. University of Chicago Press.

Rome, Adam. 2003. "'Give Earth a Chance': The Environmental Movement and the Sixties." *Journal of American History* 90: 525–554.

Rorty, Richard. 1998. *Achieving Our Country: Leftist Thought in Twentieth-Century America*. Harvard University Press.

Rossi, Jim. 2001. "Bargaining in the Shadow of Administrative Procedure: The Public Interest in Rulemaking Settlement." *Duke Law Journal* 51: 1015–1059.

Rule, Lauren M. 2000. "Enforcing Ecosystem Management under the Northwest Forest Plan." *Fordham Environmental Law Journal* 12: 211–252.

Rusnak, Eric. 2003. "The Straw That Broke the Camel's Back? Grand Staircase Escalante National Monument Antiquates the Antiquities Act." *Ohio State Law Journal* 64: 669–730.

Ryan, Clare M. 1995. "Regulatory Negotiation: Learning from Experiences at the U.S. Environmental Protection Agency." In *Mediating Environmental Conflicts*, ed. J. Blackburn and W. Bruce. Quorum Books.

Scheberle, Denise. 2004. *Federalism and Environmental Policy: Trust and the Politics of Implementation*, second edition. Georgetown University Press.

Schickler, Eric. 2001. *Disjointed Pluralism: Institutional Innovation and the Development of the U.S. Congress*. Princeton University Press.

Schlozman, Kay Lehman, and John T. Tierney. 1986. *Organized Interests and American Democracy*. Harper and Row.

Seidenfeld, Mark. 2000. "Empowering Stakeholders: Limits on Collaboration as the Basis for Flexible Regulation." *William and Mary Law Review* 41: 411–501.

Shaiko, Ronald G. 1999. *Voices and Echoes for the Environment: Public Interest Representation in the 1990s and Beyond.* Columbia University Press.

Shanley, Robert A. 1992. *Presidential Influence and Environmental Policy.* Greenwood.

Sheldon, Karin P. 1998. "Habitat Conservation Planning: Addressing the Achilles Heel of the Endangered Species Act." *New York University Environmental Law Journal* 6: 279–340.

Shellenberger, Michael, and Ted Nordhaus. 2004. "The Death of Environmentalism: Global Warming Politics in a Post-Environmental World." *Grist Magazine* (http://www.grist.org).

Shipan, Charles R., and William R. Lowry. 2001. "Environmental Policy and Party Divergence in Congress." *Political Research Quarterly* 54: 245–263.

Siegler, Ellen. 1997. "Regulatory Negotiations and Other Rulemaking Processes: Strengths and Weaknesses from an Industry Viewpoint." *Duke Law Journal* 46: 1429–1443.

Sinclair, Barbara. 2000. *Unconventional Lawmaking: New Legislative Processes in the U.S. Congress,* second edition. CQ Press.

Siy, Eric, Leo Koziol, and Darcy Rollins. 2001. *The State of the States: Assessing the Capacity of States to Achieve Sustainable Development through Green Planning.* Resource Renewal Institute.

Skowronek, Stephen. 1982. *Building a New American State: The Expansion of National Administrative Capacities, 1877–1920.* Cambridge University Press.

Skowronek, Stephen. 1997. *The Politics Presidents Make: Leadership from John Adams to Bill Clinton,* revised edition. Harvard University Press.

Slingerland, George R. 1999. The Effect of the "No Surprises" Policy on Habitat Conservation Planning and the Endangered Species Act. M.A. thesis, Virginia Polytechnic and State University.

Smith, Mark A. 2000. *American Business and Political Power: Public Opinion, Elections, and Democracy.* University of Chicago Press.

Soden, Dennis L., ed. 1999. *The Environmental Presidency.* SUNY Press.

Squillace, Mark. 2003. "The Monumental Legacy of the Antiquities Act of 1906." *Georgia Law Review* 37: 473–610.

Steinzor, Rena I. 1998. "Reinventing Environmental Regulation: The Dangerous Journey From Command to Self-Control." *Harvard Environmental Law Review* 22: 103–203.

Stephenson, Matthew C. 2003. "A Tale of Two Theories: The Legal Basis for EPA's Proposed Revision to the Routine Maintenance, Repair, and Replacement Exception, and the Implications for Administrative Law." *Environmental Law Reporter* 33: 10789–10807.

Sunstein, Cass R. 1999. "Is the Clean Air Act Unconstitutional?" *Michigan Law Review* 98: 303–395.

Sunstein, Cass. 2002. "Regulating Risks after *ATA*." *Supreme Court Review: 2001*: 1–47.

Switzer, Jacqueline Vaughn. 1997. *Green Backlash: The History and Politics of Environmental Opposition in the U.S.* Lynne Rienner.

Taylor, M. F. J., K. F. Suckling, and J. J. Rachlinsk. 2005. "The Effectiveness of the Endangered Species Act: A Quantitative Analysis." *BioScience* 55: 360–367.

Terrie, Philip G. 1997. *Contested Terrain: A New History of Nature and People in the Adirondacks.* Syracuse University Press.

Teske, Paul. 2004. *Regulation in the States.* Brookings Institution.

Truman, David. 1951. *The Governmental Process.* Knopf.

Vaughn, Jacqueline, and Hanna Cortner. 2004. "Using Parallel Strategies to Promote Change: Forest Policymaking under George W. Bush." *Review of Policy Research* 21: 767–782.

Vig, Norman J. and Michael E. Kraft, eds. 2006. *Environmental Policy: New Directions for the Twenty-First Century,* sixth edition. CQ Press.

Vogel, David. 1989. *Fluctuating Fortunes: The Political Power of Business in America.* Basic Books.

Vogel, David. 1995. *Trading Up: Consumer and Environmental Regulation in a Global Economy.* Harvard University Press.

Vogel, David. 2005 [2003]. "The Hare and the Tortoise Revisited: The New Politics of Consumer and Environmental Regulation in Europe." In *Environmental Policy in the European Union,* second edition, ed. A. Jordan. Earthscan.

Vogel, David. 2005. *The Market for Virtue: The Potential and Limits of Corporate Social Responsibility.* Brookings Institution.

Weber, Edward P. 1998. *Pluralism by the Rules.* Georgetown University Press.

Weber, Edward P. 2003. *Bringing Society Back In: Grassroots Ecosystem Management, Accountability, and Sustainable Communities.* MIT Press.

Weber, Edward P., and Ann Khademian. 1997. "From Agitation to Collaboration: Clearing the Air through Negotiation." *Public Administration Review* 57: 396–410.

Wenner, Lettie. 1982. *The Environmental Decade in Court.* University of Indiana Press.

West, Jonathan P., and Glen Sussman. 1999. "Implementation of Environmental Policy: The Chief Executive." In *The Environmental Presidency,* ed. D. Soden. SUNY Press.

Wiessner, Carol. 2002. "Regulatory Innovation: Lessons Learned from the EPA's Project XL and Three Minnesota Project XL Pilots." *Environmental Law Reporter* 32: 10075–10120.

Wilkinson, Charles F. 1992. *Crossing the Next Meridian: Land, Water, and the Future of the West*. Island.

Wondolleck, Julia M., and Steven L. Yaffee. 2000. *Making Collaboration Work: Lessons from Innovation in Natural Resource Management*. Island.

Yaffee, Steven L. 1994. *The Wisdom of the Spotted Owl: Policy Lessons for a New Century*. Island.

Zaller, John. 1992. *The Nature and Origins of Mass Opinion*. Cambridge University Press.

Index